WRITING JEWISH CULTURE

WRITING

Jewish

CULTURE

PARADOXES IN ETHNOGRAPHY

EDITED BY

ANDREAS KILCHER AND

GABRIELLA SAFRAN

INDIANA UNIVERSITY PRESS

Bloomington & Indianapolis

This book is a publication of

Indiana University Press
Office of Scholarly Publishing
Herman B Wells Library 350
1320 East 10th Street
Bloomington, Indiana 47405 USA

iupress.indiana.edu

Manufactured in the
United States of America

Library of Congress
Cataloging-in-Publication Data

Writing Jewish culture : paradoxes
in ethnography / edited by Andreas
Kilcher and Gabriella Safran.
  pages cm
  Selected papers presented at a conference
titled "Jewish ethnography between
science and literature" held in Zurich
(Switzerland) in September 2013.
  Includes bibliographical
references and index.
  ISBN 978-0-253-01962-2 (pbk. : alk.
paper) — ISBN 978-0-253-01958-5 (cloth : alk.
paper) — ISBN 978-0-253-01964-6 (ebook)
1. Jews—Europe, Eastern—Social life and
customs—Congresses. 2. Jews—Social
life and customs—Congresses. 3. Jewish
folklorists—Europe, Eastern—Congresses.
4. Folk literature, Yiddish—Congresses.
5. Jewish folk literature—Congresses.
6. Ethnology—Europe, Eastern—Congresses.
7. Europe, Eastern—Ethnic relations—
Congresses. I. Kilcher, Andreas B., 1963– editor.
II. Weissberg, Liliane. The voice of a native
informer: Salomon Maimon describes life
in Polish Lithuania. Container of (work):
  DS135.E83W75 2016
  305.892'4047—dc23

                                    2015033420

1 2 3 4 5   21 20 19 18 17 16

To our families

CONTENTS

ACKNOWLEDGMENTS

WE ARE GRATEFUL to the contributors to this volume, who have joined us in an intellectual journey that originated with the international conference "Jewish Ethnography between Science and Literature" at the ETH Zurich in Fall 2013, and that has carried almost all of us beyond the borders of our scholarly comfort zones. We want to acknowledge three participants in our Zurich conference, Sasha Senderovich, Alexander Lvov, and Bernhard Tschofen, whose work is for various reasons not included here but who offered very valuable contributions to our conversation. We thank James Clifford for consulting with us and carefully reading our introduction. Raina Polivka, Janice Frisch, Darja Malcolm-Clarke, and Jenna Whittaker shepherded the manuscript through at Indiana University Press, and Joyce Rappaport copyedited it with informed precision. At Stanford, we thank the Humanities Center, which gave Andreas the possibility of spending two months in the Bay Area and working on the volume. D. Brian Kim elegantly and carefully edited and translated from Russian; Brian Tich effectively edited multiple parts of the manuscript and organized the paperwork around it. In Zurich, we thank Victoria Laszlo, who was of great help in the organization of the conference, and Jonas Stähelin, who was responsible for the index of the volume. Thanks go also to the Swiss National Science Foundation for the support of our Zurich conference, and to the Stanford Taube Center for Jewish Studies, the Department of Slavic Languages and Literatures, and the Georges und Jenny Bloch Foundation, Zurich, who provided support for the volume. Finally, we thank the authors and artists we analyze, whose writings about Ashkenazic Jews continue to challenge and provoke us today.

NOTE ON TRANSLITERATION AND NAMES

As a rule we have used a modified Library of Congress transliteration style for Russian and Hebrew and YIVO style for Yiddish, but for personal names we have attempted to use the spelling that is most familiar in English (often following *The YIVO Encyclopedia*). With Eastern European place names, we have strived for consistency and often settled on the Russian spellings that were familiar to our subjects.

WRITING JEWISH CULTURE

Introduction

ANDREAS KILCHER AND GABRIELLA SAFRAN

PARADOXES

Ethnography by its nature is a highly complex kind of writing. Ethnographers try to describe a culture using a specific scientific language, but they know the words they use may limit their readers' understanding of that culture and betray the limitations of their own knowledge. Ethnographic writing is inevitably objective and subjective at the same time; the description of the alien reveals the self, whereas the seemingly familiar self emerges as alien and unknown. To use rhetorical and literary-critical terminology, ethnographic writing lends itself to ambivalences, contradictions, and *aporias,* or moments that give rise to philosophically systemic doubt. These *aporias* are at once *epistemic*—concerning the possibility of gaining knowledge—and *aesthetic*—concerning modes of imagination and narration, the effect of writing and art through various means of representation. Analyzing ethnographic texts consequently requires one to evaluate their success at empirical scholarly measurement and at aesthetic representation that evokes the ethnographer's experience of seeing and listening by means of drawing and storytelling in multiple media.

This constellation of scholarly and literary questions is the starting point of this volume, which concerns ethnographic writings on the Jews produced between the late eighteenth and mid-twentieth centuries. When writers worked to describe Jews as a group, they produced powerful epistemic and aesthetic aporias heightened furthermore by a *cultural* aporia: a claim and at the same time a hesitation about the consistency of Jewish culture across time and space. Even though these writers worked at times and in places where most Jews and non-Jews perceived Jewishness as an essentially fixed, unchangeable category of identity, this ethnographic writing suggests that the notion of the Jews as a single, clearly definable people commensurate with the other peoples described in ethnographies at the time is problematic.[1] This problem might seem to contradict the expectation that ethnography permits writers to construct and claim distinct cultural identities. From the eighteenth century, European scholars who encountered unfamiliar peoples wrote ethnographies about them, describing their customs, buildings, language, economic activities, and beliefs. Writing since that period on "Jewish ethnography" suggests that Jews can be described in the same secular mode: that they constitute a single body, unified across space and time by customs, beliefs, language, and economic activity. However, when we take a closer look, Jewish ethnographic texts, considered as a body, reveal the fissures in these notions, which are apparent even when the focus is narrowed to the Ashkenazic Jewish communities of Eastern and Central Europe that from the sixteenth through the mid-twentieth centuries constituted the bulk of the world's Jews and are the subject of the lion's share of Jewish ethnographic writing. A case study based on some two centuries of writing about these Ashkenazic Jews reveals problems that concern ethnography more generally.

A closer examination of this Jewish ethnography makes these fissures visible and prompts five central questions that reveal five paradoxes, which emerge from the epistemic, aesthetic, and cultural aporias evident in the texts. From the ancient Greek terms for something contrary to expectations, *paradoxes* are statements that combine contradictory features and startle their audiences. We have chosen this term to bring together the contradictory elements in the textual endeavor of Jewish ethnography. These paradoxes emerge from the distinctive position of Jewish ethnography and at the same time from its similarity to other ethnographies.

1) *Who are the Jews?* The first paradox emerges from the shifts in understandings of the Jews as adherents of a religion or, alternatively, as members of a nation or ethnos. In various historical and cultural contexts, these understandings change, or one of these definitions dominates, or

these two ideas coexist. There is thus no universal agreement about what it means to understand the Jews as a single ethnos. The ethnography of the Jews emerged out of this complex situation. That ancient Jews differed from modern ones was the departure point of Johann Gottfried Herder's late eighteenth-century writings. That ethnographers of Jewish origin who dressed, spoke, and behaved unlike the traditional Jews whom they wanted to describe were not Jewish in the same sense as their subjects was clear to both parties (in an 1891 memoir about an ethnographic expedition to Jewish market towns in southern Poland, the Yiddish writer Y. L. Peretz remembered being called "a goy who speaks Yiddish"). That Jews living in different countries differ from each other is obvious to anyone observing their habits, spoken language, clothing, and beliefs. Both the religious textual corpus and the modern discourses of Jewish nationalisms—not to speak of the reductive and stereotypical notion of the "Jews" used by antisemitism—all rely on the concept of the Jews as one people. Ethnographic encounters and the texts they have generated display both the fragmentation of this imagined unity and at the same time the literary and performative devices that are generated to restore it.

2) *How does ethnographic writing—the Jewish textual corpus—interact with ethnographic experience?* Second, the ethnography of the Jews troubles the distinction between the two roles central to the scholarly and epistemological practice of ethnography: the observer, the one who writes; and the observed, the one who is written about. In the earliest eighteenth-century ethnographies, written by the French, Germans, Iberians, or British about the "primitive" inhabitants of the colonies or borderlands of the empires (the indigenous peoples of the Americas or Eurasia), literacy marked the difference between the observer and the observed and ethnography meant producing the first written description of a given culture. Jewish ethnographers faced a completely different situation. Jewish folklore has been written for millennia in the so-called "written" and "oral" Torah, the Hebrew Bible, the Talmud, the Kabbalah, and especially Aggadah and Minhag, traditional genres of Jewish literature that describe Jewish customs. Thus ethnographers of the Jews cannot see their access to writing as something that distinguishes them from their subjects, even though their scholarly approach gives them a different methodology. Jewish ethnography is necessarily collaborative, in active conversation or

explicit competition with a bookshelf of older texts, written by Jews and held sacred by them and others, that define Jews as a people and describe Jewish customs, beliefs, and economics not in a descriptive and secular mode but in a prescriptive and religious one. The authority of the secular ethnographer, in this environment, is necessarily limited; shoring it up requires ethnographers to prove their literacy in the traditional texts and to secure the help of their producers. In this regard, the ethnography of the Jews resembles the ethnographies of other religious groups, such as the premodern and nineteenth-century Orientalist projects that understand the adherents of "Eastern" religions, Jews, Muslims, and others, by combining exegetical and ethnographical approaches, that is, by reading as well as by traveling.[2] As the writers and consumers of what could be seen as a corpus of religious autoethnography, the Jews force the student of ethnographic history to reconsider neat epistemological divisions between ethnographers and their subjects or between oral and literate cultures in general. Increasingly from the second half of the nineteenth century, Jews produced secular as well as religious autoethnographies, and we can see interaction between these two genres; at times they merge.

3) *Where are Jews located?* The location of the observer and the observed in space prompts a third paradox of Jewish ethnography. Consideration of the Ashkenazic Jews of Central and Eastern Europe in the eighteenth through twentieth centuries forces us to question the dichotomy between the indigenous and the mobile. While ethnography has traditionally distinguished between the "indigenous" peoples under observation, who are fixed in place, and the mobile investigator, the self-image of the Jews as diasporic (in spite of their centuries-long history in Europe), and the visibly transnational scope of the Jewish ethnographic project, suggest that observer and observed can be united by their mobility as well as their literacy.

4) *Who is the audience of Jewish ethnographic writing?* A fourth paradox turns our attention to the sociopolitical frame of Jewish ethnography. This ethnography has never been conducted in an apolitical vacuum; it is situated strongly, sometimes even controversially, within a field of power, involving exclusion and inclusion, self-assertion and demarcation, assimilation and dissimilation. The diasporic situation of the Jews affects the sociopolitical disposition of Jewish ethnography, differentiating it from

ethnographies based on more fixed national identities and political frameworks. Jewish ethnography confronts the fundamental nonterritoriality and transnationality of Jewish life in diaspora, problems that persist even in less diasporic Jewish contexts (such as Zionist thought). The (diasporic) politics of Jewish ethnography also draws attention to the question of the addressee, be it in Jewish or non-Jewish contexts. It is paradoxical that Jewish ethnographical texts do *not* structure their implied audience according to the division between Jews and Christians; rather, they blur that difference, whether by a dialectical relation of the particular and the universal or by addressing both in different layers of a single text, a move akin to what George Marcus labels "double agency" or "producing research for both 'us' and 'them' at the same time, in different registers."[3]

5) *How do knowledge and imagination interact?* The fifth paradox, linked to the aporias with which we began, relates to all the others and emerges from the methodological and epistemological contrast between the scholarly goals of ethnography and the aesthetic and artistic means that it employs. While all ethnographies use a range of literary forms, the heavily intertextual ethnography of the Jews reflects extensively and self-consciously on the functions of genre and language as well as of mediality and recording techniques. The Jewish ethnographic texts we consider often pause to interrogate the verbal trace—the supposed original voice—or reconstruction of the ethnographic encounter that they contain. In these texts, artistic and scholarly modes are not separated but are necessarily interwoven. Art is informed by scholarship, scholarship by art, and in many texts, the two modes cannot be disentangled. The ethnographic undertaking is revealed as simultaneously scholarly and imaginative.

KNOWLEDGE AND POETICS

The multiple connections between the observer and the observed in Jewish ethnography from its inception, as well as its hybridization of artistic and scholarly methods, have methodological implications that anticipate some of the concerns of late twentieth- and early twenty-first-century anthropology and ethnography. Recent and contemporary theorists and historians of anthropology from the late twentieth and early twenty-first centuries, such as Clifford Geertz, George Stocking, James Clifford, George Marcus, Richard Bauman, Charles Briggs, Mary Pratt, Arjun Appadurai, and Bruno Latour, take pains to situate themselves honestly in their own writing, acknowledging the limitations of their own access to information, the biases of their interpretations, and the degree to which the knowledge that they produce emerges from specific encounters with informants who may have their own agendas. Their accounts of anthropology's roots overlap with what we have identified as the paradoxes of Jewish ethnography. Indeed, even though we have been considering the specific situation of Jewish ethnography, it is not surprising that this study parallels and echoes more general and theoretical reflections on ethnography. Even while Jewish liturgy insists on the difference between Jews and other peoples, a nonexceptionalist approach to the Jews appears in the Jewish folkloric corpus. A Yiddish saying reported by the turn-of-the-century Russian Jewish folklorist Ignaz Bernstein, "*azoy vi es kristelt zikh, azoy yidelt zikh*" (as it goes for the Christians, so for the Jews),[4] goes back to a medieval formula that emerges from the proto-ethnographic reflection on *minhag* (custom) in Jewish tradition: "*kemo she-minhag ha-noẓrim kakh minhagey ha-yehudim*" (as is the custom among Christians, so is the custom among the Jews).[5] At the same time, Jewish ethnographical texts offer a set of features that allow us to paint a distinctive picture in response to the theorists of anthropology.

Theorists and historians of anthropology in the late 1970s and 1980s performed a "literary turn," drawing the attention of their field to the fact that ethnographic scholarship—and the study of culture in general—always requires literary devices. The concept of "writing culture" was inspired by Geertz; in the introduction to *Writing Culture* (1986), coedited by Clifford and Marcus, Clifford points out—following Hayden White's *Metahistory* (1973)—the rhetoric and narrative performance involved in the writing of scientific texts, be they historical or anthropological.[6] We gesture toward the Clifford and Marcus volume with the title of our own volume (and even the cover design showing the ethnographer at work), because we and our contributors find many of its insights inspirational. At the same time, as literary critics rather than anthropologists and as scholars of a different generation, writing almost thirty years after that volume came out, we recognize that much distances us from them.[7] Some of the political and theoretical battles fought by the readers of that 1986 volume (about the anthropologist's self-consciousness about power relations and the limitations to anthropological knowledge in contexts where the subaltern can be clearly distinguished from the colonizer) have been won. Others (which drew on postmodernism in a reflexive rejection of positivist approaches) have been largely abandoned. Those battles are not ours; our material does not engage in them in a single or obvious way. But in their wake, we find that the formulations that these anthropologists developed to describe the interactions between the literary and the ethnographic remain useful, and we notice that by concentrating on a particular, conceptually challenging instance of that interaction—two centuries of representations of Ashkenazic Jews in journalism, popular scholarship, poetry, prose, and visual image—we can speak back to that volume and to the conversation it engendered in ways that are useful for our own field and, we hope, beyond it. The Jews of Europe are often conceived as inhabiting history in a way that appears anomalous to their neighbors, as either disturbingly modern, strangely archaic, or both at once. Similarly, Jewish ethnography, when contrasted with the ethnography of other groups, emerges as oddly located in time: now as tied to ancient models, now as having anticipated, in the early twentieth century, twenty-first-century demands for a more self-conscious and collaborative scholarly approach. The complex and highly nuanced interactions that many secular nineteenth- and twentieth-century Ashkenazic Jewish intellectuals had with Marxism may account in part for the surprising ways that writing they produced before the Second and even the First World War smells like the anthropological scholarship of the post-1960s, much of it also informed by Marxist ideals. By bringing together Ashkenazic texts frequently identified as ethnographies with others that are rarely categorized that way and considering them through the lens of the last few decades' reconsideration of anthropology, we find an intellectual confluence useful to us, and, we hope, others.

As literary scholars, we are intrigued by the political and philosophical positioning of the texts that concern us, but we approach them first as artistic and linguistic objects, and it is in that mode that we are most inspired by Clifford, Marcus, Geertz, and other theorists of anthropology. Like them, we are interested in the poetics of ethnography as well as in the ethnography of literature. We see that Jewish ethnographic texts use literary devices in the description of their objects as well as in service of generalizable scholarly conclusions, and that literary texts serve ethnographic functions in their ability to describe travels, experiences, encounters—be they individual or social—in a subjective and autobiographical way. Drawing together texts that announce themselves as fiction or poetry with those that claim to be scholarship or journalism and responding to our fourth paradox, we propose a supra-generic category into which our texts fit (and which we suspect would be useful for ethnography in general). We call this contact zone of ethnography and literature *ethnoliterature,* a term proposed by one of our contributors, Annette Werberger. Because Jewish ethnography is so highly intertextual and so self-consciously "literary," it is particularly clear that it contains a consistent set of literary features that transcend genre.

Jewish (and non-Jewish) ethnoliterature is not limited to a specific literary genre, such as the ethnographic novel that thematizes exotic lives. The notion is more general and designates the space between the documentary and the imaginary, research and storytelling, or the techniques for recording alien voices and those for acting them out. "Ethnoliterature" thus is an interspace for the experience, performance, and description of cultural differences and transitions. Whether typeset as prose or poetry, framed as fiction or fact, as autobiography or scientific report, or as a fragmented and generically unstable mix of all these forms, Jewish ethnographic writings share the generic features of ethnoliterature. They juxtapose the perspective of an idiosyncratic individual to the vision of a society as a whole, imagined as premodern, where myth and legend interact with social reality and consciousness is unstable. They foreground medial heterogeneity, through the narratives of *writing,* through the use of the *visual* (drawings, photography), and particularly through literary gestures toward *oral* performance, situated in specific locations that are signaled through nonstandard language. They thematize the encounters of asymmetrical cultures, the folklore of the imperial periphery or colony as opposed to the elite knowledge of the metropoles. They use metonymy and synecdoche to indicate that the scenes they describe represent a larger cultural whole, Eastern European Jews in general. They frequently juxtapose the evidence available to the observer's senses with earlier texts that describe a given culture; as Galit Hasan-Rokem argues in this volume, this produces in the Jewish case a tension between the "exegetic" and the "ethnographic" imaginations, an oscillation between reading and seeing or listening, the immediate evidence of the senses, as privileged modes of understanding of the self or the other. By juxtaposing texts and images usually read as separate, the authors of this volume reveal their similarities and in the process discover patterns that, they argue persuasively, apply to ethnoliterature in general.

Jewish ethnographic writing affirms the position of semiotics in anthropological writings even while responding to it in a distinctive way. In *The Interpretation of Cultures* (1973), Geertz understands culture as "a system of inherited conceptions expressed in symbolic forms by means of which men communicate, perpetuate, and develop their knowledge about and attitudes toward life."[8] This semiotic notion of culture allows ethnoliterature to function as the location of the juxtaposition of two modes of cultural expression and interpretation, "science" and "literature." Understanding culture demands what Geertz called "thick description," meaning the description of cultural phenomena not as isolated objects, but in their contexts. Writing in 1997, almost a quarter century after Geertz, Clifford, in *Routes: Travel and Translation in the Late Twentieth Century*, asked anthropology to question the notion of culture and their codes as fixed in place, pointing out that peoples and their behaviors are more often, at present, in motion.

The inadequacy—or perhaps the purely literary, artificial, constructed quality—of the notion of place-based semiotic cultural codes is anticipated well before the late twentieth century by Jewish ethnography, as evidenced by our third paradox. Our texts inspire us to introduce a new category that surpasses the purely semiotic universe of culture: *nonrooted experience,* meaning both experience as nonrootedness and the experience of nonrootedness. This notion does not insist that the Jews exemplify an absolute (or romantic) diaspora. Rather, we argue, Jewish ethnographic textual production displays a tension between extraterritorial ideals (of diaspora, transculturation, and hybridity) and territorial ones (of cultural fixedness and national identities). Indeed, romantic notions of an "authentic," "autochthone," "exotic," "oriental," "original" Jewish culture belong to Jewish ethnography just as much as the poststructural, postmodern, and postcolonial attentiveness to the margins of the extraterritorial, the layers of the diasporic, the passages of the transnational, and the mimicry-staging of assimilations. The nonrooted ethnographic experience reinforces methods of semiotic interpretation and processes of enforcing cultural continuity and political identity. But it also troubles them: it produces no synthesizing (hermeneutic) totality but instead a constellation of heterogeneous and fragmentized differences.

Clifford reflects on the troubling ethnographic experience of the "alien" and understands ethnography as a mode of description implicated by the crisis of classical occidental paradigms of knowledge and culture. Jewish ethnography reinforces this questioning of traditional occidental notions such as nation, culture, and language, as well as binaries such as European/non-European, premodern/modern, religion/science, self/alien, subject/object, and East/West. It does so by constantly posing the question of what it means to be Jewish, offering transnational and transcultural responses, positing the ethnographer as now on one side, now on the other side of the border between subject and object, Jewish and non-Jewish, exotic and familiar.

Finally, Jewish ethnography offers anthropological theory the consistent displacement of what Clifford names "ethnographic authority" from persons onto texts, rituals, and objects. Recent historians of anthropology have probed the sources of the ethnographer's authority, the scholarly training, self-conception, and scientific discourse that give him or her the right to judge his or her subjects. As we noted in relation to our second paradox, this right is often linked to control of media, particularly writing, and to the distinction between oral and literate societies. In large and multiethnic empires like the Habsburg Monarchy or the Soviet Union, ethnographers saw themselves as literate scholars helpfully bringing the benefit of their skills to the illiterate in the margins of the empire. In contrast to this, recent critical ethnography has criticized this fetishization of orality (and its insistence on illiteracy even in spite of evidence to the contrary) and pointed out that ethnographers were in fact rarely the first people touched by literacy to encounter a given culture. Both the political instrumentalization of ethnography and the neo-Romantic concept of orality are questioned by Jewish ethnography, which profoundly complicates the oral/literate divide. The unique place of the written at the center

of traditional Jewish culture challenges normative ethnographic authority. Instead of that authority, Jewish ethnographers place what appears to
be the authentic word, gesture, or object at the center of their accounts,
and frame that word or object as possessing its own authority.

HISTORIES

The ethnographic descriptions of Eastern European Jews are manifold
and divided in many ways: by language (especially Russian, German, Hebrew, and Yiddish); by genre (memoir, journalism, prose fiction, poetry,
political polemics, religious guides, and scholarly essays or monographs);
by addressee (state policy-makers, educated non-Jews, missionaries, and
Jews themselves, imagined as secular or religious, assimilating or nationalistically minded); and by author (churchmen, state officials, amateur
and paid scholars, journalists, travelers, communists, Zionists, Yiddishists). There is no homogeneous description of the Ashkenazic Jews, but
instead a constellation of different cultural and political interpretations as
well as modes of writing, cultures of knowledge, and literary expression.

Jewish ethnoliterature developed along parallel lines simultaneously,
responding to an array of local conditions and the varying motivations of
writers and their funders. As Nathaniel Deutsch explores in this volume,
the sixteenth-century minhag books or collections of customs written in
Hebrew, such as Yosef Karo's 1563 *Shulḥan 'Arukh* (The Set Table), can be
seen as a kind of Jewish autoethnography *avant la lettre,* concerned with
recording customs for the benefit of readers who hope to preserve them by
their own diligent performance of them. (Such minhag books continued
to be published and purchased through the ensuing centuries of Jewish
civilization and remain popular in the twenty-first century.)

Since the eighteenth century, Jewish customs have been described in
secular as well as religious modes. From its inception, such ethnographic
scholarship has inspired conversation among the elites of the Russian- and
German-speaking countries where Ashkenzic Jews lived. One of the first
ethnographies of any group was produced by Gerhard Friedrich Müller,
a German scholar, hired by Peter the Great to explore Siberia during the
Kamchatka Expedition of the 1730s; he wrote an account that was use-

ful to the tsar but also accessible to anyone literate in German. Other eighteenth-century Germans wrote more descriptions of peoples to the east and south. By the end of the century, Johann Gottfried Herder offered a broad study locating peoples along a timeline that marked the differences from the most "primitive" to the most "civilized." His work inspired both anthropology, or *Völkerkunde,* the study of many peoples, and folkloristics, or *Volkskunde,* the study of the German self. As Liliane Weissberg discusses in this volume, among these peoples he situated the Jews, both ancient (whom he saw as heroic and appealing) and modern (whom he saw as neither). The sense that the study of the Jews was scholarship undertaken by erudite writers for the benefit of readers curious about the world informed the practice of Jewish ethnography by Herder's successors, Jews and non-Jews writing in German.

In this Herderian mode, Western Europe in the age of emancipation, where Jews lived among Christians without specific legal disabilities (even though many social differences remained), positioned Jewish ethnography from the early nineteenth century inside the *Wissenschaft des Judentums,* the beginning of the modern secular study of Judaism. Using the methods of philology and historiography, this field constituted and investigated new subjects such as "Jewish history," "Jewish literature," and "Jewish philosophy." Scholars such as Heinrich Graetz focused their attention on texts produced for the most part by the male Jewish elite, not the popular culture of ordinary Jews. Nevertheless, some scholars like Leopold Zunz became interested in aspects of Jewish popular life, as demonstrated by his book on *Namen der Juden* (Jewish Names, 1837), and by Adolph Jellinek's *Der jüdische Stamm* (Jewish Tribe, 1869) with the significant subtitle *Ethnographische Studien* (Ethnographic Studies); Jellinek addresses modern Jewish family life, holidays, and proverbs, using the term *ethnographic moments.*

The ethnographic situation in the multiethnic Austro-Hungarian Empire was politically more complex than in Germany: "Eastern" and "Western" Jews were seen as integral parts of a culturally heterogeneous but unified state. The Eastern Jews of the shtetl first became the object of intense ethnographic description in the scholarly-cum-literary genre of Galician and Bohemian "Ghetto literature" around 1850. The Galician writer Leo Herzberg-Fränkel understood "Ghetto stories" as "ethnographic images" (see his volume *Polnische Juden: Geschichten und Bilder,* 1867). Stemming like Herzberg-Fränkel from Brody in eastern Galicia, Joseph Roth focused on Eastern Jews, but whereas Herzberg-Fränkel's Ghetto stories describe the tension between tradition and modernity in the age of emancipation and assimilation, Roth focuses on the deterritorialization of Eastern Jews in times of war and the dissolution of the old transcultural empire after 1914. Both examples demonstrate that Jews in the Austro-Hungarian Empire were seen as a threatened people in the context of large shifts such as secularization, modernization, and the formation of nation-states.

Things looked different yet in the Russian Empire, where Jews—again as part of a large multiethnic state—resided primarily in the Pale of Settlement in the westernmost provinces and where their religious affiliation gave them a distinctive (usually disadvantageous) legal status. The ethnography of the Jews, as of the other peoples of the Russian Empire, responded to the authorities' urge to understand their population in order to administer them more effectively. Russian ethnography of the Jews participated in a dialogue between those who believed Jews to be dangerous to Christians and those who disagreed, with the government and the literate elites as the addressees of their arguments. From soon after the Polish Partitions (1772–1795), when the Russian Empire somewhat inadvertently acquired the world's largest Jewish population, books were published asserting that the Jews constituted a state within a state, that the Talmud instructed them to conspire to cheat Christians, and that they consumed Christian blood at Passover—followed by other books refuting these claims. (Converts from Judaism to Christianity spoke on both sides.)[9] Russian Jews responded by writing ethnographies or commissioning them from sympathetic Christians. Moisei Berlin, a Jew from Shklov with a German education, the court's official *Uchenyi evrei* (learned Jew), helped the government of Alexander II formulate laws concerning Jews; urged by the Imperial Geographical Society, he wrote the *Ethnographic Sketch of the Jewish Population in Russia* (1861). The convert Yakov Brafman's *Book of the Kahal* (1869), a hostile depiction of the Jews' "state-within-a-state," was answered by I. I. Shershevskii's *About the Book of the Kahal* (1872) and his *Worldview of the Talmudists* (1874). I. Liutostanskii's frightening book, *On the (Talmudic) Jews' Use of Christian Blood for Religious Purposes, in Connection with the Relations between Jews and Christians in General* (1876), was countered by Daniel Khvol'son, a convert and a defender of the Jews, in *Do Jews Use Christian Blood?* (1879). When the government set up the Pahlen Commission to draft new laws about the Jews after the 1881–1882 pogroms, a group of Jews from St. Petersburg used funding from Baron Horace Guenzburg to commission the popular writer Nikolai Leskov to write *Jews in Russia* (1884).[10] The most enduring Russian attack on Jews is the *Protocols of the Elders of Zion* (1903); the 1913 blood libel trial of Mendel Beilis in Kiev opened the floodgates for yet more pro- and anti-Jewish books and articles. The development of Jewish studies in the Russian Empire would retain a comparativist orientation and an assumption that Jewishness is defined as an attribute of a politically disadvantaged community that inhabits a geographically distinctive space.

While this debate about Jewish rituals and society continued in the 1880s, Jewish ethnographic fieldworkers fluent in Yiddish began to travel through the western parts of the Russian Empire. Jan Bloch, a convert to Christianity, hired the Yiddish writer Y. L. Peretz to research Jews in the Zamość region; Peretz then wrote *Travel Pictures from a Journey through the Tomaszów Region in the Year 1890*. S. An-sky (Shloyme-Zanvl Rappoport) led expeditions in 1911–1914 to the shtetls of Ukraine, with funding from Baron Vladimir Guenzburg (the son of the Baron Guenzburg who funded Leskov). Both Peretz and An-sky gathered Jewish folktales and songs, and an essay on Jewish folksong and an important collection of sayings appeared in 1889 in the Warsaw journal *Hoyzfranyd* (the House-friend). Jewish collectors issued calls for people to send folklore, and in 1901 Peysakh Marek and Shaul Ginzburg published *Jewish Folk Songs in Russia,* containing hundreds of songs that people had sent them.

At the end of the nineteenth century, German-language scholars turned their attention to the specifics of Jewish cultural practice and grew closer to the ethnographic approach more common in the Russian Empire, where travelogues, memoirs, and popular-scholarly articles by Jewish and Christian writers reporting on life in the Jewish Pale had been appearing regularly. Increasingly at the turn of the century, Jewish scholars in the East and West, partly inspired by "salvage ethnography" tendencies among Russian and Polish intellectuals, defined their task as the retrieval and collection of documentary traces of local history and the customs and folklore of Jewish communities, seen as under threat due to urbanization, emigration, and assimilation. In the 1890s, Max Grunwald (1871–1953) called on his fellow Jews to collect folk traditions and founded the Gesellschaft für Jüdische Volkskunde (Society for Jewish Folklore) and the Museum für Jüdische Volkskunde (Jewish Folklore Museum) in Berlin.

The Yiddish-based ethnoliterature of Russia's late imperial period, as well as the traditions of German-language scholarship, informed the Jewish ethnographic "boom" of the interwar period. Jewish folkloristics grew in independent Poland, in tandem with a movement to validate Yiddish and diasporic Jewish culture. In 1925, the Yidisher Visnshaftlekher Institut (Yiddish Scientific Institute, or YIVO) was founded in Vilna. It became the center of Jewish ethnographic research in Eastern Europe, organizing and inspiring battalions of amateur *zamlers* (collectors) who gathered stories, songs, and other materials and sent them in. Across the Soviet border, similar work was undertaken by the Jewish section of the Institute for Belorussian Culture in Minsk. As the leaders of the Soviet Union shifted among various policies toward their multiple ethnicities throughout the 1920s and into the 1930s, state resources were devoted to Yiddish publications and Jewish cultural projects that appeared to have the potential of transforming Jews into secular, productive, and loyal Soviet citizens; ethnographic and folkloristic scholarship was for a time among these projects. The international scope and multilingual faces of Jewish ethnoliterature in the interwar period are exemplified by the production history of S. An-sky's *The Dybbuk*. Based on data and impressions from his 1911–1914 ethnographic expeditions, this play circulated in the 1920s in Yiddish, Hebrew, English, Polish, German, and French (though the original Russian version had been lost); it was performed in the Soviet Union, Europe, North America, and Palestine. The appeal of this text to Jewish and non-Jewish audiences throughout the world suggests that the Jewish ethnographic enterprise had become highly translatable, able to entertain, and perhaps to educate, a variety of audiences.

In the period during and after World War I and the Russian revolution, the political meanings of Jewish ethnography became ever more urgent. For scholars in and near German territories, the growing power of German antisemitism and then of the Nazi party—a movement that relied on anthropology's definition of race in the production of its own "research" into Jewish culture—made the need to unite and inspire the Jews and to defend them against their enemies terribly obvious.[11] The methodological rapprochement between German and Russian Jewish studies coincided with a shared focus on their geographical setting. After the pogroms in tsarist Russia and again particularly during and after World War I, when the homeland of Eastern Jews became a theater of war, masses of them fled to the Western European capitals. With the migration of Jews west, their places of origin—the Pale of Settlement as well as the eastern provinces of the Imperial and Royal monarchy—came into view. German-language Jewish writers turned their attention to the "Jews of the East" (*Ostjuden*), who had become the subjects of ethnographical studies as well as literary writing in the late nineteenth century.

The presence of the "Ostjuden" in Western Europe during and after World War I on the one hand amplified the German antisemitism that now was directed against a new Jewish visibility, in contrast to the disappearing Jewishness of the assimilated German Jews. It in part inspired the cultural and political reinvention of Judaism in Zionism that claimed to save the "Ostjuden" from Russian as well as European antisemitism. The anthropology and ethnography of the Jews also played an *affirmative* political function in Zionism, which hoped to find the "essence" and "origins" of the Jews. In this quest, they looked beyond Europe's assimilated Jews to the "Ostjuden" and to "Oriental Jews" like the Caucasian "Mountain Jews," who took part in the first Zionist congresses around 1900. Zionist ethnography used methodologies from the humanities, especially philology, to explore the primordial and original customs and cultures of the Jews, as in the case of the Berlin Orientalist and librarian Heinrich Loewe, who—as a leading Zionist intellectual—wrote about Jewish languages, names, books, jokes, and rituals. Zionism also promoted the more apparently scientific study of the Jews according to the methodologies of statistics and expeditions. This was evident in the work of scholars such as the founders and promoters of Jewish sociology, statistics, and demography, Alfred Nossig, Davis Trietsch, and Arthur Ruppin.

After World War II, with the destruction of much of Ashkenazic Jewry, the remainder was split among three sites, each producing a distinctive form of ethnography. Soviet Jews, who were motivated to downplay their

official "national" identity, avoided self-ethnography until glasnost, when
the genre reappeared in Russian. Israeli ethnographers of the Jews benefited from state-supported academic institutions that carried on the Zionist vision of investigating and affirming transnational Jewish cultures.
And North American and other non-Soviet diasporic Jews, although star-
tlingly overrepresented among the social scientists of their various countries, only rarely directed their ethnographic impulses to contemporaneous Jewish populations. The many ethnographers of the Ashkenazic Jews,
writing in multiple locations, languages, periods, and genres, produced a
significant ethnoliterary corpus. The scholars whose work is collected here
consider striking selections from almost exactly two centuries of that corpus, from the conversation between Herder's 1764 depiction of "Oriental"
people and Salomon Maimon's 1792 autobiography, to a German scholar's
presentation at Hebrew University in 1961 and an Israeli scholar's reaction
to it. We hope that our examination of these texts will illuminate their
differences, similarities, and paradoxical stances.

CHAPTER OUTLINE

This book emerged from a discussion among an interdisciplinary group
of scholars who gathered in the summer of 2013 at the Swiss Federal Institute of Technology (ETH), Zürich, to think together about the multilingual and multipolar corpus of Jewish ethnography, focusing especially
on pre–World War II writing on the Jews of Europe. The majority of us are
trained as scholars of literature, while some are historians and folklore
scholars; all of us work inside the multidisciplinary framework of Jewish
Studies. Having begun with a set of texts that were more or less familiar to
us, describing Jews for various audiences, we took on the unfamiliar task
of reading them in concert, putting their linguistic and generic differences
aside in response to their functional similarities as ethnographic texts.
Whereas our field tends toward divisions along the lines of language—
German-speaking Jews are studied by German-speaking scholars, Russian-speaking Jews by Russian-speaking scholars—we, recognizing that
our subjects were more multilingual and transdisciplinary than ourselves
and that Jewish ethnography existed in multiple languages from the start,

decided to reject this boundary. The articles in our volume and this reflection inspired by them interrogate the literary techniques and generic
constants of Jewish ethnography.

The organization of this volume reflects the first four of the five paradoxes with which we began this introduction. Accordingly, the first section, reacting to the paradox of shifting definitions of "the Jews," considers
how Jews and Jewishness are defined in the many genres of ethnoliterature. The second section, prompted by the paradox of the status of the
already-written in Jewish ethnography, addresses the different medial
and aesthetic techniques of recording and representing the sound of the
informant's voice and the sight of ethnographic realia. The third section,
responding to the paradox of Jewish location, focuses on the spaces imagined by ethnographers, which oscillate between diasporic distraction and
national concentration. The fourth section, in reaction to the paradox
of the shifting addressee, addresses the political context of Jewish ethnography and the question of audience, readers, and listeners. Our fifth
paradox, which points out the interaction between literary and scholarly
modes of writing, informs all the essays and thus is not represented by its
own section.

1. *Reinventing the "Jews" in Ethnographic Writing:* The first section examines the methods of constructing and imagining the ethnographic object
in ethnographical writing, or writing strategies to produce and perform
ethnographic authenticity, to claim it but also to play with it and even
to question it. Liliane Weissberg examines the construction of an individual's authentic experience through autobiographical self-inspection
by reading Salomon Maimon's autobiography (1792–1793) as an origin
point for Jewish ethnography. Sylvia Jaworski looks at the representations
of Polish Jews as "authentic" Jews in a German Jewish literary collection
of tales, anecdotes, and images from 1916. Andreas Kilcher analyzes the
ethnographic vision of "exotic" Jews by Joseph Roth during his travels to
Soviet Russia and the Caucasus in 1926, surveying the complex constellation of Roth's journalistic and literary modes of ethnographic writing.
Jordan Finkin considers whether poetry can be seen as containing and
transmitting the sort of ethnographic data more often associated with
prose; he demonstrates that the interwar Yiddish writer Moyshe Kul-

bak's poetic work wields ethnographic authority through its references to Jewish spaces and objects, making his verse into a kind of museum, or a secular but functional amulet.

2. *Seeing, Hearing, and Reading Jews:* The second section collects essays that analyze the sound and sight of Jewish life; some focus on the voice, others on the visual. The section starts by considering the position of orality in ethnography, looking at how Jewish ethnographers depicted and experienced the listening encounter with the subject. Gabriella Safran contrasts the Polish Jewish practice of male researchers listening to Jewish women in the late nineteenth and twentieth centuries with mid-nineteenth-century writings by their Russian predecessors about gentry researchers who listen to peasants. Annette Werberger examines the use of folklore in the construction of Polish Jewish modernity in the environment of the Warsaw Yiddish writers' salons and elsewhere. In her analysis of Lion Feuchtwanger's use of the legend of the Wandering Jew in the 1925 novel *Jud Süss,* Galit Hasan-Rokem contrasts the sensory experience of the ethnographer, who hears and sees his subjects, with the reading techniques of exegesis. The visual is no less important in the construction of the immediacy of the ethnographic experience. Eva Edelmann-Ohler investigates photographs and lithographs of "eastern" Jews produced during and after World War I by German Jews eager to locate an authentic self. Samuel Spinner considers Moishe Vorobeichic's 1931 volume of Jewish photographs that refract Vilna's peddlers and rabbis through the lens of avant-garde photography without fully rejecting realism or the trope of visual authenticity. All five of these essays carefully locate the sensory encounter with a Jewish ethnographic subject inside the genre constraints relevant to the media selected for the recording of that encounter.

3. *Spaces of Jewish Ethnography between Diaspora and Nation:* The third section focuses on the use of space in Jewish ethnography, which is characterized by tension between the diasporic and the national, dissemination and territorialization. Two examples illustrate this contrast. Alexander Alon analyzes the reinterpretation of Jewish ethnography in Zionism; in this essay, travel—scientific expeditions to be more precise—plays a central role, but its aim is not to understand a diasporic disposition but to explore Palestine for Jewish colonization. Tamar Lewinsky evaluates

the concept of diaspora in Jewish ethnographic travelogues about twentieth-century Yiddish-speaking migrants from Eastern Europe to South America.

4. *Politics and the Addressee of Ethnography:* The fourth section draws attention to the political context of Jewish ethnography and especially to the addressee, be it the German Jewish west, Russian Jewish intellectuals, or Christian readers and government officials. The question forces our essayists to confront the differences among the political, economical, and cultural functions of Jewish ethnographical research in different contexts. Nathaniel Deutsch considers "minhag" or custom books produced by the religious in order to help Jews continue to follow tradition and demonstrates that they entered into a conversation with the secular mode of ethnography. Alla Sokolova considers the impressions that the Jewish built environment of the Russian Pale of Settlement produced on travelers yearning to experience the exotic Orient; she traces the interaction in their writing between their expectations formed by literature and their immediate visual impressions. Dani Schrire thinks about the study of Jewish folklore at Hebrew University and its postwar conversation with European scholars.

The volume concludes with three appendixes containing significant source texts made available in English for the first time. They include two sets of instructions to fieldworkers (one written in Vilna in the 1920s by the Yiddishist YIVO Institute for Jewish Research, another produced across the border in Soviet Minsk by Bolsheviks with similar goals but a different ideology) and the memoir of a Warsaw folklorist who goes to a brothel to collect folksongs from prostitutes and finds himself imprisoned there overnight.

We do not devote a separate section to our fifth paradox, because its topic, the interpenetrations of literary and scholarly ways of presenting words, sounds, and images, is omnipresent in all our texts and all our chapters. Because ethnographers of the Jews always know that their subjects have already been described in writing, Jewish ethnoliterature displays a particularly paradoxical set of attempts to create texts that combine the evidence of the senses with the knowledge gained through reading in order to create compelling and believable descriptions of a single people.

NOTES

1. We are grateful to James Clifford for suggesting improvements to this chapter.

2. Note the German Orientalist Johann Christoph Wagenseil (1633–1705), who traveled to Jewish communities in Europe and the Orient and at the same time collected, studied, and edited Jewish and Oriental books. Cf. Peter Blastenbrei, *Johann Christoph Wagenseil und seine Stellung zum Judentum* (Erlangen: Fischer, 2004).

3. George Marcus, "The Legacies of Writing Culture and the Near Future of the Ethnographic Form: A Sketch," *Cultural Anthropology* 27, no. 3 (2012): 433.

4. Ignaz Bernstein, *Jüdische Sprichwörter und Redensarten*, Gesammelt und erklärt unter Mitwirkung von B. W. Segel, 2. Aufl. (Warsaw, 1908), 128.

5. Jehuda ha-Chassid, *Sefer Chassidim* (Bologna, 1538), 1106.

6. James Clifford and George Marcus, ed., *Writing Culture: The Poetics and Politics of Ethnography* (Berkeley: University of California Press, 1986).

7. Some of us are inspired by a useful special issue of *Cultural Anthropology* 27, no. 3 (2012), "Writing Culture at 25," which reflects on the afterlife of this volume.

8. Clifford Geertz, *The Interpretation of Cultures: Selected Essays* (New York: Basic Books, 1973), 89.

9. Gabriella Safran, "Ethnography, Judaism, and the Art of Nikolai Leskov," *Russian Review* 59, no. 2 (April 2000): 242.

10. Ibid., 236–238.

11. On the transnational response of Jewish thinkers to the depictions of Jews in "race science," see John Efron, *Defenders of the Race: Jewish Doctors and Race Science in Fin-de-Siècle Europe* (New Haven, Conn.: Yale University Press, 1994).

PART 1.
REINVENTING THE "JEWS" IN ETHNOGRAPHIC WRITING

The Voice of a Native Informer

Salomon Maimon Describes Life in Polish Lithuania

LILIANE WEISSBERG

FIELD WORK

The discipline of ethnography, writing—*graphein*—about ethnicity as scholarly endeavor, is an invention of the late eighteenth century, when descriptions of peoples, their customs, and their cultures began to flourish. Of course, travel accounts of foreign lands and their populations existed earlier, as well as descriptions of foreign customs and lifestyles, but it was only in the late eighteenth century that these texts were viewed as "scientific," as part of a scholarly discipline, or *Wissenschaft*.

Early scientific literature in this field was mostly written in German. The historian Gerhard Friedrich Müller took part in the second Kamchatka Expedition (1733–1743) and issued descriptions of various peoples and tribes.[1] His account may be the first detailed description of a foreign encounter cast for a reading public at home. August Ludwig von Schlözer published his *Vorstellung einer Universalgeschichte* (Introduction to Universal History) in 1772, and his colleague at the University of Göttingen, Johann Christoph Gatterer, translated his genealogical knowledge into his own version of world history.[2] Both authors aimed to expand historical and geographical knowledge by turning to the East. While Müller still sought to describe peoples, or engage in "Völker-Beschreibung" (1740),[3] these scholars began to coin terms that would name the emerging discipline and separate it from the already existing field of history. The new research would be named *ethnographia* (1767–1771), *Völkerkunde* (1771–1775), or *ethnologia* (1781–1783).[4]

Later, in his monumental sketch of the development of mankind, *Ideen zur Philosophie der Geschichte der Menschheit* (Ideas for the Philosophy of History of Humanity, 1784–1791), Johann Gottfried Herder would describe human characteristics as dependent on geography and climate, thus distinguishing between peoples of the North—such as Germans—and those of the South. Not accidentally, perhaps, it was Herder, too, who devised a model of historical progress. In Herder, history combined with teleology, as human development moved in a forward direction. People not only differed from each other because of the circumstances of their surroundings; some were simply backwards, while others progressed and became more "civilized." Indeed, Herder relied on this notion of civilization throughout his work.[5]

Anthropology, another brainchild of the eighteenth century, sought to describe human beings in general; ethnography took on the task of describing peoples more specifically.[6] This development paralleled the difference between philosophy of language, with its eighteenth-century speculations on the nature and origin of speech and writing, and later linguistics, which cared about the specific characteristics of each individual tongue, beginning with the description of Sanskrit.[7] Description was also central to ethnography, while a theologian and philosopher like Herder still offered general outlines that sought universal validity. Herder lived in the small German town of Weimar; he encountered the world via books and a close reading of the Scriptures. His followers, though, were eager to travel and encounter their objects of research in their natural habitats. These traveling scholars were, by their own admission, representatives of civilized peoples, and thus able to employ the necessary distance and judgment to evaluate others whom they considered less far along in their development. Early ethnographers were less interested in the familiar, and more attracted to the far-flung and exotic.[8] Describing a people's Otherness provided, moreover, the assurance of one's own properties and characteristics. Thus, ethnography could strengthen and even define the newly emerging national idea; it could define *home*. Ethnography and the construction of nationhood went hand in hand.

Already for Herder, the description of the Jewish people caused a problem. As the people of the Bible, they are *Morgenländer* (Oriental), living in the hot climate of the eastern desert. In his early essay on "Ueber den Fleiss in mehreren gelehrten Sprachen" (On Diligence in Many Scholarly Languages, 1764), Herder wrote: "Here the Oriental [Morgenländer] glows under a hot vertex: his booming mouth brings forth a heated language, full of affect."[9] Jews as Morgenländer could be placed in the Near East and in ancient history—an ancient history that Germans in the *Abendland* (Occident) were eager to share.[10] Herder described their ancient poetry as beautiful, and Moses as a national leader who may have established a precedent for Germany's own struggle for national unity and recognition. There was a problem to be considered, though: some of these Orientals were also living in present-day German lands. Even though they were largely absent in Weimar, they were elsewhere working as money-lenders, traffickers in clothes and used merchandise, or even as beggars. There was no poetry or heroism in their way of life.

In his brief essay on the conversion of Jews, "Bekehrung der Juden" (Conversion of the Jews, 1804), Herder was thus eager to distinguish between the Then and There and the Here and Now. The Hebrews of old were admirable as the predecessors to German civilization in a sort of historical continuum. Present-day Jews, in contrast, were poor folk and even "parasites."[11] They were obstinate, and they were missing out on the historical civilizing process. Thus, Herder was not only able to distinguish between Hebrews (of the past) and Jews (of the present), but also to offer a picture of the underside of his depiction of progress, namely the possibility of evolutionary standstill or even degeneration.[12] These unfavorable paths of development were only open to the ethnographer's object of description, however. The ethnographer himself (a male and Western European figure) was firmly settled at the peak of a hierarchical order of development, a position that assured him a discerning eye and ear and a capacity for precise description.

Was Herder's essay on the "Bekehrung der Juden" already "Jewish ethnography"? "Jewish ethnography" could perhaps be simply understood as the ethnographical description of Jews in various diaspora settings. In this case, Jews would be merely the *object* of research and fact-finding missions.

For Jews to become ethnographers themselves, however, more would be needed. A Jew would have to turn from being passively observed to being the active observer, would have to assume agency and the self-confidence of a *subject* position. He would have to appear emancipated—if not for his readers, then at least for the objects of his description—and he needed to be empowered for his task.

What if "Jewish ethnography" were to cover both sides, to establish Jews as scholars and writers as well as objects of scholarship? What began with Müller or Schlözer as a way of describing different peoples and distinguishing among them has also been a way of unifying descriptions and establishing, more abstractly, the idea of nationhood. Thus, ethnography has always been a statement of division itself: between the Self and the Other. While describing other peoples, Müller and his followers achieved something else: through the ethnographical project, the German nation could define itself.

This situation would not be quite the same for the Jewish ethnographer who set out to describe Jews. The Jewish ethnographer as an active observer could not be, and did not want to be, part of the group that he would describe. He had thus to accept Jews as a diverse multitude, and to assume different customs and lifestyles for each Jewish group in different parts of the world. Still, there would be some sense of Jewishness uniting subject and object. Unlike the work of the German ethnographers, learning about the Other now meant turning against oneself, against this shared sense of Jewishness. Jews had to defamiliarize themselves to make "Jewish ethnography" possible; not the strange and the foreign, but estrangement and alienation, had to be at the core of this endeavor.

In this sense, "Jewish ethnography" is the result of Jewish diaspora existence. The Jewish people appear as tribes or groups who relate to each other with different degrees of familiarity. The readers of this ethnography's early texts were not only scholars, but also a general public eager to learn about the exotic and new, either via vivid descriptions or through paintings and illustrations. Often, these texts addressed both Jews and non-Jews. And if early Jewish readers shared the sense of estrangement from other Jews, those of the later studies focused on a kind of national self-reflection.

Once again, however, the geographical scope in these texts was limited. Jewish ethnographers who largely hailed from the so-called West turned toward the East and Slavic lands; they continued a perspective that has defined ethnography since its founding days. This point of view produced descriptions that rejected the East for the more advanced and "civilized" West, in which a steady stream of Eastern European Jewish immigrants sought economic success and political emancipation. By the end of the nineteenth century, however, life in the East became sentimentalized in the so-called *Ghettogeschichten* (tales of the ghetto) that dealt with the East nostalgically, as offering a glimpse of the Jewish past. Jewish ethnographers who traveled to the Pale were no longer looking to reject that life, but to revitalize Jewish values. The East morphed from a primitive, foreign land into a place of common roots that had to be explored; it became the phantom image of true and authentic Judaism.[13]

At its core, "Jewish Ethnography," as it was practiced throughout the nineteenth and twentieth centuries, is not related to world or universal history. It is, rather, a limited endeavor that deals most often with Jewish life in the East as viewed through Western eyes. And more often than not, it does not study Jewish life as much as the transformations of its perception, changes happening in and through the Western gaze. This direction is set with one of the earliest ethnographic studies, Salomon Maimon's description of Jewish life in Poland in the late eighteenth century.

FROM EMPIRICAL PSYCHOLOGY TO ETHNOGRAPHY

It may not be surprising, then, that the concept of "Jewish Ethnography" can be linked to another Enlightenment invention, the idea of the introspective individual. More precisely, the creation of ethnographic texts happened alongside the first efforts of German Jewish autobiography. Those autobiographical sketches were regarded as scientific studies as well, and were published in a scholarly venue.

In 1783, Karl Philipp Moritz founded his journal of empirical psychology, *Magazin zur Erfahrungsseelenkunde* (Journal of Experiential Psychology), and went on to publish it until his death in 1793. Moritz had been

friends with Moses Mendelssohn, who suggested the name for the journal
and the new scientific study it would pursue, as well as with the Kantian
scholar and doctor Marcus Herz, who offered advice in regard to medical
classification of the study of the soul. Moritz adopted terminology offered
in Herz's outline of the field, *Grundriss aller medicinischen Wissenschaften*
(Outline of All Medical Sciences, 1782).[14]

Moritz himself was a pedagogue and the director of a well-known Berlin gymnasium, the Graues Kloster, an institution of higher learning that
was partially supported by tax money from Berlin's Jewish community.[15]
Moritz's *Magazin* set out to gather case studies in which the author would
describe psychological ailments or strange behaviors noted in others, as
well as *Selbstbeobachtungen* (self-observations). These case studies were
supposed to be gathered like *facta,* without further explanations, in order
to supply the data for a later description of humankind and offer a "mirror
in which mankind could view itself."[16] This may, indeed, sound paradoxical. While psychological case studies would concentrate on an individual's
psyche, anthropological studies were to describe man in general, as well
as peoples and ethnicities often other than the one to which the author
belonged. Indeed, the issue of the "distance" required for proper observation was particularly at stake in *Selbstbeobachtungen.* The observer had to
view himself or herself as both subject and object at once, and stress his or
her specific characteristics while also generalizing. The *Magazin* was not
only the first psychological journal ever published, but also an important
contribution to anthropological research. Its case studies were, moreover,
closely related to a literary genre that stressed the author's double role as
subject and object: autobiographical discourse. In the late eighteenth century, autobiography often tried to fulfill the same twofold task of stressing
the particularities of an individual life while integrating it into a more
general framework, be it of a historical, religious, or ethnic nature.

Perhaps it was because of Moritz's social connections, or the community's involvement with his school, or the topic itself, but no other German
language paper attracted as large a number of Jewish contributors as the
Magazin. Moses Mendelssohn, Lazarus Bendavid, David Veit, and Markus
Herz wrote about themselves and others, describing mental ailments and
eccentric behavior that set people apart and were viewed as unusual or
strange. Salomon Maimon became Moritz's most important contributor,

as he offered a new manifesto for the psychological discipline that Moritz had sketched in volume one of the *Magazin*, a "Revision der Erfahrungs-seelenkunde" (Revision of Experiential Psychology) published in volumes 9 and 10 in 1792 and 1793.[17] In addition, Maimon served as the coeditor of the journal during these years, and compiled the index for the ten volumes of the *Magazin* in 1793.

Unlike Mendelssohn, Bendavid, and Veit, Maimon was not from Berlin. He grew up in Polish Lithuania and moved to the Prussian capital in 1780, a few years before Moritz founded his *Magazin*. At that time, Maimon was about twenty-five years old. Like many eighteenth-century intellectuals, he excelled in a range of pursuits not limited by contemporary disciplinary boundaries. He was a Talmud scholar of rabbinical learning who was fluent in Hebrew and conversant in Hebrew scholarship. He was interested in mathematical problems. He studied pharmacy. He immersed himself in philosophical history, especially in the works of Moses Maimonides, whose name he would eventually adopt as his own. He wrote books and essays on philosophy and engaged with Enlightenment figures like Moses Mendelssohn and, in particular, Immanuel Kant. In Berlin, where both Kant and Mendelssohn were well regarded, Maimon sought to find the center of Enlightenment thought.

Maimon had studied German while still living at home, having taught himself the language to be able to read German books. A decade after his arrival in Berlin, he was not only able to pen philosophical essays in German and set down his thoughts on *Erfahrungsseelenkunde* and the new psychology, but he was also willing to turn himself into an object of contemplation for Moritz's *Magazin*. However, while Mendelssohn would write about incidents of stammering, or Herz about episodes of dizziness, Maimon had something else to offer. He presented his entire previous life for review. Thus, the story of a poor Eastern Jew would rival accounts of odd behavior or illness, and his move from the Polish wilderness to Berlin was, at the same time, a proof of his health and of his entry into accepted civilization.

The first part of Maimon's life story was published in 1792 in volume 9 of the *Magazin*, already coedited by the author, and it was subsumed under the medical category *Seelennaturkunde* (natural study of the soul). It appeared as a case study, in the form of a third-person narrative titled

"Fragmente aus Ben Josua's Lebensgeschichte" (Fragments of the Life Story of Ben Josua), with Maimon's name given according to the Jewish tradition of patronymics. The article itself, which continued in the following issue of the *Magazin*, gives no hint of its authorship,[18] but Moritz's introduction to the account was meant to assure readers of its veracity. "As the editor of these fragments may not have to affirm, they represent a literally faithful representation of truly experienced events [*eine buchstäblich getreue Darstellung wirklich erlebter Schicksale*]," Moritz writes. "The whole narrative bears too much the faithful stamp of truth; nobody whose heart responds to it would be able to misjudge it. The editor hopes as well to offer more of this story to the public, a story that speaks from heart to heart."[19]

Moritz insists not only on the literal truth offered by the narrative that follows, but also that it would speak "from heart to heart." While offering specific glimpses of a Jewish childhood in Polish Lithuania, Maimon's tale should point, therefore, to the general suffering of humankind. Maimon himself—still known under his Jewish name, Salomon Ben Josua—is simply called "B.J." here.

According to this tale, B.J. grows up in poverty, and does not even speak a proper language, using instead a *jargon* with words plucked from Polish, Russian, and words he insists come from other sources—though it is obviously Yiddish. He knows Hebrew, a language reserved for the religious realm, and is eager to learn German, the language of *Bildung* and enlightenment. Clandestinely, B.J. deciphers German books. He encounters the writings of Maimonides, in particular his *Moreh nevukhim* (Guide for the Perplexed) and this work, as well as works by the German philosophers of the Enlightenment, encourages B.J. to leave home and move to the West. He wants to become a philosopher of the more progressive Enlightenment.

B.J. embarks for Berlin, the promised city of Enlightenment thought. Once there, he comes into his own and develops into the proper human being that he is destined to be. Traces of his past are still discernible linguistically, however. B.J.'s language is awkward at times; his grasp of German grammar is shaky. But not all of this is the author's doing; for the sake of the desired authenticity, Moritz inserted linguistic mistakes into Maimon's text.[20]

FIGURE 1.1

Salomon Maimon, *Lebensgeschichte,* 2 vols. Berlin: F. [Friedrich] Vieweg, 1792–1793, vol. I, frontispiece.

In this early autobiography, Maimon is not only the author and protagonist of his tale; he is also a witness who is certified by Moritz himself.
The article seeks to present an accurate description of a Jewish life in the
Pale. But while B.J.'s life in Polish Lithuania can be described as Jewish,
his life in Berlin resembles that of a German. With willpower and the help
of a proper education, B.J. is able to leave behind his former self, the naïve
inhabitant of a primitive, superstitious land, and transform himself into a
person almost worthy of Prussian citizenship—which, however, he would
never hold. He turns from an object of study into a discerning writer and
philosopher, ready to embark on an ethnographic project himself—even
though this one would be limited to an exploration of his own origins.

The third-person narrative signals a distance between the author and
his object. But the success of the "Fragmente" with its readers, along with
the very idea that B.J.'s story might be not unique but exemplary and re-
peatable, brought the articles into the general debate on Jewish emancipation. Indeed, Moritz felt confident enough that he persuaded Maimon to
publish his life story as a book. It promised to offer an unusual tale, and
perhaps even financial success for its author, who was chronically in need
of support.

Just as Moritz's own *Anton Reiser* (1785–1790) offered an account of a
person struggling with a puritanical upbringing and extreme poverty,
Maimon's tale was rendered as a kind of *Bildungsroman*, and like Moritz,
Maimon published early excerpts, or *Fragmente*, in the *Magazin*.[21] But
while Moritz published his autobiography as a third-person narrative
and gave its hero a different name, thus turning his life story into a novel
of sorts, Maimon instead chose the first-person singular and offered the
first autobiography written by a Jew in German. His *Lebensgeschichte* was
published in 1792, accompanied by an etched frontispiece created by the
illustrator Wilhelm Arndt. The image shows Maimon dressed in fashion-
able clothes and wearing a powdered wig.

Maimon's book differs from the earlier "Fragmente." Once Maimon
has claimed the autobiographical discourse for himself and decided to
write under his newly chosen name, *Maimon*, a first-person voice appears.
Moritz's introduction once again promises the reader the pleasure of a true
tale. But when Maimon commences, he does not begin with his own story.
Instead, he sets out to describe the place where he lived, and the town's

population. He writes about non-Jews and Jews alike, sketching a broader picture of Polish and Jewish coexistence in which an individual life like his own has to be embedded. In short, to tell his life story, he first has to become an ethnographer, describing a country in which Jews live in great numbers and coexist with a non-Jewish population. He has to describe the specific circumstances of Jewish life in Polish Lithuania.

Thus, Maimon's *Lebensgeschichte* is not only the first German autobiography written by a Jew, but is a document that marks the origin of Jewish ethnographic discourse. And while Maimon turns his mirror most obviously toward himself, it is only because of this reflection that an ethnographic study emerges. Somewhere between the medical case study and the story of the Self, ethnography is ready to be invented.

AUTOBIOGRAPHY AS ETHNOGRAPHY

Moritz would provide an introduction and endorsement for Maimon's book publication as well. Now, however, it was no mere footnote but a "Vorbericht des Herausgebers" (Preface by the Editor) that was to prepare the reader and outline the project. As Moritz insisted, however, a book such as Maimon's was so intrinsically of interest that it did not need any introduction at all:

> This book will be of interest to everyone who is willing to ponder how the task of thinking can develop in the human mind even in the most adverse circumstances, and how the true drive for science will not be hindered by the greatest obstacles, those that seem perhaps even insurmountable.[22]

Just like the contributions to Moritz's *Magazin*, Maimon's account was to provide two lessons. First he would offer a specific story that would serve as an "example"[23] and thus add to a body of evidence on human nature in general. But in contrast to the *Magazin's* earlier work, there was now a second aspect that needed to be stressed:

> There is another great value to this book; it is the impartial and unprejudiced description of Judaism. Indeed, one could say that it is the first of its kind and deserves therefore especially in the current times, in which education and enlightenment of the Jewish nation has been much discussed in its own right, particular attention.[24]

For Moritz, moreover, the Jewish *Nation* was undivided, and firmly placed in Europe's East. Maimon was a member of this nation, and a witness to Jewish life, but also a person who had left this life and the East behind. He had become somebody entirely new, namely a Jew of Western education, a person whose Bildung demanded respect. Leaving the East behind meant leaving some less civilized past in order to achieve a worthy life dedicated to scholarly and scientific discussion. In his introduction, Moritz does not mention the situation of Berlin Jews, who were obviously already living in the West. Christian Wilhelm von Dohm's *Ueber die bürgerliche Verbesserung der Juden* (On the Civil Improvement of the Jews, 1781) had been published in Berlin a few years earlier, just to name one important contribution to the ongoing and unresolved debate on Jewish emancipation in Prussia. Dohm's work had also contributed to the decision to emancipate Jews in France after the revolution.[25] Moritz was on good terms with Mendelssohn and knew Dohm and his circle, and there is no doubt that Maimon's autobiography related to the emancipation debate, even if this connection was passed over silently by Moritz. After all, the book featured a person who had become worthy of emancipation, who had provided the proof of cultivation that Prussian authorities seemed to demand of Jews. One can, indeed, detect a certain *mise en abyme* in this book. Moritz's preface provides testimony for Maimon's development, just as Maimon would provide testimony for his former brethren in the East.

To be a believable witness, Maimon must be established as the author of a trustworthy narrative. Curiously, Moritz does not even mention Maimon's name in his introduction, nor does he refer to Maimon's achievements as a philosopher in Berlin, although his reputation there was already established. Two years before the publication of his autobiography, Maimon had published his work on transcendental philosophy, *Versuch über die Transcendentalphilosophie mit einem Anhang über die symbolische Erkenntnis* (Essay on Transcendental Philosophy with an Appendix on Symbolic Knowledge, 1790), a book that he had personally sent to Kant upon Herz's recommendation. He had published his *Philosophisches Wörterbuch* (Philosophical Dictionary) in 1791, his *Streifereien im Gebiete der Philosophie* (Ramblings in the Realms of Philosophy) in 1793, and in the following year a handbook on logic, *Versuch einer neuen Logik oder Theorie des Denkens* (Essay on a New Logic or Theory of Thought). Altogether, Maimon would publish twelve books and fifty-eight articles, and at the time of the publication of his autobiography he was particularly productive—more so, indeed, than Moritz himself.[26] But Moritz's concern was not with Maimon's current scholarly standing and reputation. For the purposes of the autobiography, Maimon is not important as a philosopher or critic, but as a native informer who, at the same time, could reflect on the Eastern Europe that he had left behind. To preface Maimon's account of successful acculturation to the West, Moritz simply praises the book as the first proper description ever of Jewish life in Polish Lithuania.

Still, Maimon's account of life in Polish Lithuania presents "history" in a very limited sense only. There are no data or solid facts. Here—as elsewhere in Maimon's narrative—the author does not offer a single date; at most, we learn that something happened in the "last century."[27] What we encounter is a region that is not only "backward" in its development, but that may stand outside time altogether, that may be completely disconnected from the idea of historical processes.

For German readers, this may have been surprising, akin, perhaps, to entering the realm of myth and fairytales. For Jewish readers, it may have been more familiar. Did not the early Mendelssohn still insist that history may not be for Jews?[28] After all, Jews were God's Chosen People, receiving their laws from God Himself. These laws, and the religion they defined, were not really open to change; wisdom was not to be found in worldly events but was to come from above, and from the reading of Holy texts. In Poland, however, according to Maimon, those texts were transmitted in peculiar ways:

> For example, in the first Book of Moses it is said, "Jacob sent messengers to his brother Esau, etc." Now, the Talmudists were pleased to give out that these messengers were angels. For though the word *melakhim* in Hebrew denotes messengers as well as angels, these marvel-mongers preferred the second signification, because the first contains nothing marvelous.[29]

Similarly, superstitious explanations were preferred for events that could easily be explained otherwise, for example by simple theft:

> Very often the cows came from the pasture with empty udders. According to the superstition which prevailed there, it was said in such cases that the milk had been taken from them by witchcraft—a misfortune against which it was supposed that nothing could be done.[30]

An enlightened Maimon, unlike the Polish Jews, would distinguish between truths and superstitions, between laws and customs that could
and should be discarded. Maimon is also eager, however, to distinguish
between the core and essence of Jewish belief and Polish Jewish interpretations thereof. Indeed, Maimon places a summary of Maimonides' *Moreh
nevukhim* at the center of his book, though later editors often regarded this
section as an extraneous insert and removed it to allow the uninterrupted
flow of his life's narrative.[31] But by referring to this medieval philosopher
at the center of his book, and by treating him as a proponent of the search
for Truth, Maimon reverses the direction of his ethnographic endeavor.
The German reader should consider Maimonides' work not as an example
of "backwardness" and an old text written far from the German intellectual centers, but as a real philosophical achievement. For many German
philosophers of the Enlightenment, Spinoza's philosophy had gained in
importance, even though it drew into question their traditional Christian
beliefs. With the addition of Maimonides to his narrative, Maimon offers
additional material from another Jewish author, one whose work had been
almost unknown to Maimon's readers.

Maimon would travel West to reach the capital of the Western Enlightenment, Berlin, and become an ardent reader of Kant's work. The
Enlightenment, however, does not appear to be a Western, or non-Jewish,
phenomenon at all.[32] Its philosophical ideas can already be found in the
twelfth-century book of a Spanish Jewish philosopher of the Arabic world.
While Polish conditions signified a decline of Jewish culture, the German
Enlightenment was not German at all; Maimonides had already formulated many of its thoughts. Thus, Maimon distinguishes between Jews and
Jews, just like Herder did before him, though he does not differentiate between the Hebrews of the Bible and the Jews in present-day Germany. For
Maimon, there is simply the difference between Enlightenment thought
on the one hand, and the lack thereof on the other. In the East, this lack is
shared by both Jews and non-Jews; Maimon, as well as many of his German readers, would deny Poles any encounter with the Enlightenment.
But as Maimon shows, the Enlightenment was already part of the Jewish
tradition, even in the East. It was just forgotten or neglected, and it was
meanwhile reclaimed—not claimed—by philosophers in the German
West.

Maimon begins his book with a description of a shared land: "The inhabitants of Poland may conveniently [*füglich*] be divided into six classes: the superior nobility, the inferior nobility, the half-noble, burghers, peasants, and Jews."[33] What does this *füglich* refer to? It could mean "conveniently," or "appropriately," but also "therefore," thus demanding some preceding argument or statement. Maimon does not explain, but he continues with a description of each class. Whereas the nobles own land, fill political offices, and ask for tributes from their subjects, Maimon describes the last two orders, the peasants and the Jews, as the "most useful in the country"[34] and, indeed, as the only truly working populations:

> The former occupy themselves with agriculture, raising cattle, keeping bees—in short, with all the products of the soil. The latter engage in trade, take up the professions and handicrafts, become bakers, brewers, dealers in beer, brandy, mead, and other commodities. They are also the only people who farm estates in towns and villages, except in the case of ecclesiastical properties, where the reverend gentlemen hold it a sin to put a Jew in a position to make a living, and accordingly prefer to hand over their farms to the peasants. They suffer for this with the ruin of their farms, as the peasants have no aptitude for this sort of employment; but of course they choose to bear this with Christian resignation.[35]

Maimon's description here is far from neutral. While Herder had described Jews as unproductive, Maimon's Jews are not only engaged in trade, but also in handicrafts. These are occupations from which Jews were banned. In Herder's Germany, in turn, Jews could not become members of the guilds that controlled many crafts. According to Maimon, it is the Polish aristocrats who do not work, and neither do the men of the church. Both of these groups bar Jews in Poland from making a living by working the land. But in Maimon's account, Jews may be still better off in Poland than peasants who are bound to "Christian resignation."

Even in Poland, however, all Jews were not the same, and Maimon is eager to draw distinctions. First of all, there are the Galician Jews, who differ from the Lithuanians. They are canny, "shrewder" than all others,[36] and able to find a way to make the class structure work for themselves. An anecdote serves here as illustration: two brothers from Galicia were able to move into the area, rent land, and install an administrative system that was authoritarian, tyrannical even, but ultimately productive. This resulted in a better economy, something that neither the nobility nor the Lithuanian Jews had been able to achieve.

But even the Lithuanian Jews have to be classified in groups: "[T]he illiterate working people" and "those who make learning their profession," and finally also "those who completely devote themselves to learning without engaging in any remunerative occupation, being supported by the industrial class."[37] Rabbis, Jewish judges who served the Jewish community, and schoolmasters belonged to the second group. The last group comprised those young men who were talented and destined for a life of learning, taken in by families, and married to their daughters. "Afterwards, however," Maimon adds, "the wife is obliged to take upon herself the maintenance of the saintly idler and the children (who are usually very numerous); and for this, as is natural, she thinks a good deal of herself."[38] They lived their early married lives at their parents' expense. As the reader would learn, Maimon himself belonged to this last class, having been promised to two girls in marriage at once; he wed one of them at an exceedingly young age, shortly after he reached the age of his bar mitzvah.

Thus, there was a nonindustrial class in both Jewish and non-Jewish society. For non-Jews, it was the nobility, the class that topped the social hierarchy. For Jews, it consisted of the Talmud students, and Maimon places them at the bottom of the scale. But to what extent can Maimon censure Talmud study as idleness, if he does not wish anything more than to move to Berlin and study? Quite obviously, it is not just learning that is at stake here. Maimon considers the difference between studying religious texts and studying those of the Enlightenment. For him, it is the difference between the yeshiva and the university; he exchanges Talmud study for *Bildung*.

THE HERE AND NOW

The West and the East do not share the same time. In the West, Maimon finds historical progress and the force of civilization. The East, in turn, is stuck in some dim past; everything there moves ahead fitfully and as if by accident—if it moves ahead at all. Only random anecdotes—the tale of the Galician brothers who reformed Polish agriculture, for example—are able to document any changes. But there is a third time at stake as well, mentioned only occasionally and mostly in allusions. It is the time of the present day in which Maimon penned his autobiography.

This time is documented most poignantly in the context of a discussion of religious freedom and the social and political status of the Jews. From the beginning of the book, Maimon is eager to address the topic of religion, but as a political issue, and in terms of religious freedom. Here, he has both praise and condemnation for the Poland that he knew:

> There is perhaps no country besides Poland, where religious freedom and religious enmity are to be met with in equal degree. The Jews enjoy there a perfectly free exercise of their religion and all other civil liberties; they have even a jurisdiction of their own. On the other hand, however, religious hatred goes so far, that the name of Jew has become an abomination; and this abhorrence, which had taken root in barbarous times, continued to show its effect till about thirteen years ago.[39]

The "thirteen years" that Maimon refers to lead back to 1780, the year of his departure from Poland. But there is also an indication that the situation may have shifted in the past few years. While little had changed "on the ground," the Independent Commonwealth of Poland and Lithuania lost almost one-third of its land in the first partition of Poland by Austria, Russia, and Prussia in 1772, which turned Frederick II from a King *in* Prussia to a King *of* Prussia. By 1790, a new treaty with Prussia was signed, followed by a second partition in 1793 that added land to Russia's and Prussia's claims. Prussia, in turn, dominated most of the area's trade. Remembering life in Polish Lithuania, Maimon wrote not only about a country that was foreign and far away, but one that had drawn politically closer over the years, turning into a territory dominated by Prussian rule.

But Maimon points to something else as well. He describes a distinction between the legal framework and popular practice. Poland might have been ruled tyrannically, in adherence to a hierarchical class structure, the *Ständesystem*. But it had been open to Jewish settlers and had offered Jews civil liberties and self-jurisdiction, by which they were at least legally independent. Jews in Poland thus enjoyed a greater freedom than in Prussia, where they were not allowed such self-administration.

The religious freedom was, however, countered by the behavior of the non-Jewish population, which had not changed much since "barbarous times" and was anything but civilized.

Once again, the consideration of time is important. If Maimon describes Polish Jewish customs as superstitions, they are perhaps naïve, but not "barbarous." The Jews work against their own advantage, but they do not really mistreat others. While Jews may be "backward" in their development, Poles, although seemingly adhering to Christianity, are more dangerously backward still. They foment verbal and physical violence against Jews. The line of religious progress that would place Christianity as the successor of Judaism does not seem to be valid here at all. Considering Enlightenment thought and behavior independently from beliefs, it translates into social behavior that has little to do with religion. "But this apparent contradiction will be very easily removed, when it is realized that the religious and civil liberty, conceded to the Jews in Poland, has not its source in *any respect for the universal rights of mankind* [emphasis mine]"; Maimon continues,

> while, on the other hand, the religious hatred and persecution are by
> no means the result of a wise policy which seeks to remove out of the
> way whatever is injurious to morality and the welfare of the State. Both
> phenomena result from the political defects and laziness prevalent in
> this country. With all their defects the Jews are almost the only useful
> inhabitants of this country, and therefore the Polish people found them-
> selves obliged, for the satisfaction of their own wants, to grant all possible
> liberties to the Jews; but, on the other hand, their moral ignorance and
> indolence could not fail to produce religious hatred and persecution.[40]

Here, early on in his introduction, Maimon mentions the observation of the rights of mankind, and he highlights the notion in the original German printing: *Achtung für die allgemeinen Rechte der Menschheit.*[41]

Enlightenment philosophers such as Kant insisted on the equality of all human beings—at least theoretically. They emphasized that *Naturrecht* (Natural Law) would also have to inform individual political constitutions.

The very term *allgemeinen Rechte der Menschheit* (Human Rights) was used explicitly by Jean-Jacques Rousseau, in *Émile, ou De l'éducation*

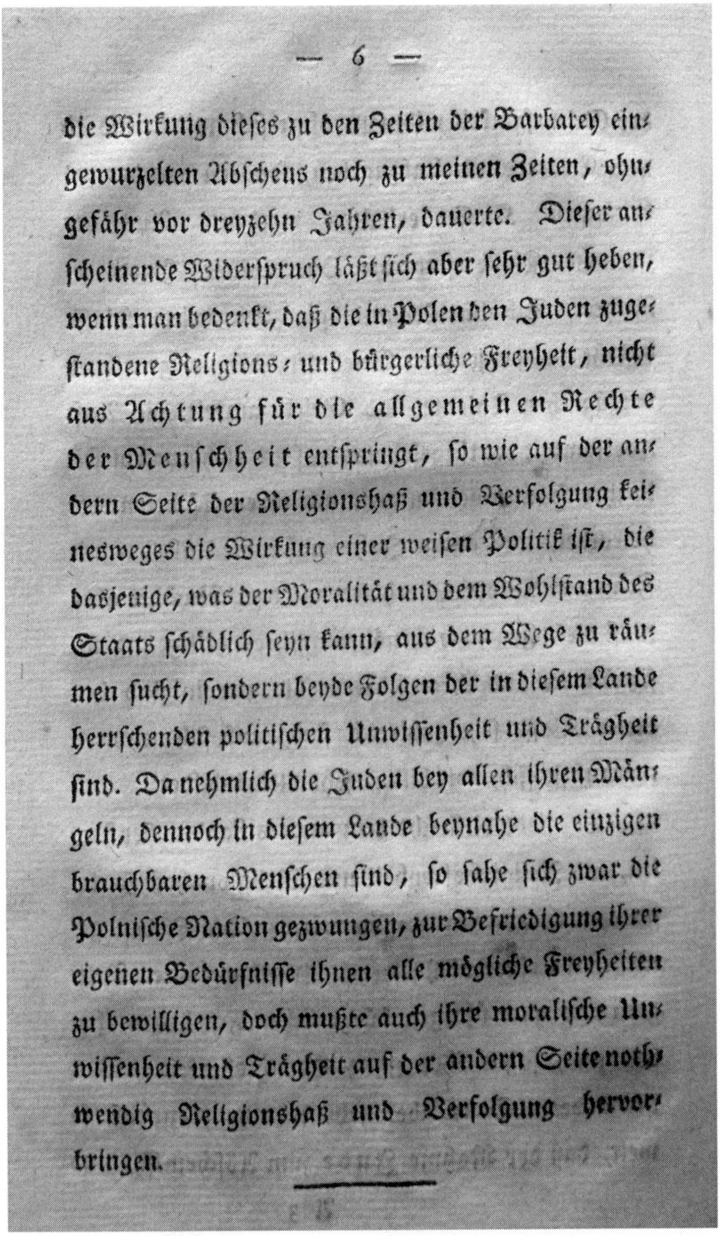

— 6 —

die Wirkung dieses zu den Zeiten der Barbarey ein-
gewurzelten Abscheus noch zu meinen Zeiten, ohn-
gefähr vor dreyzehn Jahren, dauerte. Dieser an-
scheinende Widerspruch läßt sich aber sehr gut heben,
wenn man bedenkt, daß die in Polen den Juden zuge-
standene Religions- und bürgerliche Freyheit, nicht
aus Achtung für die allgemeinen Rechte
der Menschheit entspringt, so wie auf der andern Seite der Religionshaß und Verfolgung kei-
nesweges die Wirkung einer weisen Politik ist, die
dasjenige, was der Moralität und dem Wohlstand des
Staats schädlich seyn kann, aus dem Wege zu räu-
men sucht, sondern beyde Folgen der in diesem Lande
herrschenden politischen Unwissenheit und Trägheit
sind. Da nehmlich die Juden bey allen ihren Män-
geln, dennoch in diesem Lande beynahe die einzigen
brauchbaren Menschen sind, so sahe sich zwar die
Polnische Nation gezwungen, zur Befriedigung ihrer
eigenen Bedürfnisse ihnen alle mögliche Freyheiten
zu bewilligen, doch mußte auch ihre moralische Unwissenheit und Trägheit auf der andern Seite noth-
wendig Religionshaß und Verfolgung hervor-
bringen.

FIGURE 1.2

Salomon Maimon, *Lebensgeschichte*, 2 vols. Berlin:
F. [Friedrich] Vieweg, 1792–1793, vol. I, page 6.

(Emile, or On Education, 1762). Rousseau's work influenced, in turn, that of the Marquis de La Fayette, who penned the first draft of a French Declaration of Human Rights just a few days after the revolutionaries declared the French Republic, namely on July 11, 1789. La Fayette was aided in his task by Thomas Jefferson, who had formulated much of the Declaration of Independence for the United States in 1776. Jefferson was the American ambassador to France in Paris at that time. Writing in 1792, the formulation *allgemeine Rechte der Menschheit* had to be recognized not only as a term of philosophical tradition, but also of political fervor. Thus, a reference to nothing less than the French Revolution was inauspiciously inserted into a narrative of Polish conditions.

It was precisely this idea of human rights that led to the emancipation of Jews in various areas of France beginning in 1790, only shortly before Maimon's "Fragmente" were put into print. And, after all, Poland was not the only state in which human rights were neglected; Prussia was guilty on this account as well. The question of human rights structured the Prussian debate on Jewish emancipation, just as the French translation of Dohm's treatise would guide Napoleon's final decisions vis-à-vis the Jews.

With a single formulation that he would highlight in his text, Maimon was able not only to draw a picture of what was admirable and what was abominable in his former homeland, but also to give evidence for the unstable borderlines between Poland and Prussia—just as he had done in regard to the Ancients and Moderns by reference to Maimonides and Kant. The East, it would seem, resided in the midst of the West as well. It was very much a part of Berlin.

Maimon's book thus fulfills multiple tasks. It provides an ethnographic description of Jewish life in Polish Lithuania in the late eighteenth century, and contrasts this with life in the more progressive and enlightened Prussia. In Maimon's sketching of Enlightenment ideas, the comparison between East and West is replaced by one that counters present-day Königsberg (Kant's hometown) and Berlin with the medieval South of Maimonides' time. Jews are both backward and advanced here, and one particular Jew, Salomon Maimon, can even offer implicit criticism and advice. The frame of autobiography serves as a means to hold all of this together, offering room for anecdotes, self-reflection, description, philosophical discourse, and political advice. Maimon's text documents not only the literary emancipation of a Jew—as the first autobiographical text written in the German language—but also the emancipation of the genre itself. Even in its very early stages, the autobiography brings together genres while also transgressing them, performing a sort of *Wanderschaft* itself.

NOTES

1. Gudrun Bucher, *"Von Beschreibung der Sitten und Gebräuche der Völcker": Die Instruktionen Gerhard Friedrich Müllers und ihre Bedeutung für die Geschichte der Ethnologie und der Geschichtswissenschaft* (ser.) Quellen und Studien zur Geschichte des östlichen Europa 63 (Stuttgart: Franz Steiner Verlag, 2002).

2. August Ludwig von Schlözer, *Vorstellung einer Universalgeschichte* (Göttingen: Dieterich, 1772/73; reprint Waltrop: Spenner, 1997). See also Heinz Duchhardt and Martin Espenhorst, eds., *August Ludwig (von) Schlözer in Europa* (Göttingen: Vandenhoeck & Ruprecht, 2012). See also Martin Gierl, *Geschichte als präzisierte Wissenschaft: Johann Christoph Gatterer und die Historiographie des 18. Jahrhunderts im ganzen Umfang* (Stuttgart-Bad Canstatt: Frommann-Holzboog, 2012).

3. See Wolfgang Kaschuba, *Einführung in die Europäische Ethnologie* (ser.) Studium (Munich: C.H. Beck, 1999); and Ingeborg Weber-Kellermann, Andreas C. Bimmer, and Siegfried Becker, *Einführung in die Volkskunde/Europäische Ethnologie: Eine Wissenschaftsgeschichte* (ser.) Sammlung Metzler, Third revised edition (Stuttgart: J.B. Metzler Verlag, 2003).

4. Hendrik Frederik Vermeulen, "Early History of Ethnography and Ethnology in the German Enlightenment: Anthropological Discourse in Europe and Asia, 1710–1808," (PhD thesis, University of Leiden, 2008), https://openaccess.leidenuniv.nl/handle/1887/13256.

5. See David Denby, "Herder, Culture, Anthropology and the Enlightenment," *History of the Human Sciences* 18, no. 1 (2005): 55–76.

6. See Helmut Pfotenhauer, *Literarische Anthropologie: Selbstbiographien und ihre Geschichte am Leitfaden des Lebens* (Stuttgart: Metzler, 1987).

7. See Tuska Benes, *In Babel's Shadow: Language, Philology, and the Nation in Nineteenth-Century Germany*, Kritik: German Literary Theory and Cultural Studies Series (Detroit: Wayne State University Press, 2008).

8. In this, Müller provided an example as well.

9. See, for example, Johann Gottfried Herder, "Ueber den Fleiss in mehreren gelehrten Sprachen," cited here in J. F. Haussmann, "Der junge Herder und Hamann," *Journal of English and Germanic Philology* 6 (1906–1907): 609.

10. See, for example, Herder, "Geist der Ebräischen Poesie" (1782–1783), and Wulf Koepke, "Vom Geist der Ebräischen Poesie. Biblisch-orientalische Poesie als alternatives Vorbild," in *Herder-Jahrbuch* VII (2004): 89–101.

11. See, for example, Emil Adler, "Johann Gottfried Herder und das Judentum," in *Herder Today: Contributions from the International Herder Conference*, ed. Kurt Müller-Vollmer (Berlin: DeGruyter Verlag, 1987), 382–401.

12. Liliane Weissberg, "Juden oder Hebräer? Religiöse und politische Bekehrung bei Herder," in *Johann Gottfried Herder: Geschichte und Kultur*, ed. Martin Bollacher (Würzburg: Verlag Königshausen + Neumann, 1994), 191–211.

13. Salomon Maimon's *Lebensgeschichte* (1792), and Arnold Zweig's account of Jews in Poland, *Das ostjüdische Antlitz* (1920), just to mention two of these texts, were not only separated by a century, but are worlds apart.

14. See Weissberg, "Erfahrungsseelenkunde als Akkulturation: Philosophie, Wissenschaft und Lebensgeschichte bei Salomon Maimon," in *Der ganze Mensch: Anthropologie und Literaturwissenschaft im achtzehnten Jahrhundert*, ed. Hans Jürgen Schings (Stuttgart: J.B. Metzler Verlag, 1994), 298–328.

15. See Willi Winkler, Karl Philipp Moritz (ser.), *Rowohls Monographien* (Reinbeck bei Hamburg: Rowohlt Taschenbuch Verlag, 2006); Ute Tintemann and Christoph Wingertszahn, eds., *Karl Philipp Moritz in Berlin, 1789–1793* (Hannover: Wehrhahn Verlag, 2005); Konrad Pfaff, *Salomon Maimon: Hiob der Aufklärung. Mosaiksteine zu seinem Bildnis* (Hildesheim: Olms, 1995); and Steven Lowenstein, *The Berlin Jewish Community: Enlightenment, Family, and Crisis, 1770–1830* (ser.) Studies in Jewish History (New York: Oxford University Press, 1994).

16. Karl Philipp Moritz, "Aussichten zu einer Experimentalseelenlehre," in *Werke* I–III, ed. Horst Günther (Frankfurt am Main, 1981): III (Erfahrung, Sprache, Denken), 90. See also Sheila Dickson, Stefan Goldmann, and Christof Wingertszahn, eds., *"Fakta, und kein moralisches Geschwätz. Zu Den Fallgeschichten im "Magazin zur Erfahrungsseelenkunde" (1783–1793)* (Göttingen: Wallstein, 2011).

17. Salomon Maimon, "Einleitung zur neuen Revision des *Magazins zur Erfahrungsseelenkunde*," *Gnothi Sauton oder Magazin zur Erfahrungsseelenkunde als ein Lesebuch für Gelehrte und Ungelehrte* [*MzE*] IX, iii: 1–28; "Revision der Erfahrungsseelenkunde. " *MzE* X, i:1–10; "Fortsetzung der Revision der Erfahrungsseelenkunde," *MzE* X, ii:1–7. See also Maimon, "Ueber den Plan des *Magazins zur Erfahrungsseelenkunde*," *MzE* IX, i:1–23.

18. Maimon, "Fragmente aus Ben Josua's Lebensgeschichte. Herausgegeben von K. P. Moritz," *MzE* IX, i (1792), 24–69 and *MzE* IX, ii: 41–88.

19. Moritz, footnote to the first part of Maimon, "Fragmente," *MzE* IX, i: 24.

20. This attention to linguistic detail was probably also present in the book version of Maimon's life story; later editions have corrected his German, however, and done away with what should have been forensic evidence.

21. Moritz's excerpts of Anton Reiser appeared as "Fragment aus Anton Reisers Lebensgeschichte" in *MzE* II, i:76–95, and MzE II, ii: 22–36.

22. Maimon, *Salomon Maimons Lebensgeschichte. Von ihm selbst geschrieben und herausgegeben von Karl Philipp Moritz*. Neu herausgegeben von Zwi Batscha (Frankfurt/M: Jüdischer Verlag, 1995), 7. The introduction by Moritz has not been included in most English translations, such as the following one that is used here: *The Autobiography of Solomon Maimon: With an Essay on Maimon's Philosophy by Hugo Bergmann*, trans. J. Clark Murray (London: The East and West Library, 1954).

23. Maimon, *Lebensgeschichte*, 8.

24. Ibid., 7.

25. Weissberg, "Metropole der Freiheit: Berliner Juden in Paris, 1789–1812," in *Jüdische Literatur als europäische Literatur*, ed. Caspar Battigay and Barbara Breysach, (ser.) Schriften der Gesellschaft für europäisch-jüdische Studien I (Munich: Text und Kritik, 2008), 17–43.

26. Maimon's studies were reissued in Maimon, *Gesammelte Werke*, ed. Valerio Verra, 7 vols. (Hildesheim: Olms, 1965).

27. Maimon, *Lebensgeschichte*, 11.

28. See, for example, the dissertation by Elias Reinhold Sacks, "Enacting a 'Living Script': Moses Mendelssohn on History, Practice, and Religion" (Princeton University, 2012).

29. Maimon, *Autobiography*, 33.

30. Maimon, *Lebensgeschichte*, 19.

31. In the present edition of Maimon's *Lebensgeschichte*, see pp. 240–315; this is excluded from the present edition of Maimon's *Autobiography* entirely.

32. See Weissberg, "Erfahrungsseelenkunde als Akkulturation," and Abraham P. Socher, *The Radical Enlightenment of Solomon Maimon: Judaism, Heresy, and Philosophy* (Stanford, Calif.: Stanford University Press, 2006).

33. Maimon, *Autobiography*, 11.

34. Maimon, *Lebensgeschichte*, 11.

35. Ibid., 7.

36. Ibid., 12.

37. Ibid.

38. Ibid., 13.

39. Ibid.

40. Ibid.

41. Ibid.

Legends of Authenticity

Das Buch von den polnischen Juden (1916)
by S. J. Agnon and Ahron Eliasberg

SYLVIA JAWORSKI

In his article "Deutsche und polnische Juden" (German and Polish Jews, 1897), Nathan Birnbaum (1864–1937) describes the German Jew's perception of the so-called "Polish Jew" as follows:

> When a German Jew crosses the eastern border of his fatherland, he immediately feels like he is being transferred into a new world. It is strange and significant that nothing in this new world attracts his attention more than the Jews. It is mostly them who make him shake his head. Well, no! We are better people than that, he thinks. We dress and speak like the world does, and we are polite and modest. We do not wave about that much with our hands, we do not scream as intolerably, we do not creep, hop, or walk in such a ridiculous way. It is a real blemish for . . . for . . . for—he thinks a while about what for exactly—for Judaism. . . . Since they [the German Jews] wear a white collar, these people think that they may look down on Polish Jews to the extent that, for instance, Dr. Peters does on his colored fosterlings.[1]

Birnbaum's article further develops the issue of perception, showing the reciprocal view of German and Polish Jews and their cultural differences (he speaks of *Culturgegensatz*) that in turn—according to Birnbaum—have stirred the aversion between them. Birnbaum emphasizes that in his view "Culturgegensatz" does not imply any hierarchy among the two cultures. German Jewish and Polish Jewish cultures should rather be understood as two differing cultures that are, however, on the same level and not in any hierarchical relation to each other. The German Jews are more "wandering *abstracta,* living theories . . . neither fish nor meat, aliens in European culture and dispossessed of a Jewish one."[2] The German Jew is a "person pieced together," while the Polish Jew is "complete and undivided."[3] In Birnbaum's perspective, Polish Jewish culture as

> the culture from the Middle Ages and the Jewish ghetto, that is unaesthetic for the European erudite and trained eye as well as unworldly in the highest degree, is an atrocity. Actually, as the culture of a living tribe in atrophied conditions, it is grotesque and it is doomed to be unable to develop a higher level of civilization. But, since it has the true expression, the content, the originality of the *Volksgeist,* it leaves the nation with its original completeness and the closeness [*Geschlossenheit*] of its character. Polish Jews are consistent people, without ambivalence, made of one piece.[4]

Being "consistent people . . . made of one piece," "Polish Jews" should be regarded as representatives of authentic Jewry, as "the true expression, the content, the originality of the *Volksgeist.*" In this chapter, I discuss the quest for authenticity[5] and, more precisely, the conceptualization and construction of authenticity in ethnographical literary writing that shares the Western European Jewish image of the "Polish Jew" as *the* authentic Jew. I take as a clarifying example the anthology *Das Buch von den polnischen Juden* (1916) edited by S. J. Agnon and Ahron Eliasberg. In my reading, this anthology includes a perspective on the supposedly "authentic" Eastern European Jew that opposes the Western European image of the "Polish Jew."

The introductory example offers a paradigmatic impression of the changes that the discourse on the "Polish Jew" or "*Ostjude*" undergoes on the threshold of the twentieth century. From the beginning of the nineteenth century, the idea of Eastern European Jewry is a significant topic in Jewish writing:[6] it oscillates between the rejection of the Eastern European Jew as an imagined backward-oriented Ostjude and the romanticized "authentic" Jew—whoever that may be.[7] We may assume that dealing with Eastern European Jewry becomes more and more of an obsessive quest for authenticity precisely as assimilation is depriving Western Jewry of its traditional, religious background, and, at the same time, as antisemitism is gradually emerging. While to be completely assimilated was the condition hoped for by Jews during the nineteenth cen-

tury, at the beginning of the twentieth century Jewish authenticity in the
form of a "new spiritual self-consciousness"[8] becomes—with the rise of
political Zionism—the object of desire,[9] as voiced by the so-called Jewish
Renaissance.[10]

Especially during the first two decades of the twentieth century, anthologies gathering Jewish tales, legends, and stories were published.[11]
Undoubtedly, they were mainly fostered by a widespread Zionist interest
in assembling a national collection of tales and legends that was comparable to the romantic, national "Volksmärchen" project of the Brothers
Grimm during the nineteenth century. But at the same time, the anthologies served to crystallize a specific Jewish selection that was to have a
fundamental function, for ethnographical reasons.

In this regard, the anthology *Das Buch von den polnischen Juden* occupies a peculiar position: it is a book by "Polish Jews" *about* "Polish Jews."
It includes a self-reflexive ethnographical program, since its texts were
mostly written by Eastern European Jewish writers, and it was edited
by two Eastern European Jews living in Germany. In this sense, the role
of the anthology's editors, both born and raised in Eastern Europe, is a
matter of special interest: S. J. Agnon, born 1888 in Buczacz, Galicia, lived
in Germany from 1912 to 1924. Among German Jews, he was considered
to be an "authentic" Jew, "an *Ost-Jude* . . . a category still scorned in some
circles, but regarded as exotically interesting in others."[12] During his first
years in Germany, Agnon worked with Ahron Eliasberg for the Jüdische
Verlag.[13] Eliasberg, who was born in 1879 in Pinsk, studied in Leipzig and
Heidelberg. For eight years (1911–1919), he was the head of the Jüdische
Verlag in Berlin,[14] where he worked on several anthologies gathering Jewish legends and tales. In 1919, he refers to this type of book as follows:
"The publishing house [the Jüdische Verlag] tried to create . . . new types
of Jewish books. This collection of sources, legends, and folkloristic facts
together with monuments of Jewish book art will certainly succeed in
awakening the sense of our past's depth and to help revive the elementary
feeling for historical continuity."[15] While Eliasberg seems eager to "waken
the sense of our past's dimension," Agnon's intention is not quite clear at
first glance. It therefore suggests a reading of—among others—two texts
provided by Agnon that will allow us to recognize the anthology's inherent twofold intention: I assume that the editors' awareness of their Eastern

European origins (and especially their awareness of being *perceived* as Eastern European Jews by the assimilated German Jewry) allows them to disclose their supposedly Eastern European Jewish authenticity to the assimilated German Jewish audience, while at the same time challenging the very concept of Jewish authenticity.

With reference to the described quest for authenticity, I consider the anthology *Das Buch von den polnischen Juden* not as yet another collection of texts in search of authenticity, but rather as an Eastern European Jewish response to a Western European Jewish discourse on Jewish authenticity. This observation relates to Mary Louise Pratt's assumption that "autoethnographic texts are representations that the so-defined others construct in response to or in dialogue with those texts [i.e., ethnographical texts constructing the Other]. Autoethnographic texts are not, then, what are usually thought of as autochthonous forms of expression or self-representation."[16]

In my reading, the texts of the anthology *Das Buch von den polnischen Juden* reflect and deconstruct the Western Jewish desire for authenticity as well as this desire's projection onto Eastern European Jews. I read the anthology as a compilation of texts bound to subvert the imagination of the essence of Judaism that Western society hopes to find in those texts. At the same time, the texts introduce a different and dynamic understanding of Jewish authenticity as being always constructed, fragmented, and performative.

RETHINKING AUTHENTICITY

In our contemporary culture, the term *authenticity*—like many other notions including modernity, assimilation, and secularization—is difficult to define. It is "a fickle one—on this, at least, there seems to be a universal agreement. Ontologically, it hints at the genuine origin (of things) and true essences (of selves) while at the same time resisting any attempt to distinctly identify and conceptualize such intimations of 'pure' existence."[17] Before analyzing the literary texts, we should consider the role that authenticity played in the nineteenth century and how authenticity is linked to folklore studies.

Authenticity has received increasing attention in Western European philosophy since the mid-eighteenth century, and it is closely linked to and challenged by the historical and social developments resulting from the complex changes of modernity: "The quest for authenticity is a peculiar longing, at once modern and antimodern. It is oriented toward the recovery of an essence whose loss has been realized only through modernity, and whose recovery is feasible only through methods and sentiments created in modernity."[18]

Although Jean-Jacques Rousseau's philosophy managed to formulate the important shift from the concept of sincerity to authenticity, it was Johann Gottfried Herder who intrinsically tied the imagination of authenticity to language and literature.[19] His widespread image of a cultural system structured as closed spheres implied the concept of a national culture with *one* culture for *each* nation (without any intention or possibility of mingling).[20] In this context, Herder singled out each nation's "folk poetry as a locus of folkness, inspiring contemporaries and an entire social and literary movement to absorb and imitate the authentic aesthetic of the folk."[21]

Subsequently, the collection and the rewriting of legends and tales by the Brothers Grimm played a key role in the constitution and perception of a national-cultural authenticity, which was supposedly to be found in folklore writing:[22]

> Of all that has flourished in earlier times, nothing remains, even the memory fades, except for the song of the folk, a few books, legends and these innocent household tales. . . . Inside this poetry flows the same kind of purity which makes children appear so wonderful and blessed.[23]

The Brothers Grimm formulated an authenticity with religious and moral connotations by referring to blessedness, innocence, and purity.[24] Therefore, legends and tales are believed to carry every folk's internal, pure, authentic value and core. In this sense, the editors S. J. Agnon and Ahron Eliasberg reveal the aim of their publication in their closing remarks:

> This present book wants to teach the understanding of Polish Jews on the basis of their own culture. The culture of a people finds its ideal expression in its intellectual creations, in its poetry, in its tales and legends, in its wit, in its proverbs, in its legislation and decrees. We have tried to create out of

the direct production of the people, so to speak, out of the source [*Urquell*] of the people's soul, and we believe that we have gathered material that renders a true and descriptive picture of the Polish Jews.[25]

The collected material consists of sixteen literary stories, two compilations of legal restrictions, one description of Polish synagogue architecture, an extract from an ethnographical, statistical study by Y. L. Peretz, numerous "Anekdoten, Geistergeschichten, Sprichwörter, Verschiedenes" (Anecdotes, Ghost-Stories, Proverbs, Miscellanea), and twenty-nine illustrations.

Indicating that their anthology contains omissions and therefore should be regarded neither as a scientific study nor as an anthology of every literary and cultural school, Agnon and Eliasberg focus on drawing a picture of Polish Jewry that counters the stereotyped perception of Western Jewry.[26] Furthermore, in this literary project we find the intention to answer and to weaken Western Jewish prejudices about Eastern Jewry. Therefore, a fortiori, the anthology can be regarded as influenced by ethnological motivations. Since folk narrative is supposed to express "both the individual artist and the entire ethnic group,"[27] ethnological studies specifically collect and investigate unfamiliar myths and legends[28] as well as their influence on the social structure or their function within religious practices.[29] In this respect, the role of Agnon and Eliasberg as the editors of this anthology is a special one: as they are Jews from Eastern Europe themselves, they seem (of course from a Western Jewish perspective) authorized to select adequate texts that illustrate Eastern European Jewish thinking, life, and customs, and thereby to grant the texts authentic value.[30]

Nevertheless—as in such collections in general, and in this anthology in particular—choosing, rewriting, and translating legends and tales also expose the aesthetic constructedness of authenticity. *Das Buch von den polnischen Juden* gathers mostly translated texts, which highlights the editors' intention to introduce these texts to an assimilated German-speaking Jewish audience. Paradoxically, the translation of Eastern European Jewish folk poetry into another language raises the well-known question of the mediated authentic core in the process of translation: if the authentic "essence" is—in the sense of Herder or the Brothers Grimm—supposed to be intrinsically tied to (in this specific case) the Yiddish and Hebrew languages and expressed by folk legends and tales, what happens to this authentic character in the process of translation?

Although the process of translation is not the topic of this paper, the awareness of the mediated character and the constructedness of authenticity plays a key role in the following textual analysis, which will allow us to approach a different understanding of authenticity as a fragmented and performative phenomenon[31] in Agnon's and Eliasberg's anthology.

THE CHANGING SHAPES OF AUTHENTICITY

"Agnon's use of Jewish sources and his selection of the linguistic and cultural code, with its strata and depths, create a secondary plot alongside the overt one; this hidden layer is a key for understanding the story,"[32] observes Haya Bar-Itzhak with good reason. In my analysis, I focus on three aspects of three specific texts: a) The "Genesis" of Polish Jewry in S. J. Agnon's "Polen. Die Legende von der Ankunft" (Poland. The Legend of the Arrival); b) The purity and "closeness" (*Geschlossenheit*) of Polish Jewry in "Estherkas Haus" (Estherka's House); and c) Assimilation and "authentic" Polish Jewry in Josef B. Ehrlich's "Zwischen zwei Müttern" (Between Two Mothers). As mentioned, I assume that the hidden layer in both the anthology and in Agnon's stories, as the following textual analysis will show, approaches and responds to the Western European search for authenticity on different levels and by varying strategies.

The "Genesis" of Polish Jewry: S. J. Agnon's "Polen. Die Legende von der Ankunft"

"We would not have known it, but our fathers told us how Israel came from France to Poland and settled there."[33] These are the opening words of S. J. Agnon's first contribution, "Polen. Die Legende von der Ankunft," which consists of two stories titled "Erste Kunde" (First Lore) and "Regen" (Rain). Agnon describes—as the title already suggests—different possibilities for the arrival of the Ashkenazic Jews in Poland.[34] A historical contextualization of a nation's genesis is fundamental for building a national identity.

Through the first legend, "Erste Kunde," the narrator plays with the historical vagueness of the Jews' arrival in Poland. Based on the differentiation of the Brothers Grimm between fairytale and legends, legends as a genre are "associated with a particular historical incident or personality and take place in the geographical space inhabited by the narrator."[35] Hence it is not surprising that this legend circles around questions of historical proof on the one hand and, on the other, the possibility of any recognizable magic moment in the settlement of Jews in Poland. In this story, which picks up the biblical Exodus narrative and places it in a European context, neither a certain date nor the name of the king is mentioned, without which it is impossible to contextualize this historical event. The only authenticating tool provided is a picture of coins supposedly fabricated by Polish Jews.

A divine will leads the Jews from France to Poland, suggesting that it is God who helps them to enter Poland and settle there ("And God took care of them and he dispensed mercy in front of the King and the chieftains").[36] But the first Jewish settlement on Polish ground is—according to this legend—not at all the first one. The Jews from France notice Talmudic Hebrew inscriptions on the trees in a forest near Lublin. The apparent first settlers become witnesses of an earlier settlement that has left no record in history.[37] The historical classification of the primary settlement of Jews in Poland is impossible. This hints at a central issue of the text: the impossibility of defining a first beginning.

The introductory phrase, with its strange grammatical construction "We would not have known it," points out the current lack of knowledge about the early stages of Jewish history and culture in Poland. The oral tradition passes on the information about the historical event from father to son, and it is eventually written down in the story. "In this way, the folk legend becomes the work of a specific author [kunst sage] as part of the transition from the oral to the written medium."[38] The narrative pretends to report the moment of birth of Polish Jewish history and culture. Occupying the first position of the collection, this story is the first step in constructing a chronological, almost historiographical order of events. Besides the opening position of the legend, the first sentence suggests the stance of the anthology. The reader is supposedly ignorant of the "truth" about Polish Jewry—an awareness about Polish Jewish ancestors that the reader gains while reading the texts in their predisposed sequence.

Agnon ends the first story as follows: "This is the heritage that we accept as such. Whoever wants to hear a confident account of the arrival should listen to what is about to be reported."[39] Since the information provided by the first story is insufficient, the narrator leads the reader to a more trustworthy account that replaces the first narrative: the second legend entitled "Regen." "Regen" uses strategies for authenticating the narrative, such as including the year 4653 (i.e., 892) and the historical name "Prince Leschek of the House of Piast,"[40] which raise expectations about its historical authenticity; nevertheless, the second legend fails to provide a reliable report. "Regen" is the story of the condition set by the counselors of the Polish king: that the Jews may settle in Poland as long as they agree to pray and to provide rain ("Do not allow them to enter your kingdom, except they will bring rain in due time by praying").[41]

The authentication of the Jewish arrival in Poland is confirmed by a custom of Polish peasants that is ongoing at the time of the narrative:

> Therefore, until today peasants in Poland seed their fields on Rosh Hashana and on Yom Kippur in memory of how their fathers used to do it. This is how their fathers used to do it: at a time when Israel stood bowing before its Father with an empty stomach, they [the peasants] went outside and seeded their fields. If the seed was sown on the fields during the same time as Israel stood bowing and with an empty stomach in front of its Father, the cereals rising from the soil proved to be fully eared, the soil gave its harvest, and the field was blessed. To their fathers' custom they held on.[42]

This custom turns out to be ambiguous as well: Polish peasants may have adopted it from the Tatars who settled in Polish–Lithuanian territory in the fourteenth century. We cannot be certain that Polish peasants practiced it at the time of Jewish settlement mentioned in this legend.[43]

Since both sections of this legend are constructed by connecting different legends and myths,[44] they cannot be regarded as consistent and authentic with regard to the content of one single and original text. The fact that legends claim to be linked to a historical event or person on the one hand, while on the other hand "legends are creations that are always being modified in accordance with the problems that preoccupy a society at a particular time and which reflect these problems,"[45] creates in Agnon's text a paradoxical tension, in which the search for authenticity is located and deconstructed.[46]

His short story binds together three aspects: the oral tradition, the biblical, and the ethnographical imagination. Agnon composes this story by using different textual elements, all of which tell a certain story of Jewish immigration. Yet the final and original story remains untold. Thus, the idea of authenticity as "Eigenart" is dissolved. At the same time, the mixture of seemingly historical facts and magical moments, as well as the interwovenness of Jewish and Polish history and culture, expresses the impossibility of separating European (in this case Polish) and Jewish culture as such and finding a distinct, authentic cultural core in either.

The purity and "closeness" [Geschlossenheit]
of Polish Jewry: "Estherkas Haus"

This interwovenness of Jewish and Polish history and culture is also of central importance in the second story of this analysis. While Western European Jews imagine Polish Jewry to be a hermetically closed group devoid of any cultural exchange with or influence by the surrounding majority, the text subversively hints at the opposite.

The narrator of the text "Estherkas Haus"—an educational mock-guidebook for the "daughters of Israel"[47]—refers to the legend of the Jewess Estherka, allegedly the mistress of the Polish King Casimir the Great (1310–1370). According to the "original" legend, Casimir's love for Estherka is responsible for his tolerant politics toward Jews in the fourteenth century, a narrative that recalls the biblical Esther.[48] Yet in "Estherkas Haus," the narrator concentrates on two specific points: Estherka's house, where she was meant to live; and her beautiful eyes, which Casimir framed in gold after her death.

The familiar play between "appearance" and "reality" (*Schein und Sein*, yet another marker of ambivalence) is fundamental to both the anthology and the story "Estherkas Haus," and the anonymous writer of the short story "Estherkas Haus" makes large use of it in the text.[49] In this story, accompanied by an illustration of Estherka's house, the narrator describes the house as follows: "[T]his is the house of Estherka . . . in the middle of the house you can see a door. . . . The small and nearly invisible stain on the right doorpost is the Mezuzah."[50]

The illustration serves as a means of authenticating both Estherka's existence and, in conjunction with the mention of the *mezuzah* (doorpost amulet), the fact that she was Jewish. The interaction between text and illustration is widely used in ethnographical reports. Yet in our specific case the picture raises more questions than answers: it pretends to be merely proof for authentication,[51] but since there are three houses with doors in the picture and the stain mentioned cannot be located, it is impossible to identify which house is actually Estherka's. It is left to the reader to spot the mezuzah in the picture and to imagine in which house Estherka used to live.

Quite evidently, the text merely simulates information about the Estherka legend. Several aspects of the story deal with perception, observation, and the construction of images. In this sense, the motif of Estherka's eyes is a part of this discourse of seeing. It is narrated that Estherka's ghost, who in life was too modest to sit for a portrait, can still be seen at night while she searches for her eyes. Since Casimir robbed her corpse of them after her death, she is not allowed to enter paradise. In the narrator's example of Estherka and Casimir, by stating that the legend of Estherka's eyes should be read metaphorically and by quoting Numbers 15:39,[52] the text stresses that the issue of Jewish–Christian interaction is a social, religious, and moral problem of the age. It suggests the problematic nature and theological extent of interreligious discourse by making reference to the fourteenth century, when the story is set, and by mentioning the mezuzah. The invisible or missing mezuzah highlights the lack of remembrance of the Lord's commandments, since "the Gentile king comes to the Jewess Esther through the mezuzah-bearing door."[53] Therefore it hints, mirrors, and deconstructs the Western European Jewish readers' assumptions of Eastern Jewish purity and authentic religious essence as manifested in Jewish daily life. In place of these assumptions, the narrator mentions the young Jewish girl's dream of "gentile [*fremdgläubig*] princes devout to other gods or [of] non-Jewish chieftains and earls" and states ironically that it is not his intention to use the story to frighten Jewish girls and make them forget their dreams about non-Jewish princes, dukes, and counts. Beyond that, it exemplifies the difference between the biological or "real" eye and the intellectual one (*geistiges Auge*). The biological eye is seduced and yearns for immoral things, whereas the intellectual eye, being a metaphor, distinguishes right from wrong and strives for right, real, and moral behavior in life.

The narrator also mentions that Casimir's other mistresses, who are jealous of Estherka's beauty and Casimir's love for her, "inscribed mocking verses about her on the wall. But we had them eliminated and gilded by dexterous hands in order not to spoil the beautiful view."[54] The "real" is blurred as the traces are plated with gold and thereby covered. Both the ambiguity of the localization of Estherka's house and the intervention of the narrator(s) to keep and to guarantee an adequate, beautiful—though constructed—picture of Estherka reflect and subvert the image of a real and unalterable existence.

The illustration of Estherka's house serves as a paradoxical authentication; if the image, as argued before, is bound to the eyes as a metaphor, it reveals the importance of the reader's perception. The reference to Estherka's house is the story's cardinal point, in which the act of perceiving and fantasizing happens on three different levels: first, the reader (both Jewish young women and the "Western Jew") imagines Estherka living in the (illustrated) house, waiting for the beloved gentile Casimir; second, it is insinuated that Jewish girls (who are addressed as readers) fantasize about a love affair with gentile princes; and third, this can be read as an allegory of the Western European Jewish imagination, which aims to locate and confirm its stereotypes of Eastern European Jewry in the text.

No matter how Jewish authenticity is performed or what the nature of Jewish essence is, the narrator insists on the impossibility of perceiving Jewish nature from a real/biological perspective. Jewish nature (or essence) can only be identified with the intellectual eye, which implies that the reader challenges a second and deeper level of significance bound to overcome the mere reading of historical facts and customs in the narrative. Therefore, neither authenticity nor Polish Jewry as its expression can be regarded as a singular, unalterable, and static originality. In fact, authenticity is repeatedly generated as a "performative effect," aesthetically constructed and incorporated in a communicative process.[55]

Assimilation and "Authentic" Polish Jewry: Josef B. Ehrlich

Josef B. Ehrlich's "Zwischen zwei Müttern" (Between Two Mothers) also hints at the nonexistence of one singular, authentic expression. However, this story goes a step further by opposing Jewish religiosity and assimilation, and thereby questioning an authentic Jewish essence on different levels: by playing with the metaphor of seeing and blindness.

Ehrlich tells the story of the young Jew Josef, born in Brody and raised by foster parents. The protagonist's biological father, a Talmud scholar, and his twelve siblings died of the Black Death before he was born. His biological mother Gütele—blind and therefore unable to make a living—cannot raise her child on her own.

"Zwischen zwei Müttern" stems from the memoirs *Der Weg meines Lebens. Erinnerungen eines ehemaligen Chassiden* (The Path of My Life. Memoirs of a Former Hassid, 1874) by Josef Ruben Ehrlich (1842–1899). The little-known Ehrlich was born in Brody and studied philosophy in Vienna. He wrote dramas (e.g., *Jacopus Ortis* [1876] and *Cato der Weise* ["Lustspiel" (comedy), 1898]) and he was a journalist for newspapers in Vienna.[56]

The excerpt "Zwischen zwei Müttern" is probably a fulfilling text for those readers who wish to gain insight into hasidic social structures, ways of life, and customs. While the autobiography depicts the story of the young hasidic *boher* and his educational path toward assimilation in the first half of the nineteenth century, the excerpt "Zwischen zwei Müttern" focuses on his family and on the problems arising from the coexistence of a biological and a foster mother.

By selecting this specific part of the autobiography, Agnon and Eliasberg place the anxiety and the battle for custody at the center. This gives the editors the opportunity to focus, in a codified way, on current issues closely related to the Western European Jewish imagination of an Eastern European Jewish authenticity: the concern with assimilation, which reveals the constructed character of authenticity and challenges the concept of *one* singular authentic core, as well as the tension between Eastern and Western Jewry and the search for identity by the young generation. The constellation of the protagonists and their interaction is of central importance: Josef's adoptive mother Freide is described briefly as being childless and a caring person. The adoptive father Samuel is more of a central figure. The protagonist describes him as a "bourgeois shoemaker"[57] and former soldier who, though religious, is not trained in reading the Talmud and lacks any knowledge of the Holy Scripture. "His whole knowledge was restricted to a collection of anecdotes and stories that he had heard from loquacious Hasidim."[58]

Samuel's ignorance of religious customs and knowledge is narrated several times within the text, and his awkwardness and lack of knowledge kindles the disapproval of the other Hasidim: he is anxious that his foster son might turn away from him and his wife and return to his biological mother to keep his biological father's memory as his "kadish." The other religious parishioners stimulate Samuel's doubts instead of being helpful. Samuel spares no effort to visit a rabbi who lives far away in order to obtain his advice. During Samuel's visit with the Belfer Rabbi, Josef is taken sick. After his return, Samuel is again afraid of losing Josef, so he walks directly to the *mikveh* (ritual bath) for praying and bathing.

The biological mother, Gütele, is gradually excluded from the foster family's life, though she lives in the same village. When Josef is five years old, he is sent to *kheyder*. Gütele, who suffers from not having her child with her, talks to him regularly: "At that time my mother used to go there [to the kheyder], guided by a little girl in order to talk to me and touch me with her hands. She would ask all my playmates where her child Jossele was. But I was ashamed of her deplorable figure . . . and I shouted: 'This is not my mother. My mother is called Freide and she has eyes to see.'"[59] Gütele's behavior encourages Samuel's fear of her and his irritability. The story ends with their battle for custody:

> "Do you pay me something for him, blind cow? You gave birth to a calf and I created a human being out of it. Who saved him from death if not I, who almost lost breath three times underneath the water?" But Gütele responded with an anxious and complaining voice: "But he is my child, my only one out of twelve unlucky born children! Alas, you wean him completely from my heart and he calls you father and your wife mother— and he calls me just by my name as they call a stranger, he mocks me and escapes from me."—and so they kept on quarrelling about custody, but my mother had to surrender to her fate, and wait for the future with divinely strong patience.[60]

In this part of the story Samuel is rendered as a more secularized person. He has an unclear position in the hasidic community, he seems to be illiterate and, although observant, has no knowledge of the Talmud and the Bible. Gütele, on the contrary, is the observant widow of a famous Talmudic scholar, and by being depicted ideally, she serves as a counterpart to Samuel and his wife. Without knowledge of the whole autobiography, the reader's first impression is that this story is not just about a son caught between two mothers. Although the text also represents a variety of Jewish religious movements (and therefore not *one* unaltered authentic form of Judaism) and aspects of religious life, it can—due to the anthology's context—also be read as a narrative of religion and religious alienation. The text includes a dichotomy of "enlightenment" or "progress" and pre-modern "tradition," emphasized by the metaphor of seeing and blindness. In this sense, Freide/Samuel and Gütele are allegories for two different ways to live religiously: Josef's biological, blind mother Gütele is an allegory for the "projected" Eastern traditional religious Jewish life, a supposedly "authentic" form of Judaism, which is not capable of reaching "enlightenment" or recognizing progress. Nevertheless, she is able to "see" the truth with her "inner" eye, thus recognizing that Josef is her son. However, Gütele will never be able to see again with her "real" eye. In a symbolic way, she is missing the opportunity to adjust to the challenges of modernity: she is doomed to be blind and to stay unenlightened and "backward."

In contrast, Samuel and Freide represent the progressive Western Jewish way of life; they are more and more alienated from their Jewish religious past at the same time that their anxiety over this past continues to grow. They are about to lose their bond to religiosity, as one can tell by Samuel's lack of knowledge of the Torah and the Talmud. Their way of performing hasidic religiosity is revealed to be only superficial.

Josef represents the second generation, not knowing exactly where he belongs. Because of his upbringing in a foster household, he is more and more alienated from his mother and, accordingly, from his religious roots. Therefore, he is increasingly open to enlightenment and assimilation. However, in this process he loses the ability to recognize where he actually comes from and where he belongs. Josef is rather afraid, and at times even ashamed, of the "deplorable figure" of his biological mother.

He stands for a young Jewish generation somewhere in between religious and assimilated Judaism, searching for its own Jewish identity.

The question of authenticity is brought up metaphorically by the battle for custody, but it remains unsolved in this text, since the "authentic" Jewish life as an unchangeable essence is not to be found in either way of life. The image of a supposedly "authentic" Eastern European Jewish essence expressing itself through (religious) tradition and culture is reduced to absurdity.

CLOSING REMARKS

Das Buch von den polnischen Juden as a whole, and the three analyzed texts in particular, show how literature deals with authenticity in the first half of the twentieth century. Authenticity seems to be located between a "real"/historical experience and its fictional representation.

Based on this anthology, the production of authenticity can be viewed from three different perspectives. Under the aspect of poetics, authenticity is created by the editors and authors, who are perceived as authentic. And yet, this process of authentication is virtually endless. Historically, authenticity evokes a tension between the (pointless) search for a historical *Ursprünglichkeit* (nativeness) and the use of legends that are by nature composed, constructed, and lack an original author. In this case, the constructed, fragmented character of authenticity is undeniable. On a metaphorical and narrative level, authenticity is constructed in the process of reading—in an interaction between the text and the reader. By making use of the metaphors of the "real" and "intellectual" eye, and by constructing a supposedly authenticating frame through illustrations, the text offers different starting points for authenticating readings, and likewise for a critique of authenticity.

My aim has been to show that *Das Buch von den polnischen Juden* is founded on the Western European discourse of authenticity (as nativeness and originality) in order to highlight the nonexistence of the "authentic" condition that is, in turn, imaginary. In this anthology, the editors Agnon and Eliasberg emphasize the quest for an authentic Jewish identity in order to reflect the "encounter of Self and other," which "becomes the site of ongoing power struggles and endless (re)negotiations of values and meanings that circumscribe the individual's role in and relationship to society."[61] In this sense, *Das Buch von den polnischen Juden* is a quintessentially modern text: it deals with the problematic construction of authenticity at a time when searching for Jewish authenticity—be it for Zionist or other reasons—was en vogue.

Accordingly, in November 1916 Nathan Birnbaum published a review of the anthology *Das Buch von den polnischen Juden* with the abbreviation M.A. for his pseudonym, Mathias Acher, in Martin Buber's *Der Jude*. Despite Birnbaum's critique of the term "Polish Jews," the romanticizing style, and the selection of texts, he confirms that "every 'Westler' will lay down the book with a dreadful agitation, which is the sign of the initial turmoil of the balance of the prejudices."[62]

NOTES

1. Nathan Birnbaum, "Deutsche und polnische Juden," *Die Welt* 10 (1897): 4 (my translation).

2. Ibid., 5.

3. Ibid.

4. Ibid., 4.

5. The Greek adjective *authentikos* (late Latin: *authenticus*) "designates the genuineness of an object or a circumstance, usually in the form of an attribution to a specific origin or provenance. The term 'authentic' expresses a positive, rare and singular quality, which is perceived and sought for in different contexts." Aleida Assmann, "Authenticity—The Signature of Western Exceptionalism?" in *Paradoxes of Authenticity. Studies on a Critical Concept*, ed. Julia Straub (Bielefeld: transcript, 2012), 34 f.
Authenticity, both within the nineteenth century and today, is mostly associated with notions such as nativeness, originality, and the German "Eigenheit/Eigentümlichkeit" and "Ursprünglichkeit."

6. E.g., Heinrich Heine's *Über Polen* (1823), David Friedländer's *Über die Verbesserung der Israeliten im Königreich Polen* (1834), or Leo Herzberg-Fränkel's *Polnische Juden. Geschichten und Bilder* (1867), just to give a few examples.

7. Steven E. Aschheim shows in his study *Brothers and Strangers: The East European Jew in German and German Jewish Consciousness 1800–1923* (1982) how dealing with the Eastern European Jew implied primarily a constructed opposition of the civilized *Westjude* to the backward-oriented *Ostjude*. Similar to Edward Said's thesis that the projection of the Orient as a counterpart to Europe was mainly a manifestation for self-confirmation of Europe's own culture, Aschheim suggests that "[i]n large parts this was a view formulated and propagated by West European and especially German Jews, serving as a symbolic

construct by which they could distinguish themselves from their less fortunate, uneman-cipated East European brethren." Steven E. Aschheim, *Brothers and Strangers: The East European Jew in German and German Jewish Consciousness 1800–1923* (Madison: University of Wisconsin Press, 1982), 3.

8. Hans-Jürgen Becker and Hillel Weiss, "Introduction," in *Agnon and Germany: The Presence of the German World in the Writings of S. Y. Agnon*, ed. Hans-Jürgen Becker and Hillel Weiss (Ramat Gan: Bar-Ilan University Press, 2010), 10.

9. Cf. Michael Rössner and Heidemarie Uhl, "Vorwort," in *Renaissance der Authentizität? Über die neue Sehnsucht nach dem Ursprünglichen*, ed. Michael Rössner and Heidemarie Uhl (Bielefeld: transcript, 2012), 9.

10. Cf. Becker and Weiss, "Introduction," 10.

11. Such as—among others—Martin Buber's *Die Geschichten des Rabbi Nachman* (The Stories of Rabbi Nachman, 1906) or *Die Legende des Baalschem* (The Legend of the Baalshem, 1908), Micha Josef Bin Gorion's *Die Sagen der Juden. Mythen, Legenden, Auslegungen* (The Legends of the Jews: Myths, Legends, Exegesis, 1913), Aleksander Eliasberg's *Sagen polnischer Juden* (Legends of the Polish Jews, 1916), or *Die Legenden der Juden* by Judah Bergmann (The Legends of the Jews, 1919).

12. Arnold Band, *Nostalgia and Nightmare*, 20, quoted in Andrea Weilbacher, "Agnon and the Jewish Renaissance," in *Agnon and Germany: The Presence of the German World in the Writings of S. Y. Agnon*, ed. Hans-Jürgen Becker and Hillel Weiss (Ramat Gan: Bar-Ilan University Press, 2010), 17.

13. Cf. Arnold J. Band, "Agnon, Shmuel Yosef," in *Encyclopedia Judaica*, Vol. 1, Second Edition 2007, 465–467.

14. Cf. Anatol Schenker, *Der Jüdische Verlag 1902–1938* (Tübingen: Max Niemeyer, 2003), 130–134.

15. Ahron Eliasberg, quoted in Schenker, *Der Jüdische Verlag 1902–1938*, 188 (my translation).

16. Mary-Louise Pratt, "Arts of the Contact Zone," *Profession* (1991): 35.

17. Wolfgang Funke, Florian Gross, and Irmtraud Huber, "Exploring the Empty Plinth: The Aesthetics of Authenticity," in *The Aesthetics of Authenticity: Medial Constructions of the Real*, ed. Wolfgang Funke, Florian Gross, and Irmtraud Huber (Bielefeld: transcript, 2012), 11.

18. Regina Bendix, *In Search of Authenticity: The Formation of Folklore Studies* (Madison: University of Wisconsin Press, 1997), 8.

19. Cf. Ibid., 16.

20. Cf. Johann Gottfried Herder, *Ideen zur Philosophie der Geschichte der Menschheit*, ed. Martin Bollacher (Frankfurt am Main: Deutscher Klassiker Verlag, 1989).

21. Bendix, 17.

22. Cf. Ibid., 50.

23. Brothers Grimm, quoted in Bendix, 51.

24. Cf. Ibid.

25. S. J. Agnon and Aaron Eliasberg, "Nachwort und Anmerkungen der Herausgeber," in *Das Buch von den polnischen Juden*, ed. S. J. Agnon and Aaron Eliasberg (Berlin: Jüdischer Verlag, 1916), 261 (my translation).

26. "Also an individual person cannot be illustrated by descriptions of every detail; anyhow by single drafts, gestures and deeds his image reveals itself to the watching eye." Agnon and Eliasberg, "Nachwort," 262 (my translation).

27. Haya Bar-Itzhak, *Jewish Poland Legends of Origin: Ethnopoetics and Legendary Chronicles* (Detroit: Wayne State University Press, 2001), 14.

28. The difference between *legend* and *myth*: "According to traditional definitions used in folklore studies, myth differs from legend chiefly on the time axis. Whereas a 'myth' is a sacred tale that explains the creation of the world, humanity, and the condition of both, a 'legend' takes place in the post-creation era, that is, in historical time." Bar-Itzhak, 15.

29. Cf. Elke Mader, *Ethnologische Mythenforschung: Theoretische Perspektiven und Beispiele aus Lateinamerika*, p. 8, http://www.lateinamerika-studien.at/content/kultur/mythen/pdf/mythen.pdf.

30. They stir the primary meaning of the notion of authenticity, which implies the function as a seal of quality for certain different objects, e.g. events, traditions, persons, art works, institutions, etc. Cf. Assmann, "Authenticity—The Signature of Western Exceptionalism?" 34 f.

31. Cf. Funke, Gross, and Huber, 13.

32. Bar-Itzhak, 123.

33. S. J. Agnon, "Polen: Die Legende von der Ankunft," in *Das Buch von den polnischen Juden*, ed. S. J. Agnon and Ahron Eliasberg (Berlin: Jüdischer Verlag, 1916), 3 (my translation).

34. Annette Werberger observes in her talk on *"Ein Wald voller Talmudtraktate"— 'Polin' als Migrationsmythos im imperialen Kontext*, held in January 2013 at the Zentrum für Literatur- und Kulturforschung Berlin, that it was Y. L. Peretz who wrote down the legend of the Jewish settlement in Poland for the first time at the beginning of the chapter "Asekuriert" in his *Bilder fun a provvints-rayze in tomashover poviat um 1890 yor* (1891). Werberger suggests that Peretz, as the first author of this story, was responsible for the further spread of this legend. I thank Annette Werberger both for this hint and for showing me her paper.

35. Bar-Itzhak, 14.

36. Agnon, "Polen," 3.

37. This folklore legend is discussed thoroughly in Bar-Itzhak's aforementioned study, *Jewish Poland*, in the first chapter "The Geography of Jewish Imagination: Po-Lin among Trees with Leaves from the Gemara," 27–44.

38. Bar-Itzhak, 22.

39. Agnon, "Polen," 5.

40. It is worth mentioning that during that specified time there was not a Prince Leschek ruling Poland. From about 900 on it could be Prince Lestek, but his existence is disputable in historical research.

41. Agnon, "Polen," 6.

42. Ibid., 8.

43. Cf. Marek M. Dziekan, "History and Culture of Polish Tatars," in *Muslims in Poland and Eastern Europe: Widening the European Discourse on Islam*, ed. Katarzyna Górak-Sosnowska (University of Warsaw, Faculty of Oriental Studies, 2011), 27 and 35. This custom was also practiced by Kurdistani Jews, as Erich Brauer reveals in his book *The Jews of Kurdistan* (1940/1993). Cf. Erich Brauer, *The Jews of Kurdistan*, ed. Raphael Patai (Detroit: Wayne State University Press, 1993), 323 ff. I want to thank Galit Hasan-Rokem for this hint.

44. Boris Kotlerman, "Historical Time and Space in S. Y. Agnon's *Sippure Polin*," in *Agnon and Germany: The Presence of the German World in the Writings of S. Y. Agnon*, ed.

Hans-Jürgen Becker and Hillel Weiss (Ramat Gan: Bar-Ilan University Press, 2010), 361–374.

45. Bar-Itzhak, 19.

46. As Gershon Shaked states about Agnon's literary work, "[F]or Agnon, intertextuality was neither a mere literary device nor an unconscious phenomenon. Rather, it was the very source of his creativity, perhaps even its main subject." Gershon Shaked, *Shmuel Yosef Agnon: A Revolutionary Traditionalist* (New York: New York University Press, 1989), 24, quoted in Andrea Weilbacher, "Agnon and the Jewish Renaissance," in *Agnon and Germany: The Presence of the German World in the Writings of S. Y. Agnon*, ed. Hans-Jürgen Becker and Hillel Weiss (Ramat Gan: Bar-Ilan University Press, 2010), 21.

47. Besides the intention to justify historical events, Bar-Itzhak also refers to the possibility that this legend was widely spread and a pattern for fictional stories and/or plays in order to "reinforce the taboo against sexual relations with non-Jews." Bar-Itzhak, 127.

48. Bar-Itzhak states: "In normal circumstances, such relations would be condemned, but the absence of such condemnation, and even possible legitimation, is seen from the story of the biblical Esther on, when such relations are interpreted as being decisive for the survival of the entire community. . . . Thus the legends about Esther and Casimir are used in folk tradition to explain the grant of settlement rights and the expansion of the privileges of the Jews in Poland by King Casimir." Bar-Itzhak, 113.

49. Although the story does not bear the name of the writer, Boris Kotlerman suggests in his article that it was probably written or dictated by Agnon, since in one of his following publications one can find a changed version of this text. Kotlerman, "Historical Time and Space in S. Y. Agnon's *Sippure Polin*," 371 f.

50. "Estherkas Haus," in *Das Buch von den polnischen Juden*, ed. S. J. Agnon and Ahron Eliasberg (Berlin: Jüdischer Verlag, 1916), 17 (my translation).

51. "The reference to the mezuza aims to verify the opening line that 'this is Estherke's house': the mark left by the mezuza is offered as proof." Bar-Itzhak, 131.

52. "And it shall be a tassel for you to look at and remember all the commandments of the Lord, to do them, not to follow after your own heart and your own eyes, which you are inclined to whore after" (English Standard Version).

53. Bar-Itzhak, 131.

54. "Estherkas Haus," 18.

55. Funke, Gross, and Huber, 13.

56. *Österreichisches Biographisches Lexikon 1815–1950*, s.v. "Ehrlich, Josef Ruben," http://www.biographien.ac.at/oebl/oebl_E/Ehrlich_Josef-Ruben_1842_1899.xml.

57. Josef B. Ehrlich, "Zwischen zwei Müttern," in *Das Buch von den polnischen Juden*, ed. S. J. Agnon and Ahron Eliasberg (Berlin: Jüdischer Verlag, 1916), 199 (my translation).

58. Ibid., 200.

59. Ibid., 210.

60. Ibid., 211.

61. Funke, Gross, and Huber, 13.

62. M.A., "Polnische Juden," in *Der Jude* 8 (1916): 562 (my translation).

3

The Cold Order and the Eros of Storytelling

Joseph Roth's "Exotic Jews"

ANDREAS KILCHER

In August 1926 the Austrian writer and star journalist Joseph Roth traveled to Russia for the *Frankfurter Zeitung.* Roth, himself originally from Brody in the easternmost part of Galicia, close to the Russian border, had been commissioned to write a series of articles, for a Western European readership, on the young Soviet Union, where Stalin was in the process of establishing a centralized system of governance designed to shape economic, social, and cultural life. After Lenin's death in January 1924 Stalin had emerged victorious from the power struggle with Trotsky, who was excluded from the Politburo in 1926 and, at the 15th Party Congress in late 1927, from the Communist Party of the Soviet Union.[1]

The West, where the rift between "the left" and "the right" started to escalate, had been looking at the new Russia with a mix of curiosity and skepticism. Although the Spartacist uprising in Berlin and the Munich Soviet Republic had failed in 1919, and despite relentless persecution by the German right, German communists on the far left, following Liebknecht and Trotsky, such as Ruth Fischer, Arkadij Maslow, and Werner Scholem, were still counting on a German revolution.[2] By means of the Communist International (Comintern), the long arm of Stalin reached Germany. In November 1925, the German Trotskyists lost their influence within the German Communist Party (KPD) before they were altogether banned in 1926. Considering these developments, Roth—who had signed his contributions to the social-democratic newspaper *Vorwärts* as "red

FIGURE 3.1

Aleksandr Chemeriski: *Di alfarbandishe komunistishe partei
(bolshevikes) un di yidishe masn.* Moscow: Farlag Shul un Bukh 1926.

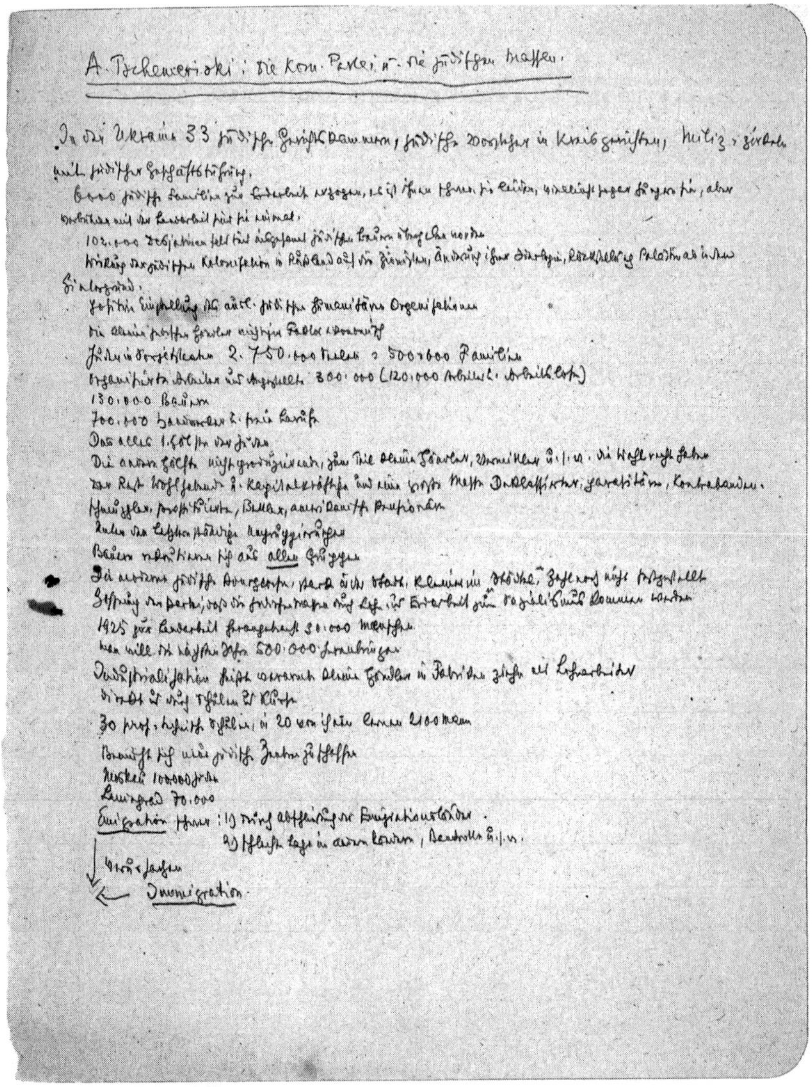

A. Tschemeriski: Die Kom. Partei u. die jüdischen Massen.

FIGURE 3.2

Joseph Roth: Excerpt from "A. Tschemeriski: Die Komm. Partei und die jüdischen Massen." Courtesy of the Leo Baeck Institute, New York, Joseph Bornstein Collection.

Joseph" and had published his first novel, *The Spider's Web* (1923), in the Viennese *Arbeiter-Zeitung*—sought to appease his features editor Benno Reifenberg even before he embarked on his travels. Roth gave him assurances that he had no intention of merely launching into panegyrics about the revolution and that he would instead be reporting factually; indeed, he would be a critical observer.

His journalist's gaze would be trained not just on the general tension between revolutionary idealism, which was close to his own heart, on the one hand, and actual circumstances in communist Russia during the establishment of Stalin's power, on the other. It would also be focused on the way in which, compared with the tsarist empire, the Soviet Union dealt with its many ethnic minorities, including the Jews, to whom Roth would devote particular attention. He did so ahead of time while preparing for his trip by reading not only contemporary travelogues by his peers, such as those of Egon Erwin Kisch, a member of the KPD who had traveled several times to "the world proletariat's fatherland" since 1925 to write enthusiastic reports, and Ernst Toller, who had participated in the Munich Soviet Republic in 1919 and then became a member of Kurt Hiller's "Group of Revolutionary Pacifists" before traveling to Moscow in the spring of 1926.[3] Roth also jotted down the keyword "Jews" on a list of topics to be studied in preparation of his journey. And indeed, he read and excerpted Aleksandr Chemeriskii's Yiddish book *Di alfarbandishe komunistishe partei (bolshevikes) un di yidishe masn* (The United Communist Party [Bolsheviks] and the Jewish Masses, 1926).[4] Chemeriskii was for many years a leading figure in the "General Union of Jewish Workers in Lithuania, Poland, and Russia," which turned to the Bolshevik side after the Russian Revolution and then entered the Jewish section of the Communist Party, with Chemeriskii becoming its secretary in 1920.[5]

Roth's view of the politics of the Soviet multiethnic state must also be seen against the backdrop of the policy of *korenizatsiia* (indigenization) adopted in 1923.[6] This policy governed the integration of non-Russian peoples into the new state. In a marked departure from tsarist "imperialism" and "chauvinism," the new principle was designed to promote, rather than discriminate against, the identities, cultures, and languages of non-Russian peoples. The promotion of regional cultures was accompanied by an education and information drive, in the course of which many of the hitherto mainly oral languages were alphabetized: for the first time written languages were created for forty-eight smaller groups of peoples, specifically in the Caucasus and Siberia, albeit in Latin script.

The science of ethnography played a particular role in this politically motivated education and information drive by the young Soviet Union. With its specific cultural and epistemological techniques it was particularly well suited to the project of including ethnic groups in the newly defined multiethnic state. Ethnography was meant to promote the cultural policy ambitions of the socialist state through research work as well as information and the education of non-Russian peoples.[7] With the policy of *korenizatsiia*, the ethnography of the socialist state was therefore pursuing a dual—and paradoxical—objective: on the one hand, non-Russian peoples were to be accepted, not to say strengthened, in their cultural identity; on the other hand, they were to be assimilated and integrated into the vast entity of the Soviet Union through nationalization, literacy, and modernization in order to broaden the path of socialism. "'National in form, socialist in content' was the motto."[8]

It is an approach that was also adopted toward Jews. The position of Jews in the young Soviet Union was initially characterized positively by the abolition of the restrictions and discrimination imposed by the tsarist minorities policy. By contrast, the emergence of a new Jewish Soviet culture was promoted at great length.[9] However, the "indigenization" of Jews went hand in hand with the abolition of traditional Jewish institutions, so-called bourgeois and more particularly religious ones, such as community leadership institutions and synagogues; it also entailed a sharp criticism of Zionism and its "bourgeois" notion of a "Jewish nation." Particular efforts were made at the same time to turn the Jews into a people compatible with the socialist state by creating new institutions such as the Jewish section of the Communist Party (the Evsektsiia [1918] or Yidishe komunistishe sektsyes). However, the most important remedy for this persecuted, landless, and unproductive people was the program of agrarian revolution and industrialization. Land and labor were the means by which the nomadic "peoples of the air"[10] were to be socialized, a view Roth was able to read also in Chemeriskii, who as secretary of the Evsektsiia was one of its leading members.[11] Roth aptly described this program endorsed by Chemeriskii in his article "Die Lage der Juden in Sowjetrussland" (Situation of the Jews in Soviet Russia), which was published in the *Frankfurter Zeitung* on November 9, 1926:

> What does theory call for?—national self-determination!—But in order to apply the prescription in full, the Jews first need to be made into a "legitimate" national minority, like the Georgians, or the Germans, or the Belarusians. The unnatural social structure of the Jews must be transformed, for this is a people that—of all the peoples in the world—has the most beggars; the most "welfare recipients" as the Americans say; the most downwardly mobile. They must be molded into a people with familiar and reliable characteristics. And because this new nationality is to live in a socialist state, its "unproductive" and lower-middle-class elements must be converted into workers and peasants. And finally they will be rewarded by their very own piece of territory somewhere.[12]

What Roth is alluding to here was promoted by institutions such as the Komzet, founded in 1921, the government Committee for the Settlement of Toiling Jews on the Land, and the Ozet, the corresponding and complementary public society. The plan for the agricultural "colonization" of the Jews was approved in June 1926, and Chemeriskii promoted it as the "solution to the problem of territorial autonomy"; the Evsektsiia endorsed his view in a resolution in September 1926.[13]

As problematic as the forced secularization of the Jews proved to be (in the course of which, in Roth's own words, "synagogues are now being transformed into workmen's clubs and Talmud schools are banned");[14] as ambiguous as the agrarian and industrial territorialization of the Jews proved to be (in the course of which they were settled in several "colonies" in Ukraine and in Crimea as well as in the Siberian region of Birobidzhan after 1927);[15] and as ambiguous as the talk of the national autonomy of the Jews proved to be (limited as it was by socialist internationalism), always foremost in the minds of the architects of the Soviet Union was the need to put right the oppression suffered by Jews in tsarist Russia. Similarly, Roth's article on Jews in the Soviet Union, despite his skepticism about the attempts at the territorialization of the "intellectual people," led to the following conclusion, which—in referring to the Jews in Russia—is entirely in keeping with Chemeriskii's line: "everyone should take notice as one people is freed from the stain of suffering and another from the stain of cruelty.... This is a great accomplishment of the Russian Revolution."[16]

It was thus against this political and ideological backdrop that Roth embarked on his travels to Russia in August 1926.[17] In the course of a voyage lasting five months to late 1926, he journeyed from Paris across Poland and Belarus to Moscow via Minsk, and from there eastward and southward by mail steamer down the Volga to Astrakhan and the Azerbaijan oil-producing center of Baku, to the Caspian Sea. On these travels to the provinces, Roth began to develop an ethnographic perspective and an ethnographic way of writing; however, both differed fundamentally— and expressly—from the aforementioned Soviet political ethnography. Roth's perception was structured rather simply initially. He was guided by difference with regard to the familiar (Western, European) in that he classified what he saw as extremely "foreign," thereby underscoring its exoticism: in late August, he wrote from Astrakhan to the editor's office in Frankfurt: "If one were to set foot on a different star, things couldn't be more different or more strange."[18] And he went on to do more of the same, traveling from there across the Caucasus via Tiflis and Sochi to Yalta, Sebastopol, and Odessa, to the shores of the Black Sea. On October 1st he wrote to Frankfurt, explaining that the tour through the mountain valley of the Caucasus in particular was taking its toll on the Western European traveler: "I'm going to ask for damages for all the torments of this exotic journey in the Caucasus, on mule, by bus— . . . and I'm dreaming of a room at the Frankfurter Hof."[19] He arrived in Odessa on September 22nd and recovered there for ten days from the outlandish Caucasus before setting off across Ukraine via Kiev and Kharkov, initially to the equally longed-for hotel with a European standard of comfort in Moscow, where he arrived in late October; according to Roth it was the "Hotel Bolshaia."[20] There he was planning to meet some of the leading intellectuals of the Soviet Union, such as the film director Sergei Eisenstein and the writer Isaac Babel. In fact, he also met Walter Benjamin, who recorded the meeting in Roth's hotel—"like a European hotel that has been transplanted far to the east"—in early December 1926 in his Moscow Diary, fittingly characterizing Roth as a disillusioned Soviet fan: "He had come to Russia as a (nearly) confirmed Bolshevik and was leaving it a royalist."[21] Indeed, Roth's conclusions about the Soviet Union at the dawn of the Stalin era were ultimately less than optimistic. As he put it in a lecture titled "Über die Verbürgerlichung der Russischen Revolution" (On the Bourgeoisification of the Russian Revolution) in Frankfurt in late January 1927, revolution had turned into bureaucracy: "In Russia the scarlet, ecstatic, bloody terror of the active revolution has given way to the dull, silent, inky-black terror of bureaucracy."[22]

ETHNOLITERATURE: MODES OF WRITING RUSSIA

At first sight, the travel journalist's approach to cultural differences hardly seems imbued with ethnographic sensitivity. Demanding ethnographic methods such as "participant observation," which Bronislaw Malinowski had only just coined while conducting research in Papua New Guinea, appear quite alien to him.[23] But the moment Roth ceased to describe to his Frankfurt employer in dramatic terms the physical exertions of his travels and, instead, conveyed his experiences through the medium of writing, a methodologically highly reflective process began to take hold, with far-reaching prospects for the *epistemic* and also *aesthetic* methods of ethnography. Indeed, by the end of December 1926 Roth had not only written a total of seventeen journalistic articles from Russia, but he also worked on other—also literary—texts: he kept a diary of his travels,[24] continued to work on the essay "The Wandering Jews," and wrote a novel about Russia, featuring a literary approach to his experiences: *The Flight without End*. The realization of his ethnography of Eastern European Jews lay precisely in this constellation of hugely diverse types of texts.

Roth's initial thoughts on ethnographic description are first apparent in a letter from Odessa dated September 26th to his colleague Bernard von Brentano. When once again he emphasizes the distance that separates the Western European from Russian Europe on the border with Asia, he does so initially to establish—as before—the claim of cultural difference: the object is positioned as the *foreign* of European culture, to which the subject feels a sense of belonging: "I feel as though I have been gone from Europe for six months. I've experienced so much here, and all of it strange to me. Never has it been brought home to me so strongly that I'm a European, a man of the Mediterranean."[25] What is crucial here for Roth's incipient ethnographic writing is not so much the constitution of the object as foreign and *exotic*—evidently a central category of Roth's, which we shall be examining in more detail—but rather the awareness of

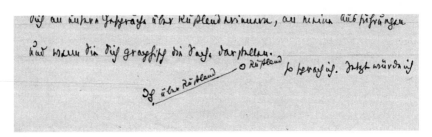

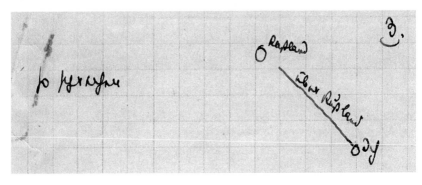

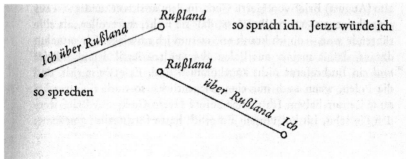

FIGURE 3.3A–C

"Me on Russia—Russia on Me." Joseph Roth: Letter to Bernhard von
Brentano, Odessa, September 26 1926, Deutsches Literaturarchiv, Marbach.

the role of observation. Here Roth achieved a significant epistemological
reversal of perspective, which gave rise to a highly differentiated form of
ethnography: while his initial starting point was that of himself as the
Western European subject of the observation confronting "Russia" as the
inaccessible foreign entity, "Russia" now became the agent of the observation, with Europe receding into the background and put into perspective

as a fixed cultural entity. At this tipping point the ethnographic object became the subject; the Western *me* of the observation, the new foreign entity: "It's a boon that I've come to Russia. I should never have gotten to know myself otherwise."[26] Roth sketched a diagram of this crucial reversal.

Roth himself explained the diagram as a Copernican reversal within ethnography, as the reversal from a "primitive" premodern colonialist objectification of the foreign, toward the recognition of the Other as a subject: "In other words, I am looking in a completely different direction. Russia is somewhere else. I was like a mariner from antiquity or the Middle Ages, setting off for the Spice Islands, in the belief that the earth was flat. If you know it's round, you know how mistaken the voyage was."[27] One of Roth's central theses is that it cannot be a matter of sizing up Eastern Europe—particularly the Eastern Europe of the Jews—from a Western European perspective and in so doing colonizing it symbolically; rather, it is about using Eastern Europe to put Western Europe into perspective, in fact to "irritate" it, thereby allowing Eastern Europe its rightful status.

This reversal also has a crucial impact on the methodology of ethnography. It is the moment of birth not just of the travel journalist, but of the writer, too—in a word, of *ethnoliterature*. Indeed, as a writer, Roth also found the ethnographical adaptation of writing itself motivating, for in the same letter of September 26, 1926 he goes on: "Finally I have the subject for the book that only I can write, and will maybe write while in Russia."[28] A day later he noted in his diary: "The novel! What should it be called?"[29] And already on October 2nd he wrote: "Started the novel. If I manage to write but three pages every day, I could have an impeccable novel within six weeks."[30] Roth would indeed go on to write large sections of the novel *The Flight without End* in the course of his travels in Russia.

This essay proposes that it was neither the novel nor the travel reportage by themselves, but in fact the constellation of factual-journalistic and narrative-literary methods that allowed Roth to produce a new form of ethnographic writing. The productive tension generated by both styles sparked a more complex ethnographic writing, an ethnoliterature that bridges the classic cultural differences. Roth was already well versed in both genres. His trip to Soviet Russia as a travel journalist for the *Frankfurter Zeitung* was not his first in that capacity: he had previously been to

Galicia in late 1924 (we shall be returning to that journey) and to France, and thereafter to Albania and Yugoslavia (May to June 1927), to Poland (May to July 1928) and to Italy (autumn 1928). Prior to that, Roth had become known as a writer with novels such as *Hotel Savoy* (1924) and *The Rebellion* (1924). But it was only as a result of the interplay between travel journalism and literature such as it emerged in the context of the trip to Russia in particular that Roth was presented with opportunities for ethnographic writing.

In fact, it would seem that Roth gave a great deal of thought to the complex relationship between these forms of writing. By no means did he see it as a static opposition, with the scientific, objectifying journalist and his reportage on the one hand and the poetically creative writer and his novels on the other. Rather, Roth shaped the relationship between journalism and literature as a dynamic and dialectical one by linking both in the context of his trip to Russia and developing both in a critical way. Thus initially around 1926 he made the factual and documentary style of journalism the focal point of literary storytelling. This gave rise to the literary texts which he himself attributed to what is referred to as *Neue Sachlichkeit* (New Objectivity) and which made the realism of documentary reporting a model for literary writing. The result was a hybridization of literature and factual text under the aegis of journalism. But Roth also saw this connection in reverse, namely under the aegis of literature. This revision was consistent with a sharp criticism (at times) of New Objectivity and a restitution of the storytelling and poetic function of literature.

In what follows, I will analyze these ethnographic constellations of literature and objectivity using examples that highlight Roth's view of the Jews in the Soviet Union in particular. This can be done by examining two pairs of texts: firstly and mainly, the constellation of the Russian travel features (considered in the second section of this essay) with the novel *The Flight without End* (examined in the third section), which look at Jews in the Russian provinces of the Caucasus; then secondly and shorter, the constellation of the essay *The Wandering Jews* with the novel *Job* (analyzed in my fourth section), which focuses on Jews in Poland, Galicia, and Russia. These two pairs of examples make it possible to track the shift in perspectives in the relationship between journalism and literature. The first is based primarily on the possibilities for factual and scientific description, so they can be postulated as a model for literature. By contrast, the second sounds out the possibility of factual documentation and sets it against the primacy of poetry. But both scenarios produce the sort of fertile space between objectivity and literature that gives rise to ethnoliterature.

"EXOTIC JEWS" OF THE CAUCASUS: ROTH'S ETHNOGRAPHIC JOURNALISM

The most remarkable of the Russian feature articles is the one on the Caucasus: *Das Völker-Labyrinth im Kaukasus* (The Labyrinth of Peoples in the Caucasus), which was printed in the *Frankfurter Zeitung* on October 26, 1926. The ethnographic view hinted at by Roth in the title follows his newly adopted method: namely, not to approach the border region between Europe and Asia in a hegemonic way using Western European categories and values, but instead to "irritate" the West with the "half-Asian"[31] East. Roth does so essentially with the main proposition that all the fundamental Western European categories of political identity such as people, nation, culture, and language have no validity in the Caucasus region. Rather, Roth the ethnographer characterizes the peoples and cultures of the Caucasus as essentially heterogeneous, as hybrid forms that have always avoided political affiliation and cultural identity and consequently cannot be integrated: "A general assimilation has never succeeded."[32]

Roth's central and striking attribute for this complex plurality and heterogeneity of small Caucasus civilizations is the "exotic." However, the exotic as stated here is no mere category of colonial experience of the foreign. Rather, it implies the assumption that the ethnographic object is irreducibly resistant and foreign for Western European observers, and in this sense also untouched, original, oriental, and authentic. Better still: this half-Asian Orient in turn becomes an agent of irritation for the Occident. It unsettles homogeneous Western categories of identity, culture, and nation. Roth's first description of the "exotic" in this sense applies to the labyrinthine and polyphonic market square in Baku: "Many narrow, dirty alleys; passageways used as market halls; countless small shops with signs in Turkish, Persian, and Armenian."[33] Equally exotic is the medley of the most heterogeneous things, which symbolically represent unrivaled cultural diversity and heterogeneity: "Jewish matzo," "Georgian belts," a "dagger in a Tula-silver scabbard," "cufflinks inscribed with Turkish blessings"—and by contrast, from the modern West only "watches without hands, fake jewels, bright green braces," which Roth dismisses as extremely slack symbols of civilization.[34] The Caucasian peoples as a whole are then "exotic," compared with the faded culture of Western Europe. In describing them, Roth departs from the otherwise predominant factual-realistic description and reaches for concepts of authenticity founded in myths of origins that have been circulating about the Caucasus for a long time, for instance the legend of the ten lost tribes of Israel: "In the inaccessible gorges and valleys of the Caucasus live the last relics of an otherwise extinct exoticism of long dissipated civilizations," he writes. Nonetheless, such mythical narratives tend to be far less prominent in the feature on the Caucasus than the more realistic description of the transnational civilizations of the Caucasus. Through Roth's eyes we see them as polyphonic, heterogeneous, uncolonizable—and therefore as an outstanding antithesis of the powerful and forceful identity concepts of the West, which had only recently given rise to a devastating war.

Roth illustrates this aspect with the Jews in particular. Indeed, he goes out of his way to present them not as assimilated Europeans of the East reading Schiller and Goethe. Living at the heart of the labyrinth of Caucasian peoples, whose number Roth estimates at around forty-five, he sees them as "the most interesting Jews in the world"—the *most exotic*. With this concept of "exotic Jews," which has played its part in shaping Jewish ethnography since 1900,[35] Roth initially means the *gerim,* Russian peasants who converted to Judaism, but mainly he refers to what are known as the "mountain Jews." They had previously attracted the attention of Zionists by attending the Zionist Congresses in Basel as "proud horsemen"—as un-European and unassimilated Jews—in their own separate delegation.[36] This is why, in his essay *Zur Kunde von den Juden im Kaukasus* (1900), the Zionist folklore expert and librarian Heinrich Loewe categorized the mountain Jews as "ethnologically all the more interesting" as they retained their authenticity amidst the "mountain peoples of the Caucasus," "yet without blunting the sharpest traits of its nationality over the course of the millennia. . . . Only the Jewish nationality has remained, immovable and immutable."[37] While Roth concurs with the above with regard to the claim of authenticity, he rejects the notion that it underpins any Zionist nationalization, territorialization, and culturization of the Caucasian "mountain Jews." Rather, he describes them as a prime example of Caucasian transculturalism that utterly repudiates any national-cultural patterns—even Judaism itself in its classic form. For Roth, they are the "most interesting Jews in the world" for the simple reason that they are *not* "Jewish Jews."

Roth first encountered a mountain Jew on the market square in Baku, where by chance he happened upon a "familiar name written in Latin script" among the babble of languages featured on the signs: "Who here might be called 'Levin'? Albeit with the first names 'Arvad Darzah.' It is a mountain Jew. He trades in sole leather. Even though, in terms of race, he belongs to the Tat people, in other words not even a Semite, he does speak broken German."[38] Roth's mountain Jew cannot be reduced to any national-cultural model, either linguistically or ethnically: he remains unintegratable among heterogeneous paradigms. It is not only by language that Roth emphasizes the transculturalism of the Caucasian mountain Jews. While they use the Tat language, there is no Tat script, and so according to Roth they hit "upon the impractical solution of using Hebrew characters for the Tat language."[39] Roth therefore contrasts the Zionist narrative of the Caucasian mountain Jews, which situates them within the territory of a national-cultural narrative of origins, with a deterritorializing transcultural ethnographic narrative that describes them in their irreducible foreignness and heterogeneity.

What is even more important to Roth than the demarcation of the mountain Jews from Zionist nationalization is the evaluation of the way in which communist Soviet Russia deals with the mountain Jews in particular and, more generally, with minorities. Does the USSR put them under the pressure of assimilation in the name of a centralizing internationalism, or does it integrate them in their resistant foreignness into a multiethnic state of cultural pluralism and heterogeneity, for which Roth had the lost Danube monarchy in mind as a role model? As in the feature on *Die Lage der Juden in Sowjetrussland*, Roth's answer in the Caucasus feature is ambivalent: unlike tsarist Russia, the Soviet Union for the first time allows "equal rights for national minorities in Russia."[40] On closer inspection, however, it becomes clear that Roth has again spotted a coercive colonialist moment. It lies, of all places, in Soviet Russia's endeavors to survey its minorities using ethnographic research. What manifests itself, initially in a somewhat covert fashion, is the force of order, systematic approach, administration, and bureaucratization in the guise of education and progress: "For now, a national labyrinth has been created, at great effort, out of the maze of peoples: it is complicated but systematic. And while the foreigner may lose his way, the locals know where they are."[41] Here Roth references the aforementioned cultural-political program adopted by the young Soviet Union aimed at the alphabetization, education, and culturalization of its non-Russian peoples, a program of which ethnography was a significant part. Its purpose was also to take the revolution and, with it, progress to the remotest regions of the multiethnic state. If, as Roth writes, minorities were to be recognized in the process, it was also clear to him in this feature that it went hand in hand with the ideological objective and, at the same time, with bureaucratization on a massive scale, which, as he then openly criticized in his lecture "Über die Verbürgerlichung der Russischen Revolution" in January 1927, ultimately affected all of intellectual life: "cultural policy, newspapers, art, literature, and a large part of science."[42]

OVERCOMING OBJECTIVISM IN THE NOVEL

In the Caucasus feature of late October 1926, the criticism of Soviet political ethnography is still comparatively reserved. In the novel *The Flight without End,* which he wrote concurrently, that criticism becomes more explicit, albeit in quite a different—namely a literary—form, put into perspective by an alternative type of ethnography: ethnoliterature. What is remarkable first of all is how much Roth is in accord with the novel's protagonist: the Austrian first lieutenant Franz Tunda bears marked traits of Roth himself. He is introduced as an old friend of Roth's, writing letters to him. In the spring of 1917 Roth himself arrived in the Lvov region of Galicia as a soldier with the press corps; at the end of the war and following Austria's collapse he went to Brody, but became caught up in the conflict between Polish and Ukrainian troops and fled to Vienna. Roth later claimed that, as an officer, he was a prisoner of war and was sent to Siberia;

this claim has to be seen as a product of Roth's tendencies as a creator of myths, even if some people believed it.[43] That is precisely what happened to Roth's literary alter ego, Franz Tunda, who as a prisoner of war finds himself taken to Siberia by the Russians and then, after the war, having set off for Vienna under a false name, happens across a revolutionary group in Ukraine, which he joins more by accident than out of any conviction, as he himself is not a revolutionary; indeed, if anything, he is far more in tune ideologically with the notion of the old Danube monarchy. Stranded there, he falls in love with the leader Natasha Alexandrovna; however, her ideology is incompatible with the bourgeois notion of love; instead, she assigns him the role of cultural propaganda writer for the group so that he, too, can participate in the new socialist world order. He initially writes newspaper articles in Moscow before being dispatched to the Caucasus to conduct scientific research on the labyrinth of peoples and to push ahead with the implementation of the revolution through its program of alphabetization. No ideologist himself, Tunda comes to typify the Soviet ethnographer at the service of the revolution. Indeed, at this point Tunda's ethnographic work is entirely in the service of the new Soviet cultural policy:

> He sat in the office of a newly founded institute whose task it was to create new national cultures for some small peoples in the Caucasus by furnishing them with a new alphabet, primers, and primitive newspapers. Tunda was commissioned to travel to the Caucasus with specimens of newspapers, magazines, and propaganda material, to the River Terek, on whose banks lived a small people which according to ancient statistics numbered some twelve thousand souls. He lived for some weeks in the house of a relatively well-to-do Kumyk, who practiced hospitality on religious grounds and treated inconvenient strangers with friendly solicitude. Little remained for Tunda to do. Some of the young folk had already taken control of culture, formed clubs, and composed wall-newspapers. It emerged that the people were not learning fast enough. They had to be helped with films. Tunda became the director of a cinema.[44]

The use of film also ties in with the use of this emerging medium to disseminate the communist idea. It is no coincidence that Roth was keen to meet Eisenstein, whose *Battleship Potemkin* had premiered in Moscow in late 1925 and was now the showcase of Soviet film.[45]

But ultimately Tunda is unable to embrace the role of socialist education colonialist and cultural propagandist that has been imposed on him.
Rather, he undergoes precisely the same Copernican reversal toward an
alternative ethnography as had Roth on his travels to Russia: the reversal
from colonizing to compassionate ethnography, which acknowledges the
foreign in its cultural difference and does not annihilate it. And indeed,
for a while, Tunda immerses himself entirely in the world that he initially came to observe, by falling in love and marrying a "girl called Alja,
daughter of a Georgian father and a Tadzhik mother,"[46] and moving with
her to Baku. Like the cold, antibourgeois relationship with the garrulous
Natasha, the marriage to Alja is also symptomatic of an ethnographic
model: while the former is aimed at domination, colonization, politicization, and the literacy drive, the latter is guided by a love that sees the person one faces as foreign, exotic, wild, and speechless—this is how Alja is
described: "The girl was silent, her great brown eyes lay in dark blue pools,
she walked as erect as if she carried a pitcher on her head."[47] And while
Tunda is compelled as above to "make films for a scientific institute,"[48]
with hindsight he is critical of that very fact in a letter "to his friend Roth"
sent from Baku. His criticism is levied quite specifically at the colonialist
way in which the new Soviet centralism deals with its Caucasian minorities. Under the pretext of scientific ethnographic research, they are subject
to a system of order and administration:

> My work consisted of making or commissioning photographic and
> cinematographic records of the life of the Caucasian peoples. I did not
> exert myself. But the administrative system of the Soviet state is large and
> extensive and intricate—a deliberate, skilled, and very refined intricacy
> within which every individual is only a smaller or larger point, linked with
> the next larger point and with no notion of his significance in relation to
> the whole.[49]

Tunda's criticism of Soviet political ethnography, which turns science
into the instrument of revolutionary colonization and administration,
also has essential methodological and literary implications. Roth shows
that socialist political ethnography was pursued using the objectivizing
methods of realism and scientific objectivity. At first sight it seems that
Roth's Russia novel is committed to that very objectivity, given that it is
referred to as *A Report* in its subtitle and the foreword programmatically

states: "In what follows I tell the story of my friend, comrade, and spiritual associate, Franz Tunda. I follow in part his notes, in part his narrative. I have invented nothing, made up nothing. The question of 'poetic invention' is no longer relevant. Observed fact is all that counts."[50] On closer inspection, however, it becomes clear that the program set out under the name Joseph Roth is only one aspect of the text, which Tunda initially adheres to in his role as ethnographer for the ever more bureaucratic revolution, even if he in turn gradually becomes ever more critical of it.

What is crucial is his search for an alternative. It is based on his capacity for love, which is rejected by his revolutionary comrades as a bourgeois relic. At the methodological-ethnographical level the cold, realistic regulatory force of the Soviet state therefore clashes with affection, which is a kind of participant observation. Therefore, Tunda as a journalist increasingly resists the formulaic language of the revolution with its clichés—"one cliché for protests and invocations, a second for sketches and memories, a third for outrage and accusation." In its place Tunda uses an aesthetically creative language that describes the real world rather than pressing it into formulas: "Writers experience everything in terms of language, no experience is authentic if it cannot be formulated."[51] Tunda is thus working on overcoming the tenets of New Objectivity. In the place of the doctrine of objective reporting, he is campaigning for the role of artistic creativity, or poetic storytelling.

What the novel cautiously preempts, Roth addresses concisely in a programmatic newspaper article in early 1930, emphatically entitled "Schluss mit der 'neuen Sachlichkeit'" (Enough of the New Objectivity). The feature article picks up where the novel leaves off, inasmuch as it situates politically the new objective call for the documentary as a demand of the Russian revolution in particular, against which he now takes an openly critical stand: "The bureaucratic administrators of the Russian revolution instructed writers as follows: Write the facts we supply you with. . . . As the Soviets see it . . . writers no longer need to 'invent' anything. Here are the drafts; now just copy them please!"[52] Roth recognizes therein a primitive and naïve realism, and the Russian revolutionaries were taken in by it.

This is precisely what Roth refers to as *die kalte Ordnung* (the cold order). The eloquent phrase is a retranslation of the French term for New Objectivity: *l'ordre froid,* which Roth had come across in Félix Bertaux.[53]

Cold is the ordered classification and administration of the foreign using the methods of a scientific realism in the name of a postbourgeois, revolutionary political agenda. It is the regulatory force from which Tunda, with his prerevolutionary notions of "love" and "poetry," tries to escape in *The Flight without End*. In "Schluss mit der 'neuen Sachlichkeit'" Roth uses analogous reasoning. He demystifies "primitive" realism with his belief in the documentary possibilities of the factual as "objective naiveté,"[54] and, by contrast, he restores subjective artistic creativity and "linguistic expression" to its rightful place: "The fact and the detail make up the entire content of the evidence. They are the raw material of the report. In order to 'reflect' the incident, it takes a composed, that is an artistic expression, which contains the raw material in the same way as ore is contained in steel, or mercury in a mirror."[55] What Roth is doing here is performing the *linguistic, narrative,* and *poetic turn* of ethnography. The work of the observing and expert narrator does not provide the real facts of the case, *"rather reality transformed into truth (through the means of language)."*[56]

COMPASSIONATE WRITING: ETHNOGRAPHY OF HASIDISM

That is precisely the starting point of Roth's most elaborate ethnographic essay, *The Wandering Jews*. In its genre, the text itself is extremely heterogeneous: it features autobiographical traits, factual journalistic descriptions, and literary traits, implementing what Roth was calling for in counteracting New Objectivity. It shapes the real in linguistic and narrative terms. For all that, the text is also fundamentally subjective, in that it not only construes Eastern European Jews through storytelling, but also idealizes them. It is precisely in its heterogeneity that the essay represents that hybrid mix of subjectivity, objectivity, and literature that characterizes postcolonial, ethnoliterary writing, which no longer territorializes the subject matter, but recognizes it as foreign.

This thesis is confirmed by the context of the essay's creation. Roth wrote the essay within the context of his travels to Russia: the larger part in Paris in summer 1926 while preparing for his trip, and other parts during the journey. In the foreword, he dissociates himself from any colonialist Western points of view that disqualify Eastern European Jews as precivilized and superstitious, as Theodor Lessing did in his *Impressions from Galicia* (1909)[57] or Alfred Döblin in his *Travel to Poland* (1926). Roth had criticized Döblin's book in a review in early 1926[58] directed precisely at the colonialist tendency. Empathy and passion become the emotional prerequisite for ethnographic writing, which in this way actually becomes a form of participatory observation. Empathy suspends the conventional boundaries between subject and object, thus making it possible to describe Eastern European Jews beyond Western European cultural differences and colonialist tendencies, from an insider's view. Roth formulates this point in the foreword programmatically:

> This book is not interested in the plaudits and endorsements, much less in the cavils or criticisms of those who despise, hate, and persecute the Eastern European Jews. It does not address itself to those Western Europeans who, by virtue of the fact that they grew up with elevators and flush toilets, allow themselves to make bad jokes about Romanian lice, Galician cockroaches, or Russian fleas. This book is not interested in those objective readers who peer down with a cheap and sour benevolence from the rickety towers of their Western civilization upon the nearby East and its inhabitants; who, out of sheer humanity, are struck with pity at inadequate sewage systems, and whose fear of contagion leads them to lock up poor immigrants in tenements where social problems are solved by simple epidemics. . . . This book has not been written for readers who would blame the author for treating the subjects of his account with love, and not with "scientific detachment" better known as indifference. . . . In what follows, I will attempt to describe how he [the Eastern Jew] and his kind live, first at home and then abroad.[59]

Roth's description of Eastern European Jews in their home in the chapter "The Jewish Shtetl" is of particular interest. He is alluding here to his travels to Galicia in late autumn of 1924 for the *Frankfurter Zeitung*. Lvov and Kraków were on the route, accounting initially for three articles published in November 1924. Roth made use of his impressions of that journey also in *The Wandering Jews*, together with his own experiences, all of which he assembled into narrative form in 1926. One outstanding example of this is his description of the Hasidim. It is no coincidence that Roth's description of the Caucasian mountain Jews, again described in the essay as resistant to Western European categories of nation and culture,[60] is consistent with that of the Hasidim in one crucial point: the exotic as the guiding concept of ethnographic construction. Specifically, Roth exoticizes Hasidim by using a remarkable comparison with a mountain people located even more remotely than the mountain dwellers of the Caucasus, namely in the Himalayas:

> Still bitter and unreconciled, however, are a great many Hasids, who occupy a very remarkable position within Judaism. To the Western European they are as exotic and remote as, say, the inhabitants of the Himalayan region, who are now so much in fashion. In fact they are even more mysterious, because, being more prudent than those other helpless objects of European inquisitiveness, they have already come to know the superficial civilization of Europe, and they are resolutely unimpressed by such things as film projectors, or binoculars, or airplanes. But even if their naiveté and their hospitality had been as great as those of other people who have suffered at the hands of our desire for knowledge, even then it would be hard to persuade a European man of learning to embark on a voyage of discovery among the Hasids. The Jew, because he lives everywhere in our midst, has ostensibly already been "researched." Meanwhile the things that happen at the court of a wonder-rabbi are at least as interesting as with your Indian fakir.[61]

Hasidim are the Foreign Ones in our midst: the fakirs of Europe, the ones to whom science, in Roth's view, should be turning its attention. However, Roth's plea for their study is also accompanied by an increased awareness of the problems involved. Such research runs the same risk that Tunda recognized when dealing with the peoples of the Caucasus: that the Hasidim are misused by a hegemonic knowledge system: they are reified, objectified, colonized, administered, and bureaucratized.

Roth proves to be an ethnographically highly critical observer when describing his visit to a miracle rabbi. The visit dates not only from Roth's travels to Galicia in "late autumn" 1924, but also from experience: his father Nachum Roth came from a Hasidic background, one to which he returned when after his mental illness he went to live at the court of a miracle rabbi in Russian Poland until his death in 1907.[62] At the same time, Roth's description of the visit to the miracle rabbi is also characterized by a high level of literary and ethnographic structure. That includes the self-reflection of his standpoint as an observer: Roth positions himself as a necessarily foreign intruder into the world of the Hasidim, defined symbolically and spatially by both location and attire. In order to gain admission, he first had to pass the gatekeeper, to whom Roth pays particular attention as a symbolic threshold figure. The fact that he is described as a "red-haired Jew" refers to a recurring figuration of the Jewish exotic that has existed since Roth's youth and has now turned into something more eerie:[63]

> It was a day in late autumn that I set out to call on the rabbi.... Outside the rabbi's house stood a red-haired Jew, the master of ceremonies ... a man of influence who knew no mercy. He repelled the imploring and the scolding alike with a kind of measured roughness.... I gave the man a signal I thought he'd understand. It meant: Here is something rather out of the ordinary, something we need to talk about in private. He vanished. He slammed the door, locked it, and, parting the crowds, came up to me. "I'm not from here, I've come from afar, and I would like to speak to the rabbi."[64]

Roth thus constructs a spatial scenario that allows him, as an outsider, to advance to the innermost chamber of Hasidism and unlock the mystery of the wonder-working rabbi. However, the miracle worker proves to be far less exotic than a fakir.[65] Nevertheless, Roth does describe other aspects of religious life among the Hasidim as exotic, particularly the holy day Simchat Torah in a little town in which "there were many red-haired Jews living." According to Roth, among the Hasidim the feast of joy and rejoicing that marks the day on which the Torah was received on Sinai is celebrated with the "energy given by a fanatical faith." The participatory observer describes this phenomenon of religious ecstasy with particular "emotion":

> It moved me deeply to see a whole people that didn't separate physical cravings from spiritual joys but united them, consecrating its sensual pleasure to its God.... There was fervor and ardor together, dancing as a form of worship, an orgy of prayer.[66]

The transition from factual description to poetic storytelling about Eastern European Jews is finally accomplished by the novel that may be regarded as the literary counterpart to the essay *The Wandering Jews: Job* (1930). As part of Roth's comprehensive ethnoliterary project on Eastern European Jews, the novel systematically implements the postulate of the "account rendered with love," and achieves the ethnographic possibilities of poetic writing. It combines in literary and narrative form what the essay puts forward in a hybrid mix of genres.

The novel specifically tells the story of the sickly young boy Menuchim and his father Mendel Singer, a simple and pious teacher living in a shtetl in western Russia around 1900. Like Job he gradually loses everything, beginning with his aforementioned son, who is severely handicapped both physically and mentally. The pivotal hub of the novel is the question of how healing is achieved in the pious world of the Eastern European Jews. Two answers are explored. Either one endures all manner of suffering as part of the divine plan of creation, or one chooses to intervene in the divine plan and seek out the Hasidic miracle rabbi. In the novel, Mendel Singer's wife Deborah sets off to see such a "holy man." It is striking that her visit to the miracle rabbi in the novel is described in structurally analogous terms to Roth's own visit in *The Wandering Jews:* the arduous journey to the rabbi, the wait outside in the hallway, the exceptional admission, the rabbi's appearance, and the conversation with him. But while the scene in the essay is described in realistic terms as viewed from the outside, in the course of the novel's narrative it is raised to the inner and performative level of magic. Not only does the miracle rabbi appear as a wise man, but he is also capable of performing miracles.

The highlight of the audience with the rabbi is an act of healing. In Roth's ethnoliterary narrative, the miraculous gift of the rabbi is demonstrated in dramatic terms: he appears as an all-knowing seer, predicting a *messianic* future for Menuchim, over and beyond his *medical* health:

> very close to her she heard the voice of the rabbi, though he only whispered: "Menuchim, Mendel's son, will grow healthy. There will not be many like him in Israel. Pain will make him wise, ugliness kind, bitterness gentle, and illness strong. His eyes will be far and deep, his ears clear and full of echoes. His mouth will be silent, but when he opens his lips, they will herald good things."[67]

The novel thus goes far beyond the possibilities of the essay. While the essay only conveys a view of the external circumstances of the scene featuring the visit to the miracle rabbi, the novel imagines the magical effect of the miraculous act in a dramatic narrative context. The juxtaposition of the ethnographic photograph featuring the image of an observation made from the outside becomes a narrative literary stage-setting that transposes the reader to the very heart of the miraculous events. Only literature then—as ethnoliterature—is capable of fulfilling ethnography's great promise through imagination, the promise to venture deep into the innermost space of the exotic and foreign and to participate in the magical actions of the fakirs among the Jews.

NOTES

1. For this Paperny used the term "Culture Two." See Vladimir Paperny, *Architecture in the Age of Stalin: Culture Two* (Cambridge: Cambridge University Press, 2002).

2. See Mirjam Zadoff, *Der rote Hiob: Das Leben des Werner Scholem* (München: Carl Hanser, 2014).

3. Egon Erwin Kisch, *Zaren, Popen, Bolschewiken* (Berlin: Erich Reiss, 1927); Ernst Toller, *Quer durch. Reisebilder und Reden* (Berlin: G. Kiepenhauer, 1930).

4. Joseph Roth, *Reise nach Russland: Feuilletons, Reportagen, Tagebuchnotizen 1919–1930*, ed. Klaus Westermann (Cologne: Kiepenheuer und Witsch, 1995), 284.

5. See Arkadi Zeltser, "Chemeriskii, Aleksandr," trans. Yisrael Cohen, in Gershon David Hundert, ed. *The YIVO Encyclopedia of Jews in Eastern Europe*, vol. 1 (New Haven, Conn.: Yale University Press, 2008), 310–311.

6. Terry Martin, *The Affirmative Action Empire: Nations and Nationalism in the Soviet Union, 1923–1938* (Ithaca, N.Y.: Cornell University Press, 2001); Uwe Halbach, *Das sowjetische Vielvölkerimperium: Nationalitätenpolitik und nationale Frage* (Mannheim: B.I.-Taschenbuchverlag, 1992), 32–39; Andreas Kappeler, *Russland als Vielvölkerreich: Entstehung, Geschichte, Zerfall* (Munich: C.H. Beck, 1992), 300–306.

7. Francine Hirsch, *Empire of Nations: Ethnographic Knowledge and the Making of the Soviet Union* (Ithaca, N.Y.: Cornell University Press, 2005); Markus Hirnsperger, "Rote Ethnographie: Strategien der Repräsentation indigener Völker in ethnologischen Werken der Sowjetunion," in *Bruchlinien im Eis: Ethnologie des zirkumpolaren Nordens*, ed. Stefan Bauer, with the help of Rahel Baumgartner (Vienna: LIT, 2005), 245–262; see also Ministerium für Hoch- und Fachschulwesen, *Lehrprogramm für das Lehrgebiet Ethnographie der Völker der Sowjetunion zur Ausbildung in der Fachrichtung Ethnographie innerhalb der Grundstudieneinrichtung Regionalwissenschaften* (Zwickau [DDR]: Zentralstelle für Lehr- und Organisationsmittel des Ministeriums für Hoch- und Fachschulwesen, 1978).

8. Andreas Kappeler, 305.

9. Edmund Silberner, *Kommunisten zur Judenfrage. Zur Geschichte von Theorie und Praxis des Kommunismus* (Opladen: Westdeutscher Verlag, 1983).

10. See also the quotation from the speech by Esther Frumkin in Silberner, 157.

11. Aleksandr Chemeriskii, *Di alfarbandishe komunistishe partei (bolshevikes) un di yidishe masn* (Moscow, 1926), 12 and 19. Due to his earlier activities within the Bund (i.e., the *Algemeyner Yidisher Arbeter Bund in Lite, Poyln, un Rusland* or General Union of Jewish Workers in Lithuania, Poland, and Russia), Chemeriskii fell out of favor with the Stalinist regime in the 1930s and died a camp prisoner in 1942.

12. Joseph Roth, *The Wandering Jews*, trans. Michael Hofman (New York: W.W. Norton and Company, 2001), 109.

13. Silberner, 152.

14. Roth, *The Wandering Jews*, 112.

15. See *Kommunisten zur Judenfrage: Zur Geschichte von Theorie und Praxis des Kommunismus*, 159ff.

16. Roth, *The Wandering Jews*, 114.

17. On Roth's travels to Russia see Wolfgang Müller-Funk, *Joseph Roth* (Vienna: Sonderzahl, 2012), 155–177.

18. Joseph Roth, *Briefe 1911–1939*, ed. Hermann Kesten (Cologne: Kiepenheuer und Witsch, 1970), 93.

19. Ibid., 97.

20. It is telling of Roth's dual journalistic and literary writing that the novel *The Silent Prophet*, which he began writing in 1927 and which represents a literary rendition of Roth's own travels to Russia, tells the story of the Odessa revolutionary Friedrich Kargan in that very same hotel: "On New Year's Eve 1926–1927 I was sitting with some friends and acquaintances in Moscow in room Number Nine of the Bolshaia Moskovskaia Hotel" (Joseph Roth, *The Silent Prophet* [London: Peter Owen Publishers, 1979], 7). There was a hotel of that name in Odessa, but not in Moscow. Evidently Roth confused the two.

21. Walter Benjamin, *Moscow Diary* (Cambridge, Mass.: Harvard University Press, 1986), 29f.

22. Joseph Roth, "Russland-Tagebuch," in *Das journalistische Werk*, vol. 2 of *Joseph Roth Werke*, ed. Klaus Westermann (Cologne: Kiepenheuer und Witsch, 1989–1991), 1026.

23. Brigitta Hauser-Schäublin, "Teilnehmende Beobachtung," in *Methoden und Techniken der Feldforschung*, ed. Bettina Beer (Berlin: Reimer, 2003), 33–54; Harvey R. Bernard, *Research Methods in Anthropology: Qualitative and Quantitative Methods* (Lanham, Md.: Altamira Press, 2006).

24. Some of the diaries are printed in the German edition of Roth's collected works: Roth, *Das journalistische Werk*, vol. 2 of *Joseph Roth Werke*, 1007–1022. The archive material on Roth's journey to Russia can be accessed online at the Leo Baeck Institute.

25. Roth, *Briefe 1911–1939*, 95.

26. Ibid., item, 38.

27. Ibid.

28. Ibid.

29. Roth, "Russland-Tagebuch," in vol. 2 of *Joseph Roth Werke*, 1011.

30. Ibid., 1015.

31. *Half-Asia* is a literary ethnographic term coined by Karl Emil Franzos for the Jewish shtetls of Eastern Europe. See Karl Emil Franzos, *Aus Halb-Asien: Culturbilder aus Galizien, Südrußland, der Bukowina und Rumänien* (1914). Originally published under the title *Halb-Asien: Land und Leute des östlichen Europa* (1897).

32. Roth, "Völker-Labyrinth," in vol. 2 of *Joseph Roth Werke*, 619.

33. Ibid., 616.

34. Ibid., 619.

35. The term *exotic Jews* was used after 1900 mainly for non-Ashkenazi Jews. See Y., "Exotische Juden," *Ost und West: Illustrierte Monatsschrift für das gesamte Judentum* 12 (1901): 934–938, which refers to Jews in India and China; Esriel Carlebach, *Exotische Juden* (Berlin: Heine-bund, 1932). Carlebach describes Sephardic Jews and Marranos.

36. See N., "Programm der Zusammenkunft der Zionisten des Kaukasus und des Donaugebietes," *Die Welt* 5, no. 34 (1901): 16. The stenographic minutes of the Sixth Zionist Congress state: "As living witnesses of the spread of Zionism in Russia the Congress

has been attended by delegates from Siberia, Tashkent, and also representatives of the Caucasian mountain Jews, whom we are particularly delighted to welcome." *Stenographisches Protokoll der Verhandlungen des VI. Zionistenkongresses* (Vienna, 1903), 23.

37. Heinrich Loewe, *Zur Kunde von den Juden im Kaukasus aus zwei alten deutschen Zeitungen* (Charlottenburg: Vollrath in Leipzig, 1900), 5f.

38. Roth, "Völker-Labyrinth," in vol. 2 of *Joseph Roth Werke*, 615.

39. Ibid., 618.

40. Ibid., 619.

41. Ibid.

42. Roth, *Reise nach Russland: Feuilletons, Reportagen, Tagebuchnotizen 1919–1930*, 238.

43. See for example Roth's friend, Joseph Gottfarstein, who was convinced of the story. Heinz Lunzer and Victoria Lunzer-Talos, eds., *Joseph Roth im Exil in Paris 1933 bis 1939* (Vienna: Dokumentationsstelle für neuere österreichische Literatur, 2008), 186.

44. Joseph Roth, *Flight without End* (New York: Overlook Press, 1977), 30.

45. Christine Engel, ed., *Geschichte des sowjetischen und russischen Films* (Stuttgart: Metzler, 1999).

46. Roth, *Flight without End*, 30.

47. Ibid., 31.

48. Ibid., 36.

49. Ibid., 54.

50. Ibid., 5.

51. Ibid., 25.

52. Roth, in vol. 3 of *Joseph Roth Werke*, 159.

53. Ibid., 158; Félix Bertaux, *Panorama de la littérature allemande contemporaine* (Paris: Éditions du Sagittaire, 1928).

54. Roth, "Neue Sachlichkeit," in vol. 3 of *Joseph Roth Werke*, 161.

55. Ibid., 155.

56. Ibid., 157.

57. Theodor Lessing, "Eindrücke aus Galizien," *Allgemeine Zeitung des Judentums* 49 (1909): 587–588; 51 (1909): 610–611; 52 (1909): 620–622; 53 (1909): 634–635.

58. Roth, "Döblin im Osten," in vol. 2 of *Joseph Roth Werke*, 532–535.

59. Roth, *The Wandering Jews*, 1.

60. Caucasian Jews once again feature as an example of Roth's core theory that the Jews of Eastern Europe "are unconcerned about their 'nationality' in the Western European sense, i.e., as belonging to a particular 'nation.' They speak several languages and are themselves the product of several generations of mixed marriages. . . ." Ibid., 14.

61. Ibid., 32.

62. David Bronsen, *Joseph Roth. Eine Biographie* (Cologne: Kiepenheuer und Witsch, 1974), 41f.

63. See Heinz Lunzer and Victoria Lunzer-Talos, eds., *Joseph Roth im Exil in Paris 1933 bis 1939*, 180. See also Roth, "Reise durch Galizien," in vol. 2 of *Joseph Roth Werke*, 283; Bronsen, *Joseph Roth. Eine Biographie*, 78.

64. Roth, *The Wandering Jews*, 35–37.

65. Ibid., 38.

66. Ibid., 40.

67. Joseph Roth, *Job* (New York: Archipelago 2010), 20.

Yiddish Ethnographic Poetics and
Moyshe Kulbak's "Vilne"

JORDAN FINKIN

At the conclusion of one of the poet Moyshe Kulbak's (1896–1937) few essays, "The Yiddish Word" (1918), having sketched out what Yiddish literature has achieved in prose, Kulbak turns to what is still to be achieved in poetry. "The Yiddish word was synthesized by the finest spirits of the people, and it carries with it the musical rhythm of singing Jewish souls. If our language still has something to conquer, it will achieve more through its flowers than through its publicistic paper swords."[1] Here as elsewhere Kulbak regards folksong as the beating heart of cultural creativity. In ethnographically resonant language he notes how Yiddish folksong "breathes with the primitive refinement of folk creativity."[2] It is not by chance that he regularly returns to the well of folklore and folksong in his efforts to be precisely that conqueror of the final frontier of Yiddish literary art.

In a letter some six years later, Kulbak makes a tantalizing off-hand mission statement: "I cannot express myself fully except in short or longer poems, and therefore I want to devise such a form which can in a large space, with the help of various shapes, express not an epic world-concept but a pure lyric poetry."[3] Kulbak's ambitious desire to create a new form for Yiddish poetry that can both encompass his personal aesthetic aims and fulfill his duty to folk creativity sets as one of the hinges between the two a deep reflection on Jewish ethnography. In what follows I outline a model of Jewish ethnographic engagement as it appears in the work of those committed

94

to Yiddish cultural creativity in the early twentieth century, and then I show how Kulbak's work and his dual engagement, nearly unrivaled in Yiddish literature for its sensitivity if not its lyricism, allows us a glimpse at the intersection of poetry and ethnography, their mutual influences, and how they were understood by the cultural activists committed to both. To do this, I focus on a reading of his poem "Vilne," stressing its reliance not only on modes of contemporary Jewish autoethnography but also on an understanding of ethnography rooted more in authenticity than authority. That is, whether an ethnography or an ethnographic poem, if it is based in authenticity then it relies on the data themselves rather than extrinsic warrants (especially authority) to provide legitimacy. The literature and poetry that attuned themselves to the specific shifts in conceptual emphases of Jewish ethnography, as in the case of Moyshe Kulbak, offer remarkable insights into Jewish self-understanding.

LITERARY GENRE

No matter what demands of content are placed on it, ethnography as a written text must also submit to the demands of a narrative genre. Many literary forms include ethnographic information or observations. Histories of ethnography frequently cite the ancients as offering vivid early examples of the narrative embedding of ethnographic data; and in poetic literature it may be older still.[4] But other forms, including travelogues, journals and diaries, letters, detailed administrative reports, and so on, also can be found in ethnographic space.

In addition to nonfictive areas, such as journalism, which often in their narratives make use of observations from the field, belles lettres also deploy ethnographic data in distinctive ways. The presence of verisimilar data in a fictive context may offer insights into the ethnographic pursuit more generally. In Thomas More's *Utopia* and Jonathan Swift's *Gulliver's Travels,* the novels' central conceit coincides with the central conceit of ethnography: the participant observation of an "other" culture. There not only do the ethnographic self and the narrative "I" coalesce, but they open a window to another culture that is simultaneously a mirror on the self.

Jewish maskilic satires, produced by writers such as Yoysef Perl, Yitsk-hok Linetski, and Sholem Abramovitsh, sought to lampoon the foibles of traditional Jewish society in order to advocate for reform. Such sat-ires—which were "[f]or the better part of the nineteenth century, the primary genre of Jewish 'ethnography'"[5]—dispense with precisely this kind of roman à clef of other superimposed on self. Rather, they are "eth-nographic burlesques,"[6] which can be read less as explorations of the idea of ethnography per se than as insightful meditations (and lampoons) in the mode of what we now call native ethnography or autoethnography. That is, instead of "look at the silly Lilliputian, aha!, that's you English-man" we find "look at our fellow Jew from Foolston, aha!, now do you see how foolish we Jews are?"

In the majority of cases, the genres that incorporate ethnographic data to any significant degree are narrative ones.[7] Indeed, the forms of prose literature may "blur"[8] into and out of ethnography more felicitously be-cause of the narrative structure of ethnography itself (or at least the pre-sumptions about ethnography's narrative conventions).[9] Moreover, the ethnography as such is itself a *modern* genre because all ethnographies are in part narratives about ethnographic work, which accounts for the concord between the authorial presence in many narratives and the tra-ditional emphasis on authority in ethnography.

In general terms, modern Jewish ethnographic practice—embodied notably in the Jewish Historic-Ethnographic Society in Russia, the various folkist groups in Poland, YIVO, and Soviet ethnographic trends—follows the larger trends of ethnography in Europe and Russia. Ethnographic thinking among Jews was part of a larger engagement with and partici-pation in non-Jewish cultural and intellectual life, and it *emplaced* Jews as significant, unique, and full-fledged cultural actors. And herein lay the paradox for many ethnographic thinkers: (1) from the point of view of ethnographic science, Jews become simply one people among many peoples (unum in pluribus), subject to the same analytic tools and the same historical contingency; (2) from the point of view of ethnographic ideology, Jews (like other people studied by a member of that group) are something special (unum e pluribus), not only subject to but deserving of the same analytic tools, offering a unique and essential value and playing a distinct historical role. Nineteenth- and early twentieth-century Jewish ethnography, like other autoethnographies of the period, tacks somewhat uneasily between these poles.

These ways of thinking also often had implications for the choice of methodology employed. Two of the most important of these were (1) the expeditional, in which an actual physical expedition was organized to go out to record ethnographic data, a method influenced by expeditions within the Russian Empire;[10] and, in a more folkloric tradition, (2) the deputative, in which information was solicited from informants, by such means as public advertisements, questionnaires, and surveys.[11] (The ethos of this latter model can be found, for example, in their programmatic texts, including most notably, YIVO's *Vos iz azoyns yidishe etnografye? (Handbikhl far zamler)* (What Is Jewish Ethnography? Handbook for Collectors)[12] and H. Aleksandrov's *Forsht ayer shtetl!* (Study Your Shtetl!).[13] (See the appendices for these texts.)

No method, however, was absolute, nor did undertaking one entail necessarily the rejection of another. For example, S. An-sky expanded the dimensions of his own expedition for the Jewish Historic-Ethnographic Society by composing a remarkable documentary questionnaire, which in its book-length volume and detail was effectively unusable as an enchiridion for fieldworkers. That he felt the need to produce such a document, to overlay a particular ethnographic worldview onto a finely graded landscape of sought-after data, reveals something of a perceived intellectual gap unbridgeable by one ethnographic means alone.

Equally revealing is the conceptual shift that An-sky's questionnaire straddles. As Gabriella Safran notes, at around the time when he wrote it, An-sky had begun to use "a newly urgent tone in describing the ethnographer's task. Whereas in 1912 he had written and spoken about the need to gather material to inspire artists to produce a secular Jewish culture to replace the religion of the past, in 1914 he put more emphasis on the need to *salvage* all that remained."[14] One needs little imagination to note the resonance with the important concept of "salvage ethnography."[15] Indeed, salvage and rescue are key metaphorical rationales in many of the Jewish ethnographic projects in the modern period. But what exactly is being salvaged? From the point of view of the dominant ethnographic modes discussed above, the answer would be only *valuable* things, leaving open the question of what has "value." For the Yiddishists or the Polish Jewish folkists, for example, most valuable were first and foremost linguistic things—what we think of as traditional "folklore"—because in its essence culture was constituted through language. For An-sky, by contrast, as well as for Jewish ethnographers influenced by Russian Populism, what was most valued were lifeways, especially on a birth-to-death spectrum, and particularly religious or "belief" systems and structures.[16] And taking just the maskilic literary satire, we see that those texts also focused only on such elements within the larger ethnographic system that serve the critique (such as features that expose religious obscurantism, sexism, and other social ills). All ethnographic constructions are by definition selective, even those whose goal is to salvage.

AUTHENTICITY AND AUTHORITY

The larger point of this brief excursion on method is that what one seeks to achieve through ethnography shapes the genres and methods one chooses; and the methods and genres one chooses shape how one views the nature of ethnography. "Jewish ethnography," in the forms with which we are dealing here, was sufficiently inchoate[17] to offer a range of valid options in this regard. Their one unifying premise involved the nature of the relationship between the two mutually implicated allegiances in the ethnographic enterprise, namely authenticity[18] and authority.

Authority involves a command over attention, influence over opinion, a warrant of credibility, and possession of appropriate competence. Authenticity offers a kind of qualitative truth, genuineness. Traditional academic ethnography has tended to focus its attention on the centrality of forms and models of authority.[19] And while narratives themselves hold some kind of authority, that is largely derived from the authority of the ethnographer him- or herself, based on such factors as training and experience. It is not fortuitous that Kenneth Stoddart phrases one of his guiding questions of ethnography: "How will the ethnographer structure a textual account so that it achieves its effect as knowledge of 'others,' as an objective account about subjects among whom the fieldwork was conducted, as *authoritative*?"[20]

Or take another example, a passage from Jomo Kenyatta's preface to his ethnography *Facing Mount Kenya* (1938): "The reader will undoubtedly wish to know my credentials for writing the book. Merely to have been born and bred in the Gikuyu country may seem to him a vague qualification, so I will give a more explicit account of the sources of my knowledge."[21] These include some of the specific experiences of his upbringing, especially as they relate to the primary topics of the book itself, and the quasi-governmental, committee, and other roles he served in the administration of his people. This passage and its elaboration are classic demonstrations of ethnographic authority.

Equally influential is the convention of the experiential authority of participant observation itself. Take Joseph Roth's "ethnographic" description of part of a funeral in the shtetl: "It [the coffin] is not wheeled but carried, by four Jews running at a brisk clip along the shortest possible way— I'm not sure whether this is part of the ceremonial or because a slower walk would double the weight for the bearers."[22] The author's physical presence and writerly eye for detail are not in doubt, but his descriptive and tonal certainty is matched by his intellectual uncertainty. This is by design. The "authority" of the observer is actually enhanced not only by the detail of his description but more so by his willingness to be uncertain about his interpretation, the importance of the latter being the impression he means to give his reader that he knows where he is supposed to be uncertain. (It is of course also meant to be humorous.)

Authority organizes and orients the narrative. Put in its most basic form, this authoritative model centers on the ethnographer him- or herself and presumes that "the experience of the researcher can serve as a unifying source of authority in the field."[23]

The second model, however, which focuses on authenticity, emphasizes the data themselves and less so those who accredit them. Relying as it does on the *feel* of the data, on their ability to be taken as genuine, authenticity is more slippery and less methodologically regulatable than authority. In a 1918 essay, the Georgian poet Ioseb Grishashvili writes: "Many people think that folk literature can be found only in the countryside, not in the city. By folk literature people often mean the work of authors who are unknown or forgotten. But in my opinion any work that flows unrestrained

from the heart of a son of the people can be called 'folk.'"[24] Grishashvili
was arguing that the works of urban intellectuals and cosmopolitan artists
were no less valid or genuine as "Georgian" than what was produced by
the "rural folk." His argument rests on authenticity above all else, on how
a work that "flows unrestrained from the heart of a son of the people" is
somehow verifiable by feel alone or by some feature other than the identity
of the author.

I do not mean to say that the work of ethnography requires choosing
one model or the other; they are matters of focus or emphasis more than
of strict methodology. Indeed, one can sometimes see them enacted side
by side in a single text.

Moreover, in the kinds of Jewish ethnography we are dealing with, an
apprehension of authenticity is often privileged, especially for deputative
and expeditional ethnography. *What is Jewish Ethnography?* and *Study
Your Shtetl!* both offer guidelines for the fieldworker; these suggestions,
however, are of limited scale. Far more important—and lengthy—is their
detailed exposition of the kinds of data to collect. Authority is evidently
subordinate to authenticity. And alongside An-sky's "authoritative" expeditions, organized around his own experiences in the field, his book-
length questionnaire even more dramatically presents the centrality of
authentic data to the project.

What authority there is in ethnographic work focused on authenticity
rests in the project's status and the collectors' passion. The folklorically
oriented programs in particular evince this kind of authority. The first
stanza of Avrom Reyzen's 1931 poem "Mir zamlen..." (We Collect...), for
example, presents the scope and content of YIVO's ethnographic program
(to which the poem is dedicated):

> We collect everything which is dear to us
> In our long path to Now;
> A page from back then, a book from this year,
> Let them all be protected with love.[25]

The authority of the poem's collective "we" derives from their commitment to collecting and from their "love." Moreover, it is precisely that love
which the poet singles out as the instrument of protection, a key term in
salvage-oriented ethnography.[26]

Given that there are no completely satisfactory means of gauging authenticity, this opens a space for different forms to enter, ponder, and even attempt to constitute authenticity—among them, to wit, poetry. And if "ethnographic fiction"[27] may be permitted within ethnography by dint of its incorporation of ethnographic observation and the felicitous overlap of many narrative conventions, it stands to ask what other aesthetic or literary genres might be equally permissible. Which brings this discussion to the question posed at the very outset, whether Yiddish poetry could be *ethnographic*. Put another way, genre matters, whether for the data of ethnographic collecting or for the text the ethnographer produces. And while narrative forms easily take to being understood ethnographically, I would maintain that poetry needs to be taken so as well. Indeed, insofar as "authentic" ethnography conceived of the discrete datum as the core unit of knowledge—rather than the narrative web that makes intricate use of those data—its outlook was more consistent with the aims of poetry.

Poetry is self-reflective on form and language in a less mediated way than narrative. In this it resembles other arts that also incorporated ethnographic content in this period, especially in sound and image. The "I" of modernist poetry gets deemphasized in favor of the poet's ethnographic eye. All ethnography is, after all, a filter. Ethnographic poetry is able to use a lyrical, as opposed to a narrative, filter, one attuned to aesthetic modulations (such as sound, rhyme, form, color, rhythm, and so forth). Moyshe Kulbak, for example, as we saw at the beginning of this essay, saw folksong as a, if not the, cultural storehouse—not only of concepts, imagery, tropes, and emotions, but also of language, rhythm, rhyme, sound, and music. And as we will see, Kulbak's investment in the form and language of folksong became an integral part of his own poetic project, as he experimented and expanded them into new poetic possibilities for Yiddish poetry and self-consciously produced specifically ethnographic effects.

MOYSHE KULBAK

Innumerable Yiddish poems include ethnographic data; that fact needs little elaboration. More interesting are those poems that have ethnographic goals, poems that are conscious of and comment on ethno-

graphic issues. What, therefore, does Yiddish poetry have to say of the
Jew as ethnographic object? This question is large. Instead of a canvas of
Yiddish literature, I propose taking one poet's view of Jewish ethnography
as a fascinating case on its own and an invitation for further thinking on
the relationship between ethnography and poetry.

The biography of Moyshe Kulbak resembles that of many of the Yiddish
authors of the period. Born in a provincial town, Smorgon, and having
received a traditional education, he began his writing career by trying his
hand at Hebrew poetry before deciding to write in Yiddish. In a fairly typical peripatetic fashion he moved first to Kovno, then Minsk, Berlin, and
Vilna, finally ending up again in Minsk, following the vagaries of history,
ideology, family, and employment opportunity. Though he started out
writing romantically inflected verses, his writing came of age in contact
with various Jewish and non-Jewish modernisms, which he encountered
during his sojourn (1920–1923) among the Eastern European Jewish ex-
patriate community in Berlin.

It was during this Berlin period that Kulbak cultivated an eye for ethnographic detail. Though his primary backdrops oscillate between the
metropolis on the one hand and rural or natural spaces on the other, he
began to take an interest in other locales, including the shtetl and the
Jewish hinterlands. Among his Berlin lyrics, for example, is the poem "In
shenk" (In the Tavern), a gloomy look at a motley group of carousers and
wayfarers at that common communal topos of Jewish Eastern Europe.
(One of An-sky's early prose works, the Russian story "In the Tavern," also
focuses on the tavern as a site of ethnographic observation.)[28]

Also from this period is the long poem "Raysn" (White Russia), a series
of sketches from the life of an extended family of Jewish raftsmen and
peasants. Kulbak lays out an array of primitive characteristics for these
simple, rustic Jews, at odds with more traditional literary descriptions
of shtetl-centric Jewry. With their brawn and vigor and earthy language,
the poems defamiliarize these characters as Jews. Moreover, Kulbak intimately connects their daily life and culture to that of the non-Jewish population, placing what we would now call their cultural life in the context
of that interethnic contact. The eleventh section of the poem, "Antoshe
shpilt af der bandure . . ." (Antoshe Plays the Bandura . . .),[29] takes the
form of a folksong that the Jewish family calls for the non-Jew Antoshe

to sing while accompanying himself on his bandura, a local folk instrument. Their calls to sing become part of the folksong's own refrain. The collection of folksongs was a staple of Jewish ethnography. The chorus of "Raysn" underscores a key intuition of his era's Jewish ethnography: that folk cultures exhibit hybridity.

Kulbak left Berlin for Vilna in 1923, unable to fit in or make a living in the German city. In Vilna he became something of a culture figure; he was a popular high school literature teacher and was involved in the city's Jewish cultural organizations. A confluence of ideological sympathy with the revolution and family considerations ultimately persuaded him to move to Minsk. It was there that he wrote not only his great mock epic of interwar Berlin, *Dizner Childe Harold* (1933), but also the novel *Zelmenyaner* (1931–1935).[30]

This masterpiece is a comic tale of the Sovietification of an extended Jewish family outside of Minsk. The novel shares with "White Russia" a keen interest in extended familial relations, or, in ethnographic terms, kinship groups. In *Zelmenyaner* the three generations of offspring of Reb Zelmele all live in the courtyard complex he built, and the novel follows them in and around that space. It can be read as an extended humorous meditation on Jewish life as an ethnographic experience, with the Soviet world as the hegemonic supercontext, and the lives of these "Zelmenyaners" (though their family name is Khvost) as a kind of *tribe:* They live in a circumscribed precinct, the courtyard house;[31] they have their own mannerisms and way of talking; they have a distinct physique and physiognomy, and even their own particular smell. These aspects make the Zelmenyaners more than a curiosity; they are an "ethnicity" in need of study. Interwar Jewish ethnography demanded salvage, the recording of what was being lost, while the upheaval of the revolution and Soviet experimentation meant that the rate of "loss" was inevitably, and from an ideological perspective desirably, accelerated. Kulbak's novel is a study in the humorous dimension of the ambivalence between salvage and revolution.

Zelmenyaner can be read as an extended meditation on ethnographic inquiry, as is supported by two circumstantial facts. Kulbak lived in Vilna and was active in its cultural circles during the time YIVO was established in that city; and he was living in Minsk when Aleksandrov's *Study Your Shtetl!* was promulgated by the Jewish Section of the Institute for

Belarusian Culture in Minsk. It would be reasonable to assume that their ideas, as touchstone events for far more wide-reaching thinking and activity on Jewish ethnography, were familiar to Kulbak. Indeed, it is my impression that parts of Kulbak's novel are designed to offer a humorous send-up of Aleksandrov's text and by extension of Jewish ethnographic practice.

The centerpiece of Kulbak's ethnographic meditation in *Zelmenyaner* is chapter 12 (of the second volume), entitled "Zelmeniad,"[32] which is subheaded "A scientific investigation concerning the material culture, lore, characteristics and other mores and customs of the Reb's courtyard, collected and edited by the young scientific field worker[33] Tsalel Khvost, a native of that courtyard."[34] The chapter is presented as the found notes of Tsalel—one of Zelmele's grandchildren—who is a would-be intellectual and frequent though inept attempter of suicide. These notes constitute an "ethnographic" investigation of the courtyard and the Zelmenyaner way of life.[35] (Tsalel is a self-professed "native" ethnographer of the Zelmenyaner tribe.) Tsalel divides his ethnography into the following categories: (1) Material Culture of the Courtyard; (2) Medicine in the Courtyard; (3) Zelmanyanish Geography; (4) Zelmenyanish Zoology; (5) Zelmenyanish Botany;[36] and (6) Zelmenyanish Philology. The parody of Jewish ethnography of the period is fairly clear-cut and terribly funny.

The Zelmeniad, however, stands at the end-point[37] of Kulbak's ethnographic thinking. As a parody, it adopts the narrative form and dry expository style typical of ethnography. For ethnographic poetry, however, we have to return to Kulbak's Vilna period (1923–1928), and to a work that reads as an experiment in ethnographic poetry that investigated issues later elaborated in *Zelmenyaner.*

Kulbak's compact six-canto "Vilne" (1926) remains one of the poet's most celebrated works, a haunting evocation of the city he loved. Reverberating with the city's cultural cachet, which was magnified by the intellectual ferment accompanying the founding of YIVO the year before, Kulbak's poem presents itself in conversation with the ethnographic discourse of (interwar) Jewish culture. The poem offers simultaneously a praise of tradition and traditional lifeways and an elegy on their loss. In the very first canto, for example, we read "Your joy is sadness—the joy of deep basses / In a choir, holidays are funerals, / And consolation—the clear, shining poverty, / Like quiet summer-mists on the street corners of the city."[38] The emotive and creative forces encounter here the ethos of salvage.

However, Kulbak's primary goal is not to talk about ethnographic data. Had that been his aim, given the dominant folkloric-philologic bent of Vilna's ethnographic community, doubtless he would have deployed an array of Yiddish dialectal and idiomatic variants, at which he was adept, as we see in many other of his works. This, however, is not the case in "Vilne." What Kulbak contemplates is ethnography itself.

Having neither regular rhyme nor meter, the cantos connect by loose echoes of lines or phrases, like inchoate internal refrains. As in an echo, where exact repetition is impossible, the openings of the first two cantos make a telling transition, one which offers in miniature the ethnographic ethos of the poet's vision. The poem opens as follows:

> Upon your walls someone is walking around in a tallis.
> At night in the city he alone, awake, is sad.

The initial image evokes Baudelaire's *flâneur*, but Kulbak's details go on to dampen that suggestiveness. The nocturnal wanderer is marked by his traditional religious garment, the tallis (prayer shawl). However, the *tallis* is not worn at night. Kulbak removes an object of material culture from its original and appropriate context. No traditional Jew would have used a tallis at such a time and in that way. Instead, it becomes a cultural artifact put on view, ready for a new use. That is where Kulbak inserts it, as a token of ethnographic representation, connoting religion but out of context.

Moreover, the wanderer's placement on the walls suggests the image of a guard or watchman. There may well be a biblical echo here of Isaiah 62:6—"Upon your walls, Jerusalem, have I set watchmen; neither day nor night shall they ever be still." The points of contact—an apostrophe to a city, the station on the city walls, constant motion and activity, as well as Vilna's famous epithet "Jerusalem of Lithuania"—color our reading of the poem. The prophetic text offers a vision of the redemption of the Jewish people and of Jerusalem. "No more," the prophet says, "will you be called 'abandoned'; nor will your land be any longer called a desolate place. For you will be called 'My delight is in her . . . '" (Isaiah 62:4). The culture work of ethnography is designed to convert salvage into salvation, and Kulbak's carefully chosen biblical imagery gestures to the prophetic context from which it was excerpted.

As was seen in An-sky and as is clear in Kulbak's poem, "culture work" was conceived of as central to the ethnographic gaze. In the Hebrew poet Shaul Tshernikhovski's (1875–1943) poem, "le-Nokhaḥ Pesel 'Apolo" (Before the Statue of Apollo, 1899), for example, the modern Jew stands before the beautiful Greek statue of Apollo and ruminates on the grandeur and awesome power, now degraded, of the God of the Bible. Tshernikhovski envisions the ancient as containing the potential for contemporary vitality. Indeed, unlike modes of traditional anthropology and ethnography that constructed their object outside of time,[39] unconnected to forward-moving modern peoples, as virginal and perennially "new," and unlike others for whom newness was connected to youth, for Jewish ethnographic modernism the "ethnographic" was a vehicle for converting ancientness into the new. That is why Kulbak's "ancient" city of Vilna is the catalyst for a modernist understanding of Jewishness.

This night watchman of sorts is stationed on the wall clothed in a religious token emptied of its religious content; the tallis-bearer has, therefore, a curious subjectivity. And to this description the second line adds the typical conditions of the modern individual: sadness and solitude. The oblique syntax only enhances the sense of disorientation.

The first line of the very next canto repeats the preceding canto's second line, with one small but significant change: "At night in the city I alone, awake, am sad." Here, we have moved from "he" to "I." In the transition from third to first person in a line that is otherwise exactly the same, the poet not only sympathizes but identifies with this "traditional" yet modern figure. He describes himself as engaging in the same activity as the originally observed subject, the very definition of participant observation. In the mechanics of this complicated association, the contact situation of authoritative ethnography between Self and Other is transmuted in this modern poetic model into one between Self and Self-*as*-Other.

Implicit in the poem's ethnographic construction is a critique of at least one important aspect of Jewish ethnographic practice. Eight times throughout the poem the word "city" appears, including the near programmatic lines quoted above. The urban subjects here—the observer ("I") and the observed ("he")—question the prevailing presumption of the village, or in the Jewish case the shtetl, as the default locus of authenticity. Echoing Grishashvili, Kulbak lays claim to an urban folk creativity and the ability of an urban intellectual to produce literature that can represent it from within.

Kulbak offers images that fall into the two primary categories of Jewish ethnographic collecting: material culture and verbal or linguistic culture. From the mention of the tallis in the first line we are introduced to material folk culture, and in that case, as was said earlier, what is highlighted is that object's cultural, not its religious significance. A mere four lines later: "You are a Psalter laid out in clay and iron." In one common translation, this line reads: "You are a psalm, spelled in clay and in iron."[40] Such a rendering, however, neutralizes the physicality of the image. The word *thilim* in this case refers to a concrete copy of the book of Psalms, not to a psalm itself. The distinction is important because Kulbak is not describing the city as a text to be read but as an object to be experienced sensorially (if not sensually). This material importance is reflected in the YIVO pamphlet, *What Is Jewish Ethnography?*, whose section on "Folk Art" opens as follows:

> A friend writes of a Polish shtetl: In their synagogue one finds an old volume of Psalms, its pages are adorned with drawings. Sometimes German artists would come and copy the drawings; today it lies about somewhere with the synagogue wardens.
>
> Our synagogues and study-houses are, in part, little museums of old Jewish folk art: the curtains of the ark, candelabra, fescues, paintings, alms plates, adornments on the walls, etc. The largest portion of Jewish art used to be concentrated in the synagogues. Today everything is abandoned, covered in dust; and how many relics have been lost![41]

Again, it is the Psalter's physicality, its artistry, the plastic testament to cultural creativity that the poet chooses to prize—an important distinction insofar as texts are a poet's usual stock in trade—and which is its chief relevance to ethnography.

It is seven lines further that we find one of the poem's most famous images of Vilna: "You are a dark amulet set in Lithuania." The amulet (*kameye*), that essential part of Jewish folk art and of folk belief, points to the blend of creativity and credulity that marks any folk culture. The darkness of the charm resonates with the somber elegiac mood of the work as

a whole. But in focusing on the "setting" of the amulet, Kulbak singles out
its material artistry. The natural beauty of Lithuania (*Lite*) is the inscription on that amulet ("written all over, grey and old, with moss and with
lichens"). And an amulet is designed to protect, to guard against danger,
recapitulating the earlier theme of the watchman as well as the idea underlying salvage ethnography. Two sets of images therefore predominate
in this introductory canto: those of age and desuetude or even decay and
those of guarding or protecting. One hears Kulbak's somber-voiced per-
mutation of the YIVO ethnographers' clarion call, "Today everything is
abandoned, covered in dust; and how many relics have been lost!"

Just as important as the mood and setting of the amulet is how that
single object sits emblematically at an intersection of classic ethnographic
rubrics, including religious folkways, architecture, superstition, and material culture. All things are focused through it, just as the poet sees Jewish
folk culture concentrated in the art and artifacts of Vilna. And the protec-
tive inscription on the amulet—the organic tracing on the city walls by
moss[42] and lichen—makes a case for the "organic" and ancient presence
of Jewish culture in that land and landscape.

As if to confirm in structure what is so particularly salient in theme
and image, Kulbak recapitulates these two lines ("You are a Psalter . . ."
and "You are a dark amulet . . .") at the beginnings of cantos 3 and 5, re-
spectively. In the first of these, material and indeed physical culture are
primary: occupations, quotidian practices, the look of real physical bodies. The climactic move, however, comes in the latter canto, where Kulbak shifts from material to verbal culture. The often religiously oriented
practices outlined earlier in the poem have given way here to two essential
types: "The fiery red shirt of the steely Bundist; / The blue student sitting
at [his] grey Bergelson." The Bund, the major Jewish labor organization,
had been founded in Vilna at the end of the nineteenth century and was
commonly associated with that city, as was the ardor of its adherents.
Equally connected with the city, and with Jewish Lithuania more broadly,
was the intellectual acumen of its scholars, often echoing the influence and
image of the famous Vilna Gaon. Here, however, the one explicit name
is that of Dovid Bergelson, one of the premiere prose stylists of Yiddish
modernism.[43] His works chronicled what has been called the decline of

the shtetl, with its unmoored intellectuals and unfulfilled desires. Kulbak may be offering a subtle critique of the centrality of the shtetl to Jewish cultural consciousness. More important, though, is the prominence given to Yiddish literature, and especially Yiddish literary modernism, within the "ethnographic" profile of Vilna.

Indeed, Kulbak writes more explicitly in the next lines:

And Yiddish is the simple wreath of oak leaves
Over the gates, sacred and secular, of the city.
Grey Yiddish is the candle that sparkles in the window—
Oh, like a wanderer [*geyer*] at an old well on the road
I sit here and listen to the raw voice of Yiddish.

What unites everything is Yiddish, a language whose cultural expression is definitively marked as secular, and whose secularity is in turn a sign of its sanctity. And by Yiddish Kulbak does not mean Yiddish texts, but rather how the language is spoken and heard: "raw" and unrefined, therefore pure in an ethnographic sense. We are not dealing with meaning per se, but sensory and even spiritual apprehension. That is how Kulbak identifies *Yiddish* as an object of ethnographic investigation.

In the wake of these atmospheric impressions of the details of the city's Jewish culture, Kulbak reaches his climactic statement: "I am the city!" Addressor and addressee have now merged; identification has moved to identity. Unlike the authoritative model, where the "I" *controls* the data and the discourse, the "I" of the poem "Vilne" diffuses itself throughout the material it observed and collects. It *becomes* its material ("I *am* the city!"). And in that way it both dissolves the importance of authority and constitutes its authenticity. Kulbak offers a vision of his city as ethnographic space and his poem as a meditation on what that means.

This essay began by trying to match the contours of Jewish cultural thinking to the landscape of ethnography. Jewish ethnography carved its own space out of the influential ideas and methods with which it was in conversation, shifting the emphases in consonance with its own concerns. The problematics of alterity become the benefits of identification; authority yields to authenticity. The literary ramifications of this reorientation do not pervade Yiddish letters. Ethnography was of interest to many Yiddish poets, just as many Yiddish poets deployed ethnographic details. Few, however, were the poets who devoted sustained literary attention to exploring what is modern and what is Jewish precisely in the connection of poetry to ethnography. Because it does just that, Kulbak's work deserves our continued attention as an entry point to this subject.

*   *   *

Moyshe Kulbak, "Vilne"[44]

1.

Upon your walls someone is walking around in a tallis.
At night in the city he alone, awake, is sad.
He listens: the old veins of grey alleys and synagogues
Are awake, resounding like a hoarse, dusty heart.
You are a Psalter laid out in clay and iron;
A prayer is every stone, a melody every—wall,
When the moon trickles down into your alleys of tradition,
And the naked and ugly-cold beauty blanches forth.
Your joy is sadness—the joy of deep basses
In a choir, holidays are funerals,
And consolation—the clear, shining poverty,
Like quiet summer-mists on the street corners of the city.
You are a dark amulet set in Lithuania,
Written all over, grey and old, with moss and with lichens;
A book [seyfer] is every stone, a parchment—every wall,
Paged-through mysteriously and opened in the night,
When on the old synagogue a frozen water-carrier,—
His little beard turned up,—stands and counts the stars.

2.

At night in the city I alone, awake, am sad:
Not a sound. The houses freeze—heaps of rags.
But somewhere high up a tallow candle drips and flickers,—
A kabbalist sits enwebbed in his attic room,
Like a spider, and pulls forth the grey thread of his life:
—"Is there someone there in the distant, cold waste
Whose lost cries we, the deaf, hear?"
And Raziel stands before him leaden-grey in the darkness
With old, worn-through parchment wings,

And eyes—holes filled in with sand and spider webs:
—"No one. Besides sadness there's no one anymore! . . ."
The candle drips. The sickly Jew listens stone-still
And sucks the darkness from the angel's eye sockets,
And attic room after room breathes relief—the lungs
Of the hunchbacked creature who slumbers in the mountains.
Oh, maybe you, City, are a dream of a kabbalist,
Floating about grey, like spider webs at the start of Autumn.

3.
You are a Psalter laid out in clay and iron,
And your letters wander, stray worn-through:
Jews as stiff as logs, women like loaves of bread;
Cold, mysterious beards, their shoulders hammered-out,
And eyes trembling, long, like boats on a river————
Your Jews over a silvery herring late at night
Strike their chests *for our sins:* "Oh, God, we sin, we sin . . ."
And the moon like a white eye stares through the little panes—
There rags hanging over the string turn silver,
The children in their beds—yellow, slippery worms,
And girls already half undressed with bodies like boards————
Narrow, like your streets, are your gloomy Jews;
Mute foreheads like the broad frozen walls of the synagogue courtyard,
And mossy brows like the roofs over your ruins.
You are a Psalter inscribed on the fields,
And like a raven I sing of you in the moonlight,
For the sun has never risen over Lithuania.

4.
Your joy is sadness—the joy of deep basses
In a choir, dark is your quiet springtime.
Saplings grow from the city-wall, grasses from the walls;
The grey blossoms creep out drowsily from the old tree
And the cold nettle stands muddily on the ground,
Only filth and ever-frozen walls are in the dampness.
And it happens at night, a breeze plays tricks on stone and roof,
And an image made of waterdrops and moonlight
Slinks through the streets silvery and tremblingly a-dream—
The Viliya rose cool and misty,
And fresh, and bare-naked, with long, watery hands,
Into the city. The blind little panes look out warped,

The little bridges thrown off rounded towards the city-walls.
Oh, no one will open a door, stick out his head
To the Viliya and her thin, blue nakedness.
The city-walls with their beards are amazed, like the mountains all around,
And quietly, and quietly———

5.
You are a dark amulet set in Lithuania,
And figures faintly glow in your restless ground:
The white, shining geniuses of a distant light,
With narrow, hard bones whet by toil;
The fiery red shirt of the steely Bundist;
The blue student sitting at his grey Bergelson,
And Yiddish is the simple wreath of oak leaves
Over the gates, sacred and secular, of the city.
Grey Yiddish is the candle that sparkles in the window—
Oh, like a wanderer at an old well on the road
I sit here and listen to the raw voice of Yiddish.
And perhaps the blood in my limbs rushes so strongly?
I am the city! The thousand narrow doors to the world,
The roofs upon roofs to the muddy-cold blue.
I am the black flame that here hungrily licks the walls
And glows in the cuttingly sharp eye of the Litvak abroad.
I am the grey! I am the black flame! I am the city!

6.
And on the old synagogue, a frozen water-carrier,—
His little beard turned up,—stands and counts the stars.

NOTES

My thanks to Gabriella Safran for her suggestions of incalculable value in the improvement and clarification of my arguments.

1. Moyshe Kulbak, "Dos yidishe vort," *Sovetish heymland* 21 (1981): 100.
2. Kulbak, "Dos yidishe vort," 97–98. *Folksshafung* ("folk creativity") can also be translated as "folklore."
3. Moyshe Kulbak, "Finf briv fun m. kulbak tsu sh. nigern," *Sovetish heymland* 21 (1981): 103.
4. On this point see Marianna Torgovnick's analysis of Odysseus' escapade with the Cyclops in Homer's *Odyssey*. Marianna Torgovnick, *Gone Primitive: Savage Intellects, Modern Loves* (Chicago: The University of Chicago Press, 1990), 23–26.

5. Barbara Kirshenblatt-Gimblett, "Folklore, Ethnography, and Anthropology," in Gershon David Hundert, ed., *The YIVO Encyclopedia of Jews in Eastern Europe*, vol. 1 (New Haven, Conn.: Yale University Press, 2008), 522.

6. Kirshenblatt-Gimblett, "Folklore, Ethnography, and Anthropology," 522.

7. See, for example, John B. Gatewood, "A Short Typology of Ethnographic Genres: Or Ways to Write about Other Peoples," *Anthropology and Humanism Quarterly* 9, no. 4 (1984): 5–10; Richard Handler and Daniel Segal, "Narrating Multiple Realities: Some Lessons from Jane Austen for Ethnographers," *Anthropology and Humanism Quarterly* 9, no. 4 (1984): 15–21.

8. I piggyback here on Clifford Geertz's "blurred genres." Clifford Geertz, *Local Knowledge: Further Essays in Interpretive Anthropology* (New York: Basic Books, 1983), 19–35.

9. John Van Maanen, *Tales of the Field: On Writing Ethnography* (Chicago: University of Chicago Press, 1988), 11n7.

10. See, for example, Yuri Slezkine, *Arctic Mirrors: Russia and the Small Peoples of the North* (Ithaca, N.Y.: Cornell University Press, 1994).

11. Questionnaires and other forms of data solicitation had been part of the machinery of folkloristics since the mid-nineteenth century and gained renewed strength in the first decades of the twentieth. See, for example, Nathaniel Deutsch, *The Jewish Dark Continent: Life and Death in the Russian Pale of Settlement* (Cambridge, Mass.: Harvard University Press, 2011), 32, 62–65; Mark W. Kiel, "Vox Populi, Vox Dei: The Centrality of Peretz in Jewish Folkloristics," *Polin: A Journal of Polish-Jewish Studies* 7 (1992): 94, 94n45; Kalman Weiser, *Jewish People, Yiddish Nation: Noah Prylucki and the Folkists in Poland* (Toronto: University of Toronto Press, 2011), 94–118.). In an important essay on the modern concept of Jewish ethnography the noted historian Yitskhok (Ignacy) Shiper regularly singles out the drawbacks and deficiencies of Jewish ethnographic practice. To Shiper's mind, Jewish ethnography had long been dominated by enthusiasts, by amateur or "dilettantish" "collectors" (*zamler*), inspired by a passion and love for the "people (*folk*)," but unprepared in scientific methods (Y[itskhok] Shiper, "Araynfir-verter in der yidisher folkskentenish" *Landkentenish* 1 (1933): 68.

12. *Vos iz azoyns yidishe etnografye? (Handbikhl far zamler)* (Vilna: Yidisher Visnshaftlekher Institut, Serye "Organizatsye fun der yidisher visnshaft," no. 6, 1931). The authors, Naftoli Vaynig and Khayim Khayes, are not credited in the pamphlet (Itzik Nakhmen Gottesman, *Defining the Yiddish Nation: The Jewish Folklorists of Poland* [Detroit: Wayne State University Press: 2003], 206n125).

13. H. Aleksandrov, *Forsht ayer shtetl!* (Minsk: Institut far vaysruslendisher kultur, Yidisher sektor, Sotsyal-ekonomishe komisye—Byuro far kantkentenish, 1928).

14. Gabriella Safran, *Wandering Soul: The Dybbuk's Creator, S. An-sky* (Cambridge, Mass.: Harvard University Press, 2010), 224. (Emphasis my own.)

15. See George E. Marcus, "Contemporary Problems of Ethnography in the Modern World System," in *Writing Culture: The Poetics and Politics of Ethnography*, ed. James Clifford and George E. Marcus (Berkeley: University of California Press, 1986), 165–193, especially 165n1.

16. Each specific project in some sense defines for itself, either explicitly or implicitly, the parameters of "value." That An-sky, for example, collected all kinds of materials during his expeditions does not controvert the fact that some principle of discernment was employed during collection.

17. For evidence of this developmental phase merely look at the volume of terminological experiments (Barbara Kirshenblatt-Gimblett, "*Di folkloristik*: A Good Yiddish Word," *Journal of American Folklore* 98 [1985]: 331–334).

18. For more on the constructed nature of authenticity in Jewish ethnography see Sylvia Jaworski's contribution to the present volume. Julia Straub notes a concept-historical shift in "authenticity" in the Romantic period based in changing concepts of the self. Julia Straub, "Introduction: The Paradoxes of Authenticity," in *Paradoxes of Authenticity: Studies on a Critical Concept*, ed. Julia Straub (Bielefeld: transcript Verlag, 2012), 14.

19. See most notably James Clifford's classic essay "On Ethnographic Authority."

20. Kenneth Stoddart, "The Presentation of Everyday Life: Some Textual Strategies for 'Adequate Ethnography'," *Urban Life* 15, no. 1 (1986): 104.

21. Jomo Kenyatta, *Facing Mount Kenya: The Traditional Life of the Gikuyu* (1938, London: Heinemann, 1979), xviii.

22. Joseph Roth, *The Wandering Jews*, trans. Michael Hofmann (New York: W.W. Norton & Co., 2011), 43–44.

23. James Clifford, "On Ethnographic Authority," *Representations* 1, no. 2 (1983): 128.

24. Quoted in Harsha Ram, "The Sonnet and the Mukhambazi: Genre Wars on the Edges of the Russian Empire," *PMLA* 122, no. 5 (2007): 1556.

25. Avrom Reyzen, *Di lider fun Avrom Reyzen in tsvelf teyln (1891–1951)* (New York: Abraham Reisen, 1951), 264. For a description and partial translation of this poem see Kiel, "Vox Populi, Vox Dei," 106.

26. Of course, the extremes of this salvific love for the objects of ethnography are ripe for satire, and the zealous Jewish collector did open some space for ridicule. In his book on the ardent folklorist Noah Prylucki, Kalman Weiser quotes a poem that sets side by side Prylucki's work in folklore and his political activities as member of the Warsaw city council. Throngs have come to their civic and political leader, begging for help to alleviate their miseries: "They are taking Jews' livelihoods away, / 'O, save us, Councillor, Sir'; / Noah has but one request, / 'Repeat that saying carefully' . . ." (trans. Kalman Weiser; Weiser, *Jewish People, Yiddish Nation*, 273).

27. Gatewood, 7–8.

28. Safran, 12–13.

29. Moyshe Kulbak, *Naye lider* (Warsaw: Farlag "Kultur-lige," 1922), 43–45.

30. Moyshe Kulbak, *Zelmenyaner*, vol. 1 (Moscow, Kharkov, Minsk: Tsentraler felker-farlag fun f.s.s.r., 1931), vol. 2 (Minsk: Melukhe-farlag fun vaysrusland, 1935).

31. This mirrors the image of the "domestic other" of the Jews and their shtetls in Eastern Europe.

32. "*Zelmenyade*" (Kulbak, *Zelmenyaner*, vol. 2, 97–108).

33. Sasha Senderovich in a paper presented at our Zurich conference translates this as "research associate" as a calque from a Russian term, based on Kulbak's own work experience for the Belarusian Academy of Sciences. I have kept "field worker" because it captures the in-situ observational perspective of Tsalel's work in the family's courtyard complex.

34. For a fuller treatment of the *Zelmeniad* see Sasha Senderovich's forthcoming book, tentatively titled "Seekers of Happiness: Mobility, Culture, and the Creation of the Soviet Jew, 1917–1939."

35. Samples of other of Tsalel's "field notes" are discovered in volume 1, chapter 9. Additionally, in volume 2, chapter 4, some of Tsalel's "collection" practices are mentioned, including searching for old charms (*sheymes*) and moldering women's prayer books.

36. The whole of the section "Zelmenyanish botany," for example, consists of "a birch tree." The stereotype of Yiddish having a dire paucity of words for the objects of nature is taken to its comic extreme.

37. Kulbak was murdered in one of Stalin's repressive purges in 1937, two years after the second volume of *Zelmenyaner* was published.

38. Moyshe Kulbak, *Ale verk fun Moyshe Kulbak*, vol. 2: *Poemen un lider* (Vilna: B. Kletskin, 1929), 179. All quotations from this poem are taken from this edition (the full poem is found pp. 179–184). Five of the six cantos are either 17 or 18 lines in length, and the concluding canto has only two lines.

39. For a full treatment of this idea see Johannes Fabian, *Time and the Other: How Anthropology Makes Its Object* (New York: Columbia University Press, 1983).

40. Nathan Halper's translation is anthologized in, inter alia, Irving Howe and Eliezer Greenberg, eds., *A Treasury of Yiddish Poetry* (New York: Holt, Rinehart and Winston, 1969), 216–219.

41. *Vos iz azoyns yidishe etnografye?*, 12.

42. I have elsewhere noted Kulbak's affinity for moss imagery, which often indicates "the temporal stasis of nature" among other things (Jordan Finkin, "'Like Fires in Overgrown Forests': Moyshe Kulbak's Contemporary Berlin Poetics," in *Yiddish in Weimar Berlin: At the Crossroads of Diaspora Politics and Culture*, Studies in Yiddish 8, ed. Gennady Estraikh and Mikhail Krutikov [London: Legenda, 2010], 84).

43. In Kulbak's essay "The Yiddish Word" he gives Bergelson pride of place as such a prose stylist non pareil (Kulbak, *"Dos yidishe vort,"* 99–100).

44. Moyshe Kulbak, *Ale verk fun Moyshe Kulbak*, vol. 2: *Poemen un lider* (Vilna: B. Kletskin, 1929), 179–184.

PART 2.
SEEING, HEARING,
AND READING JEWS

Listening in the Dark

The Yiddish Folklorists' Claim of a Russian Genealogy

GABRIELLA SAFRAN

The Lodz Yiddish writer Hershele (Hershl Danilevitsh, 1882–1941) explained why he collected Yiddish folksongs by linking himself to a Russian Christian born almost a century earlier, Aleksei Kol'tsov (1809–1842), a cattle merchant's son celebrated for his poems spoken in the voice of the Russian peasant. "I am a folk poet," Hershele asserted, "the Jewish Kol'tsov! I write and collect folk songs."[1] Other Yiddish folklorists during Poland's productive interwar Jewish "folklore mania" years were also inspired by the Russian writers of the early and mid-nineteenth century. Noah Prylucki (1882–1941), Warsaw's leading Jewish philologist, editor, and folklore scholar, began to write down Yiddish tales (translating them into Russian as he did so) after having read the Russian peasant tales anthologized by Aleksandr Afanas'ev (1826–1871); in the introduction to his first volume of folk songs, he quoted Nikolai Gogol (1809–1852); and when he urged the Yiddish writer Sholem Asch to develop a version of Yiddish that would be beautiful, authentic, and appropriate for upper-class speakers, he told him to model himself on the Russian Romantic writers Aleksandr Griboedov (1795–1829), Aleksandr Pushkin (1799–1837),[2] and Mikhail Lermontov (1814–1841).[3]

In his biography of Prylucki, the historian Kalman Weiser explains the link between these Yiddish folklorists and a set of Russian writers as primarily ideological:

Like other forms of European populism, Yiddishism reproached intellectuals with betrayal and abandonment of the loyal *folk* . . . the idealized
guardians of the national soul and identity, through the adoption of
foreign tongues and cultures. Taking inspiration from the Russian *narodniki,* these wayward sons and daughters were exhorted to return to their
people, to help awaken in them a secular national consciousness, and to
educate and modernize them in their own language. In return, the alienated intellectuals were to be inspired with and reinvigorated by the unre-
flective naturalness of the *folksmentsh*'s (the simple person of the masses)
assumedly uncomplicated and unembarrassed identity. Yiddish was to
undergo a process akin to that by which other European vernaculars were
transformed into standardized, national languages in the eighteenth and
nineteenth centuries . . . eventually, it would become the primary vehicle
of both high and low culture.[4]

This ideological link would have made sense to the Yiddish folklorists
themselves. But when they claimed the Russian *narodniki* (Populists) as
their predecessors, they needed to ignore some significant differences
between themselves and these putative ancestors, to smooth out the ideological differences among the various Russians they cited and between
Populist ideology and their own. Most obviously, the narodniki wanted,
in the wake of the 1861 emancipation of the serfs, to preserve and celebrate
aspects of traditional Slavic peasant ways and to help the peasants avoid
what they saw as the pernicious effects of capitalism; their anticapitalist biases made them a poor model for activists working with a population such
as Ashkenazi Jews, so many of whom were employed in trade or crafts and
so few in agriculture. In addition, most of the early nineteenth-century
writers whom Pryłucki and Hershele found inspirational—Kol'tsov, Gogol, Griboedov, Pushkin, and Lermontov—are not conventionally identified with the narodniki.

While these ideological differences are clearly visible, another paradox
underlies the Yiddish folklorists' claim of a Russian Romantic genealogy,
one that requires acknowledging the shifts in the sensory experience of
folklore collecting—or more broadly, in the history of listening. That listening could be difficult, that communication was likely to be fraught,
was a factor that troubled European thinkers in Kol'tsov's 1830s as in Hershele's 1920s. During this century, as John Durham Peters argues, the
"breaches between individual minds" gained a "wider social and political

relevance" and the concept of communication, especially its potential failures and gaps, acquired a new "grandeur and pathos."[5] The writings of folklorists and ethnographers, who were so attentive to cultural differences and linguistic details, offer rich material for consideration of the shifting perceptions of the barriers to listening and the methods for overcoming them. I begin this chapter by describing these barriers, distinguishing between the difficulties Russian intellectuals faced listening to peasants in the period before 1861 and those that secularizing Jews faced listening to more traditional Jews from the 1870s through the 1930s. I then evaluate scenes of difficult listening in Yiddish ethnoliterature, first looking at late maskilic memoirs and prose fiction by Mendele Moykher Sforim (S. Y. Abramovitsh, 1836–1917) and Y. L. Peretz (1852–1915), and second considering memoirs and stories from the interwar period and later by A. Almi (Eliyahu Hayim Sheps, 1892–1963), Avrom Karpinowitz (1913–2004), and others. Taken together, these texts show that a set of distinctive listening practices and ideologies of communication characterized the Yiddish folkloristic endeavor. For the Yiddish folklorists as for the Russians whom they admired, darkness, by removing the visible link between the speaking body and the sounds it produced, seemed to hold out the possibility of overcoming the internal and external censors that separated listeners from speakers, a fantasy that recalls the work of another early twentieth-century European Jew, Sigmund Freud (1856–1939). However, the sources—including Freud's own work—complicate any easy equation of Slavic and Jewish modes of listening.

LISTENING THROUGH BARRIERS

In rural places and small market towns in Eastern Europe at the start of the nineteenth century, both Russian peasants and traditionally observant Jews experienced much of their speaking and listening in environments segregated by gender, class, language, ethnicity, religious practice, and family ties. Women and men possessed separate folksong repertoires, performed some separate rituals, and engaged in work patterns that created gender-specific linguistic corpora. Language mastery was linked to class and gender: in Jewish society, only elite men knew and read Hebrew, and non-elite women might know only Yiddish and be illiterate; in Russian society, only the elite knew and read French, and peasants usually knew only Russian or another Slavic language and were illiterate. Jewish men listened to stories in the Hasidic court and in the study house, while Jewish women heard stories from other women at home or in the marketplace.[6] Folklorists see themselves as tasked with collecting, categorizing, and publicizing the creative production of people who have no access to the prestige lent by the printed word, and in Eastern Europe, the evident linguistic and literacy markers of class and gender helped them find the proper targets for their investigations. At the same time, gender- and class-segregated customs of storytelling and singing made folklorists' work more difficult, as demonstrated by the frequent references in their writing to the barriers making it hard for educated people to listen to peasants, or for men to listen to women, and to their own ingenuity in overcoming these difficulties.

Some of the iconic scenes of ethnographic listening in the "heroic period" of Russian folkloristics, the 1850s, on the eve of the 1861 emancipation of the serfs, figure a particularly ingenious method of surmounting the barrier: the listener is either asleep or feigning sleep. The hunter in Ivan Turgenev's 1840s–50s story sequence *Notes of a Hunter,* the imprisoned narrator in Fedor Dostoevsky's 1861 fictionalized prison memoir *Notes from the House of the Dead,* and Pavel Rybnikov, the folklorist who discovered that the bylina (Russian epic song) tradition was still alive in 1859 on the shores of Lake Ladoga, all have their eyes closed and appear to be asleep at the moment when they hear the remarkable stories voiced by the peasants. As I argue elsewhere, the Russian literary device of the sleeping listener evokes both the psychological theories and the political realities of the day. The revelation of ethnographic detail at the edge of sleep emerged from a mid-nineteenth-century discourse around sleep and the brain. In 1848, the French scholar Alfred Maury named the sounds heard or imagined on the edge of sleep "hypnogogic" hallucinations; Freud would theorize that such impressions give access to the uncensored psyche.[7] At the same time, it was only in the dark that the enormous class difference between speaker and listener, until 1861 the difference between slave and slave owner, could be forgotten, and the stories of the folk—which, it appeared, resonated with the inner voice of the listener—could be heard. In the darkness, both the serf speaker and the educated listener could forget that their politically suspect act of communication put both of them at risk, and the reader could understand that if internal and external censors could be overpowered, then upper and lower classes would experience a true connection. (Why, one might wonder, would the tsarist government want to limit noblemen listening to peasant fairytales? Although this might seem counterintuitive to those familiar with the nationalistically oriented folkloristics of Central Europe, the Russian peasants, enslaved until 1861, were not consistently seen by their rulers as the privileged bearers of a national identity linked to the state.[8] The disconnect between nationalist folkloristics and imperial politics was heightened by the fact that many of the empire's ethnographers were themselves undergoing punishment; having exiled these intellectuals for various infractions to the borders of the empire, the authorities then recruited them to study the natives and benefited from their passion for folklore.)[9]

Even while it evoked the psychological and political discourse of its era, the repeating scenes of listening in the dark could also reference real communication practices. While many listening environments in pre-nineteenth-century Eastern Europe were class and gender segregated, those that occurred in darkness were less so. In a Jewish context, men of different classes might listen to stories together in a prayer house at dusk, between the afternoon and evening prayers (*tsvishn minkhe un mayrev*). For Jews and Slavs, evening storytelling to children was relatively unsegregated. The children of the nobility, their class status in a sense mitigated by their age, might hear peasant songs or stories from a serf nanny. And in a Jewish context, boys could hear songs or stories told by their mothers or grandmothers in the evenings, even after spending the day in a male-only environment. For both Jews and Slavs, evening storytelling by adults to children had something in common with the sort of listening figured in Turgenev, Dostoevsky, and Rybnikov, in that it was virtuosic rather than in-the-round: the listener could admire the speaker's words without ever having to take a turn. In a distinction central to Peters's history of communication, this kind of virtuosic and less segregated storytelling is disseminatory, not dialogical. Peters persuasively defends the disseminatory model, with its acknowledgement of what he sees as the generosity in speech that does not demand an immediate answer.[10] The words of the storyteller may or may not evoke the desired response in any given listener; they may not even be heard. Because listeners are not obligated to respond, the storyteller has no way of knowing. When Turgenev, Dostoevsky, and Rybnikov publish what they advertise as the words of the folk, they situate themselves in that same position, disseminating their texts broadly in a written medium that requires no immediate oral response.

The need to police this disseminatory mode of communication is evident in the politics of gender and listening among Jews in early nineteenth-century Eastern Europe. Even while men and women could listen together in public to stories told by a man, such as a wedding jester or a traveling preacher, the religious definition of the aural boundaries between the genders hardened in the nineteenth century, in response to the pressures of modernization and the early Haskalah (the enlightenment movement that urged Jews to master non-Jewish languages and secular sciences). In 1814, the conservative Hungarian halakhic authority, the Ḥatam Sofer (Moshe Sofer, 1762–1839), determined that the Talmudic statement that "a woman's voice is nakedness" (kol b'isha 'ervah, Berakhot 24A) should be interpreted as forbidding men from listening to women singing. He heard women's voices as distracting to men and thus needing to be hushed. Since that time, some rabbinic scholars have worked to extend the prohibitions of kol isha, while others have attempted to relax them.[11] Kol isha has been used to justify the separate seating of men and women in synagogues, allowing women's voices to be heard in prayer, if at all, only by other women.

In spite of the irritation of cultural conservatives, Jewish listening practices in Eastern Europe shifted over the nineteenth century. The migration of Jews from market towns to regional cities, or overseas, placed them into streets and businesses where they could hear the voices of Jews and non-Jews, men and women, and people of different classes and professions. The rise of the periodical press in Hebrew, Russian, and Yiddish meant that the factual and fictional tales that circulated in print from metropolitan centers could be revoiced in the shtetls. As Jeffrey Veidlinger shows, by the early twentieth century, even in small towns in the Russian empire, Jews were inviting visiting lecturers, performing in amateur theatricals, and embracing other modern listening experiences.[12]

Like the Russian ethnoliterature of the mid-nineteenth century, the Yiddish ethnoliterature of the late nineteenth and twentieth centuries dwells persistently on listening—what makes it possible, what prevents it, and what price is paid by those who cross the borders that prevent people in one category from hearing people in another. The long nineteenth century that they shared was characterized, as Peters has it, by "the agony of solitude and the yearning for unity," both felt more intensely than ever before.[13] Both Russian and Yiddish folklorists felt anxious about trespassing the boundaries separating the educated secular ethnographer from the uneducated members of the folk. But where that boundary, for the Russians, was above all one of class, for the Yiddish folklorists the boundary between the genders is depicted with the most concern. In an undoubtedly related phenomenon, the sense that speakers and listeners make themselves vulnerable through an illicit act of listening is tied in the Russian texts to the state and its ambition to regulate both peasants and intellectuals, whereas in the Jewish texts, religious regulations and expectations for men and women, and the hierarchies and categories that they enforce, create the sense of danger. However the system is constructed, ethnoliterature speaks simultaneously of the desire for illicit listening and of the fear of its results.

"WHEN HE READS, SHE FALLS ASLEEP"

The ambivalence about ethnographic listening implicit in Turgenev, Dostoevsky, and Rybnikov's accounts of the sleeping intellectual among the peasants becomes explicit in the Yiddish writing of Abramovitsh and Peretz, texts that can be characterized as late maskilic prose. The late nineteenth-century *maskilim* (adherents of the Haskalah) were literate in Russian and familiar with Turgenev and Dostoevsky. Their attitude toward Jewish folklore was complex. On the one hand, they tended to depict it satirically, as part of the irrational traditional ways that they wanted Jews to reject. On the other hand, as Dan Miron notes, the maskilic satire of Jewish traditions often gave way to a "sense of sheer artistic joy with the material, which is unhampered by ideological considerations."[14] Miron writes that maskilim such as Abramovitsh used inset genres (the Anatomy, the Autobiography, the Story with a Bogus Folkloric Focus, and the Parodied or Poeticized Folktale) that "allowed for a direct and detailed representation of ethnographic material within a satirical framework. The author could thus . . . display his interest in folklore and wallow in its details, as well as criticize and satirize it."[15]

I propose that in addition to these subgenres, Abramovitsh used the technique of Turgenev, Dostoevsky, and Rybnikov to get access to folklore: employing the sleeping listener. In his novella *Di kliatshe* (The Nag, 1873), the narrator Yisrolik needs to study Russian literature in order to enter university. What is hardest to absorb is Russian folklore: "crazy fairy tales, stories of frightening heroes, terrible drunkards and famous robbers, tales of shape-changers, male and female witches, living and dead waters, golden apples and golden birds."[16] Constantly studying, Yisrolik grows thin and gloomy. One day he faints while walking and has a vision of a bedraggled, beaten talking horse, in whom he recognizes the Jewish people. He wakes up to hear two Jewish folk healers reciting incantations, which they claim have rescued him from the demons that had enchanted him. His mother blames his illness on the Russian fairytales.

> It's no joke to spend so long repeating out loud a story about a hero who
> cleared the horses out of thirty-six stables; or a story about Nightingale
> the Robber and a great knight who could drink up a Jordan River of liquor
> and pull up huge oaks as though he was plucking hair; or fairy tales about
> Kashchei the sorcerer and Baba Yaga, who could turn the whole world
> over and whose horses spoke like human beings; or tales of a stepmother
> who turned her stepson into a goat, and other such stories of fights, battles,
> wars, plagues, troubles and calamities, and who knows what else.[17]

After Yisrolik fails his exam, sleep brings him terrible visions: "I would just have closed one eye when wild shapes would appear before me as though rising from the earth, looking at me with sour faces."[18] He sees Kashchei from the Russian fairytales, the demon Ashmedai, who carries him around the world, and the abused nag. Finally, his mother brings back the folk healers. "It's those fairy tales that you jammed into your head" that made him ill, she explains.[19]

Yisrolik's mother's diagnosis seems to make sense, since Russian folklore characters fill his dreams: Kashchei the Deathless and Baba Yaga are from the fairytales, Nightingale the Robber from the byliny. Russian folklore, it seems, allows Yisrolik, once he closes his eyes, to hear the tale of the abused Jewish horse. As in Turgenev and Rybnikov, when an educated person listens with his eyes closed, he can learn the truth about the political subjugation of the folk; having abandoned his intelligentsia self-consciousness, even his status as the possessor of a gentry body, he can merge with the folk. However, while Turgenev's and Rybnikov's sleepers gain access to the seemingly equally disembodied voice of the folk and hear heroic stories, Abramovitsh's sleeping listener has nightmares in which he is bodily transported through the air, shown appalling visions, and asked to respond. Rather than the dissemination model of the Russian cases, Yisrolik enters into a tormented dialogue with folklore, prompted by the need to memorize Russian fairytales well enough to recite them to an examiner. As his mother complains, folklore makes him sick.

The educated listener's ambivalence about the folk voice appears even more strongly in two later works of Yiddish ethnoliterature. Peretz had just had his lawyer's license revoked when he was hired to research Jews in the Zamość region, and he then wrote *Travel Pictures from a Journey through the Tomaszów Region in the Year 1890.* Unlike the Russian peasants who only speak when they believe the masters are asleep, Peretz depicts many of his subjects as eager to tell their tales.[20] In an episode he later added to his memoir, the ethnographer is riding on a starlit night in a coach, driven by Maciej, a Christian peasant, who, taking him (due to his modern clothing and Polish speech) for a non-Jewish gentleman, tells him frankly about the tensions between the local Jews and Christians. His stories feature a Jewish merchant and tavern-keeper, Moyshe. Coincidentally, Moyshe himself then gets into the coach. He immediately recognizes the narrator as a Jew and tells him—in Yiddish—that he is preparing to recite *mayrev* (the evening prayers); thus Peretz lets the Yiddish reader know that it is *tsvishn minkhe un mayrev,* the time between the afternoon and evening prayers when Jewish men tell stories. After inquiring into the motives of this evidently secular Jew, and making some formal protests, Moyshe tells a story.

"I don't want to offend you. . . . So, say, a German Jew becomes *frum* [religiously observant], it's his mother's *yortsayt* [the anniversary of her

death], and he goes into a Jewish restaurant and for the repose of her soul
he orders kugel [noodle or potato casserole]. His Jewishness is kugel. . . .
Maybe your Jewishness is stories. Is it yortsayt for you?"

And yet he told me this story. Maybe he wanted to tell it more than I
wanted to hear it![21]

In this account, darkness facilitates listening, giving the secular narrator
access to the communal story-listening circle of traditional Galician Jews.
But darkness is not able to eliminate the barriers and resistance that Peretz
suspects lie within himself.

In the 1891 story "In the Mail Coach," Peretz indicates that of all the
listening boundaries in traditional Jewish life, the one between the genders is felt to be the most difficult to cross. This, too, is a tale set at night,
in a form of transportation that brings varied people together. It begins
with the narrator seated next to Chaim, a Jew from the small market town
of Konskivola, who "all at once, in a single breath," tells him everything
about his life, his family, and his wife.[22] His wife Chana came from Warsaw and had a secular education; she felt desperately bored, even trapped,
in Konskivola with her traditional husband, who spent all his time working or studying Talmud. The couple tries to find textual common ground,
but to no effect.

> "I used to translate a page of Gemara for her each evening . . . but I
> knew from the start what the ending would be."
> "And what was the ending?"
> "Don't ask! I translated a page from 'The Four Categories of
> Damages'—the ox and the pit, the grazing animal, and the incendiary—
> and with Rashi, the Tosaphot, and the Maharsha. I recited the lesson in
> the traditional singsong, and she fell asleep as I read to her, night after
> night—it is not for a woman! I was lucky when a peddler strayed into
> Konskivola during the great blizzard that year. I brought home a whole
> pood [16.38 kilos] of storybooks. Now the situation was reversed. She read
> to me and I fell asleep. To this very day," he continued, "I can't understand
> what there is in these storybooks. Men surely won't find anything in them!
> Maybe you write only for women?"[23]

After Chaim leaves the coach, the narrator mulls over his words. "When
he reads, she falls asleep; when she reads, he falls asleep. We should, I
think, at least unite the two worlds. It is the debt of every Yiddish writer—
but Yiddish writers have too many debts of their own."[24]

In the second half of the story, Janek Polniewski, the narrator's Polish childhood friend, unexpectedly boards the coach. The narrator fears that he may have become an antisemite, like other members of his class, but Janek assures him that he has not been infected—in part thanks to the friendship he had developed with Sarah, a Jewish woman who, like Chaim's wife, had been bored by small-town Jewish life. The story's final line insists on its ethnographic quality, identifying Sarah and Chana as two examples of a larger phenomenon. Janek's and Chaim's tales and the story of the narrator's interactions with them all turn on the difficulty of listening across boundaries—between men and women, the secular and the religious, Jews and Christians. The narrator fantasizes that his writing could cross these borders, but he recognizes their strength and his own residual hostility to both Chaim and Janek and the stories they tell.

Peretz's story confronts the folklorist's conflicting desires to listen and not to listen, to encourage another's words (in the disseminatory mode) and to escape the demands those words might make on their listener (should they begin a dialogue). The story brings us from the problem of the distance between the intellectual and the peasants, which vanishes once the listener appears to falls asleep, to the less tractable gender barrier, which is only reinforced by darkness. Unable to listen to each other, Chaim and Chana escape into slumber, and Peretz knows that Yiddish literature cannot combat their drowsiness. The distance between Chaim and Chana is like the distance between the ethnographer and Moyshe, who may want to speak more than Peretz wants to listen. Whereas sleep is a help to the mid-century Russian ethnographers, it is a hindrance for Peretz and his narrator, but in both cases, darkness allows the ethnographer to reflect on his own inadequacy as a listener.

"DIFFICULT, PAINFUL HOURS"

The boundaries between genders, and the tensions produced when folklorists are compelled to enter into dialogue with their subjects, resurface three decades later in the writing of interwar Polish Yiddish folklorists. These writers were not worried about the class differences that Dostoevsky and Turgenev saw between ethnographers and their subjects or the differences in religious practice that emerge in Mendele and Peretz. They had much in common with their subjects, many of them also literate and urban. These folklorists collected from their relatives and even from themselves.[25] In A. Litvin's collections, towns seem populated entirely by people eager to share local lore.[26] Nonetheless, interactions between male folklorists and female subjects are difficult. For instance, Shmuel Zaynvil and Oyzer Pipe get a woman to sing for them, but her husband is angry when he comes home to find them with her.[27]

Some Polish Jewish ethnographic memoirs describe subjects—including female ones—who use the ethnographer and his pen for their own purposes. The prolific collector Shmuel Lehman wrote about a twelve-year-old girl who sang for candy and a prostitute who sang, asked for money, then asked Lehman to marry her. (He refused, and entitled the episode, "She wanted to catch a sucker [a *frayer*]."[28]) In a similar mode, A. Almi wrote in 1921 about a visit to a brothel to collect prostitutes' songs. After negotiating with the madam and a skeptical guard and paying for the prostitutes' time, he was allowed in. One young woman quietly began to sing an improvised "song" revealing that she had been forced into prostitution. Another prostitute heard her plea for help and told the guard, who pulled Almi away, took his pens and paper, and locked him in a storeroom. The next morning the guard released Almi, who saw that the whole brothel had been evacuated overnight. Although Almi is not unsympathetic to the trafficked woman, his account stresses his own trauma. "Those were difficult, painful hours. This is how a person who has been sentenced to death must feel in the execution room."[29]

Almi's memoir, which we include in English translation in this volume, insists on the link between the folklorist and his subject. When he was imprisoned by the brothel guard, he became like the trafficked girl, who could not leave the brothel. As the girl was bodily assaulted by customers, so the guard assaulted the folklorist. When the guard took the folklorist's papers and pens away, he made him be like the trafficked girl, unable to voice complaints about his treatment. His imprisonment in a dark room— lit only by one small window, and presumably not lit at all as he waited there overnight—created another situation in which darkness united a folklorist and his subject.

Almi's account of his ill-fated visit to the brothel circulated widely in print and orally. Its popularity may have resulted from the way it engaged prevalent anxieties about listening. The guard who separated Almi from the trafficked girl could represent an internal censor that protected the folklorist from kol isha, what one strain of rabbinic thought imagined as the dangerous effect of a woman's voice, the sound that lured the listener to the body from which it originated. At the same time, the memoir reproduces a canonical vision of the ethnographer and his subject. As Arjun Appadurai notes, anthropologists tend to envision their proper subjects as "natives" who "are assumed to represent their selves and their history, without distortion or residue." This unmediated representation is linked to the natives' fixed location: "natives are not only persons who are from certain places, and belong to those places, but they are also those who are somehow *incarcerated,* or confined, in those places."[30] The trafficked woman, literally imprisoned in the brothel, takes on the legitimacy as an ethnographic subject that Almi and his readers may have craved. And if Almi's model for ethnographic legitimacy was the Russian writers of the 1850s who collected from peasants whose mobility was highly limited (by serfdom in Turgenev's case; by the Siberian prison in Dostoevsky's) and who themselves were in exile like Rybnikov or actually imprisoned like Dostoevsky, then Almi's own incarceration in the brothel drew him closer to them.

Did male Polish Jewish folklorists such as Almi and Lehman, in spite of their avowed secularism, fear kol isha, and could this fear account for the ambivalence in their memoirs about their encounters with female subjects? This conclusion is suggested in the stories of Avrom Karpinowitz, who wrote about the interwar Vilna of his youth throughout a long career that continued into the 1990s. "Der Folklorist" (The Folklorist, 1967) and its continuation "Khane-Merke fun di fish" (Khane-Merke the Fishwife, published much later, in 1993), describe Rubinshteyn, a lame folklorist who learns from the authorities at YIVO that the best curses could be heard from fishwives. He goes to the fish market and encounters the sharp-tongued widow Khane-Merke. After she initially chases him off, the two of them each start to feel drawn to each other, and he returns to the market:

Khane-Merke spun around in his head and kept him from thinking about anything else. She welcomed him. "Oh, the gentleman from the curses is here. I'll chop up the little door for firewood and fry you some flea giblets. Such a guest." Rubinshteyn felt warm in all his limbs. He could smell folklore. Unobtrusively he unbuttoned his raincoat, took out his notebook, and quickly started writing.[31]

The description brings out the sensual overtones of ethnographic listening and shows that the sound of a woman's voice could threaten a man's powers of concentration.

At the end of that story, Khane-Merke gets angry at Rubinsteyn for leading her on, and he leaves for another city. In the later story, Khane-Merke visits the YIVO office, learns how to collect folklore, and wins Max Weinreich's approval for her collection. At the end, Rubinshteyn returns and the two of them end up back in her room eating gefilte fish. Karpinowitz's stories make explicit what is hinted at in the memoirs of Lehman and Almi: that male folklorists' anxiety around their lower-class female informants could have been a fear of transgressing the boundaries between genders, of the distraction produced by a woman's embodied voice, and perhaps of the very commitment to the Jewish lower classes that their folkloric work was imagined to affirm.

CONCLUSION

The interwar Yiddish folklorists' depictions of informants as threatening could reflect what Itzik Gottesman, in his invaluable study of the Polish Jewish folklorists, describes as one case of a broader phenomenon:

The collection of folklore represented a power struggle. The narratives reveal that the folk, ironically, was a hindrance to the folklorists' nationalist agenda. This dynamic between the scholar or collector and the "other" exists . . . for the entire history of folkloristics and anthropology. In nineteenth-century romantic terms, it was the folk poetry, which the folk created communally, that was aesthetically prized, not the folk itself.[32]

Although Gottesman masterfully brings Polish Jewish folklorists to life, he might be too quick to categorize them as exemplifying a broader phenomenon in the history of folkloristics.[33] Close reading of the depictions of listening in ethnographic memoirs and fiction shows that the Polish Jewish case was unlike earlier Russian peasant folkloristics. Some iconic Russian folkloristic texts from before 1861 depicted peasants as so foreign and vulnerable that no real interaction was possible until the gentry listeners somehow tuned down their own consciousness and made themselves appear absent by falling asleep, which allowed them to access the peasants' words, across the boundaries of class, in a disseminatory mode. The Polish Jewish folklorists, in contrast, described their subjects as actively demanding their attention. With their insistence on being heard and their demand that the folklorists enter into a dialogue with them, the Polish Jewish informants asked for more than the folklorists were willing to give.

Of course, much does connect Russian, Yiddish, and other folklore collectors. They shared the conviction that the way to access the valuable, heretofore ignored creative production of the powerless is by listening; the belief that sound connects you to something "real" but suppressed is widespread and persuasive. Regina Bendix's historicization of the concept of authenticity links it precisely to the experience of listening:

> After years of reading and thinking about what, if anything, could still be authentic, I saw authenticity at best as a quality of experience: the chills running down one's spine during musical performances, for instance, moments that may stir one to tears, laughter, elation—which on reflection crystallize into categories and in the process lose the immediacy that characterizes authenticity.[34]

Similarly widespread is the notion that the kind of listening experience that offers an aperture to the authentic is not available all the time, but requires the sort of separation from ordinary time made possible by a musical performance or by an interval of altered consciousness, such as what we experience on the edge of sleep. As Sigmund Freud suggested in 1899, the visual and auditory perceptions experienced in this state might reveal authentic fears and desires that are ordinarily censored: "As we fall asleep, 'involuntary ideas' emerge, owing to the relaxation of a certain deliberate (and no doubt also critical) activity, which we allow to influence the course of our ideas while we are awake. . . . As the involuntary ideas emerge they change into visual and acoustic images."[35] Following Freud, intellectuals could fantasize that if you closed your eyes and listened, you would be able to attain contact with your true self—that innocent, primeval core that linked you to the folk, whether Russian peasant or shtetl Jew.

Appadurai points out another ethnoliterary constant: the tendency to imagine the informant as fixed in place as in signification, in a sense incarcerated. It is an unusual feature of the history of Russian imperial anthropology that ethnographers, like their subjects, were often limited in their mobility, if not literally incarcerated (like Dostoevsky), then exiled to the peripheries for their political views. The popularity of Almi's piece about his own incarceration might be understood as testimony to his Russian influence and as acknowledgment of his attempt to situate himself among the generations of Russian exile-ethnographers. He wanted to claim their position of the heroic listener, working against the authorities to give printed voice to the disempowered.

The work of historians of communication such as Peters warns us that in evaluating the Yiddish folklorists' claim of a Russian heritage, we should remember that modes of listening vary. The Russian literary conceit of the ethnographer who gains perfect access to the words and the mind of the folk when he appears to be asleep suits a disseminatory mode of listening and the labors of those writers who made what had been purely oral genres accessible in print; this trope fits virtuosic long genres (such as the byliny Rybnikov collected), and it maps neatly onto Freud's depiction of the mind made open to uncensored sounds at the edge of sleep. The Yiddish folklorists' insistence on their Russian genealogy is undermined by their tendency to depict themselves as engaging in a different mode of listening, what Peters calls the dialogic. Their informants are not satisfied just to be recorded. They want to engage the folklorists in conversation, to elicit at least a verbal response. The dominance of the chatty, demanding informant in the memoirs of the Yiddish ethnographers echoes Freud's own work in Jewish folkloristics. In his 1905 *Jokes and their Relation to the Unconscious,* he cites Jewish jokes in the form of mini-dialogues: between marriage-brokers and their clientele, rich men and beggars, the followers of Hasidic rebbes and the skeptical, as in this example:

> The *Schadchen* was defending the girl he had proposed against the young man's protests. "I don't care for the mother-in-law," said the latter. "She's a disagreeable, stupid person."—"But after all you're not marrying the

mother-in-law. What you want is her daughter."—"Yes, but she's not young any longer, and she's not precisely a beauty."—"No matter. If she's neither young nor beautiful she'll be all the more faithful to you."—"And she hasn't much money."—"Who's talking about money? Are you marrying money then? After all it's a wife that you want."—"But she's got a hunchback too."—"Well, what *do* you want? Isn't she to have a single fault?"[36]

Neither interlocutor wants to let the other have the last word: these speakers, like the informants depicted in Yiddish ethnoliterature, insist on engagement.

The dominance of the disseminatory mode of listening in the classical Russian ethnoliterature of the mid-nineteenth century contrasts with the dialogic mode dominant in the Yiddish ethnoliterature of a century later. The difference in listening modes helps us evaluate the Yiddish folklorists' claim to a Russian heritage. Yiddish folklorists were inspired by Russian folklore and performed their own folkloristic endeavors in a Russian spirit. They wanted not so much to believe what the Russians did (indeed, the Russians had varied beliefs) as to listen in the same ways. Their writings, though, suggest that they listened differently, and that their informants spoke differently.

NOTES

I am grateful to Naomi Seidman, Israel Bartal, and Fred Turner, as well as to the participants in our Zurich conference, for their help as I thought through the ideas in this chapter.

1. Hershele is described in Itzik Nakhman Gottesman, *Defining the Yiddish Nation: The Jewish Folklorists of Poland* (Detroit: Wayne State University Press, 2003), 51–56. On p. 52 he cites Tsipore Katsenelson-Nakhumov, *Yitskhok Katsenelson: zayn lebn un shafn* (Buenos Aires: Tsentral farband fun poylishe yidn in Argentina, 1948), 171. Gottesman, 52.

2. On Pushkin as a collector, see Vladimir Yakovlevich Propp, *The Russian Folktale*, ed. and trans. Sibelan Forrester (Detroit: Wayne State University Press, 2012), 47–50.

3. Gottesman, 31, 36; Kalman Weiser, *Jewish People, Yiddish Nation: Noah Prylucki and the Folkists in Poland* (Toronto: University of Toronto Press, 2011), 107.

4. Weiser, 75.

5. John Durham Peters, *Speaking into the Air: A History of the Idea of Communication* (Chicago: University of Chicago Press, 1999), 5.

6. Barbara Kirshenblatt-Gimblett, "The Concept and Varieties of Narrative Performance in East European Jewish Culture," in *Explorations in the Ethnography of Speaking*, ed. Richard Bauman and Joel Sherzer (Cambridge: Cambridge University Press, 1974).

7. Gabriella Safran, "The Sleeping Listener and the Devil in the Machine: Russian Stories of Resistance to Ethnographic Recording and their Hypnogogic Prehistory" (unpublished paper).

8. Nathaniel Knight, "*Narodnost'* and Modernity in Imperial Russia," in *Russian Modernity: Politics, Knowledge, Practices*, ed. David L. Hoffmann and Yanni Kotsonis (New York: St. Martin's Press, 2000), 59; Vera Tolz, *Russia (Inventing the Nation)* (London: Arnold, 2001).

9. See Nikolai Ssorin-Chaikov, "Political Fieldwork, Ethnographic Exile and State Theory: Peasant Socialism and Anthropology in Late-Nineteenth-Century Russia," in *New History of Anthropology*, ed. Henrika Kuklick (Malden, Mass.: Blackwell, 2008), 191–206. See Propp on Ivan Khudiakov (1842–1876) and Ivan Pryzhkov (1827–1885), 56–59.

10. Peters, 35.

11. Saul J. Berman, "Kol 'Isha," in *Rabbi Joseph H. Lookstein Memorial Volume*, ed. Leo Landman (New York: Ktav, 1980); Rabbi David Golinkin, "'Kol b'ishah ervah'—Is It Really Forbidden for Jewish Men to Listen to Women Singing?," *Responsa in a Moment* 6, no. 2 (November 2011): http://www.schechter.edu/responsa.aspx?ID=62.

12. Jeffrey Veidlinger, *Jewish Public Culture in the Late Russian Empire* (Bloomington: Indiana University Press, 2009), esp. chapters 4 and 7.

13. Peters, 89.

14. Dan Miron, "Folklore and Antifolklore in the Yiddish Fiction of the Haskala," in *The Image of the Shtetl and Other Studies of Modern Jewish Literary Imagination* (Syracuse, N.Y.: Syracuse University Press, 2000), 60.

15. Ibid., 73.

16. S. Y. Abramovitsh, *Ale verk fun Mendele Moykher Sforim* (Warsaw: Ferlag "Mendele," 1927), 5:16. "Gilgulim" is translated as "Werewolves" in *The Nag by Mendele Mocher Sforim*, trans. Moshe Spiegel (New York: Beechhurst, 1955), 18.

17. Ibid., 5:47. I suspect Abramovitsh is thinking about the tale "Mariia Morevna."

18. Ibid., 5:62.

19. Ibid., 5:180.

20. Y. L. Peretz, "Bilder fun a provints-rayze," in *Ale verk* (New York: CYCO bicher-farlag, 1947), 2:161. See I. L. Peretz, "Impressions of a Journey," trans. Milton Himmelfarb, in *The I. L. Peretz Reader*, ed. Ruth Wisse (New Haven, Conn.: Yale University Press, 2002).

21. Ibid., 2:197.

22. Ibid., 2:67.

23. Ibid., 2:73, with gratitude to *The I. L. Peretz Reader*, 109.

24. Ibid., 2:75.

25. Gottesman, 172.

26. A. Litvin, *Yudishe neshomes*, vol. 1, Lite (New York: Arbeter Ring, 1916), "Di kdoishim fun Rozhinoi," 1–2.

27. Shmuel Zaynvil and Oyzer Pipe, "Yidishe folkslider fun galitsye," *YIVO-bleter* 11, nos. 1–2 (January–February 1937): 54–55.

28. *Shmuel Lehman: zamlbukh* (Warsaw: Self-published, 1937), 24–26.

29. A. Almi, *Momentn fun a lebn: Zikhroynes, bilder un epizodn* (Buenos Aires: Tsentralferlag fun poylishe yidn in argentine, 1948), 125.

30. Arjun Appadurai, "Putting Hierarchy in Its Place," *Cultural Anthropology* 3, no. 1 (1988): 37. Cf. James Clifford, *Routes: Travel and Translation in the Late Twentieth Century* (Cambridge: Harvard University Press, 1997).

31. A. Karpinowitz, "Der folklorist," *Baym Vilner durkhhoyf* (Tel Aviv: I. L. Peretz Publishing House, 1976), 72–73; Karpinowitz, "Khane-Merke fun di Fish," *Vilne mayn Vilne* (Tel Aviv: I. L. Peretz Publishing House, 1993). Translation cited with permission from Abraham Karpinowitz, *Vilna My Vilna*, trans. Helen Mintz (Syracuse University Press, forthcoming).

32. Gottesman, 173.

33. Charles L. Briggs cautions against too quickly accepting anthropology's own genealogies in "What We Should Have Learned from Américo Paredes: The Politics of Communicability and the Making of Folkloristics," *Journal of American Folklore* 125, no. 495 (Winter 2012), esp. 105.

34. Regina Bendix, *In Search of Authenticity: The Formation of Folklore Studies* (Madison: University of Wisconsin Press, 1997), 14.

35. Sigmund Freud, *The Interpretation of Dreams* (first edition 1899), trans. James Strachey (New York: Basic Books, 1910), 127.

36. Sigmund Freud, *Jokes and their Relation to the Unconscious* (first edition 1905), trans. James Strachey (New York: W.W. Norton & Company, 1960), 71.

Ethnoliterary Modernity

Jewish Ethnography and Literature in the Russian Empire and Poland (1890–1930)

ANNETTE WERBERGER

JEWISH ETHNOGRAPHY WITHIN ETHNOLITERARY MODERNITY

In ethnoliterary texts, modernity is expressed in relation to culture or "ethnos." Authors seek this kind of modernity by exploring folklore and ethnology, which provide access to a certain "vanishing" premodern culture and deal with all forms of otherness: the near, the distant, and the alien. The catalyst of ethnoliterary texts is often the expressed notion of a crisis or rupture within "tradition" and the need to salvage the threatened lore of one's own or a foreign "folk," who still live outside modernity as a "survival" of ancient times.

I consider ethnoliterary texts, scenes, and motifs from Eastern Europe that show the special interest of Jewish authors in the "near" and not the "elsewhere" (Marc Augé). There had been great transformations and challenges within the Russian empire and Poland by 1900. The "modern" person (or *undzer modern* as Y. L. Peretz writes in Yiddish) need not look far to find tradition in the supposedly premodern ways of living and thinking, exotic clothing, or practices of superstition and magic outside of Warsaw, Kiev, or Vilna.[1] The interest in folklore affected a people who thought of themselves as modern; they searched in the Pale of Settlement and the Warsaw underground for primordial Jewish expression, hoping to rescue themselves and to salvage their own modernity, although they preferred to see themselves as the saviors of the folk and tradition. Peretz wrote in 1911:

Jewish life must bloom anew, the Bible must be brought to the folk as seed, and Jewish folk symbols and legends, newly refreshed, will be the dew and the rain! The field will revive, the folk will revive and awaken to suffer for truth and with unwavering faith in its victory![2]

Important representatives of this "revival" of Jewish folklore used oral legends and vernacular motifs as their raw material. Alexander Mukdoni remembers the valuable "wares," in the form of ethnographic transcripts of oral folklore, that S. An-sky brought in his field notebooks to Peretz's Warsaw salon.[3] In his memoir on Peretz, An-sky describes the circulation of folkloristic knowledge between the ethnographic field and the urban cultural centers, meaning the salons and intellectual circles in Warsaw, Vilna, or Moscow:

> Our friendship strengthened two or three years ago during the organiza-
> tion of the ethnographic expedition and after I started to visit towns and
> shtetls to collect folktales, legends, songs, melodies [*folks-mayses, legendes,
> lider, nigunim*], etc.
>
> Peretz and [Yankev] Dinezon were delighted by the undertaking. Every
> time I was in Warsaw, Peretz would "sit me down" to tell him Hasidic tales.
> Often I would sit for hours and tell him one story after another. He lis-
> tened and couldn't get enough of them. Meanwhile I had the opportunity
> to gain insight into the artistic workings of Peretz's mind [*sheferishe arbeyt
> fun Perets's gayst*]. As I was telling the story, Peretz would hear it, assimilate
> it, throw out the inartistic strands, add new ones, join it with details from
> another story [*hot Perets zi shoyn oyfgenumen, asimilirt, aroysgevorfn fun ir
> di nisht kinstlerishe shtrikhen, tsugegeben naye, tsuzamengebunden mit protim
> fun an'ander mayse*]. And I had scarcely finished when Peretz was already
> telling me the same story, revised into one of his *Folktales* [*Folkstimlikhe
> geshikhtn*], which was as far from the original version as a polished dia-
> mond is from a raw stone that has just been unearthed. The next day one
> such story had been written down, and in a few days it was printed with
> the dedication: "To An-sky, the collector."[4]

The rough diamond that is the oral folktale is polished and transformed into a written story presumably in Peretz's collections of *Khsidish* (Hasidic Tales) or *Folkstimlekhe geshikhtn* (Tales in a Folk Vein). The preservation of authenticity in the folkloristic material is obviously not a problem for An-sky. Folklore is, in the Herderian vision, part of the "natural" expres-sion of the folk and hence a natural resource for the cultural activity of the elite.[5] Peretz's stories have been, and still are, a success. Even today they are often read outside (and sometimes even inside) the academic world as authentic expressions of Eastern European lore and *Yiddishkeyt*.

In the above self-portrayal, An-sky (the "storytaker") acts as an agent who brings the collected folkloristic narratives from the informant in the field (mostly from the Russian Pale of Settlement) to the literary groups in Warsaw. In his memoir, An-sky informs us about the circulation of ethnographic knowledge among intellectuals in Warsaw while simultaneously telling us about the invention of Yiddish folklore within the system of European written culture.[6]

My main focus in the following analysis is on the relation between folklore and literature, or the transmission between the field and the salon through the analysis of the "collector's narrative[s]" and ethnoliterary writing devices like the mimicry of orality.[7] I see the quotation from An-sky as a typical example of the relationship at the beginning of the twentieth century between the ethnographic field and the literary scene. It was a relationship between oral and written (or literary) culture, between the traditional and the modern, as I will elaborate in the following pages. In the first part of this chapter I stress that the Jewish ethnographic enterprise is connected to the European attempt to produce tradition and traditionality. The attempt was part of the project of modernity, which is intimately linked to such factors as nationhood, progress, and science. My focus in the second part lies in the interactions of Yiddish ethnographers and writers. I examine how they generated ethnoliterary texts, with special attention to the "oral-literate conjunction" as a medial interface between orality and the literary, and the field and the salon.[8] I concentrate on Peretz (1852–1915), who participated in nearly every part of the "ethnoliterary project": he collected, by 1890, stories on a statistics expedition; he ran the most influential literary salon on Ceglana Street in Warsaw, which served as transfer site or trading zone for ethnographers and literati; and he published stories allegedly based on *mayses* (oral Yiddish tales).

An-sky and Peretz used folklore to build a Jewish culture beyond doxa or religion,[9] a project undertaken not only, but especially, in the Central and Eastern European empires. Ethnographic fieldwork and folklore collection were modes of creating a new cultural resource to provide symbols, images, narrations, myths, and a timeline for this undertaking.

What motivated this enterprise? The transnational European empires (the Habsburg Monarchy and the Russian Empire), with their often "premodern" structures, changed rapidly in the second half of the nineteenth century. In recent years, scholars[10] have challenged the opinion that imperial rule (in opposition to nation-state governance) was incompatible with modernity. In fact, the relation between nation-states, empires, and modernity is complex: both systems of governance "learned" from each other. Nation-states like England and France imperialized and the Habsburg, Russian, and Ottoman Empires nationalized in the nineteenth and twentieth centuries.[11] Both developments generated difficulties for certain ethnic or religious groups that had to adjust to a new situation. The transnational empires adopted several techniques from the nation-states, for example the gathering of statistics (as Peretz did), as well as holding a census. As collectives, groups like the Eastern European Jews had more freedoms in the premodern corporate society of the empires; they lost, under the new mononational terms, important institutions like the *kehilot* (Jewish community councils or executive boards that were chosen to run the autonomous Jewish communities), which had guaranteed a certain level of autonomy.[12]

Within the new framework of concepts like folk, nation, and *narod* (the term in several Slavic languages for people or folk), ethnic-religious groups including Ukrainians, Jews, and Belarusians had to start their own national projects. The folklore project was an important one, intended to secure cultural independence and visibility. It is not surprising that we find similarities among the folklore projects of the different ethnic groups within the transnational empires. Ukrainian folklore studies share interests with those of Yiddish at the beginning of the twentieth century: both ethnic groups confronted the lack of statehood or a single national literary tradition.

Why should we still be interested in the Eastern European folklore project today? It is because our understanding of modernity, for instance of modern literature, culture, or music, is still affected by the notion of traditionality. In his book *We Have Never Been Modern* (*Nous n'avons jamais été modernes. Essai d'anthropologie symétrique*, 1991), the French sociologist of science, Bruno Latour, is severely critical of the institution of modernity,[13] and ethnologists and anthropologists such as Charles Briggs,

Richard Bauman, and Pertti J. Anttonen refer to him in their critical analyses of the creation of tradition. As the Finnish scholar Anttonen writes in *Tradition through Modernity: Postmodernism and the Nation-State in Folklore Scholarship:* "I would contend that folklore is a rhetorical construction that has possibly outlived its modernist agenda, but still, I see its value in identifying a discursive field that makes the production of tradition and traditionality its main target of scientific analysis."[14]

An-sky and Peretz are probably the best representatives of this endeavor of tradition-making within Yiddish modern culture. Both participated in producing folklore on at least two levels: through scientific expeditions and artistic and literary experiments. Regina Lilientalowa (sometimes also written Lilienthal), A. Almi, Moyshe-Yoysef Dikshteyn (Vanvild), Pinkhes Graubard, and others remain more notable for their scholarly contribution to folklore studies. Literary and ethnographic activities have contributed decisively to the shaping of Jewish culture as a European modern culture.

In this chapter, I refer to the literature arising from this engagement between ethnography and the literary production of tradition and modernity as *ethnoliterary modernity*. Texts of ethnoliterary modernity were generated mostly during the height of globalization before World War II, that is from 1870 to 1945.[15] Famous examples include Freud's *Totem und Tabu. Einige Übereinstimmungen im Seelenleben der Wilden und der Neurotiker* (Totem and Taboo: Resemblances Between the Mental Lives of Savages and Neurotics, 1913), Paul Radin's *Primitive Man as Philosopher* (1927), An-sky's *Dybbuk* (Dibek, 1915ff),[16] Aby Warburg's *Das Schlangenritual. Ein Reisebericht* (The Ritual of the Snake, 1923), Michel Leiris's *L'Afrique fantôme* (Phantom Africa, 1934), Stanisław Vincenz's *Na wysokiej połoninie, First Volume: Prawda starowieku* (On the High Uplands. Sagas, Songs, Tales and Legends of the Carpathians, 1936), Carlo Levi's *Cristo si è fermato a Eboli* (Christ Stopped at Eboli, 1948), Lévi-Strauss's *Tristes tropiques* (1955), and as a late example Elias Canetti's *Masse und Macht* (Crowds and Power, 1960), which refers to Wilhelm H. Bleek's and Lucy C. Lloyd's *Specimens of Bushman Folklore* (1911). These texts help us gain a critical understanding of our idea of modernity, modern literature, or modern consciousness; their analysis shows that Arrièregarde and Avantgarde are closely united and demonstrate the working of modern modes of existence. These texts are affected not only by the notion of Modernity, but also by the notion of the Primitive, which Johannes Fabian calls "a category, not an object, of Western thought."[17]

I propose some characteristics of the ethnoliterary text. Ethnoliterary texts are mostly a result of *cultural contact or cultural encounter,* especially between a modern scholar, writer, or observer of a culture that is partly or completely regarded as premodern. Through this approach, the culture–nature divide is inscribed in the text and produces other binary codes like archaic/progressive, magical/scientific, enlightened/superstitious, and traditional/modern. The differentiation is important. Many Yiddish folklorists were born into the "folk." However, as ethnographers or *zamlers* they regarded themselves as partly detached from this kind of living. This allowed them to have a view from afar at their former *lebenswelt* and to depict it as a "survival" (Edward Burnett Tylor) of the past in the modern world, which relates to what Ernst Bloch calls the simultaneity of the nonsimultaneous and Johannes Fabian refers to as allochronism—the notion that all people do not inhabit the same kind of time.

Ethnoliterary texts express a *heterogeneity* within modern culture; the most obvious instance of this is the constant reference to, or imitation of, *orality* and performance in such texts.[18] Orality becomes an indicator of tradition, as we will see in the second part of this chapter. In his introduction to the important anthology of Yiddish folklore *Bay unz Yuden. Zamelbukh far folklor un filologye* (Among us Jews. Collection of Folklore and Philology), Vanvild alludes to *shebiksav* and *shebalpe,* or the written and the oral/verbal (terms usually used to refer to the Torah and the oral rabbinic teachings), and remarks that oral discourse should be part of the "literary canon."[19] The divide between the oral and written is linked to the vision of their reunion—a typical modern dynamic. An-sky also refers to the oral Torah, and Mark Kiel recalls Shmuel Niger, who "observed that for Peretz and for writers such as An-sky and Bialik, the oral lore began to assume the dimensions of a new oral law (Torah shebe-'al-peh) which in turn, in writings such as *Khsidish* and the *Folkstimlikhe geshikhten,* became a new "scripture" (Torah shebi-khtav)."[20]

Because they refer to a "field" or are partly the result of "fieldwork," ethnoliterary texts are very often *localized or geographically placed* through deixis, description, or linguistic markers (e.g., dialects). They tend to describe a group or *society often as a whole or an entity*. This seems possible only within the frame of the primitive or the premodern. Consider Latour's notion of the "seamlessness" of premodern culture. According to Latour, "moderns" live in an institutionally and socially differentiated society that cannot easily be described through anthropology: "Yes but we are not savages; no anthropologist studies us that way, and it is impossible to do with our own culture—or should I say nature-culture?—what can be done elsewhere, with others. Why? Because we are modern. Our fabric is no longer seamless [*notre tissu n'est plus sans couture*]. Analytic continuity has become impossible. For traditional anthropologists, there is not—there cannot be, there should not be—an anthropology of the modern world."[21]

Ethnoliterary texts are soaked with the *material culture* of a more or less foreign culture; they combine data with fiction, fact with fantasy, ethnographic observation with literary devices. With regard to *genre,* they often show a certain amount of *flexibility*. Classical boundaries of genres are crossed. For example, Levi-Strauss's *Tristes tropiques* is often considered a novel and not an ethnographic monograph.

Most literary texts of the ethnographic genre are the result of *primitivism*. The writers are fascinated by passive states (pathos) such as trance, ecstasy, magic, or spirit possession.[22] One can find descriptions of these states of consciousness frequently in ethnoliterary texts such as Leiris's description of the zar cult (a kind of spirit possession), which he found in Gondar, or in An-sky's figure of the dybbuk. Sorcery and superstition are also frequently found in texts of ethnoliterary modernity; for example, Regina Lilientalowa refers to the evil eye, superstition, and amulets in *Dziecko żydowskie* (The Jewish Child, 1904).

Some features are shared by ethnoliterary texts and modern literature in general; others are not. For example, extensive descriptions and the copious use of ethnographic detail in ethnoliterary texts are often seen as antimodern devices.

There is an important difference between ethnoliterary texts in empires and in nation-states. In empires, ethnoliterary texts use folklore as a tool for creating nationalized narratives. By contrast, ethnoliterary texts in nation-states are, in the Age of Imperialism, often the result of an anthropological encounter with the ethnology of colonized countries. Folklorists are sometimes part of the ethnographic field; ethnologists are almost never "native anthropologists."

Ethnoliterary texts result in cultural contact and reproduce hierarchies that evolved from the process of modernization. In the Pale of Settlement or in the Carpathian Mountains, the folklorist from the urban center encounters a supposed representative of an ancient or archaic way of life and thought, the Hasid or the Hutsul. Latour describes this process as a work of purification and separation that attempts to divide the natural and the cultural spheres. In our field of research, it is more accurately described as the divide between "natural" traditional cultures and modernized culture, between past and future, and between the archaic and the progressive.[23] In any case, we always find in ethnoliterary texts the description of an encounter between *asymmetric cultures* (cultures that are not regarded as equals). One culture is mostly regarded as primitive, marginal, or subaltern. This archaic illusion and the trace of the real field encounter remain part of the allure of these texts.

COLLECTORS' NARRATIVES AND THE SELF-REFLECTION OF ETHNOLITERARY WRITING

The influences and contacts between folklorists and writers, between zamlers and poets, are not easy to grasp. It is only through a close reading of the transmission of folkloric knowledge that we are able to understand how this worked in early twentieth-century ethnoliterature in Poland. We have to rely on letters or memoirs, such as A. Almi's (Eliyahu Hayim Sheps) *Momentn fun a lebn: zikhroynes, bilder un epizodn* (Moments from a Life. Memories, Pictures and Episodes),[24] Hersh Nomberg's *A literarisher dor: vegn Y. L. Perets* (Isaac Leibush Peretz as We Knew Him, 1946), or A. Mukdoni's *I.L. Perets derzeylt a folkstimlekhe geshikhte* (How I. L. Peretz Wrote His Folk Tales, 1949).[25] In addition, Sholem Asch was convinced that "the foundation of neo-Yiddish literature was laid" at 1 Ceglana Street through the gathering and production of folk literature, especially folksongs.[26] The ethnographer did not always coincide with the writer, as in the case of An-sky. A. Almi was a zamler and a poet; his collections of *lider*, such as *Far di likht* (Before the Light, 1927) especially reflect his experience with gathering folksongs, but he is remembered as an ethnographer who

not only showed an interest in Jewish folklore, but later in the folklore of
the First Nations in Canada, where he saw parallels between the oppression of the Indians and of the Jews.[27]

Gottesman enumerates four Yiddish literary salons that existed in Warsaw between 1905 and 1915. "Y. L. Peretz's home was the most prestigious
gathering place; it was not easy to gain entrance."[28] There were also the
salon of Hillel Zeitlin, the salon of Yehoshua Perle, and the salon of Noah
Pryłucki, where from 1909 to 1912 an informal folklore circle gathered with
folklorists and poets who later became famous, like Pinkhes Graubard, A.
Almi, and Shmuel Lehman.[29]

The relation between the folk and the folklorist is mentioned in autobiographical essays or in the paratext of ethnographic books by zamlers
and ethnographers. Very often, a misunderstanding between the informant and zamler is expressed. Gottesman provides us with several famous
examples, which I interpret more closely in order to frame the dynamics
in the ethnographic field.[30]

In his *Zamelbukh* of 1912, Pryłucki gives an example of the difficulties
of recording singing without a phonograph. Pryłucki was more interested
in the linguistic data of the song than in the performance or the melody.
He tried to slow down the singer, but without the usual rhythm, the singer
couldn't remember the words.[31] Such difficulties with recording led this
folklorist to criticize the folk's lack of helpfulness and readiness in his
important task, which reveals the ambivalent relationship between zamler
and informant. Although the "natural" and artless musicality of the folk
performers is usually viewed as admirable, sometimes exhaustion could
make the ethnographer unfair and hostile. Avrom-Moyshe Bernshteyn,
for example, mentions the lack of rhythm or musical knowledge among
folk musicians, factors that complicated recording.[32]

Some informants were found through family connections, but often
the informant was far removed from the social circle of the ethnographer.
Almi, famously, was held captive in a brothel while gathering songs and
narratives in the underworld of Warsaw (Appendix C) (see the section on
*Thieves and Thievery. Folk expressions, Proverbs, Questions, Rhymes, Anec-
dotes, and Tales* in *Bay unz yuden* [1923]). In this urban field his collecting
activities were mostly regarded as intrusive, and the people reacted (as in
the Peretz case below) with hostility.[33] There is a similar narrative from

Shmuel Lehman about an interview with a prostitute. The incident is mentioned in an autobiographic text in the *Shmuel Lehman Zamlbukh*.[34] The prostitute sings several songs for him, among them one song about being exploited by her pimp. Lehman reflects in the subsequent passages on the uncanny parallel between his exploitation of the prostitute as a provider of folksongs and the exploitation of the woman by her pimp. The asymmetry in this encounter is social and gendered.

Folklore in the Yiddish context is often regarded in a romantic way as a people's ancient lore, the ideal basis for nation building and tradition making. But in another episode from Lehman's autobiographical writing, folklore appears very prominently as a living progressive force that sometimes burdens the ethnographer. Furthermore, the text shows that folklore "evolves in peculiar cycles of innovation and conservatism" and is therefore not always the archaic Other of modern literature.[35] Lehman mentions an episode in which the creator of folklore reacts to the intrusion of the ethnographer and zamler. The zamler even becomes part of the folklore: while a young girl is singing a song, Lehman transcribes her words at a table in her home. He pays in chocolate and meals. People come in the room to catch a glimpse of the unusual scene and "while she sang, the bystanders nudged and poked him. The informant joined in, banged on his hat, and began to sing a popular song:

> Where is the guy in the brimmed hat and his free meals?
> His hat gets banged up, and he's sent home for the Sabbath.
> Here is the guy in the brimmed hat with his jokes.
> When his hat gets banged up, he begins to sweat."[36]

In collecting, Lehman leaves traces in the folklore of the underworld. The divide between the folklorist and the folk is suspended, indirectly revealing the dynamics and vitality of folklore, which was not exclusively "old," but also a contemporary and agile instrument for individuals to utilize to interpret their living conditions or interact with their environment. Despite these examples of contemporary and progressive folkloric expression, it remains to be emphasized that in ethnoliterary texts folkloric elements mostly served to bring color to a so-called modern way of life.

When considering the relation between Yiddish folklore and literature, why has Peretz received so much attention among scholars over the last

ten years? Like Stéphane Mallarmé's famous *mardis* in the Rue de Rome
in Paris, Peretz hosted the most prominent salon in Warsaw, probably as
early as 1880.[37] A mixed group of writers and ethnographers came to his
circle on Ceglana Street in Warsaw and submitted themselves to his criticism. Mukdoni uses economic vocabulary to describe Peretz's salon as a
trading zone for folklore: Peretz craves the "wares" that An-sky brought
in his "little notebook" from the Pale of Settlement—the simple forms of
literature, as André Jolles called folkloristic genres such as song, myths,
legend, fairytale, and riddle. He also interrogates An-sky tenaciously on
the derivation and style of the "wares," a fascination that Mukdoni had
the privilege of observing:

> I was rather surprised at this display of unusual interest in a story that
> struck me as neither peculiarly new or original; on the face of it, of a piece
> with the thousand and one folk stories that could be heard in Peretz's
> home. For it was a veritable clearing-house for folklore material of every
> kind.[38]

Peretz's attraction to young, ambitious Yiddish writers and ethnographers
and his need for "an audience in the flesh" complemented each other.[39]
Furthermore, An-sky was not the only one bringing material from the
field; Regina Lilientalowa, who wrote in Polish, was also a frequent visitor
to Peretz's apartment.[40] However, Peretz's link to ethnography predates
this. By 1890, he had already done ethnographic fieldwork *avant la lettre*
as a statistician.

PERETZ IN THE FIELD

Ethnoliterary texts are produced by writers who did fieldwork, or read
folklore and ethnographic literature collected by others. Peretz wrote
what could be called the first ethnoliterary text in Yiddish literature: *Bilder
fun a provints-rayze in tomashover poviat um 1890 yor* (Travel Pictures from
a Journey through the Tomaszów Region in the year 1890). *Travel Pictures*
originated from a statistics expedition, in which Peretz participated, to
discern the economic situation of the Jewish population in the Kingdom
of Poland.[41] The text was written before the formation of the various institutions dedicated to Yiddish folklore studies in this region (such as the

"Jewish Historical-Ethnographic Society" in St. Petersburg in 1908 and the "Jewish Historical-Ethnographic Society in Vilna" in 1919), but is it still important for our context because the ethnographer and writer coincide. The writer Peretz reflects on his own experience as a travelling *farshreyber*. I would like to draw attention to these elements of "writing culture" and "poetic self-reflection" in the following passages.

The *Travel Pictures* of smaller and larger towns in the region of To-maszów consist of twenty-two short prose pieces, published in 1891 in *Di yidishe biblyotek* (Yiddish Library). They are regarded as semifictional texts because the experience of the expedition is mixed with memories of Peretz's childhood. The findings of the expedition, including the question-naires, have been lost and we are only able to reconstruct them through some memoirs of the participants. The references to the expedition, how-ever, give *Travel Pictures* the effect of realism through narrative devices such as paratext, polyphony, and place-names. But the realism ends at the same point at which the statistical work ended; the non-Jewish popula-tion is almost never mentioned (except for the Polish coachman Maciej): "Typical of Yiddish literature of this period, the text omits Gentiles to focus exclusively on Jewish society: the narrator takes professional mea-sure of the townspeople, who return his scrutiny with varying degrees of suspicion, curiosity, hostility, and fear."[42]

What problems does Peretz encounter due to his position as an out-sider? Because of the fear of the authorities and his position, the townspeo-ple are very cautious or even hostile. Peretz encounters similar problems as a *farshreyber* or statistician in the field as an ethnographer. His questions about people's income, marital status, and children, for example, often cause him to be taken for a military recruiter or tax agent. In the first chap-ter, "Betokhn" (Faith and Trust), he refers to the suspicion of him among the folks from Tishevits. The narrator alludes to the common reaction to his "modern" clothing and his lack of a beard, or more precisely, his Polish moustache. Later on, a child calls him "a gentile who speaks Yiddish" (*a goy, vos redt yidish*).[43]

When we read the text today, the asymmetry of the encounter is obvi-ous. In Peretz's *Travel Pictures*, the narrator-statistician with his new tech-nique (statistics) encounters the traditional interviewee from the shtetl. The travel notes are some of the first texts in Yiddish literature where the "traditionality" of the inhabitants of a shtetl is created through the description of a particular life in the cultural periphery. Their life is described in contrast to life in the urban centers where the narrator lives. Mendele (S. Y. Abramovitsh) and his narrators still want to change the customs and traditions of the "folk." Peretz's intention, however, is to "study" every peculiar cultural phenomenon of the folk, to show their singularities and translate the "native" point of view for the moderns. Peretz's most important device is not plot, but form. Whereas Mendele still feels like part of the world he depicts, Peretz creates a more temporal and spatial distance and acts like an observer.

In *Travel Pictures*, we already find the whole range of Hasidic topics that in the following years dominate Yiddish and Slavic Jewish literature in the works of Der Nister, Moyshe Kulbak, and others. The fictional Peretz mentions a *lamed-vovnik* (one of the 36 righteous people on whom the world is believed to depend), a dybbuk (the soul of a dead person that cannot find rest), the sitr'a aḥr'a (the devil or the force of evil), the magic of names, and several rites of superstition. The colorfulness of Hasidic folklore is present and framed in a realistic setting.

The enlightenment plot has vanished in Peretz's text. The protagonist is no longer depicted in his struggle for *Bildung*. In *Travel Pictures*, the barrier between the enlightened *deytsh* (*di deytshn fun die groyse shtet*, or modern-appearing Jews from big cities)[44] and the inhabitants of the shtetl seems insurmountable. Peretz clearly attempts "salvage ethnography" with his ethnoliterary text; he thus registers the distinctive disappearing features of Jewish shtetl life. As James Clifford writes: "The theme of the vanishing primitive, of the end of traditional society (the very act of naming it traditional implies a rupture), is pervasive in ethnographic writing. . . . The persistent and repetitious 'disappearance' of social forms at the moment of their ethnographic representation demands analysis as a narrative structure."[45] Peretz is no longer a proponent of the Haskalah; he has already become a craftsman of tradition, a storytaker and storymaker who publishes for a readership in Warsaw, Vilna, Kraków, or Kiev.

In the chapter "In shoykhets hoyz" (At the Slaughterer's), the narrator reflects on the environment and knowledge of the local slaughterer's son and son-in-law, who know everything about ritual slaughter and kashrut:

No, only our two young men, the slaughterer's son and son-in-law, are to be envied. There is no contact between the world of "a blemish in the sacred offerings" and our world with its swine, nothing in common between the world of Them and of Us, no bridge, no overlap [*tsvishn zeyer velt un undzer velt iz gor keyn shaykhes, keyn brik, keyn tsuzamenhang nishto*].[46]

The narrator calls his world and the world of his readers (*undzer velt*) *treyf;* he believes in the sad rupture between the sphere of the young man and himself. The gaze of the narrator freezes the world of tradition into a static image. Peretz intentionally refers to a "camera obscura" in *Travel Pictures*.

In spite of this allegoric view of the ethnographic Other, Peretz's text still has its subversive merits. He does not control the voice and message of the others, and he crafts a wonderful, ironic self-critique. In one picture, he reverses the interview situation and becomes the interviewee in a severe interrogation by the local *maskil*. One could regard this passage as a subaltern counter-questioning. He asks Peretz to refrain from his *bobe-mayses* (fairytales) and to admit that he intends to act in bad faith. The maskil even interrupts the narrator's declaration:

"The object, I tell him, is to show that Jews are poor, and thereby...."
"Thereby nothing, ..."[47]

The narrator is "modern" and *deytsh* and gives other moderns insight into the so-called traditional world, which the statistical team seeks to defend from the antisemitism of the late tsarist regime (the kingdom of Poland is part of the Russian Empire). In contrast to countless German-speaking authors, Peretz does not romanticize the shtetl. In a certain sense he, who was born in Zamość, lets the subaltern speak.[48] In some small passages, the townspeople reflect on the modern world, and there are countless intradiegetic narrators and protagonists from all social levels and different professions. Still more important is the narrator's ironic self-reflection, his confession that he is affected by the traditional world and needs rescuing.[49]

In "Dos vaserl" (The Pond), one of the most important chapters of the Journey, a dialogue unfurls between the narrator and Moyshe. Crossing the pond, Moyshe tells the fictional Peretz about the mythical creation narrative (*Gründungserzählung*) of the pond and his Atlantis-like shtetl beyond the surface. At first, Moyshe is reluctant to tell the story and Peretz has to pressure him. At the end, Moyshe ventures a guess as to why the narrator is so keen to hear stories. He conjectures that the narrator attains *Yiddishkayt* through storytelling, and in some way Moyshe criticizes the exploitation of oral storytelling by urban writers. Moyshe's critique discloses the fact that the folklore project does not rescue traditional life or the folk, but the ideology-seeking elites.

> "What do you suggest? What shall I tell you?"
> "Tell me a little about the pond. You do have a story to tell about the pond?"
> "Suppose I have. You want to hear it so you'll have something to laugh about?"
> "God forbid!"
> "Then again," he says, changing his mind, "maybe not. Such crazy times! Zionism...."
> "What has Zionism to do with anything?"
> "How should I know? All of a sudden everything is topsy-turvy. Young men in the yeshiva become Zionists, and then they throw away the Talmud and do all kinds of wicked things. Contrariwise, when German Jews become Zionists they recover their Judaism. Shaven beards, and Judaism! You mustn't think I'm referring to you." He smiles apologetically.
> "What has that to do with the pond?"
> "What has it to do.... Please don't take this amiss. Let's assume a German Jew becomes religious again and it's the anniversary of his mother's death. He goes to a Jewish restaurant and for the repose of her soul orders kugel. Kugel is his Judaism. Maybe your Judaism is stories. Is this the anniversary of a death for you [*zayn yidishkayt iz kugl . . . ayer yidishkayt iz efsher mayselekh, ir hobt yortsayt*]?"
> He told me the story anyway. Perhaps he wanted to tell it even more than I wanted to hear it.[50]

In this early text, the ethnoliterary turn in literature is described through plot and dialogue. The statistician Peretz eventually becomes the storytaker of a Hasidic wondertale. Marc Caplan describes the narrator as a "mediator between cosmopolitan modernity and traditional Jewishness."[51] In my opinion, one might regard Peretz more as a creator of tradition, who represents tradition as the "Other of Modernity." The dialogic orality in *Travel Pictures* reflects the mode by which stories are collected in the field and becomes a central method to prove authenticity in Yiddish literature.

Orality remains an important source of traditionality and is often discussed. It seems that the accentuation of a dichotomy between the oral culture of the "folk" (and non-European groups) and the written culture of the elites is the outcome of a new understanding of modern society. The growing literacy of the Europeans is combined with an "Othering" of the oral as an archaic field of expression. Even in regard to Jewish culture, with its strong relation to the "Talmudic frame" (*talmudischer Bezugsrahmen*), as Victor Karady defined it, discussions can be found about oral text and orality, dating back to the end of the nineteenth century.[52] Orality is discussed in relation to Hasidism, to Yiddish (in contrast to Hebrew), to *skaz* (direct monologue) as a device, and to polyphony, among others.[53]

As an example, I would like to conclude with a short text from Alexander Mukdoni on "How Y. L. Peretz Wrote His Folk Tales," a piece that stresses the importance of orality for avant-garde Yiddish writers in the salons. This text in some ways responds to my first quotation at the beginning of this paper. Mukdoni describes a scene in which Peretz retells a story from An-sky "orally, without a scrap of paper before him"; An-sky is present, astonished and "spellbound, without missing a syllable and staring into Peretz's eyes in amazement" after the performance.[54] Afterwards, Peretz tells Mukdoni his "theory about the writing of folk stories" (*gants teorye vegn dem vi men darf shreybn folkstimlekhe geshikhtn*).[55] Emphasizing the difference between the spoken and the written word, the oral style of the folk and the written style of professional writers, Peretz tells Mukdoni that he has changed his way of writing stories. He tries to imitate oral literature by creating it without paper and writing:

> I take my time in writing down a folk story that I hear from a collector of folklore or directly from a man of the people. I first fashion it as an oral narrative. I bear in mind, too, that every folk story is told differently by every narrator, depending for one thing on the degree of narrative skill that he possesses. When I hear several versions of a story, I can tell the true and the beautiful from the false and the ugly. Poor dear An-sky, for example, kills the stories that he hears, by trying to give them a literary polish. I get them from him in that vitiated form. All he thinks about is the moral of the story, as if ordinary folk were constantly in search of wisdom and

considered the plot of secondary importance. An-sky's stories give me a
lot of trouble. I first have to peel off their literary rind, and restore them to
their oral version. I try hard to find another variant of the same tale before
deciding on its final shape.[56]

With this glimpse into Peretz's "literary laboratory" and new style of writing, which was for a long time the talk of the literary circles and salons in
Warsaw, we get insight into his creation of ethnoliterary stories.[57] Orality
becomes an important device for stressing the folkish status of the ethnoliterary modern text. Modernists and avant-gardists were both fascinated
by oral communication and art. Hugo Ball's invention of the sound poem
at the Cabaret Voltaire 1916 in Zurich is perhaps the most famous example
of the allure of orality in modern times, because oral culture is nonlinear
and synesthetic, and enables participation and mimics authenticity. Orality is labeled in modernity as an "amodern" (Latour), ancient, traditional,
or foreign way of storytelling, inadequate for the demands of modern
society but a fascinating, living force. In his 1930s essay "Der Erzähler,"
Walter Benjamin sees "survivals" of oral storytelling in the non-European
Russian literary tradition of Nikolai Leskov.[58] The ethnoliterary writer ad-
mires archaic orality and paradoxically underlines his modernity through
this device. It is important, however, to face the fact that when ethnoliterary writers and folklorists regard the underworld of Warsaw or Jewish life
in the Pale of Settlement as an oral culture, this is part of the process of
separation between the modern and the traditional. In his stories, Peretz
refers to different approaches to and modes of oral culture. He mimics
informants by using *skaz* (for example, in "Shtraimel"). He frequently imitates folkloristic genres like the Hasidic fairytale or the legend, and depicts
several typical nonpsychologized protagonists like the (holy) simpleton,
the poor and the rich man ("The Orphan"), a lamed-vovnik or the prophet
Elijah in disguise, two rabbis as ideological opponents ("Reb Noah and
the Rabbi of Brest"), and many others.

In ethnoliterary stories we can always find traces of a collective life of
lower social circles or different cultures, but they are still fundamentally
the expression of modern people and their nostalgia and longings. Nomberg writes about the shared ecstatic feeling in singing songs in Peretz's
salon. He recounts that the Sabbath gatherings were spent "singing folk-

songs in a strangely high-spirited mood, orgies of poetic delight."[59] Folk life was a spiritual event in Peretz's salon, providing the Yiddish avant-garde with the necessary tradition to live a modern life.

NOTES

1. See, for example, Joshua Trachtenberg's book on Jewish magic and superstition from 1939 in which he expresses his opinion: "To understand a people—and through it, humankind—is to see its life whole." Joshua Trachtenberg, *Jewish Magic and Superstition: A Study in Folk Religion* (Philadelphia: University of Philadelphia Press, [1939] 2004), xxvii; Yitskhok Leybush Peretz, *Ale verk. Bd. 9: gedanken un ideyen* (New York: Cyco bikher-farlag, 1947), 164.

2. I. L. Peretz, "Paths That Lead Away from Yidishkayt," in *Jews and Diaspora Nationalism: Writings on Jewish Peoplehood in Europe and the United States*, ed. Simon Rabinovitch (Waltham, Mass.: Brandeis University Press, 2012), 76.

3. "I recall An-sky's entries into Peretz's house, his cordial, grandfatherly smile and his Russian-Jewish warmth. After embracing and kissing each other in Russian fashion, Peretz would ask: 'Are you bringing along any wares this time?' We knew what wares he was talking about. . . . Peretz would sit down beside his friend and with his big smiling eyes fixed on him, he would exhort him: 'Well, out with those wares of yours!' and then An-sky would produce a little notebook, search through it and begin narrating. Peretz was all ears." A. Mukdoni, "How I. L. Peretz Wrote His Folk Tales," in I. L. Peretz, *In This World and the Next: Selected Writings of I. L. Peretz*, trans. Moshe Spiegel (New York: Thomas Yoseloff, 1958), 353f.

4. See Sh. An-sky, "Y. L. Peretz," in *Gezamelte shriftn in fuftsehn bender*, vol. 10 (Vilna: Farlag "An-ski," 1925), 166f. For Yiddish I have used the YIVO transliteration system. Unless otherwise stated, translations are my own. The second part of the English translation follows Ken Frieden, *Classic Yiddish Fiction: Abramovitsh, Sholem Aleichem, and Peretz* (Albany: State University of New York Press, 1995), 249.

5. For Herder's concept of "Naturpoesie," see Richard Bauman and Charles L. Briggs, *Voices of Modernity: Language Ideologies and the Politics of Inequality* (Cambridge: Cambridge University Press, 2003), 163–196.

6. The oral sources are often mentioned, but written sources were also important to Peretz, Bastomski, and others. Cf. Mark W. Kiel, "Vox populi, vox dei: The Centrality of Peretz in Jewish Folkloristics," *Polin* 7 (1992): 99; Itzik Nakhmen Gottesman, *Defining the Yiddish Nation: The Jewish Folklorists of Poland* (Detroit: Wayne State University Press, 2003), 106. There exist other memoirs of how Peretz gathered oral production from the folk. For example, Y. L. Cahan mentions Peretz buying songs for a ruble from some girls singing in his street in Warsaw (cf. Kiel, 7).

7. Gottesman, 63.

8. Maureen M. McLane, *Balladeering, Minstrelsy, and the Making of British Romantic Poetry* (Cambridge: Cambridge University Press, 2008), 9.

9. In a Russian short story called "Kniga" (The Book) from 1910, An-sky's narrator speaks about disciples or representatives of a "new Jewishness," who must find a way to

unite and condense the people "beyond religion." Cf. Sh. Markish, ed., *Rodnoi golos: Stra-nitsy russko-evreiskoi literatury kontsa XIX–nachala XX v.* (Kiev: Dukh i litera, 2001), 294: "Vse, na chem do sikh por derzhalos' evreistvo: religiia, tora, talmud,—palo, razrusheno. I vot my, predstaviteli novogo evreistva, pytaemsia sozdat' nechto takoe, chto, pomimo religii, ob"edinilo i sgustilo by narod v odno tseloe. Ob etom ia i pishu."

10. See, for example, the publications of Jörn Leonhard and Ulrike von Hirschhausen or the research outline on "Jews between Empires and Nation-States Research" at the Simon Dubnow Institut in Leipzig, http://www.dubnow.de/Jews-Between-Empires-and -Nation-States.117.0.html?&L=1.

11. Jörn Leonhard and Ulrike von Hirschhausen, eds., *Comparing Empires: Encounters and Transfers in the Long Nineteenth Century* (Göttingen: Vandenhoeck und Ruprecht, 2010). See also Jörn Leonhard and Ulrike von Hirschhausen, *Empires und Nationalstaaten im 19. Jahrhundert* (Göttingen: Vandenhoeck und Ruprecht, 2009), 13.

12. For the history of the Jewish autonomous *kehilot* see Antony Polonsky, *The Jews in Poland and Russia*, vol. 1: 1350–1881 (Portland, Ore.: The Littman Library of Jewish Civilisation, 2010), 48–67, 177–250; François Guesnet, *Polnische Juden im 19. Jahrhundert* (Cologne: Böhlau, 1998).

13. Bruno Latour, *We Have Never Been Modern* (Cambridge, Mass.: Harvard University Press, 1993).

14. Pertti J. Anttonen, *Tradition through Modernity: Postmodernism and the Nation-State in Folklore Scholarship* (Helsinki: Finnish Literature Society, 2005), 14.

15. For the historical framework, see Emily S. Rosenberg, ed., *A World Connecting, 1870–1945* (Cambridge, Mass.: Belknap Press, 2012).

16. Cf. Annette Werberger, "Eine Stimme der Moderne—Der Dibbuk als Medium von 'Tradition,'" in *Trance-Medien und Neue Medien um 1900*, ed. Markus Hahn and Erhard Schüttpelz (Bielefeld: transcript, 2009), 199–225. For an in-depth analysis of ethnoliterary texts see Schüttpelz's important book on primitivism. Erhard Schüttpelz, *Die Moderne im Spiegel des Primitiven* (Munich: Wilhelm Fink, 2005).

17. Johannes Fabian, *Time and the Other: How Anthropology Makes Its Object* (New York: Columbia University Press, 1983), 18.

18. Cf. Schüttpelz, *Die Moderne im Spiegel*, 17ff.; Erhard Schüttpelz, "Mündlichkeit/Schriftlichkeit," in *Handbuch Medien der Literatur*, ed. Natalie Binczek, Till Dembeck, and Jörgen Schäfer (Berlin: de Gruyter, 2013), 27–40.

19. M. B. Vanvild, ed., *Bey unz yuden: Zamelbukh far folklor un filologye* (Warsaw: P. Graubard, 1923), 2.

20. Kiel, 99.

21. Latour, *We Have Never Been Modern*, 7.

22. Cf. Kathrin Busch and Iris Därmann, eds., *Pathos: Konturen eines kulturwissen-schaftlichen Grundbegriffs* (Bielefeld: transcript, 2007).

23. One has to remember the appeal of the division between modernity and tradition in the academic community: "We have already forgotten this period, thank goodness, but let me remind you of the mountains of discussion, documentary films, newspaper articles, theses and studies of peoples 'pushed and pulled,' 'torn' or 'divided' between 'modernity' and 'tradition.' Of course, this idea still crops up from time to time, but the fervency is gone. . . ." See Bruno Latour, "The Recall of Modernity," 2007, http://www.bruno-latour .fr/sites/default/files/downloads/91-RECALL-MODERNITY-GB.pdf.

24. A. Almi, *Momentn fun a lebn. Zikhroynes, bilder un epizodn* (Buenos Aires, 1948).

25. Important monographs on this issue are by Gottesman (*Defining the Yiddish Nation*) and Kalman Weiser, *Jewish People, Yiddish Nation: Noah Prylucki and the Folkists in Poland* (Toronto: University of Toronto Press, 2011). An early article is from Mark Kiel, "Vox populi, vox dei."

26. I. L. Peretz, *In This World and the Next*, 346.

27. Cf. the reference to Almi in Rachel Rubinstein, *Members of the Tribe: Native America in the Jewish Imagination* (Detroit: Wayne State University Press, 2010), 14ff.

28. Gottesman, 5.

29. Weiser, 99.

30. Gottesman, 26ff. and 50.

31. Ibid., 50.

32. Ibid., 85.

33. Weiser, 99; Almi, 121–128.

34. Gottesman, 26.

35. Regina F. Bendix and Galit Hasan-Rokem, *A Companion to Folklore* (Malden, Mass.: Wiley-Blackwell, 2012), 4.

36. Gottesman, 26.

37. Weiser, 92.

38. Mukdoni, "How I. L. Peretz Wrote His Folk Tales," 354.

39. Ibid., 355.

40. Gottesman, 5.

41. The economist and financier Jan Bloch founded a special statistical bureau in Warsaw in 1884. He initiated the statistical expedition. Cf. the excellent French edition of I. L. Peretz, *Les oubliés du shtetl. Yiddishland* (Paris: Plon, 2007).

42. Ruth Wisse, *I. L. Peretz and the Making of Modern Jewish Culture* (Seattle: University of Washington Press, 1991), 19.

43. Yitskhok Leybush Peretz, *Ale verk. Bd. 2: dertseylungen, mayselekh, bilder* (New York: Cyco bikher-farlag, 1947), 161.

44. Ibid., 159.

45. James Clifford, "On Ethnographic Allegory," in *Writing Culture: The Poetics and Politics of Ethnography*, ed. James Clifford and George E. Marcus (Berkeley: University of California Press, 1986), 112.

46. Ruth Wisse, ed., *The I. L. Peretz Reader* (New Haven, Conn.: Yale University Press, 2002), 54. See also Peretz, *Ale verk. Bd. 2*, 164.

47. "I. L. Peretz: Impressions of a Journey through the Tomaszow Region," in *The I. L. Pertez Reader*, 31.

48. Interestingly, Gayatri Chakravorty Spivak refers in her notion of *subaltern* in *Can the Subaltern Speak?* (1988) to an important article on Folkore (*Osservazioni sul folclore*) by Antonio Gramsci from the 1930s, published in 1950.

49. In a dialogue about a *lamed-vovnik*, for example, Peretz is cautioned about the "sitr'a aḥr'a," which may threaten Peretz in his unholy task. The warning ends the passage and remains without commentary of the narrator: "Di sitr'a aḥr'a iz oykh nisht keyn kleynikeyt," in Peretz, *Ale verk. Bd. 2*, 187.

50. Wisse, *The I. L. Peretz Reader*, 78; see also Peretz, *Ale verk. Bd. 2*, 197.

51. Marc Caplan, "The Fragmentation of Narrative Perspective in Y. L. Peretz's *Bilder fun a Provints-Rayze,*" *Jewish Social Studies: History, Culture, Society* 14, no. 1 (2007): 63.

52. Victor Karady, *Gewalterfahrung und Utopie. Juden in der Europaischen Moderne* (Frankfurt: Fischer, 1999), 22f.

53. I only want to mention for this context the monograph by Marc Caplan, *How Strange the Change: Language, Temporality, and Narrative Form in Peripheral Modernisms* (Stanford, Calif.: Stanford University Press, 2011).

54. Mukdoni, "How I. L. Peretz Wrote His Folk Tales," 357.

55. Ibid., 358. See also A. Mukdoni, "Y. L. Perets dertseylt a folkstimlekhe geshikhte," in *Y. L. Perets un dos yidishe teater* (New York: Ikuf farlag, 1949), 262.

56. Mukdoni, "How I. L. Peretz Wrote His Folk Tales," 358f.

57. Ibid.

58. Walter Benjamin, "Der Erzähler," in *Gesammelte Schriften* II. 2 (Frankfurt: Suhrkamp, 1991), 438–463.

59. Hersh D. Nomberg, "Isaac Leibush Peretz As We Knew Him," in *The Golden Tradition: Jewish Life and Thought in Eastern Europe*, ed. Lucy S. Dawidowicz (Syracuse: Syracuse University Press, [1967] 1996), 296.

Imagining the Wandering Jew in Modernity

Exegesis and Ethnography in Leon Feuchtwanger's *Jud Süss*

GALIT HASAN-ROKEM

Folklore as a mode of human creativity and behavior has existed since humans have communicated amongst themselves, but the study of folklore as a category of intellectual pursuit and systematic research is modern. In their awareness of continuous traditions and the changes that they undergo, moderns have distinguished their cultural situation precisely as moderns: in a judicious relationship to tradition.[1] Rather than thinking of modernity as a sequence of premodern and then modern, I suggest that it may be more adequate for our multimigrating and pluricultural era to recognize the parallel existences of multiple modernities, postmodernities, and post-post-modernities. Combining research methodologies developed in folklore studies and the study of literature, I interpret Leon Feuchtwanger's novel *Jud Süß*'s engagement with the figure of the Wandering Jew as grappling with threatening forms of modernity growing out of medieval traditions, while I demonstrate the role of cultural imagination as the weaver of tradition, as well as what unravels it. Imagination is here conceptualized as a cultural construct characterizing a period or a place,[2] and as a creative capacity characterizing groups or individuals.[3] The two aspects of imagination shown here to be of special relevance to the study of the figure of the Wandering Jew in general, and particularly in the case of this novel, are the exegetic imagination and the ethnographic imagination.[4] The exegetic imagination is best defined as a hermeneutic and semiotic potential, active in creative performances in cultural media of various reflections, elaborations, and interpretations of texts, especially of sacred and canonical texts.[5] The ethnographic imagination, a concept that has been developed in the context of the present work, draws on the sphere of experience, reflection, and action best understood under the phenomenological concept of *Lebenswelt;*[6] its presence in a work of fiction is characterized by reference to details of everyday life, of ethnically and culturally identifiable mores, and sometimes by descriptive elements of a recognizable historical and cultural context.

THE WANDERING JEW IN THE EUROPEAN IMAGINATION

It is likely that Jews have been associated by Europeans with wandering and itinerancy since the first age when Jews appeared on the continent, in the first half of the first millennium C E at the latest. The figure of the Wandering Jew has persisted as a strong semiotic focus in the continuous—not necessarily irenic—coproduction of European culture by Christians and Jews. Its manifestations in European art, literature, and folklore communicate stereotypical stigmas projected by European Christians on Jews, as well as Jewish conceptions of their own lifestyle, history, and destiny.[7] As a powerful hermeneutic meta-figure extant in various European cultural discourses, the Wandering Jew figure has on varying levels of explicitness served to interpret Jewish modernity, mobility, and related matters.[8] It has also contributed to the Europeans' not altogether realistic construction of their own identity as stable and sedentary.[9] In the figure of Ahasver,[10] as he is often called, the partly overlapping categories of ethnographic imagination and exegetic imagination[11] meet as privileged expressive formations of the imagination of Europeans.

The exegetic imagination has continually produced biblical and parabiblical elements of the Wandering Jew and the traditions surrounding him; the ethnographic imagination weaves in observations and conceptualizations that are rooted in the real and imaginary lives of Jews, in particular European Jews and their tendency toward mobility.

Feuchtwanger's novel *Jud Süß* (1925)[12] is one of many literary works from the last two centuries engaging the figure of the Wandering Jew. It exhibits a remarkably wide perspective on the transformations of the

Wandering Jew figure from its crystallization as a legendary being in early modernity to its emphatically symbolic manifestations in modernity. This wide perspective is articulated in the diverse positions of enunciation that the Wandering Jew occupies in the novel, contributing to the *heterological*—disjunctive and subversive—characteristic of the genre as theorized by Mikhail Bakhtin.[13] The Wandering Jew functions as a versatile embodiment of the central tension of this novel: the Jew as part of the community of Europeans, or as an exception and an alien.

EXEGETIC IMAGINATION IN *JUD SÜSS: JOSEPH AND ESTHER*

The application of exegetic imagination in *Jud Süß* is rooted in Feuchtwanger's familial and educational background. He has been seen as a personification and a producer of a certain kind of Jewish modernity, an active participant in the production of national and universal values, as well as literary genres. Lion Feuchtwanger was born in Munich in 1884 to a family of neo-Orthodox Jewish Germans who had a long history in the country.[14] His forefathers were expelled in the sixteenth century from Feuchtwangen in central Bavaria to Fürth farther east in Bavaria and, as wandering Jews often did, carried with them the name of their former hometown. He served as a soldier in the German imperial army in World War I, fled in the mid-1930s to France, and in 1940 undertook a risky sea journey to the United States. He died in Los Angeles in 1958, barred by McCarthyism from ever revisiting his country of birth. When the novel *Jud Süß* was published in 1925, Feuchtwanger was already a rather famous author in Germany; the novel greatly enhanced his reputation,[15] although it was received with mixed reviews. Some considered Feuchtwanger one of the three most important prose writers of the Weimar Republic (1919–1933). Paul Levesque has suggested the novel as opening a new, superior stage in the German historical novel's development, preparing for Thomas Mann's *Joseph and His Brothers* and Hermann Broch's *The Death of Virgil*.[16] Paul Gerhard Klussman has compared *Jud Süss* to Mann's *Magic Mountain*, as well as to Alfred Döblin's *Berlin Alexanderplatz*.[17]

Jud Süß elaborates on a documented historical event from the early eighteenth century, focusing on the life of a "court Jew" by the name of

Josef Süss Oppenheimer (c. 1698–1738).[18] Oppenheimer's career surpassed all other court Jews' in its spectacular and scandalous details, presumably including riches, expensive clothing, amorous affairs, and pandering to the duke whom he loyally served. A number of attempts have been made by historians to redeem a "real" account of his life from the materials documenting his activities, successes, and demise.[19]

Jewish and particularly Biblical traditions provide a fundamental cultural semiotic framework as well as a repertoire of intertexts for Feuchtwanger's *Jud Süß*, demonstrating the author's exegetic imagination. Biblical associations reveal the double resonance of Scripture as a shibboleth between Jews and Christians: as a common canon of revelation, it marks belonging; when divergent, post-biblical interpretations are emphasized, they distinguish between Jews and Christians.

An important key for the biblical and traditional references in the novel is the status of Joseph Süss Oppenheimer as the personal banker and economic consultant for the newly appointed Duke of Württemberg, Karl Alexander, a war hero who fought against the Turks and served as the emperor's envoy in Serbia. The double bind of the Jewish wish—to be included in "we Europeans," non-Jew and Jew alike, and unlike the non-European Turk—looms from the beginning. Isaac Landauer, who had served as the Court Jew of the Duke's predecessor and cousin, Duke Eberhard Ludwig, is the perfect foil to the well-adapted, assimilated Süss; Landauer sticks to traditional Jewish apparel, caftan and sidelocks, in spite of his clearly nonpious, rationalistic views based on apparent knowledge of European philosophy. He criticizes Oppenheimer's appearance and behavior, since Oppenheimer imitates his non-Jewish lords and tops them by importing the newest fashions from Paris. The comparison between Landauer and Oppenheimer has been understood as a direct reflection of how contemporary German Jews in Feuchtwanger's time coped with being rejected by their German environment as Oriental: they obliterated, as much as possible, any similarity between themselves and "Orientals," *Ostjuden*.[20]

Süss's ambitions and success, as well as the privileges bestowed on him by the Duke, who is financially dependent on him and owes him gratitude for his many and diverse services, arouse envy but also admiration. The Catholic duke uses "his" Jew to play against each other the predominantly Protestant estates and burghers and the various other religious groups under his rule—and when he fails, the Jew serves as a convenient scapegoat to avert fury from the Duke.

Süss's insatiable desire for women is, in the novel, motivated by the untimely death of his beloved wife, which leaves him alone with his daughter Naemi.[21] Naemi is raised by Süss's uncle, the Kabbalist Rabbi Gabriel, who is explicitly characterized as the Wandering Jew. Gabriel instructs Naemi in the Bible and instills in her the admiration and love of its heroes, of whom she often fantasizes, including her father among them.

The upbringing of Naemi by Gabriel is written in terms directly referring to the relationship between the biblical Esther and her uncle, Mordekhai, who has adopted her.[22] Süss's fantasies of his daughter's future as a Queen Esther—married to the non-Jewish king—turn into an unhappy omen: Naemi dies escaping the duke's seduction, which had turned into an attempted rape.[23]

The biblical story of Esther also resonates in the masquerade ball that Süss, overstepping his old friend Landauer's advice that Jews should act inconspicuously, organizes in his luxurious apartment in Stuttgart. Echoing Jewish Purim customs based on Esther's book, the masquerade inevitably—and ironically—recalls the rescue of the Jews of Persia.[24] Thus, the historically documented hanging scene of Süss stands in harsh contrast to the victory scene of Mordekhai in the Bible, where his adversary Haman is hanged alongside his sons. Feuchtwanger may have been aware of the latent violence of Purim in the history of Jewish–Christian relations,[25] which resonates in the scene where Süss traps Magdalene Sibylle Weissensee, the innocent daughter of a powerful clergyman, at the masquerade, intending to make her the duke's mistress. Demonstrating the application of exegetic imagination to Christian Scripture, the young woman's name refers to the beloved disciple of Jesus, whose transformation from prostitute to devotee was the opposite of the downward turn taken by Magdalene Sibylle's life. The sibyls echoed in her name reinforce the persistence in the novel of various modes of divination and prophecy among Jews and Christians alike, highlighting the shared registers of popular beliefs as a facet of the intergroup relationship, as well as Feuchtwanger's active use of ethnographic imagination. While Magdalene Sibylle, complicit in the popular demonization of Jews,[26] attempted to convert Süss to the Christian God, her ruin is harshly settled by her father, Pastor Weissensee,[27] who leads the duke to Naemi's hiding place. It is at this point that Naemi, to escape rape, throws herself off the roof of her hideaway.[28] Süss's success story is revealed as a pompous masquerade, and the image of the Court Jew with the elegant house on Seegasse crumbles under the Wandering Jew's cyclic fate, here projected onto Süss himself.

The Esther theme is associated with yet another biblical figure: Joseph in the house of Pharaoh. Süss is related to Joseph in many ways, most obviously by the shared first name, which was of course not chosen by Feuchtwanger; however, he makes elegant use of it. Both Josephs juggle hiding their real ethnic and religious identity—the biblical Joseph more extremely—with expressions of their particularity, such as the talent for dream interpretation (in *Jud Süß* such practices are transposed on Rabbi Gabriel) and resisting temptations, sexual for biblical Joseph, and conversion in the case of Süss. The resulting dramatic tension charges both figures with powerful symbolic meaning and enables the intricate interplay between self-image and the image projected by others through them. Both embody a folk narrative stock figure, the minister of lowly or foreign background who has risen to greatness and remains constantly tested and repeatedly compromised by visible and invisible enemies.[29] The reference to an existing tale type interweaves modern identity-related sensibilities (e.g., the case of Rathenau) and folk narrative traditions. The interweaving results in a mixture of reverence for tradition—for instance in the admirable figure of Uncle Gabriel *qua* the Wandering Jew—with an ironic reflection on tradition.

The sexual attractiveness of Süss, especially for Christian women, has been richly embroidered by Feuchtwanger and others. The dangerous desire of a majority individual for a minority person materializes as biblical Joseph is thrown into jail after having resisted Potiphar's wife's seduction. But Joseph Oppenheimer—sharing the almost supernatural sex appeal of biblical Joseph, elaborated in both rabbinic literature and the Quran—does not resist; on the contrary, he very often seduces both his own victims and the duke's.[30] Similarities between Joseph Süss Oppenheimer of the novel and the biblical tales of Esther and Joseph reach beyond mere isolated motifs and events, displaying an entire network of associations of the milieu surrounding a minority person at the court of a powerful ruler.

The tale type of the Court Jew advising a foreign ruler appears in Jewish folk narratives of all periods.[31] The plot, however, usually runs contrary to the events in the tale of Süss: an unduly accused Jewish advisor gains the favor of the ruler and consequently also more power and riches, thanks to his intelligence. Feuchtwanger's novel thereby makes an ironic comment on popular and ancient Jewish traditions in an antitraditionalist gesture.

The tale type involves a series of historical contexts that reinforce the genre aspect of the historical novel within which Feuchtwanger consciously operates. The Biblical Joseph forecasts the future of his fellow prisoners, and Rabbi Gabriel in *Jud Süß* predicts the future rise of Karl Alexander, who will be the benefactor of Süss. A similar scene appears in prophesies of Vespasian's rise to emperor.[32] Whereas Josephus Flavius, in his version of the event, is both the advisor and the prophet, in *Jud Süß* the roles are split between Joseph Süss Oppenheimer, the advisor, and Rabbi Gabriel, the diviner. Feuchtwanger may well have also known the Talmudic-Midrashic parallel to the Josephus story in which Rabban Yohannan Ben-Zakkai, in a typically rabbinical rhetorical act, addresses Vespasian with a piece of Bible exegesis as an omen of his imminent coronation. The verse "He will cut down the forest thickets with an ax; Lebanon will fall before the Mighty One" (Isaiah 10:34 NIV), says Yohannan Ben-Zakkai, means that only a ruler could have destroyed the Temple of Jerusalem.[33] Feuchtwanger published his Josephus trilogy—another tale of a brilliant Jewish man oscillating between identities in royal courts—in the early 1930s, less than ten years after the publication of *Jud Süß*, and included in it the prophesy episode figuring both Josephus and Yohannan Ben-Zakkai![34]

The peak of Süss Oppenheimer's ambitions is to become part of European high society by acquiring a real title of nobility—without conversion to Christianity—awarded by the emperor in Vienna, where his banker relatives still exerted influence during his lifetime; this ambition was aborted by his precarious position between the duke, the estates, and the burghers, and in the wider context between Protestants and Catholics. Instead Süss is convicted for various economic transgressions. The court first rules him innocent but the ruling is overturned by his powerful enemies. His fellow Jews make great efforts to ransom him after the verdict, but they fail and Süss is brutally hanged in an iron cage on the town square. Still, his refusal to convert seems, in the end, to be rewarded. Describing Süss's last hours in jail before his execution, Feuchtwanger again exhibits his familiarity with Jewish sources, here the Kabbalah mysticism that thrived among the Jews of Europe in the protagonist's lifetime. Süss reconciles himself to his religion and mystically unites with his dead daughter. During those hours he also becomes more and more like his uncle Gabriel, so that the Court Jew blends with the Wandering, Eternal Jew, finally stamped by the letter *shin* that appears on his brow, like the sign on Rabbi Gabriel's brow.[35] And very much like the damned Eternal Jew, Süss ends up yearning for death rather than fearing it. Süss's last encounter with his mother is, however, fraught by devastating alienation. Having adored his youthful success, she now rejects him as an old, suffering, wandering Jew; she remains entrenched in her narcissistic love of the unattainable *puer aeternus*, the eternal youngster, now forever lost.[36] This powerful clash, and mesh, of self-image and image in the eyes of another makes sense—and not only in its centrality to the ethnographic production of reality, but also, I suggest, in terms of a Lacanian "mirror stage."[37] At this late stage in the novel, the author diverts the focus from historical and political issues to the sphere of the intimately personal, a turn that can be illuminated by Jane Gallop's astute description of the failure of the mirror stage when the immature self looks at the more mature other with anticipation of becoming something that never was and never will be; thus, a mistaken image is produced, as the image of the whole body is retrieved when it has already fallen apart.[38] A parallel symbolic process takes place in the novel: the Jewish self that has constructed its identity and status by mirroring itself in non-Jewish eyes, undergoes a total disintegration. But Süss Oppenheimer and the Jewish community to which he insists he belongs are not alone in this demise. The mutuality of the Jewish and Christian gazes produces in parallel and in interaction a potential disintegration of the European self, mirroring itself in its Jews.[39]

JUD SÜSS BETWEEN HISTORY AND FICTION: ETHNOGRAPHIC IMAGINATION

The Wandering Jew is introduced into *Jud Süß* as a focus of the ethnographic imagination activated in the novel. The figure is devised to communicate the diasporic experience of Central European Jews' Lebens-welt—in phenomenological and critical terms—as well as the Europeans' experience of them.[40] In this communication, the borders between history and fiction are sophisticatedly intertwined and blurred. Feuchtwanger introduced the Wandering Jew legend that was especially widely distrib-uted in the seventeenth and eighteenth centuries—the "real time" of the novel—as a narrative told within the novel,[41] challenging the dichotomy between the two categories.[42] By making the Swabians and Württember-gians of the early eighteenth century the transmitters of rumors about the Wandering Jew who visits their region, Feuchtwanger introduces history into fiction, while at the same time recognizing fiction as part of history, and revealing his profound familiarity with the European ethnographic imagination:

> During these weeks the Wandering Jew had been seen in the Swabian districts, now in one place, now in another. In Tübingen it was reported by some that he had driven through the town in a private carriage; others would have it that they had seen him on foot on the highway, or in the stage-coach; the gatekeeper at Weinsberg told a tale of a queer stranger who gave a curious name and had an extraordinary appearance; and when he pressed him for identification papers the uncanny visitor pierced him through and through with such a malevolent look that he was completely dazed and had to let him go, and he could still feel the effects of that diabolical look as a shooting pain in all his limbs. The rumors spread everywhere; children were warned to beware the stranger's eye; and Weil, the town where he had been last seen, gave its gatekeeper the strictest instructions.
>
> A little later he appeared in Hall. At the town gate he declared boldly that he was Ahasverus, the Wandering [in the original German: Eternal] Jew. The Magistrate was sent for at once, and ordained that for the present he should be allowed into the suburbs. Anxious and curious crowds gath-ered. He looked like any peddling Jew, with a caftan and side-curls. He spoke freely, in a gurgling voice, often unintelligibly. Before the Crucifix he prostrated himself wailing and beating his breast. For the rest, he sold small-wares, and disposed of many amulets and souvenirs. Finally he was brought before the magistrate and proved to be a swindler, and was flogged.
>
> But those who had seen him pointed out that he was certainly not the right one. The other had had nothing remarkable in his garb: he was clad in a respectable Dutch coat like other people, a little old-fashioned in cut;

he looked like a superior official or a comfortable citizen. It was only his face, and his general atmosphere, above all, his eye; in short, one felt immediately that he was the Wandering [Eternal] Jew. This was the story in which the most diverse people concurred, in all corners of the land.[43]

Feuchtwanger's report of Ahasver's advent demonstrates his thorough knowledge of the details of the Wandering Jew's chapbook traditions, from the diverse and contradictory descriptions of attire to the general atmosphere of anxiety. But the novelist naturally does not limit himself to the well-known clichés and formulae of the chapbooks, as he moves heterologically between the various positions of enunciation—the author, the readers, the Wandering Jew—but most of all the collective voice of the rumor genre. This collective voice is balanced by the author's rationalizing explanation that the person identified by the Swabians as Ahasver is none other than Süss Oppenheimer's uncle Gabriel. The people's belief that Gabriel is the Eternal Jew in the fictional world of the novel is based on recognition of the popularity of the chapbooks in the real world. Moreover, Rabbi Gabriel's characterization, replete with Kabbalistic knowledge and mystery, emphasizes his close relationship with the quasi-fantastic realm in which the plot of the Eternal Jew has been shaped, reflecting the often unreal image of real Jews in the eyes of their neighbors.

Half a century before Feuchtwanger's novel, Manfred Zimmermann produced the earliest historical account of Oppenheimer's case that was free of antisemitic bias, attempting to explain Oppenheimer's fate against the background of Catholics and Protestants wrestling over power. History and fiction sometimes blur in his account, too, especially when the Wandering Jew appears, as in the following "seltsame Episode" (rare episode) revealing Duke Karl Alexander's *eigenthümlich* (outlandish) beliefs: "A so-called Magus, an old grey-bearded interpreter of stars and signs, had arrived a couple of days before the court ball at Ludwigsburg.—[he] promised the duke to interpret the results of his enterprise within a few days."[44] Zimmermann's ethnographic imagination accounts for the detailed description of the magician's practices and devices, characterized by the author himself as the necessary cultural historical background of the eighteenth century. Similarly, Zimmermann's contribution, unique for its time, has to be understood in the context of his own period, when the Wandering Jew often emerged in antisemitic discourse.[45] The episode quoted from Zimmermann may have served Feuchtwanger in composing the scene of the prophecy of the duke's future, in addition to the folk narrative sources discussed above. In *Jud Süß*, Feuchtwanger activates his ethnographic imagination by elaborating on the historical context in which the tradition about Ahasver flourished, as shown by the many editions of the chapbook on this theme in the seventeenth- and eighteenth-century German-speaking lands.[46]

The reference to the story being told by actual people thus serves the historical documentary aspect of the novel. The fact that Feuchtwanger does not pinpoint a particular narrator of the Wandering Jew tale reveals his awareness of its collective and traditional mode of production, transcending any specific historical moment and flowing into the passing time between the historical past and the present moment of the author and his audiences, in a mode that strongly echoes the experiential, phenomenological basis of his cultural work.[47] Feuchtwanger not only reconstructed the Ahasver of the seventeenth and eighteenth centuries, including some of the allegorical and symbolic traits inspired by the adoption of the figure by the English and German Romantics,[48] but he also reconstructed the system of cultural communication by which the tradition of the Wandering Jew was transmitted. This invites an interpretation of the Wandering Jew theme and figure in *Jud Süß* that takes into account both the context of the author and his audience and the evolution of the Ahasver tradition in European, especially German, culture.[49]

A fascinating connection signals the vagueness of the borders between history and fiction in the novel, namely the fact that the early accounts of the story of Joseph Oppenheimer were distributed in the same medium as the Wandering Jew traditions, chapbooks.[50] Thus, the historical reconstructions of what really happened to Süss are as equally reliable—or rather unreliable—as the testimonies of the visits of the Wandering Jew. Rumor, the wandering genre, is indeed the characteristic mode of distribution of the Wandering Jew traditions in Europe, especially in premodern times.[51]

The dichotomy between folk literature and belletristic literature also becomes blurred as *Jud Süß* interweaves the Wandering Jew motifs into the reality of the eighteenth century. Rabbi Gabriel's tendency to appear suddenly and to disappear even more suddenly, as well as his introducing himself as a Dutchman and wearing clothes of a Dutch burgher, remind us of the many similarities between the legends of the Wandering Jew and the Flying Dutchman. Feuchtwanger, too, must have been aware of that, having in 1907 submitted a doctoral dissertation on a text by Heinrich Heine,[52] who famously characterized the Flying Dutchman as "the Eternal Jew of the ocean."[53] The phrase is by many erroneously attributed to Richard Wagner, who probably borrowed it, as well as the tale of the Flying Dutchman itself, from Heine.[54] Feuchtwanger's representation of the Wandering Jew figure in *Jud Süß* must be understood in light of the marks that Wagner—the harsh opponent of Jews—and especially Heine—"the lost brother"—left on that tradition. Heine himself was titled "the Wandering Jew" at least twice.[55] Rabbi Gabriel's mysterious walks in the forest also associate him with another related legendary figure, namely Odin or Wotan, who in folk belief is embodied in the wind in the forest.[56]

The most striking elements in Rabbi Gabriel's description are the furrows on his forehead that create the letter *shin*. The author explicitly associated this letter with the divine name Shaddai, which renders Gabriel almost a walking mezuzah (often adorned with a *shin*) and emphasizes the visual aspect of his peculiar identity, while also reminding the readers about his piety—unlike Süss—and the daily practice of laying *tefillin* (phylacteries) on which this letter is also inscribed. But the same initial on Rabbi Gabriel's forehead could of course also refer to Satan, spelled in Hebrew with an orthographically identical *sin*—a fact that Feuchtwanger, with his neo-Orthodox education, must have known. The mark on the brow is seldom mentioned in the Christian traditions of the Wandering Jew that I have encountered,[57] but it is associated directly with that other, earlier eternal wanderer cursed by God—Cain.[58] In one of his most acrimonious attacks on Jews, Augustine compares them with the first murderer, developing a theme suggested by Jerome.[59] This attack has unquestionably influenced the character of the legendary Wandering Jew's punishment from the motif's earliest versions.

Feuchtwanger's Gabriel is, however, not a mere version of the folk narrative motif.[60] Working within the genre framework of the historical novel, of which he has been hailed as an innovator introducing universal rather than national standards,[61] Feuchtwanger's novel exemplifies the heterological potential of the genre and sets the historical materials in a dialogic tension with his own subject position, informed both by Jewish traditions and the experience of being a modern Jew. Gabriel accordingly lacks a central trait of the Eternal Jew in European folklore: he is not a penitent Christian, as Ahasver is often described, but a believing and practicing Jew. Moreover, his rich education makes him—in the novel—a partner in dialogue and polemics with one of the most contentious figures of early modern Central European Jewish history, Jonathan Eybeschütz (1690–1764).[62] Eybeschütz's presence in the novel provides yet another explication for the letter on Gabriel's brow, reminding us that one of Eybeschütz's most ardent opponents, Rabbi Jacob Emden, somewhat later than the events in the novel, accused Eybeschütz of Sabbateanism—that is, that he was among those persisting in the belief that Shabbetai Zevi (1626–1676) was the Messiah. Such belief was still vibrant among European Jews many years after his conversion in 1666 and his death in 1676.[63] Thus, Rabbi Gabriel's *shin* could of course be much "worse" than Shaddai—it could mean Shabbetai.[64] The Wandering Jew figure in Feuchtwanger's novel is ostensibly a folkloristic reference to the Sabbatean movement, one of the major earthquakes that shook Jewish life in Europe after the expulsion from the Iberian Peninsula in the late 1490s and the many partial expulsions from the British Isles and Central Europe from the Crusades on, while it also introduced into early modern Jewish culture many of its creative, restless elements.[65]

In *Jud Süß*, Feuchtwanger as a modern Jew and author processed multiple sensibilities of modern Jewish literatures as part of the semiotics of modern Jewish culture, emphasizing the radical cultural work performed by folklore in general, and particularly by the figure of the Wandering Jew in modern culture.

CONCLUDING MOMENTS

The Wandering Jew is a multivalent sign in Jewish culture and acts as a reflection on Jews. At every instance of its use, it represents a number of unresolved oppositions between center and periphery, between history and redemption, nationhood and universality, in a "unity of nearness and remoteness."[66] These oppositions have, especially from the early nineteenth century on, charged the Wandering Jew figure with rich symbolic connotations derived from complex, often oppositional semantic configurations. The Wandering Jew is a peripatetic stranger who carries the European cognitive universe everywhere. More specifically, he carries the intimate, mythical cognizance sacred to Christian society and therefore embodies the fear held by Jew and Christian alike: that the stranger may possess knowledge of one's own primordial symbols, hidden from oneself.[67]

Lion Feuchtwanger did live to witness the infamous Nazi adaptation of *Jud Süss* (1940), a violent appropriation, if not of the Jewish author's text, then at least of the earlier Jew's life story. Highly praised by critics, the film was designed to prepare the minds of the Germans for the extermination of European Jewry, and the evil deviousness of the enterprise was emphasized by the substantial artistic investment in the film's quality and the manipulative enlisting of great talents as actors and director.[68] The casting of Ferdinand Marian as Süss himself reveals the demonic plotting of the production, as the actor was known for his brilliant portrayal of Iago in stage productions of Shakespeare's *Othello*.[69] Oppenheimer's uncle Gabriel, the Wandering Jew of the novel, is played by Werner Krauss, who earlier performed the title role in the Expressionist horror film *The Cabinet of Dr. Caligari* (1920).[70] The producer and director of the film were thus conscientiously manipulating the demonizing elements associated by the audience with these actors to ensure the hateful effect of their work.[71]

The Wandering Jew, possibly an Augustinian residue in the Reformation cosmology making room for Jews as a necessary reminder of salvation by embodying its painful postponement, permeates the world of Feuchtwanger's novel. Relegated—indeed almost expelled—from Veit Harlan's film, the Wandering Jew's shadow nonetheless hovers over the film and its figures, persistent in its suppressed presence.[72] The Eternal Jew, ousted from Harlan's film, emerges as a horrendous specter in Fritz Hippler's almost contemporaneous film, *The Eternal Jew*, where the stereotype is entirely disconnected from the legendary and theological context. Unlike the Nazi production of the *Jud Süss*, this Nazi movie, titled *Der ewige Jude*—a would-be documentary of Jewish customs with grueling visuals of kosher slaughtering and Jewish faces marked by irregular features to prove their racial inferiority, at worst presenting the migrations of Jews as rats crawling around the world—did not make it in the box offices. It remains a harrowing testimony of cultural creativity involving the Wandering Jew, if only by name, in the most horrendous moment of the history of Europe.[73]

In the novel *Jud Süß*, the figure of the Wandering Jew acts in the liminal spaces between Jews and Christians on one hand, and between reality and legend on the other. To borrow the notion of "the bridge and the door"—formulated by Feuchtwanger's contemporary, Georg Simmel, in his essay on "the sociology of space"—these liminal spaces both connect two separately conceived categories and also mark their separation,[74] in a much more complex dynamic of similarity and difference than the dichotomously encoded categories of "hybridity" or "mimicry," which remain entrenched in division. The Wandering Jew figure also amply informs the text with an indelible interweaving of folklore and literature, identified by Bakhtin as a new, productive wave inspiring the shaping of the historical novel from the second half of the eighteenth century onward.[75] In *Jud Süß*—the work of a modern Jewish author, situated at a specific moment in European history between the twentieth century's two World Wars—the dialogue between folklore and literature points to the meeting, and sometimes clashing, of various sources of authority and information in the interplay of Jewish tradition and European, especially German, folklore.

Feuchtwanger's version of the legend of the Wandering Jew, taken from the best-selling chapbooks of the seventeenth century, seems at least partly to deviate from the symbolic turn of the Romantics and their successors in describing the figure.[76] On the one hand, he constructed a traditional, legendary Wandering Jew straight out of the historical period and the communicative system in which the figure flourished in German-speaking Europe. But on the other hand, Feuchtwanger projected into his novel the symbolic shadow of the Wandering Jew as a collective representation, embodied in the complex figure of Joseph Süss Oppenheimer himself, and enhanced by the biblical echoes of Esther and Joseph. Feuchtwanger's treatment of these topics reveals a double—German and Jewish—cultural literacy and an active engagement with European imagination, in both its exegetic and ethnographic aspects, shared by its Jewish and Christian populations. It is a distinct example of the vital presence of folklore on multiple levels of culture, especially in literature, and invites the application of methodologies developed in the study of folklore into the study of cultural production at large.

NOTES

1. Regina Bendix, *In Search of Authenticity: The Formation of Folklore Studies* (Madison: University of Wisconsin Press, 1997); Diarmuid Ó Giolláin, *Locating Irish Folklore: Tradition, Modernity, Identity* (Cork: Cork University Press, 2000); Richard Bauman and Charles L. Briggs, *Voices of Modernity: Language Ideologies and the Politics of Inequality* (Cambridge: Cambridge University Press, 2003). See also Dan Ben-Amos, "The Seven Strands of Tradition: Varieties in Its Meaning in American Folklore Studies," *Journal of Folklore Research* 21, nos. 2–3 (1984): 97–131; Dorothy Noyes, "Tradition: Three Traditions," *Journal of Folklore Research* 46, no. 3 (2011): 233–268; Galit Hasan-Rokem, "Contemporary Perspectives on Tradition: Moving on with the Wandering Jew," in *Konstellationen: über Geschichte, Erfahrung und Erkenntnis* (Festschrift for Dan Diner), ed. N. Berg, O. Kamil, and M. Kirchhoff (Göttingen: Vandenhoeck & Ruprecht 2011), 309–331.

2. Jacque Le Goff, *The Medieval Imagination*, trans. Arthur Goldhammer (Chicago: University of Chicago Press, 1988).

3. Vincent Crapanzano, *Imaginative Horizons: An Essay in Literary-Philosophical Anthropology* (Chicago: The University of Chicago Press, 2004).

4. Richard Cohen, Ruth Hacohen, Ilana Pardes, Israel Yuval, Vered Madar, Shai Secunda, Ora Limor, Joshua Levinson, Hagar Salamon, Dani Schrire, Dina Stein, Haim Weiss and Freddie Rokem have all contributed to my thinking on this topic. This article is for my friend Richard I. Cohen, exquisite historian, inspired scholar of the Wandering Jew, and fellow traveler.

5. Galit Hasan-Rokem, "Leviticus Rabbah 16, 1—'Odysseus and the Sirens'" in the "Beit Leontis Mosaic from Beit She'an," in *Talmuda de-Eretz Israel: Archaelogy and the Rabbis in Late Antique Palestine*, ed. Steven Fine and Aaron Koller (Berlin: De Gruyter, 2014), 159–189.

6. Among the numerous post-Husserlian elaborations of the concept, the one most illuminating and edifying for my discussion has been Hans Blumenberg, *Theorie der Lebenswelt*, ed. Manfred Sommer (Berlin: Suhrkamp, 2010), in its consistent tracing of the interaction between the experiential worlds of individuals and the various expressive modes of culture, especially traditional and collective modes encompassed in Blumenberg's complex understanding of "myth."

7. The most comprehensive historical overview of the Wandering Jew materials is George K. Anderson, *The Legend of the Wandering Jew*, 3rd printing (Hanover, N.H.: University Press of New England, 1991) (originally: Providence: Brown University Press, 1965). I also thank Dr. Dominique Coulombe at the John Hay Library of Special Collections and Archives of the Brown University Library, who guided me through the "Wandering Jew Collection": https://library.brown.edu/collatoz/info.php?id=112. See also: *The Wandering Jew: Interpretations of a Christian Legend*, ed. Galit Hasan-Rokem and Alan Dundes (Bloomington: Indiana University Press, 1986); *Le juif errant: un témoin du temps,*

ed. Laurence Sigal-Klagsblad and Richard I. Cohen (Paris: Adam Biro & Musée d'art et d'histoire du Judaisme, 2001).

8. Richard I. Cohen, "The 'Wandering Jew' from Medieval Legend to Modern Metaphor," *The Art of Being Jewish in Modern Times*, ed. Barbara Kirshenblatt-Gimblett and Jonathan Karp (Philadelphia: University of Pennsylvania Press, 2008), 147–175.

9. Galit Hasan-Rokem, "L'Image du juif errant et la construction de l'identité européenne," in Sigal-Klagsblad and Cohen, 45–54.

10. David Daube, "Ahasver," *Jewish Quarterly Review* 45, no. 3 (1955): 243–244, reprinted in Hasan-Rokem and Dundes, 36–38; Galit Hasan-Rokem, "Ahasver—The Enigma of a Name," *Jewish Quarterly Review* 100, no. 4 (2010): 544–550; Alfred Bodenheimer, *Wandernde Schatten: Ahasver, Moses und die Authentizität der jüdischen Moderne* (Göttingen: Wallstein, 2002), 219–220n6.

11. A volume coedited by R. I. Cohen, R. Hacohen, G. Hasan-Rokem, and I. Pardes on "Exegetical Imagination" is in preparation.

12. Lion Feuchtwanger, *Jud Süß* (Berlin: Knaur Verlag, 1931) (Munich: Drei Masken Verlag, 1925). Here German orthography is used for the novel, Süss when the person of Joseph Süss Oppenheimer is indicated; the orthographies of various sources are kept. I quote from the 2011, 9th edition from Berlin: Aufbau-Verlag, based on Lion Feuchtwanger, *Gesammelte Werke in Einzelbänden*, Band 1 (Berlin: Aufbau-Verlag, Berlin und Weimar GmbH, 1991).

13. Mikhail Bakhtin, "Discourse in the Novel," in *The Dialogic Imagination*, ed. Michael Holquist, trans. Caryl Emerson and Michael Holquist (Austin: University of Texas Press, 1981), 259–422.

14. Main biographical source: Wilhelm von Sternburg, *Lion Feuchtwanger: Ein deutsches Schriftstellerleben* (Königstein/Ts.: Athenäum, 1984).

15. Feuchtwanger wrote an eponymous play in 1916, performed in Munich in 1917. Wilhelm Hauff published a short story about Süss Oppenheimer in 1824; see Jefferson S. Chase, "The Wandering Court Jew and the Hand of God: Wilhelm Hauff's 'Jud Süss' as Historical Fiction," *Modern Language Review* 93, no. 3 (1998): 724–740; Susanne Tegel, *Jew Süss: Life, Legend, Fiction, Film* (London: Continuum, 2011), 61–77. Hauff also published literary versions of folktales; see Gabriele von Glasenapp, "Literarische Popularisierungsprozesse eines antijüdischen Stereotyps: Wilhelm Hauff's Erzählung *Jud Süss*," in *"Jud Süss": Hofjude. literarische Figur, antisemitisches Zerrbild*, ed. Alexandra Przyrembel and Jörg Schönert (Frankfurt: Campus, 2006), 125–138, esp. 126. Some consider his short story antisemitic, while others stress the empathy that the author expressed toward the Jewish protagonist's sister, Leah, and his critique of the unfair trial of the protagonist.

16. Paul Levesque, "Mapping the Other: Lion Feuchtwanger's Topographies of the Orient," *German Quarterly* 71, no. 2 (1998): 145–165.

17. Paul Gerhard Klussmann, "Lion Feuchtwangers Roman *Jud Süss*: Gedichtete Psychologie und prophetischer Mythos des Juden," *Zeitschrift für Deutsche Philologie* 9 (1978): 87–107.

18. Selma Stern, *Jud Süss: Ein Beitrag zur deutschen und zur jüdischen Geschichte* (Munich: G. Müller, 1973) (orig. Berlin 1929).

19. Hellmut G. Haasis, *Joseph Süß Oppenheimer genannt Jud Süß: Finanzier, Freidenker, Justizopfer* (Reinbek by Hamburg: Rowohlt, 1998); Barbara Gerber, *Jud Süss: Aufstieg und Fall im frühen 18. Jahrhundert; ein Beitrag zur historischen Antisemitismus- und Rezeptions-*

forschung (Hamburg: H. Christians, 1990), esp. 17–33; Mona Körte, "Figur ohne original: *Jud Süß* und *Ewiger Jude* als Metafiguren der Geschichte bei Lion Feuchtwanger," in *Jud Süß: Hofjude, literarische Figur, antisemitisches Zerrbild*, ed. Alexandra Przyrembel and Jörg Schönert (Frankfurt am Main: Campus, 2006), 175–188, collocated the Wandering Jew figure and *Jud Süß* illuminating the use of the historical novel with Feuchtwanger's own theories with regard to the genre: Körte has also published a more comprehensive book on the Wandering Jew figure in literature: *Die Uneinholbarkeit Des Verfolgten: Der Ewige Jude in der Literarischen Phantastik* (Frankfurt am Main: Campus, 2000).

20. Levesque, 1998; cf. Galit Hasan-Rokem, "*Ex Oriente Fluxus:* The Wandering Jew— Oriental Crossings of the Paths of Europe," in *L'orient dans l'histoire religieuse de l'Europe: l'invention des origins*, ed. Mohammad Ali Amir-Moezzi and John Scheid (Turnhout, Belgium: EPHE & Brepols, 2000), 153–164. Feuchtwanger mentioned in his diary that he had wanted to write on Walther Rathenau.

21. Cf. Feuchtwanger's own life's tragedy, the early death of his only daughter Tamar, whose name was given to the daughter in the drama version (1916–1917).

22. Feuchtwanger's "Ester" remained an incomplete sketch for a novel, now published in Tanja Kinkel, *Naemi, Ester, Raquel und Ja'ala: Väter, Töchter, Machtmenschen und Judentum bei Lion Feuchtwanger* (Bonn: Bouvier, 1998), 130–182. Yosef Kaplan sets the Mordekhai and Esther tale as the prototype of "Jewish courtiership," in "Court Jews before the *Hofjuden*," in *From Court Jews to the Rothschilds*, ed. Vivian Mann and Richard I. Cohen (Munich: Prestel, 1996), 11; 24. Cf. the comparison of Süss to Haman in a German rhymed verse on the topic introduced in Richard I. Cohen and Vivian Mann, "Melding Worlds: Court Jews and the Art of Baroque," Mann and Cohen, 1996, 106.

23. The name of Esther's husband, Persian king Ahasverus, as the most popular name of the Eternal Wandering Jew figure in German narrative traditions (see above references to Daube 1955 and Hasan-Rokem 2010) seems to play no role in the novel.

24. The masquerade was possibly the insightful invention of Wilhelm Hauff. Jefferson S. Chase, "The Wandering Court Jew and the Hand of God: Wilhelm Hauff's 'Jud Süss' as Historical Fiction," *Modern Language Review* 93, no. 3 (1998): 724–740, esp. 727.

25. Elliott Horowitz, *Reckless Rites: Purim and the Legacy of Jewish Violence* (Princeton, N.J.: Princeton University Press, 2006).

26. Joshua Trachtenberg, *The Devil and the Jews: Medieval Conceptions of the Jew and Its Relation to Modern Anti-Semitism* (New Haven, Conn.: Yale University Press, 1943).

27. A prelate with that name is documented in contemporary sources: August Gottlieb Spangenberg, *The Life of Nicholas Lewis Count Zinzendorf: Bishop and Ordinary of the Church of the United, or Moravian, Brethren* (n.p.: Ulan Press, 2012) (reprint of 1923 edition; the author lived in the years 1753–1807 and wrote in German), http://books.google.com /books?id=Xmg3AAAAMAAJ&pg=PA171&lpg=PA171&dq=Prelate+Weissensee &source=bl&ots=oA9fOvSUjw&sig=Wb5NcxgvMv2eA1xWU7uN_R1KtoY&hl =en&sa=X&ei=obd7UtXGDZT9yAHJnIHYCg&ved=0CCwQ6AEwAA#v=onepage&q =Prelate%20Weissensee&f=false.

28. Jumping off the roof is a Jewish female martyrological topos, e.g., in the legend of the mother of seven martyrs, e.g., Galit Hasan-Rokem, *Web of Life: Folklore and Midrash in Rabbinic Literature* (Stanford, Calif.: Stanford University Press, 2000), 117–119.

29. Antti Aarne and Stith Thompson, *The Types of the Folktale: A Classification and Bibliography*. Folklore Fellows Communications, no. 184 (Helsinki: Academia Scientiarum Fennica, 1973), type number 922 or 922A.

30. In the Koran: Surat Yusuf, 12:23 ff. esp. verses 31–32; in the Rabbinic literature, e.g., Midrash Tanhuma: on Genesis 39:7 (Tanhuma [Warsaw] Vayeshev, 5). Cf. Joshua Levinson, "An-Other Woman: Joseph and Potiphar's Wife, Staging the Body Politic," *Jewish Quarterly Review* 87 (1997): 269–301.

31. Antti Aarne and Stith Thompson, *The Types of the Folktale: A Classification and Bibliography* (Helsinki: Academia Scientiarum Fennica, 1973), 322, no. 922A, "Achikar"; Eli Yassif, *The Hebrew Folktale: History, Genre, Meaning*, trans. Jacqueline S. Teitelbaum, (Bloomington: Indiana University Press, 1999), 63–64, 102–103, 214–215, 485n34, 506n124, and numerous versions in The Israeli Folktale Archives (IFA) at the University of Haifa.

32. Suetonius, *The Lives of the Twelve Caesars*, accessed November 7, 2013, http://www .gutenberg.org/files/6400/6400-h/6400-h.htm#link2H_4_0011; Josephus, *War* 3.399– 408. Rebecca Gray, *Prophetic Figures in Late Second Temple Jewish Palestine: The Evidence from Josephus* (Oxford: Oxford University Press, 1993), 35–38; David Edward Aune, *Prophecy in Early Christianity and the Ancient Mediterranean World* (Grand Rapids, Mich: Eerdmans, 1991, orig. 1983), 140; Robert Karl Gnuse, *Dreams and Dream Reports in the Writings of Josephus: A Traditio-Historical Analysis* (Leiden: Brill, 1996), 136–142. With gratitude to Daniel R. Schwartz.

33. The story became the foundation legend for the institutionalization of Rabbinic culture and authority. Many treatments are referred to in Hasan-Rokem 2000, 171–189 and listed in detail in note 74, 242–245. See also Daniel Boyarin, "Tricksters, Martyrs, and Collaborators: Diaspora and the Gendered Politics of Resistance," in Jonathan Boyarin and Daniel Boyarin, *Powers of Diaspora: Two Essays on the Relevance of Jewish Culture* (Minneapolis: University of Minnesota Press, 2002), 37–102, discussion of Yavneh on 46–54.

34. *Der jüdische Krieg* (The Jewish War) (Amsterdam: Querido, 1937) (orig. Berlin: Propyläen-Verlag, 1932). 190, 193, 219, 221, 227–234, 251–253; in the English translation titled *Josephus*, trans. Willa and Edwin Muir (New York: The Viking Press, 1932), 236, 246–250, 270, 274, 278. The other two volumes: *Die Söhne* (The Jew of Rome) (Amsterdam: Querido, 1935); *Der Tag wird kommen* (The Day Will Come, Josephus and the Emperor) (Stockholm: Bermann-Fischer, 1945).

35. Feuchtwanger, *Jud Süß* 2011, 524; Feuchtwanger, *Jud Süß* 1926, 414.

36. On the complex entanglements between the archetype of the forever young male ("Peter Pan") and the archetype of the great mother, see e.g., Marie-Louise von Franz, *The Problem of the Puer Aeternus*, 3rd edition (Toronto: Inner City Books, 2000).

37. Jacques Lacan, *Écrits—a selection*, trans. Alan Sheridan (London: Tavistock Publications, 1977), 1–7.

38. Jane Gallop, "Lacan's 'Mirror Stage': Where to Begin," *SubStance* 11/12, nos. 37–38: A Special Issue from the Center for Twentieth Century Studies (1982/1983): 121, 123–124 [118–128].

39. Hasan-Rokem, "L'Image du juif errant," 45–54.

40. On the cultural-critical potentials of the term *Lebenswelt*, see Blumenberg, 38.

41. Gérard Genette's "intra-diegetic narration"; see Remigius Bunia, "Diegesis and Representation: Beyond the Fictional World, on the Margins of Story and Narrative," *Poetics Today* 31, no. 4 (2010): 679–720, esp. 681.

42. In this I differ from Tegel, *Jew Süss*, dividing her sources into "The Legend" (chapter 4) and "The Historians" (chapter 7).

43. Lion Feuchtwanger, *Power* [Jud Süß], trans. Willa and Edwin Muir (New York: The Viking Press, 1926), 25–26; Feuchtwanger, *Jud Süß* 2011, 32–33. The change of the title merits a separate discussion. The passage is quoted verbatim in Anderson, 368–369; see note 60 below.

44. Manfred Zimmermann, *Josef Süss Oppenheimer, ein Finanzmann des 18. Jahrhunderts. Ein Stück Absolutismus- und Jesuitengeschichte*. Nach den Vertheidigungs-Akten und den Schriften der Zeitgenossens bearbeitet von M.Z. (Stuttgart: Riegersche Verlagsbuchhandlung, 1874), 99. The translation from the German is mine. Zimmermann does not mention his sources specifically.

45. Tuvia Singer, "Navadut u-moderniut: ha-siaḥ ha-antishemi 'al dmut ha-yehudi ha-noded be-mifneh ha-me'ot ha-tsh'a-'esreh ve-ha-'esrim be-Germaniah u-ve-'Ostriah [Nomadism and Modernity: The Antisemitic discourse on the Wandering Jew in the turn of the nineteenth–twentieth century in Germany and Austria]" (MA thesis, Hebrew University of Jerusalem, 2013).

46. Leonhard Neubaur, *Die Sage vom ewigen Juden* (Leipzig: Hinrichs, 1884), https://archive.org/details/diesagevomewige02neubgoog, reprinted with his *Neue Mitteilungen über die Sage vom ewigen Juden* (Leipzig: Hinrichs, 1893); idem, "Bibliographie der Sage vom ewigen Juden," *Centralblatt für Bibliothekswesen* X, 1895, 249–67, 297–316; idem, "Zur Geschichte der Sage vom ewigen Juden," *Zeitschrift für Bücherfreunde* 5, 1914, 211–223.

47. Blumenberg, 55.

48. Anderson, 174–211; Galit Hasan-Rokem, "The Jewish Tradition of the Wandering Jew: The Poetics of Long Duration" (in press).

49. Anderson, 169–177, 190–200, 213–227, 239–242, 245–266, 266–284, 293–310, 318–328, 334–340, 345–352, 355–358, 366–369, 372–374, 377–380; see also *Ahasvers Spur: Dichtungen und Dokumente vom "ewigen Juden,"* ed. Mona Körte and Robert Stockhammer (Leipzig: Reclam, 1995); Mona Körte, *Die Uneinholbarkeit des Verfolgten: der ewige Jude in der literarischen Phantastik* (Frankfurt am Main: Campus, 2000).

50. Chase, 728; Glasenapp, esp. 131. The bibliographies published on them also parallel chronologically Neubaur's publications mentioned above, Tegel, 231n 43. Richard I. Cohen and Vivian Mann emphasize the "sensationalism per se," characterizing the visual representations in the chapbooks, "Melding Worlds: Court Jews and the Art of Baroque," Mann and Cohen, 1996, 109.

51. E.g., *Rumor Mills: The Social Impact of Rumor and Legend*, ed. Gary Allan Fine, Veronique Campion-Vincent, and Chip Heath (New Brunswick N.J.: Aldine Transaction, 2005).

52. Wulf Köpke, *Lion Feuchtwanger* (Munich: Beck & Verlag, edition Text u. Kritik 1983), 16; Heinrich Heine, "Der Rabbi von Bacherach. Ein Fragment," *Sämtliche Schriften* Bd 1, 459–501.

53. Heinrich Heine, "Aus den Memoiren des Herren von Schnabelewopski," *Sämtliche Schrifte*, vol. 1, 504–556, esp. 528–532, on page 529 the famous coinage "den ewigen Juden des Ozeans." I thank Na'ama Rokem.

54. E.g., Ruth Hacohen, *The Music Libel against the Jews* (New Haven, Conn.: Yale University Press, 2011), 243–251; see also Singer, "Navadut u-moderniut."

55. Na'ama Rokem, *Prosaic Conditions: Heinrich Heine and the Spaces of Zionist Literature* (Evanston, Ill.: Northwestern University Press, 2013), mentions, on p. 54, a poem by Richard Dehmel (1867–1920) and on p. 55 H. N. Bialik's essay based on his speech at the Second Conference for Hebrew Language and Culture, convened in Vienna in conjunction with the Eleventh Zionist Congress in 1913, where incidentally a postcard featuring

the Wandering Jew painting by Fabian was officially distributed; see Hasan-Rokem, "Contemporary Perspectives on Tradition," 322. Anderson, p. 295, briefly mentions the Dehmel poem but not Heine's own reference to the figure.

56. Karl Blind, "Wodan, the Wild Huntsman, and the Wandering Jew," Hasan-Rokem and Dundes, 169–189, reprinted from *Gentleman's Magazine* 2449 (1880): 32–48.

57. Also confirmed by Cohen, "'The Wandering Jew' from Medieval Legend to Modern Metaphor," 2008, 409n38; see, however, James Martin Harding, *Adorno and "A Writing on the Ruins": Essays on Modern Aesthetics and Anglo-American Literature and Culture* (Albany: State University of New York Press, 1997), 142 and 177n41.

58. Hyam Maccoby, *The Sacred Executioner: Human Sacrifice and the Legacy of Guilt* (London: Thames and Hudson, 1983); idem, "The Wandering Jew as Sacred Executioner," Hasan-Rokem and Dundes, 236–260, esp. 241–243; Ruth Mellinkoff, *The Mark of Cain* (Berkeley: University of California Press, 1981).

59. Jerome, *On Psalms*, Homily 35; Augustine, *Contra Faustum*, Book XII (preceded also by Ambrose *De Cain et Abel* 2.9.34–37); Paula Fredriksen, *Augustine and the Jews: A Christian Defense of Jews and Judaism* (New York: Doubleday, 2008), 320–324.

60. Although Anderson's short mention of the novel is strangely included in a paragraph titled "Folk-Tale Variants," 1965, 368.

61. E.g., F[riedrich] S[ally] Grosshut, "Lion Feuchtwanger and the Historical Novel," *Books Abroad* 34, no. 1 (1960), esp. 9 [9–12].

62. Gershom Scholem, *The Messianic Idea in Judaism and Other Essays on Jewish Spirituality* (New York: Schocken, 1971), "Redemption through Sin" [78–141], gives some insight into the social context, esp. 82; 93; 114–115; 135 and in other essays in the volume; idem, *Indices to the Emden-Eybeschuetz Controversy Literature*, introduction by Yehuda Liebes (Jerusalem: Magnes, 2006) (Hebrew); the topic exceeds the scope of the article as well as my expertise.

63. Scholem's critics' resistance has not changed this picture, e.g., Barukh Kurzweil, *Sifrutenu ha-hadashah—hemshekh o mahapekha* [Our Modern Literature—Continuity or Revolution] (Tel Aviv: Schocken, 1959), 80–96. Among the numerous discussions on the persistence of such belief, see Paweł Maciejko, *The Mixed Multitude: Jacob Frank and the Frankist Movement, 1755–1816* (Philadelphia: University of Pennsylvania Press, 2011), 6–12; Maoz Kahana, "The Allure of Forbidden Knowledge: The Temptation of Sabbatean Literature for Mainstream Rabbis in the Frankist Moment, 1756–1761," *Jewish Quarterly Review* 102, no. 4 (2012): 589–616.

64. Apparently what most infuriated Emden was Eybeschütz's use of the Magen David in amulets, interpreted as a messianic symbol: Scholem, in *The Messianic Idea in Judaism*, "The Star of David," 257–281, esp. 266–267, 272–273.

65. In Scholem, *The Messianic Idea in Judaism*, "Toward an Understanding of the Messianic Idea," 1–36, esp. 16, the author emphasizes the Jewish–Christian coproduction of messianic ideas. Historian Simon Dubnow (1860–1941) brilliantly pointed out what he called the Wandering Jew legend's strange historical connection to Sabbatean messianic expectations (record in Y. T. Lewinsky's Wandering Jew archives at the Folklore Research Center of the Hebrew University of Jerusalem). This association also inspired Jakob Wasserman, whose *Shabtai Zevi* (The first part of *The Jews of Zirndorf*, 1897) may have influenced Feuchtwanger (apparently unaware of their families' common roots in Fürth). In Gerber, 82 an anonymous satirical text in the popular chapbook genre of "Discourses after Death," stages a meeting between Sabbatai Sevi (Zwi) [her orthography] and Süss in the world hereafter, comparing their fates.

66. Paul Mendes-Flohr, "The Study of the Jewish Intellectual: Some Methodological Proposals," in F. Malino and R. Albert-Cohen, *Essays in Modern Jewish History* (Rutherford, N.J.: Fairleigh Dickinson University Press; London: Associated University Presses,1982), 152, quoting Georg Simmel.

67. Dina Stein, *Textual Mirrors: Reflexivity, Midrash and the Rabbinic Self* (Philadelphia: University of Pennsylvania Press, 2012), 75n72, 162n94, 238, on the ancient roots of the theme.

68. *Jud Süß*, directed by Veit Harlan. The Deluxe Restored Version, Chicago: International Historic Films 2008, essay by David Culbert. Ruth Hacohen, *The Music Libel against the Jews*, 341 analyzes the manipulation of the musical score for ideological purposes; on 481n1 an account of our common experience watching the film, and *Der ewige Jude* described below, at the Bundesarchiv on Ferbelliner Platz in Berlin, tightly guarded since in Germany the distribution of both films is prohibited by law.

69. David Culbert's essay appended to the film. Josef Škvorecký at http://www .filmreference.com/Films-Jo-Ko/Jud-S-ss.html claims that Marian had been married to a Jew and rescued his second wife's ex-husband by hiding him in his home.

70. Also cast as Jack the Ripper; cf. Siefried Kracauer, *From Caligari to Hitler: A Psychological History of the German Film*. Revised and expanded edition, edited by Leonardo Quaresima (Princeton, N.J.: Princeton University Press, 2004 [1947]), 69; 85; and as Pontius Pilatus in the film *I.N.R.I* (1923), ibid., 109; and as a brutal butcher in "Die Freudlose Gasse" (1925), ibid., 168.

71. Gabriel's role in the film is much less impressive than in Feuchtwanger's novel, and Oppenheimer's daughter Naemi is totally absent from the film.

72. Cf. Bodenheimer's focus on the metaphor of "shadows" for Jewish German existence; on suppression of the Wandering Jew, see Galit Hasan-Rokem, "Carl Schmitt and Ahasver: The Idea of the State and the Wandering Jew," *Behemoth, a Journal on Civilization* 2 (2008): 4–25, http://ojs.ub.uni-freiburg.de/behemoth/article/view/737.

73. *Der ewige Jude: ein Dokumentarfilm über das Weltjudentum*, Gestaltung: Fritz Hippler. "The Eternal Jew," English translation of the original German narration. A&M Productions 2004.

74. Georg Simmel, "Bridge and Door," *Simmel on Culture*, ed. David Frisby and Mike Firestone (London: Sage Publications, 1997), 170–174.

75. M[ikhail] M. Bakhtin, *Speech Genres and Other Late Essays*, ed. Carol Emerson and Michael Holquist, trans. Vern W. McGee (Austin: University of Texas Press, 1986), 52–53.

76. An extensive discussion of this transformation is in my Hebrew article on the Wandering Jew in Feuchtwanger's *Jud Süß* (in press).

8

Exclusion and Inclusion

Ethnography of War in *Kriegsgefangene* (1916) and *Das ostjüdische Antlitz* (1920)

EVA EDELMANN-OHLER

World War I can be considered "*the* great seminal catastrophe"[1] of the twentieth century in Europe, having unsettled politics, culture, media, and social life.[2] These extensive changes in the wake of the war also had consequences for the relationship between "Eastern" and "Western" Jews, consequences that were, in a broader sense, part of the so-called "Rediscovery of the Eastern Jews."[3] As Steven Aschheim has pointed out, there was a long history of contact between "East" and "West" in the period from 1800 to 1923, divisible into several stages.[4] The idea of the "Eastern Jew" arose in the first half of the nineteenth century; the concept had diverse manifestations over the course of time and varied at the beginning of the twentieth century across, for instance, Zionism and Liberal Judaism. Furthermore, before World War I, Martin Buber acknowledged Eastern cultural and literary traditions in a positive light, taking them as an example for an ideal Jewish community.[5] This rather cultural and philosophical approach was totally different from the questions about "Eastern Jews" that arose after the outbreak of World War I. During the war, "Eastern Jews" became for many soldiers a subject of personal experience—or as Aschheim has described it, a "strange encounter."[6] "Western Jews" found their prejudices confirmed: "the Ostjude was no figment of the overheated anti-Semitic imagination but a stark reality."[7] At that time, cultural differences became visible and had to be faced. The press and other media addressed these cultural differences in numerous

181

articles, using various metaphors for the "brothers" in the East and for related political issues.[8] Thus the question of Eastern European Jewry turned from a cultural issue into a political one. In this process, the spaces of one's own and the alien were interchanged:

> Instead of the ghetto coming to Germany, Germany came to the ghetto
> ... German Jews were forced to confront the problem. Their responses
> to the challenge not only mirrored their changing feelings and attitudes
> towards the Ostjuden but also provided a sensitive measure of their own
> self-conceptions.[9]

The encounter with the "brothers in the East" also caused changes in concepts of Jewish identity and affiliation. The fact that Jews fought in this war in every European army accentuated the transnational and diasporic condition of the category *Jew* and was therefore related to a number of problematic "confrontations." On the one hand, Jews were forced to fight against each other despite their common religious system and shared cultural practices and identities, just because they were members of opposing armies. More generally speaking, war nationalizes identities by declaring them essential for warfare, therefore causing a conflict between the diasporic Jewish identity and the nationalized identities of war. On the other hand, the war also had internal Jewish consequences, because it unsettled the relations and distinctions between "East" and "West" through personal experience—diversifying these categories and making it necessary to revalue self-conceptions.

The two books discussed here—Felix von Luschan's and Hermann Struck's *Kriegsgefangene* (Prisoners of War, 1916) and Arnold Zweig's and Hermann Struck's *Das ostjüdische Antlitz* (The Face of East European Jewry, 1920)—are two examples marking this changing relationship between "Eastern" and "Western Jews," and they furthermore echo the different ethnographic experiences of their authors. *Kriegsgefangene* was the product of a collaboration between the anthropologist Felix von Luschan and the German Jewish artist Hermann Struck. The project was based on the suggestion of Graf von Oppersdorff, a member of the German Reichstag who asked Struck for lithographs for a book project. At the beginning of World War I Struck went voluntarily to war,[10] and in 1915 he was deployed on the eastern front in the territory of "Ober-Ost," which covered parts of Lithuania, Latvia, Estonia, Belarus, Poland, and Courland, all formerly regions of the Russian Empire.[11] During his military service, Struck became an expert on Jewish affairs; by 1917 he was commandant of the Dezernat für jüdische Angelegenheiten Ober-Ost (Department for Jewish Affairs)[12] and used this post to address the problems of the poor Jews there.[13] In addition to his military service, he engaged in documenting war, especially its Jewish dimension, in various drawings and lithographs that were later published in books such as *In Russisch-Polen* (In Russo-Poland, 1915),[14] *Skizzen aus Litauen, Weissrussland und Kurland* (Sketches from Lithuania, Belarus and Courland, 1916),[15] and *Das ostjüdische Antlitz*. His partner in this project, Felix von Luschan, was one of the central figures in Germanophone anthropology during the war, especially given his role in the Royal Prussian Phonographic Commission, which contained a section for physical anthropology, which he chaired.[16] This section used POW camps to conduct "racial studies" of Prussia's enemies and, in a broader sense, to "link anthropological science to the war effort."[17] Besides his position as a researcher of war anthropology, von Luschan was famous for his "studies in race," especially of Jews as a "race,"[18] and for his book *Völker, Rassen, Sprachen* (Peoples, Races, Languages, 1922), in which he pleaded for a more descriptive definition of race and argued against the devalorization of special races.[19]

The second book discussed here, *Das ostjüdische Antlitz*,[20] originated from a cooperative effort between Struck and Arnold Zweig. After time spent on the western front in Verdun, Arnold Zweig—the German Jewish writer and Kleist Prize winner—was redeployed to the eastern front. Also stationed in "Ober-Ost," he was a member of the press department, writing articles for many war journals and also working as a censor of books and articles. In "Ober-Ost" he met Struck and many other German intellectuals, including Richard Dehmel, Herbert Eulenberg, Magnus Zeller, and Sammy Gronemann,[21] all in the "Club of Former Intellectuals,"[22] a group of artists and writers deployed at the Eastern front who met every Monday to discuss literary and philosophic topics. There at the Eastern front, Zweig also had the chance to fulfill his "tremendously intense wish to see Eastern Jews personally."[23] At that time, he also intensified his correspondence about Jewish topics with Martin Buber. During the development of Zweig's increasing interest in Jewish questions, Struck's art played an important role in amplifying his understanding of "Eastern Jews" and related political questions, as witnessed by an article from 1918 on "Struck's Eastern Jews" about a collection of drawings[24] from Struck which was printed at the publishing house "Ober-Ost," Zweig wrote:

> The most beautiful feature and the specific political aspect of Struck's portfolio is this: in the struggle for the destiny of this people . . . it is possible to stand up—relentlessly and with scorn—to those who roll the dice for this destiny without knowing how precious the effort is to us. Look here! these faces shout; Look! they urge. The language of the artist is his art; the politics of the artist are the convictions of his form—they are the intensity of his creation and its language.[25]

According to this context, we can see that the ethnographic experience of the authors and the purpose of the books are strongly linked to war experience and to the participation of their authors in war as artists, writers, and scientists. The fact that war intensified contact between "Eastern" and "Western" Jews, especially at the eastern front in "Ober-Ost," entails also the need to write and bear testimony about the conditions of war, and especially about the "Eastern Jews" there. The two books therefore not only mirror new, developing relations between "East" and "West," but can also show basic mechanisms of Jewish ethnographic writing by presenting its function in detail. The function of a Jewish ethnography of World War I is thus to reevaluate the transformation of Jewish identity by scrutinizing the changing relation between "East" and "West" that could be witnessed at the eastern front. This approach to ethnography is based on the structure of ethnographic writing: according to research on the literary form of ethnography, the compound "ethno-graphic" refers to a process of understanding in which the ethnographer is confronted with the alien, which leads to an act of writing, because the ethnographic situation itself calls for an eyewitness who documents his objects.[26] Through this documentary process of frequently approaching the Other, "the writing I" and the "object" strike up a circulating relationship: writing about the Other is at the same time always also writing about oneself. Or, with appeal to Claude Levi-Strauss's well-known formulation: "Rousseau . . . anticipates the famous formula 'I is another.' Ethnographic experience

must establish this formula before proceeding to its demonstration: that
the other is an I."[27] This basic procedure of ethnographic writing cor-
relates with the situation that Struck and Zweig had to face when they
were on the eastern front and wanted to speak as Jews about the Jews
they met there. Thus, this writing about the Other as an "I" had its own
wartime peculiarity. Jewish ethnography during World War I had to face
two problems simultaneously: externally, there was a need to fix and to
nationalize Jewish identity so as to submit to the order of war; internally,
the unsettled relationship between "East" and "West" had to be reinvented
and consolidated. This external and internal process of both changing and
reinforcing one's own identity had two stages, which can be studied in
the two above-mentioned publications on the basis of the two operations
"exclusion" and "inclusion."

EXCLUSION—ETHNOGRAPHY OF WAR AND
THE NATIONALIZING OF IDENTITY

The book *Kriegsgefangene* was intended as a "Contribution to Ethnogra-
phy/Ethnology during World War I,"[28] as its subtitle indicates. It contains
one hundred lithographs of prisoners of war by Struck, prefaced with an
illustrated text by von Luschan titled "Introduction to Anthropology." According to this, the intention of the book is not merely to present a visual
and aesthetic archive of prisoners of war, but also to evoke a scientific,
anthropological perspective, contributing to a more objective treatment
of the topic. In the introduction, von Luschan emphasizes the exceptional
quality of Struck's lithographs and commends their documentary function for the study of anthropological matters. He also draws a distinction
between anthropology and art, when he declares that the POW camps
are crucial sites for research on the "anthropology of race" and stresses, at
the same time, the scientific relevance of Struck's lithographs. It becomes
evident that von Luschan considers the lithographs as scientific data with
an objective value.[29] For the same reason, he even illustrates his introduction with photographs of several "racial types."

These illustrations correspond to his introduction's scientific contents:
he wants to settle the question of whether all people descend from a single
human "race." This leads him to a thoroughly ethnographic question:

maus zurückschlägt. Ebenso ist es längst bekannt, daß Kreuzung zwischen zwei extrem weit von einander gezüchteten Taubenvarietäten bei einem Teil der Nachkommen wieder zur alten Stammform, zur gewöhnlichen grauen Wildtaube zurückführt.

So sind wir also nicht in Verlegenheit, auch bei strengem Festhalten an einer durchaus einheitlichen Abstammung der Menschheit das Auftreten verschiedener Haar- und Schädelformen zu erklären.

Für sehr viele andere Eigenschaften genügt die Annahme von Wanderungen in eine neue, völlig anders geartete

33./34. Ainu von der Insel Jesso. Die Ainu bilden eine ältere Schichte der Bevölkerung von Japan und sind sowohl von der malaiis-mongolischen Hauptmasse der heutigen Japaner als von ihrer koreanisch-manschurischen Oberschicht somatisch, wie in ihrer geistigen und materiellen Kultur durchaus verschieden; auch sind sie durch besonderen Haarreichtum ausgezeichnet, so daß sie sich beim Essen eines flachen Stäbchens bedienen, um den Bart der Oberlippe hochzuhalten.

35./36. Turkmene, mit ganz besonders schlichtem Bartbaar, vielleicht als Zeige ostasiatischer Blutmischung.

Umwelt. So pflegt man z. B. das Auftreten eines blonden Typus meist dadurch zu erklären, daß die ursprünglich sicher brünetten Ahnen der Blonden sich lange Zeiträume hindurch in sonnenarmen und nebelreichen Gegenden aufgehalten hätten, in denen sie einen großen Teil ihres Pigments verlieren konnten, ohne dadurch irgendwie geschädigt zu sein. Dabei bleibt freilich die Frage noch offen, ob jenes Blondwerden sich nur einmal und an einer Stelle vollzogen hat, oder ob zu verschiedenen Zeiten und an verschiedenen Orten brünette Menschen blond geworden sind. An sich ist es natürlich nicht ausgeschlossen, daß wirkliche Blondheit auch unabhängig von der Umwelt durch bloße zufällige Mutation entstehen konnte, und dann müßten wir uns wohl mit dem Gedanken vertraut machen, daß blonde Menschen auch im sonnenreichen Süden entstehen konnten. Diese Frage, die sicher gerade für uns Europäer von, ich möchte sagen persönlichem, Interesse ist, wird akut, wenn wir hören, wie ein nicht geringer Teil der berberischen Bevölkerung von Nordwestafrika blond ist. Nun ist die ganze Nordküste

FIGURE 8.1

Kriegsgefangene. Hundert Steinzeichnungen von Hermann Struck. Mit Begleitworten von Prof. Dr. F. von Luschan. Ein Beitrag zur Völkerkunde im Weltkriege. Mit Genehmigung des königlichen Kriegsministeriums herausgegeben. (Prisoners of War. One Hundred Lithographs by Hermann Struck. Preface by Felix von Luschan. A Contribution to Ethnography/ Ethnology during World War I. Edited with Permit of the Royal Ministry of War.) Berlin: Reimer, 1916, page 17.

what caused the phenotypic difference between the ethnic groups? Are these differences characteristics of "race," or are they influenced by external criteria like climate? It is remarkable that he declares the importance of climate and mutation as the main causes for the visible differences between people of various ethnicities.[30] With this approach he differs partly from other research of his time, which aimed at explaining the differences of the "races" on the assumption of three "archimorph races."[31] Von Luschan mentions, among others, Joseph Arthur de Gobineau—who argued for the superiority of the "Aryan race"—and declares these theorems unscientific.[32] Thus, the central theme of von Luschan's introduction is the influence of the environment and mutation on the visual differences of men.

Apart from the anthropological nature of this key assumption, the form through which the anthropological information is provided is also important for the reconstruction of the ethnographic purpose of the book. As stated, von Luschan illustrates his introduction with anthropological photographs. These photographs, showing both frontal and profile views of their subjects, are on the one hand printed to illustrate the general difference of men and, on the other hand, to manifest again the scientific claim of the publication. The photographs follow the iconography of anthropological illustrations, as adopted from the mug-shot images used in police investigations.[33] The twofold depiction is meant to guarantee a highly scientific character by capturing all characteristics relevant in physiognomy.[34]

Furthermore, it is remarkable that von Luschan chose no photographs of prisoners of war for the introduction. In a publication on that topic from 1916, one would not expect the majority of photographs to be anthropological and unrelated to war. This suggests that the underlying function of these photographs is—beside the evocation of the aforementioned scientific context—to establish a reference to an objective form of anthropology and its methods.[35] By referring to the stereotypical form of "anthropological representation," the introduction provides a scientific background or context and reveals how the following lithographs of Struck should be read. Struck, too, portrays some of the prisoners of war twice, once in frontal and once in profile view.

FIGURE 8.2

Smolin, Russe, 30 Jahre, Offizierstellvertreter, aus
Nischmy=Nowgorod [*sic*]. (Smolin, Russian, 30 years, Officer
Deputy from Nizhnii Novgorod.) *Kriegsgefangene,* ill. 14 and 15.

FIGURE 8.3

Smolin, Russe, 30 Jahre, Offizierstellvertreter, aus
Nischmy=Nowgorod [*sic*]. (Smolin, Russian, 30 years, Officer
Deputy from Nizhnii Novgorod.) *Kriegsgefangene,* ill. 14 and 15.

The anthropological iconography is supplemented by cultural and military characteristics. Most of Struck's prisoners of war wear a specific headdress or uniform that identifies them as members of a certain ethnic group or army.

We can read this as a nationalization of anthropological information, which is also confirmed by the captions. These captions nearly always mention the nationality or origin of the depicted prisoner: "William Bimstead, Engländer, P.O. (1st Class) Petty Officer, Feldwebel, Coast Guard, East Cowes, I.O.W. Marinesoldat, 46 Jahre" (William Bimstead, Englishman, P.O. [1st Class] Petty Officer, Sergeant, Coast-Guard, East Cowes, I.C.W. Marine, 46 years old) or "Jagor Sgurski, aus Minsk-Gouvernment, 41 Jahre, Landarbeiter, 170. Infant.-Regt" (Jagor Sgurski, from Minsk-Government, 41 years old, agricultural worker, 170th infantry regiment). This general perspective, which is a result of intermediality as well as a phenomenon of contextualization, allows for further considerations about the purpose of the book as well as about the function of ethnography in times of war. If we compare the ethnographic perspective of the book to similar publications such as *Die Gegner Deutschlands im Weltkriege* (The Opponents of Germany in Word War I, published in 1925),[36] which employs a similar iconography, we have to consider the function of the uniform. Obviously, the uniform is a sign of affiliation, a characteristic of nationality, and also—as attested by the additional texts of this book—a sign of hostile and violent behavior. Furthermore, this collection of different combatants gathers together information that might be useful in forthcoming times of war. It also functions as a visual archive of potential enemies.

The photographs in von Luschan's introduction differ from this perspective, but not the lithographs by Struck that follow them. While the photographs show mostly neutral clothing, Struck's lithographs show mostly uniforms (cf. figure 8.1, 8.4, 8.5). This combination of anthropological information and bellicose signification is surely not unintended. We can understand the depiction of uniforms in this ethnographic context as a wartime strategy of cultural exclusion. The prisoners are marked as enemies; the captions confirm this by mentioning their nationality. What Stuart Hall has written about "stereotyping as a signifying practice"

FIGURE 8.4

William Bimstead, Engländer, P.O. (1st Class) Petty Officer, Feldwebel, Coast Guard, East Cowes, I.C.W. Marinesoldat, 46 Jahre. (William Bimstead, Englishman, P.O. [1st Class] Petty Officer, Sergeant, Coast-Guard, East Cowes, I.O.W. Marine, 46 years old.) *Kriegsgefangene,* ill. 1.

FIGURE 8.5

Jagor Sgurski, aus Minsk-Gouvernment, 41 Jahre, Landarbeiter, 170.
Infant.-Regt. (Jagor Sgurski, from Minsk-Government, 41 years old,
agricultural worker, 170th infantry regiment.) *Kriegsgefangene,* ill. 11.

strengthens this hypothesis: the depiction of the prisoners as enemies is a result of a cultural signifying practice that demarcates between the Self and the Other, between one's own people and the enemy. For that reason, Struck, who as a German soldier witnesses the prisoners in the POW camps, depicts uniforms, and declares their wearers members of a certain army. In this cultural empowerment process, the characteristics of the enemy are "reduced, essentialized, naturalized, and difference is fixed."[37] Against the background of ubiquitous war propaganda, which contributes to the fact that every contemporary reader of Struck and von Luschan would recognize the enemy uniforms as such, it becomes clear that the intended purpose of the lithographs is also to stabilize a particular symbolic order.[38] This perspective is supported by the recourse to "anthropology of race" made by orienting the introduction around its pictures. The superimposition of war iconography and "anthropology of race" in the lithographs naturalizes this symbolically fixed order. And reference to scientific data also identifies it as a natural order that manifests itself as visible difference. Therefore, the aesthetics of anthropology produces difference and the exclusion of wartime enemies.

In this particular context we have to consider the illustrations of "Eastern Jews" (figures 8.6, 8.7, 8.8), and therefore Struck's ethnographic objective, from a Jewish perspective. While the military perspective stresses his approach as a soldier, the Jewish perspective has a twofold base. Researchers such as Margret Olin have mentioned that Struck's depictions of Jews in this publication are less stereotypes of "Eastern Jews" than "*military* images"[39] that "disrupt Jewish stereotypes."[40] I, however, argue that we can find in Struck's and von Luschan's book a twofold exclusion process that corresponds to the perception of "Eastern Jews" as described by Aschheim, and which can also be found in the war press between 1914 and 1918. Aschheim, for example, has written about the above-mentioned "strange encounter" of "East" and "West":

> The war placed German Jews directly in the middle: they were poised
> between the Jews of the Eastern ghettoes and the German authorities
> (ranging from the soldier at the Front to the civil administration and the
> political policy makers in Berlin). As patriots they had to confront the
> Ostjuden within a German political perspective; as Jews they had to act

FIGURE 8.6

Chajus Krasikow, Jude aus Lubin, Gouv. Poltawa, 22 Jahre, Buchhalter, 39.
Sibirisches Regt. (Chajus Krasikow, Jew from Lubin, government of Poltawa,
22 years old, accountant, 39th Siberian regiment.) *Kriegsgefangene,* ill. 33.

FIGURE 8.7

Bomblatt, David, Polnischer Jude aus Warschau, Tempelbeamter. (Bomblatt, Polish Jew from Warsaw, temple official.) *Kriegsgefangene,* ill. 35.

FIGURE 8.8

Isaak Chotoran, Jude aus Kiewer Gouv., 38 Jahre Vorbeter, 79. Artill.-
Regt (Isaak Chotoran, Jew from government of Kiev, 38 years old,
prayer leader, 79th artillery regiment.) *Kriegsgefangene*, ill. 34.

as champions and mediators of the Ostjuden in their encounters with the German authorities.[41]

This twofold political requirement of being a patriot and at the same time being stirred by the Jewish dimension of the *Ostjudenfrage* is also the signature of "Eastern Jews" as represented in Struck's lithographs, and it can be considered his ethnographic objective. The wartime iconography depicts them as enemies, while at the same time the captions declare them to be fellow Jews. The lithographs hence are not only depictions of prisoners but, in a general sense, figurations of the destiny of Judaism in times of war.

This ambivalence embodies exactly the ethnographic writing process as it is described above: the exclusion at work in von Luschan's and Struck's *Kriegsgefangene* is nothing other than a cultural strategy for facing the problem of Jewish national affiliation in times of war. By exposing both characteristics of "Eastern Jews," Struck also reveals the underlying paradox of the Ostjudenfrage: firstly, that the Other is an "I," and secondly, that this "I" is at the same time an enemy. Struck's lithographs show visually what his contemporaries put into words. His student Joseph Budko[42] declared in an article in the *Jüdische Rundschau* (Jewish Panorama) that *Kriegsgefangene* provides useful information about the enemies "that fought in this war against Germany."[43] Furthermore, he mentioned the Jewish dimension of the book:

> Here you can see not only the artist but also the Jew Struck; it is no coincidence that the master shows exactly these three in his work. The young Jew from Lublin tells us with his great, bright, and at the same time deeply melancholic eyes about the grief of a people; the prayer leader Isaak Chtoran [sic] tells us how much he yearns for his prayer desk in his faraway synagogue, and the temple official from Warsaw shows us that even in captivity he doesn't leave his Talmud.[44]

In summary, it can be stated that Struck's lithographs are not the product of an intentional cultural exclusion process, but they show to a greater degree the Janus-faced conditions of war. Struck reveals that World War I for Jewry can only be understood as an exclusion, as a fragmentation process, in which the "I" transforms as well as the Other. By using lithographs and by adopting the means of scientific anthropology, *Kriegsgefangene* manifests objectively the changing relationship between "East" and "West" and culminates in a hybrid exclusion process, one that establishes the borders between the Self and the Other and simultaneously queries these borders and attributions.

BLURRED DISTINCTIONS—INCLUSION OF "THE OTHER"

Arnold Zweig's and Hermann Struck's *Das ostjüdische Antlitz* takes a completely different approach to "Eastern Jews," one more poetically and aesthetically motivated. While *Kriegsgefangene* reduces the images of "Eastern Jews" to a few lithographs, *Das ostjüdische Antlitz* contains fifty-two drawings of "Eastern Jews" by Struck and a framing essay by Arnold Zweig. Zweig's and Struck's book discusses the realities of life for the "brothers in the East," while the text of *Kriegsgefangene* focuses on the more scientific issues of descent and anthropology. *Das ostjüdische Antlitz* pursues another objective: "This book speaks about the Eastern Jews as somebody who is seeking truly to see them"[45] (*Dieses Buch spricht über die Ostjuden als jemand, der sie zu sehen versuchte*).[46] In this astonishing formulation, the personification of the book as a speaker who tried to look truthfully at Eastern Jews reveals the perspective on the subject. The aim is not a *representation of* "Eastern Jews" but rather real appreciation. It is an attempt to explain the strange outward appearance of "Eastern Jews" not as an effect of anthropology or "race" but rather as a result of the history of the Jewish diaspora. The ethnographic interest of *Das ostjüdische Antlitz* lies in capturing the essence of the "Eastern Jew."

Both Zweig's admittedly emotive style and his line of argumentation are characteristic of his way of thinking as well as of his ethnographic writing. He starts his remarks by evoking a "look into the face" of the "Eastern Jew" and then describing what he sees:

> He turns his eye away from me and into the distance, a distance that is nothing but time. His profile leads like a waterfall into his beard, which dissolves into spray and clouds. The nobility of his posture and his nose, the spirituality of his pensive and furrowed brow, contrast the hard, defiant ear and meet in his gaze, a gaze that neither demands nor renounces,

FIGURE 8.9

Arnold Zweig. *Das Ostjüdische Antlitz. Zu fünfzig Steinzeichnungen von Hermann Struck.* (The Face of East European Jewry. With reference to fifty lithographs of Hermann Struck.) Berlin: Welt-Verlag, 1920, without page reference.

neither longs for nor laments what it is. And his gaze draws upon itself a distance about which we know that it is nothing but time.[47]

It becomes evident that this "textual profile view" differs in many aspects from the scientific approach of *Kriegsgefangene.* Zweig uses a language full of comparisons and images. His purpose is not an accurate, ethnographic measurement of facial features to explain visual and cultural differences, but rather an explanation of how this face got its shape:

> For nearly five generations it has shaped us, this European fate and its freedom, its new air, its wonderful and artistic values, its integrating and liberating aura. And then it took the most explicit crisis of all to bring us to our senses: crisis of the heart, crisis of memory, crisis of countenance [*Antlitz*]. For it is out of the stern, modest, forward-turned face of the Jew—the witness to the indolence of our times and to the mightiness of a wilfully chosen national substance—that the bloated, transparent, and flat caricature of the Jewish trader on Nordic terrain is made, destined to disappear in the muck of eternal "newness" [*Jetztzeit*] in all big cities . . . The old Jew of the East, however, preserved his face.[48]

Based on this general assumption of the suggestibility of "the face" through the history of the Jewish diaspora, Zweig continues to comment on Struck's drawings. He shows that not only the Jewish diaspora but also World War I is engraved in *Das ostjüdische Antlitz*. To describe these effects of war on the "Jewish face," it is important to focus on what aspects of history Zweig locates "in this face":

> Inconspicuous and serene is the way of the Eastern Jewish community, an ordinary life that characterizes itself, a life that is lived to the fullest; it is an everyday life, which one encounters with piercing, bright eyes, a face full of wrinkles, and lips firmly sealed—there is, incidentally, always a pipe between the Eastern Jew's teeth. The human being must live and not allow others to live for him, and the experience of many failures, successes, and half-successes teaches that half-failures are the most common.[49]

In the "East European face" Zweig sees aspects of the simple life of a down-to-earth human being, which also recalls Zionist conceptions of the colonization of Palestine. Zweig mentions that the "Eastern Jew" has an innate knowledge of Zionist goals:

> the man of the people, has just now worked out for himself the meaning of the appeal for a Jewish homeland in Canaan, because it merely expressed in a new political form what he always knew: that this land was his land. Yet the old Jew of the East did not see in Herzl's message a utopia, as the Western Jew did, but rather, he recognized with passionate agreement the real, the actual, the indisputable and natural essence of it.[50]

Zweig elaborates on the implicit coherence between physiognomic characteristics and political issues:

> Time and again he raises his sorrowful eye out of the depths of affliction, his great hope glimmering in the stars of the blackened night sky: the hope for eternity. . . . with the heroic patience of the old Jew, he knows that the composed passivity of his courage must be stronger than the violent act that undeveloped and rapacious people inflict on him now and then—those who bestow upon his white beard an incriminating honor, even if the same beard is red from the blood of the murdered Jew who lies trampled in the filth of an Eastern alleyway. Even then. Again yesterday, as now and then, we read, in the bloodied pages of the history of this people, that cowardly Ukrainian and Polish soldiers, in acts of brutality and debasement, murdered and violated Eastern Jews—human beings who did not defend themselves. . . . Judah is eternal and Amalek, who massacred the weak who did not defend themselves, is merely long-lived. Should he rise up in a shameful time, his eye will always catch sight of the shimmering hair, the pure, thoughtful forehead, and the raised eye of the Jew, and he, Cain-Amalek, formerly a Roman and a German, now a Romanian, a Hungarian, a Ukrainian and Pole, will spill the blood of the Jew, and in that he will find his defeat, his sin, his final death.[51]

The face of the "Eastern Jew" mirrors all the violence of the war and is at the same time a symbol for nonviolent resistance. Due to these characteristics, the "Eastern Jew" is seen as a proxy for all the sufferings of the whole of Jewry.

Taking the "Face of the Eastern Jew" as a symbol for the aftermath of the war, especially as it was experienced by the whole of Jewry, motivates the inclusion of Eastern Jews, which Zweig argues in the text. His "physiognomy of war" pursues a goal different from the scientific perspective of *Kriegsgefangene*. While the scientific perspective seeks to make explanations with reference to the general facial characteristics of certain groups, Zweig's poetic ethnography emphasizes the particular. It is not surprising that he chooses the face[52] as a paradigm—as *the* place of identity. But it is not Zweig's aim to explain only the outward characteristics of this "Eastern Face." He wants to give an "aetiology of the specific" that manifests in this "face"—and this might also be the reason why he describes fifty-two individual faces. Zweig recognizes, by observing Struck's drawings, that "Eastern Jews" are a subject of ethnography understood as a writing process in a scientific context: he refers implicitly to this by taking the face as an example. On the one hand, he can thereby provide a more objective perspective on his topic; on the other hand—and this should not be underestimated—by referring to Struck's drawings he can go back to a point of "discourse"[53] in the recent past: the publication of the *Kriegsgefangene* was only a few years earlier, and the discourse about "Eastern Jews" that Zweig refers to was still present among his readers. The fact that the same artist contributed the lithographs that were produced in "Ober-Ost" stresses this relation.[54] Clearly, then, the references to the iconography of war in *Das ostjüdische Antlitz* are carefully selected. While the *Kriegsgefangene* depicts "Eastern Jews" as enemies wearing uniforms, *Das ostjüdische Antlitz* hides these uniforms. The drawings either show only the faces of Eastern European Jews or observe them during their daily routine—reading, praying, working. While *Kriegsgefangene* depicts "Eastern Jews" as wartime enemies and therefore—from the perspective of Judaism—as tragic war victims, in *Das ostjüdische Antlitz* they are also stigmatized by war and violence. Only the results of the books differ strongly from each other. By depicting "Eastern Jews" as enemies, *Kriegsgefangene* shows an *exclusion process* caused by war. But in drawing an analogy between the fate of "Eastern Jews" and the diaspora existence of the whole of Jewry, Zweig's *Face of East European Jewry* initiates an *inclusion process,* one that incorporates "Eastern Jews" into a notional collective of all Jewry. And this marks the second step I mentioned in the beginning, the second step of an internal and external change of identity. First, the statement of an exclusion caused by war, and second, a poetic inclusion influenced by totally different parameters.

The relevance of these two books for research on ethnographic writing, which includes both literary forms and scientific texts, is obvious. The two books reflect precisely the process of ethnographic writing that mirrors the dialectic between the "I" and the Other. Considering its form of representation, the exclusion process of the *Kriegsgefangene* aims to show that in times of war, the experience of the Other as an "I" and at the same time as an enemy became reality for thousands of Jewish soldiers on the eastern front. Zweig's book, on the contrary, uses the Other to access the "I." By imposing desirable properties (cf. above "has just now worked out for himself the meaning of the appeal for a Jewish homeland in Canaan") on the "Eastern Jews," Zweig becomes an ethnographer, as in Levi-Strauss's terms:

> Every time he is in the field, the ethnologist finds himself open to a world where everything is foreign and often hostile to him. He has only this self still at his disposal, enabling him to survive and to pursue his research.... It is a self which, in this strange conjuncture, is crippled and maimed by all the blows of personal history responsible at the outset for his vocation, but which will affect its future course. Hence, in ethnographic experience the observer apprehends himself as his own instrument of observation. Clearly, he must learn to know himself, to obtain, from a *self* who reveals himself as *another* to the *I* who uses him, an evaluation which will become an integral part of the observation of other selves.[55]

This interaction of the observer and the object of study is crucial, especially for the Jewish perspective concerning "East" and "West." Zweig's text can be read as paradigmatic for all the cultural reconfiguration processes in the postwar era that deal with a reevaluation of self-conceptions. And this can be considered the true ethnographic question of the postwar era. In order to describe and study the Other, Zweig has to appraise the "I," which is revealed during this process "as another." Zweig thus develops a circulating[56] notion of the I and the Other, and distinctions become blurred. The properties and characteristics of the Other become desirable for the "I," and—as Zweig notes conclusively—he can see the goals of the I already inherent in the Other. Regarding Zionist subjects, it is especially remarkable that his "subject," the Other, might also achieve goals which are worthwhile for the "I." Zweig finishes his text with a few portraits of children. In his description, the children stand for the achievement of the main Zionist goals. Therefore, during Zweig's ethnographic work the inclusion process progresses so far that the "I" and the Other reintegrate into a prospective whole, where the aftermath of the war is no longer visible. *Das ostjüdische Antlitz* has thus been rejuvenated from an old man into a child:

FIGURE 8.10

Arnold Zweig. *Das ostjüdische Antlitz. Zu fünfzig Steinzeichnungen*
von Hermann Struck. (The Face of East European Jewry.
With reference to fifty lithographs of Hermann Struck.)
Berlin: Welt-Verlag, 1920, without page reference.

Because you yourself are a young boy, Israel, an extremely young people,
astray like the youth and striving for the right path, like youth once again,
so that a voice calls out to you: "Come home, Israel, to your father, for you
shall be consoled!" Israel is a young boy on earth, innocent, disoriented,
defiant, and ready to return home if somebody approaches him with the
righteous and benevolent word to ease his shame. Listen, the times have
begun to utter this word.[57]

NOTES

1. George F. Kennan, *The Decline of Bismarck's European Order: Franco-Russian Relations, 1875–1890* (Princeton, N.J.: Princeton University Press, 1979), 3.

2. Bernd Hüppauf, "Kriegsliteratur," in *Enzyklopädie Erster Weltkrieg*, ed. Gerhard Hirschfeld, Gerd Krumeich, and Irina Renz (Paderborn: Schöningh, 2009), 177–191.

3. Sander L. Gilman, "The Rediscovery of the Eastern Jews: German Jews in the East, 1890–1918," in *Jews and Germans from 1860–1933*, ed. David Bronsen (Heidelberg: Winter, 1979), 338–365.

4. Steven Aschheim, *Brothers and Strangers: The East European Jew in German and German Jewish Consciousness 1800–1923* (Madison: University of Wisconsin Press, 1982).

5. Cf. Martin Buber, *Die Geschichten des Rabbi Nachman* (Frankfurt am Main: Rütten & Loening, 1906); Martin Buber, *Die Legende des Baal-schem* (Frankfurt am Main: Rütten & Loening, 1908); Martin Buber, *Drei Reden über das Judentum* (Frankfurt am Main: Rütten & Loening, 1911).

6. Aschheim, 139–148.

7. Ibid., 143.

8. Cf. "Die Ostjudenfrage," *Ost und West* 2–3 (1916): 73–112 [*Ostjudenfrage* as "ghost"]; Berthold Viertel, "Ostjuden [I]," *Selbstwehr* 47 (1916): 2–4; Berthold Viertel, "Ostjuden [II]," *Selbstwehr* 1 (1917): 11–12; Berthold Viertel, "Ostjuden [III]," *Selbstwehr* 2 (1917): 2–4.

9. Aschheim, 139, 141.

10. Cf. Gilya Gerda Schmidt, *The Art and Artists of the Fifth Zionist Congress, 1901: Heralds of a New Age* (Syracuse, N.Y.: Syracuse University Press, 2003), 104.

11. For a Jewish Russian ethnographic perspective cf. S. An-sky, *The Enemy at His Pleasure: A Journey through the Jewish Pale of Settlement during World War I* (New York: Metropolitan Books, 2003).

12. Cf. Schmidt, 109.

13. Cf. Ibid., 107.

14. Hermann Struck, *In Russisch-Polen. Ein Kriegstagebuch* (Berlin: Bard, 1915).

15. Hermann Struck and Herbert Eulenberg, *Skizzen aus Litauen, Weissrussland und Kurland: 60 Steinzeichnungen* (Berlin: Stilke, 1916).

16. Cf. Andrew D. Evans, *Anthropology at War: World War I and the Science of Race in Germany* (Chicago: University of Chicago Press, 2010), 135.

17. Ibid., 3.

18. Felix von Luschan, *Völker, Rassen, Sprachen* (Berlin: Welt-Verlag, 1922); cf. also Felix von Luschan, "Zur physischen Anthropologie der Juden," *Zeitschrift für Demographie und Statistik der Juden* 1 (1905): 1–4.

19. Cf. Fritz Kahn, "Luschan, Felix von" in *Jüdisches Lexikon: Ein enzyklopädisches Handbuch des jüdischen Wissens in vier Bänden mit über 2000 Illustrationen, Beilagen, Karten und Tabellen*, vol. 3., ed. Georg Herlitz and Bruno Kirschner (Berlin: Jüdischer Verlag, 1928), 1252–1253.

20. Arnold Zweig, *Das ostjüdische Antlitz: Zu fünfzig Steinzeichnungen von Hermann Struck* (Berlin: Welt-Verlag, 1920).

21. Georg Wenzel, ed., *Arnold Zweig 1887–1968: Werk und Leben in Dokumenten und Bildern. Mit unveröffentlichten Manuskripten aus dem Nachlaß* (Berlin: Aufbau-Verlag, 1978), 77.

22. "Klub ehemaliger Intellektueller," Sammy Gronemann, *Hawdoloh und Zapfenstreich: Erinnerungen an die ostjüdische Etappe 1916–1918* (Berlin: Jüdischer Verlag 1914), 45 and 50.

23. Cf. Wenzel, *Arnold Zweig 1887–1968*, 75 (my translation).

24. "Ostjuden," *Fünfzig Originalsteinzeichnungen in Vorzugsdrucken auf Japan. Vom Künstler signiert. 50 num. Exemplare in Mappe. Druckerei des Ob.-Ost.* (Frankfurt am Main: Baer, 1918).

25. Arnold Zweig, "Strucks 'Ostjuden,'" *Vossische Zeitung* 554 (1918): 2. "Dies aber ist an Strucks Mappe das Schönste und das Politische. Denn im Streite um die Bestimmung dieses Volkes, . . . kann wenigstens denen, die um dies Geschick würfeln, ohne den uns kostbaren Einsatz zu kennen, . . . ein unablässiges und spöttisches Paroli geboten werden. Hersehen! rufen diese Gesichter; Sehen! verlangen sie. Die Sprache des Künstlers ist die Sprache seines Werks; die Politik des Künstlers ist die Gesinnung seiner Form, ist die Intensität des Geschaffenen und seine Sprache."

26. Alexander Honold, "Das Fremde verstehen—das Verstehen verfremden: Ethnographie als Herausforderung für Literatur- und Kulturwissenschaft," *TRANS. Internet-Zeitschrift für Kulturwissenschaften* 1 (1997), http://www.inst.at/trans/1Nr/honold.htm .14.7.2015.

27. Claude Levi-Strauss, "Jean Jacques Rousseau, Founder of the Sciences of Man," in *Structural Anthropology*, vol. 2 (New York: Basic Books, 1976), 33–43. On Rousseau and Levi-Strauss cf. Tanya Marie Luhrmann, "Our Master, Our Brother: Levi-Strauss's Debt to Rousseau," *Cultural Anthropology* 4 (1990): 396–413.

28. "Ein Beitrag zur Völkerkunde im Weltkriege."

29. Evans, 163f.: "By placing photographs such as these in a volume with the drawings, the two forms were essentially equated as having scientific worth—but both were primarily subjective, rather than positivistic documents."

30. *Kriegsgefangene. Hundert Steinzeichnungen von Hermann Struck. Mit Begleitworten von Prof. Dr. F. von Luschan. Ein Beitrag zur Völkerkunde im Weltkriege.* Mit Genehmigung des königlichen Kriegsministeriums herausgegeben (Berlin: Reimer, 1916), 26.

31. Cf. ibid., 4, 26.

32. Cf. ibid., 26.

33. Cf. Evans, 156.

34. Cf. ibid., 162.

35. Cf. ibid., ill. 2, 142.

36. The pictures were painted between 1914 and 1918.

37. "Stereotyping, in other words, is part of the maintenance of social and symbolic order. It sets up a symbolic frontier between the 'normal' and the 'deviant,' the 'normal' and the 'pathological,' the 'acceptable' and the 'unacceptable,' what 'belongs' and what does not or is 'Other,' between 'insiders' and 'outsiders,' Us and Them. . . . And it sends into a symbolic exile all of Them—'the Others'—who are in some way different—'beyond the pale.'" Stuart Hall, "The Spectacle of the Other," in *Representation: Cultural Representations and Signifying Practices*, ed. Stuart Hall (London: Sage, 1997), 258.

38. Ibid.

39. Margret Olin, "Jews among the Peoples: Visual Archives in German Prisoner of War Camps during the Great War," in *Anthropology in Wartime and War Zones*, ed. Monika Sheer and Reinhard Johler (Bielefeld: transcript, 2010), 263 (my italics).

40. Ibid.

41. Aschheim, 142.

42. Cf. Elisheva Cohen, "Joseph Budko," in *Encyclopaedia Judaica*, vol. 4, ed. Fred Skolnik (2007).

43. Joseph Budko, "Kriegsgefangene," *Jüdische Rundschau* 15 (1918): 109.

44. Ibid. "Hier sieht man außer dem Künstler auch den Juden Struck; denn es ist kein Zufall, wenn der Meister gerade diese drei in seinem Werke vorführt. Der junge Jude aus Lublin erzählt uns mit seinen großen hellerleuchtenden [sic] und zugleich tief melancholischen Augen vom Kummer eines Volkes; der Vorbeter Isaak Chtoran [sic] sagt uns, wie sehr er sich nach dem Gebetpult seiner fernen Synagoge sehnt und der Tempelbeamte aus Warschau zeigt uns, daß er auch in der Gefangenschaft seinen Talmud nicht verläßt."

45. Adapted from Arnold Zweig, *The Face of East European Jewry: With Fifty-Two Drawings by Hermann Struck*, trans. and ed. Noah Isenberg (Berkeley: University of California Press, 2004), xxxi.

46. Cf. also Zweig, *Das ostjüdische Antlitz*, without page numbers.

47. Zweig, *The Face of East European Jewry*, 1.

48. Ibid., 2.

49. Ibid., 20.

50. Ibid.

51. Ibid., 24–25.

52. Cf. Sarah Mohi-von Känel, "Krieg und Gesicht. Sprache der Entstellung bei Joseph Roth, Erich Kuttner und Vicki Baum," in *Nachkriegskörper: Prekäre Korporealitäten in der deutschsprachigen Literatur des 20. Jahrhunderts*, ed. Christoph Steier and Sarah Mohi-von Känel (Würzburg: Königshausen & Neumann, 2013), 97–114.

53. Cf. Michel Foucault, *The Archaeology of Knowledge* (New York: Pantheon Books, 1972).

54. In the German edition there is a note that the lithographs were produced in "Ober-Ost."

55. Levi-Strauss, 36.

56. Cf. Jan Assmann, *Das kulturelle Gedächtnis. Schrift, Erinnerung und politische Identität in frühen Hochkulturen* (Munich: Beck, 2007), 140; Philipp Sarasin and Andreas Kilcher, editorial, "Zirkulationen," *Nach Feierabend. Zürcher Jahrbuch für Wissensgeschichte* 7 (2011): 7–11.

57. Zweig, *The Face of East European Jewry*, 148.

Avant-Garde Authenticity

M. Vorobeichic's Photographic Modernism
and the East European Jew

SAMUEL SPINNER

"... [it is] a kind of museum [*bet osef*] for all the evening shadows of the [Jewish] street—shadows that tremble on the border of the traditional past and the modern present."[1]

So wrote the prominent Hebrew and Yiddish writer Zalman Shneour in an introductory essay to Moyshe Vorobeichic's 1931 photobook, *Ein Ghetto im Osten. Wilna* (A Ghetto in the East: Vilna; see figure 9.1).[2] This book, containing both elaborate photomontages and "straight" photographs of the Jewish quarter of Vilna, was released in the *Schaubücher* series of the Orell Füssli Verlag of Zurich. *Ein Ghetto im Osten* was, like the rest of the *Schaubücher*, a small-format, mass-produced book of approximately sixty-five images. The series was an idiosyncratic combination of high and low culture, of avant-garde and straight photography. With titles like *Befreites Wohnen* (Living Free—on modern home architecture) and *Technische Schönheit* (Technical Beauty—with images of factories and machines), it was clearly hospitable to modernist themes and tropes. The *Schaubücher* series encompassed another popular theme of the period: popular ethnography.[3] Such books, including *Negertypen des Schwarzen Erdteils* (Negro Types of the Dark Continent) and *Nias: Die Insel der Götzen* (Nias: Island of Idols), comprised a total of six of the *Schaubücher*.[4] *Ein Ghetto im Osten* seems to fit in the latter category.[5] East European Jews and the shtetls from which many of them came were popular subjects in the Jewish press and belles-lettres from the latter half of the nineteenth century onward.

FIGURE 9.1

Moyshe Vorobeichic. "Ḥanuyot bi-reḥov ha-yehudim" (Shops in
the Jewish Street), Hebrew cover, in *Ein Ghetto im Osten—Wilna. 65
Bilder von M. Vorobeichic. Eingeleitet von S. Chnéour,* German cover.
Zurich: Orell Füssli Verlag, 1931. Courtesy of Yossi Raviv.

But the book foregoes the bland realism and prurient exoticism of the more generically popular series titles, embracing a striking avant-garde idiom that surpasses that of even those books on modernist themes. The book thus scrambles the dichotomy between realist and avant-garde, between high and low, that is represented by the other *Schaubücher*. More significantly, this tactic placed Vorobeichic at the center of a modernist approach to ethnography that had only just begun to take shape at large and, significantly, was unprecedented in the photographic representation of Eastern European Jews.[6]

Vorobeichic simultaneously accommodated and interrogated the often conflicting demands of the traditions on which his photobook was based: those of popular ethnography, the valorization of the Eastern European Jew, the modernist photobook, and the avant-garde engagement with ethnography. This multifarious genealogy creates taxonomical and interpretive problems: a book that capitalizes on a popular nostalgic trope of Jewish identity in an avant-garde idiom would seem to be a paradox. I propose to situate the book in a network of discourses characterized by the collision of the avant-garde and ethnography and often called, using James Clifford's term, "ethnographic surrealism."[7] It is in this context that Vorobeichic's effort begins to become clear.

I will show how *Ein Ghetto im Osten* expresses an awareness of the opposed trajectories of ethnographic and avant-garde idioms in the photographic representation of Jews. The book is, however, not an avant-garde rejection of the ethnographic tradition, but an exploitation of it, inherently reifying the underpinnings of the ethnographic project, namely the creation of ethnographic objects out of subjects designated primitive or exotic. Vorobeichic's challenge to ethnography, which also formed a goal of the modernist critique of ethnography, was to attempt to turn these objects back into subjects. But turning ethnography against itself creates an ambiguity of meaning that becomes the chief statement of the work. Rather than a standard instantiation of the trope of the Ostjude or an all-out critique of ethnography, Vorobeichic's photographs suggest a multiplicity of interpretive possibilities without affirming any single one.[8] The sentimental gaze and the ethnographic impulse are pulled back from the foreground and are removed as the only possible interpretive modes for representations of the Ostjude. New possibilities are opened that direct the viewer away from the heavily tropic representation of Ostjuden in contemporary culture.

It is, in fact, the metaphor of opening and the exploration of alternatives with which Vorobeichic introduces his work (see figure 9.1).[9] The image on the book's cover is a montage of numerous doors, some overlapping, all cluttered together in a jumble, suggesting a playful attitude toward a subject typically treated with heavy-handed sentiment, but also evoking the interpretive conundrum of the work: behind which door lies the meaning of the book? Throughout the work, the very lack of an answer is articulated through Vorobeichic's characteristic techniques of repetition, doubling, visual puns, ironic captions and layouts, and use of negative space. All contribute to a work that points toward the semiotic status of photography while undermining the possibilities for interpretation through the proliferation of signs.[10]

The demand for multiple meanings is articulated not only through the polysemy of its images, but also through its very materiality: the year 1931 saw three simultaneous editions of *Ein Ghetto im Osten* from its publisher. Each edition was bilingual, featuring dual versions of the cover, the captions, and the introduction: one was in German and Hebrew, one in English and Hebrew, and one in German and Yiddish. The rather strange production of three bilingual editions sharpens the interpretive challenge posed by the image of doors: not only does the cover pose the riddle of which door is the correct entryway to the book, but we must now ask, for whom are these doors? With these four languages—German, English, Hebrew, and Yiddish—the target audience would seem to be the entire Ashkenazi diaspora.[11]

Although the duality of the three editions is primarily textual, with the various languages surrounding the same images, it is not entirely so. The image of doors forms the cover of the Hebrew and Yiddish sides of the three editions, but not the covers of the sides in German and English. These sides have a different image—an unmanipulated shot with a slightly elevated perspective onto a crowded, filthy alley (figure 9.2). At the far end of the alley is a sunlit façade blocked by an archway, which in turn is obstructed by pedestrians and partially obscured by shadow. The face of the book presented to a "Western" audience thus displays the clutter and darkness of the ghetto with an only partly visible single point of egress

FIGURE 9.2

Moyshe Vorobeichic. "Judengasse mit Balkon der grossen Synagoge" (The Jewish Street with the Balcony of the Great Synagogue), German cover, in *Ein Ghetto im Osten*. Zurich: Orell Füssli Verlag, 1931. Courtesy of Yossi Raviv.

at the image's vanishing point. For the eye that possesses this downward view on to the crowded alley, is the point of interest what is in the ghetto or what is tantalizingly just visible outside its gate? By contrast, the doors of the "Eastern" or "Jewish" cover are all closed but unblocked and lit evenly, seeming to offer many (too many) choices for entry, but no clue as to what may lie behind them. To whom is interpretive access offered and to whom is it denied? Which view is inside and which outside? Is the speaker of Hebrew and Yiddish—the returning Ostjude—barred from reentry? Is the speaker of English and German—the exploring European—trapped and prevented from exiting? The self-reflexivity of this question-asking is characteristic of the avant-garde approach to ethnography; it resists universalized approaches and produces no definitive answer.

This is in stark contrast to the dominant and heavily tropic understanding of Eastern European Jewish identity in the period, typified, in fact, by Zalman Shneour's introduction to *Ein Ghetto im Osten*. Shneour's understanding of the book emerges from the discourses governing the representation of Eastern European Jews in modernity, discourses conditioned in large part by ethnography and against which Vorobeichic, together with other representatives of the avant-garde engagement with ethnography, was reacting. In the line quoted above, Shneour characterizes the book as a museum, the site par excellence for the popular mediation of ethnography.[12] He writes that the photographs are a "museum for all the evening shadows of the street—shadows that tremble on the border of the traditional past and the modern present,"[13] and thus perched on the border between then and now, tradition and modernity, without a stable chronological identity. For Shneour, the metaphor of the museum mirrors the chronological and evolutionary conceit behind the ethnographic conception of the primitive, namely the trope of primitive timelessness.[14]

Ethnography likewise lurks behind other aspects of Shneour's understanding of *Ein Ghetto im Osten*. He concludes his introduction as follows: "This album is not an extravagance for aesthetes and connoisseurs of one kind or another, but has something for everyone: it is a collection of pictures for the masses; a delight for parents and children; a resource for researchers; a wealth of ethnographic material; an example of Jewish art; and a guide for the performance of plays on Jewish life."[15] The last clause appears only in the Hebrew; the translator(s) into Yiddish, German, and English seem to have thought this phrase out of place. All of the non-Hebrew versions end with a variation of the Yiddish conclusion: "a wealth of ethnographic material of Jewish life." Whether or not Shneour's final phrase in Hebrew was meant literally or metaphorically, it hinges on a discourse entirely in keeping with the interpretation of these photographs as ethnographic material. The performative aspects of the ethnographic showcases of the late nineteenth and early twentieth centuries were fodder for satire (as with Kafka's "A Report to an Academy") and also grounds for the modernist performance of primitive authenticity (as with Peter Altenberg's *Ashantee*). Yet they remained "scientific" sources at a time before ethnography had sufficient institutional presence to police its disciplinary borders and control its methodologies. The tradition of ethnographic display and viewing in the modern period had always encompassed both the popular and the scientific, the performative and the documentary, and did not always distinguish between the different registers. This is clearly how Shneour saw Vorobeichic's work, identifying it unambiguously as a source for the ethnography of Jews.

But Vorobeichic's images were not primarily a product of this tradition of popular ethnography, though he exploits its tropes. *Ein Ghetto im Osten* emerges more directly from the avant-garde approach to photography—to which he was exposed during his studies under László Moholy-Nagy at the Bauhaus in the late 1920s—and its approach to ethnography, which had resulted most prominently in Georges Bataille's journal *Documents,* published from 1929–1930 in Paris, where Vorobeichic had settled after his time in Dessau. Although he had begun his studies at the Bauhaus focusing on painting, by the time he left he had switched his allegiance to photography. While in Paris he worked as a photographer for the press and produced the two signal achievements of his career, the seminal avant-garde photography book *Paris* and *Ein Ghetto im Osten,* both from 1931. Despite a long career—he emigrated to Palestine in the mid-1930s, where he was a founder of the artists' colony in Safed and had a successful career as a painter and graphic designer until his death in 1995—his reputation rests largely, if not exclusively, on the publication of *Paris.* For *Paris* he went by the pseudonym Moï Ver, which has become his most common appellation.[16] *Paris* is a consummate expression, a codification even, of high modernist photomontage. In one representative image, old and new

FIGURE 9.3

Moyshe Vorobeichic. Handcart and automobiles in *Paris*. Paris:
Editions Jeanne Walter, 1931. Courtesy of Yossi Raviv.

collide in urban space as an automobile seems to drive right through a
handcart and its driver (figure 9.3). In another, the superimposed—indeed, almost abstracted—forms of trees and the Eiffel Tower suggest a
destabilized relationship between nature and machine.

Paris was an appropriate subject for a modernist photobook. It was,
after all, a capital of the avant-garde and a destination for artists like Vorobeichic. Moreover, the formal composition of the images matches their
content in attitude and orientation—the images dramatize the collision
of tradition and modernity encapsulated by the idea of Paris. But his Vilna
book seems far from appropriate—if Paris was a capital of the avant-garde,
Vilna was not even on the map. On the map of Jewish Europe, however,
Vilna was the so-called "Jerusalem of Lithuania," a major cultural center.
As indicated by this moniker, it was also a focal point for stereotypes of
Eastern European Jewry—Vilna was the home of the saintly sage and
the stooped peddler. Such characters, in fact, are the stock in trade of

Ein Ghetto im Osten. Moreoever, there are no cars, no steel structures, no cinemas: no traces at all of modern life. Nor is there any collision of nature and modernity, for nature is equally absent: the book represents the shtetl reduced to synagogue and Jew. But the images are composed and arranged in Vorobeichic's relentlessly avant-garde idiom, so much so that it demands to be read alongside *Paris* as a companion piece, the two books presenting two sites, or perhaps even two kinds, of modernity. In this collision of form and subject, *Ein Ghetto im Osten* would seem at once to affirm and to interrogate the era's stereotyped picture of Eastern European Jews. By engaging the idioms of ethnographic realism but also those of modernism, the book forces us to recognize that the visual representation of the classic Eastern European primitivist subject is not an either/ or proposition between realism and abstraction, or between critique and promotion of the authentic Ostjude.

Vorobeichic's instantiation of the dual—and often dueling—modes of ethnographic realism and avant-garde photography was sui generis for the photographic representation of the Eastern European Jew.[17] But, more broadly, he was not alone in his use of an equivocal stance toward the ethnographization of his subject. In fact, this move had become characteristic of (but not limited to) the Paris-based artists, writers, and ethnographers of the circle around Georges Bataille and his journal *Documents,* the special focus of which was the intersection of ethnography and representation. They produced the body of work that James Clifford named "ethnographic surrealism." A focus of Clifford's analysis is Michel Leiris, whose *Phantom Africa* serves as the paradigm of a surrealist ethnography (an inversion of his category in discipline, but not intention). Leiris's text was a diaristic ethnography resulting from his participation in the famous Mission Dakar-Djibouti ethnographic expedition of 1931–1933. He gained his place on the expedition, so goes the story, due to Luis Buñuel's decision not to take part. Instead, Buñuel returned to Spain from Paris and made *Las Hurdes* (also known as *Tierra sin pan* [Land without Bread]), a thirty-minute ethnographic film that articulates many of the suppositions and enacts many of the forms of ethnographic surrealism.

As the debate that followed in the wake of Clifford's article made clear, ethnographic surrealism was neither ethnography nor surrealism per se.[18]

It was, rather, a posture—most frequently adopted by artists and writers associated with surrealism—that sought to expose and undermine the representational and subject-making capacities of ethnography. It was a posture that found a clear expression in Buñuel's engagement with ethnography, and, so I argue, in Vorobeichic's avant-garde Jewish ethnography. The substantial links between the formal and polemic approaches of the two works will become clear by means of James Lastra's apposite and convincing reading of Buñuel's film.[19]

Las Hurdes is sometimes interpreted as a typically exploitative ethnographic film; sometimes as a powerful critique of capitalism; and sometimes as a profoundly self-aware parody of ethnography. It is all three, and perhaps more. The film is, according to James Lastra, fully in control of what he identifies not as an ambivalent posture but an "equivocal strategy."[20] Its subject, the remote Spanish region of Las Hurdes, is presented as hopelessly woebegone: mired in extreme poverty, filth, disease, and hunger. The residents of this barren, remote region are also presented as forlorn and without hope. But the film is also cut through with parodic elements, some of them undeniably humorous. Most notorious of these is the scene in which the narrator describes the scarcity of meat among the Hurdanos; one rare source of such is the mountain goats that occasionally plummet to their deaths among the sheer crags. Such an eventuality is shown, but with an unmistakable puff of gunfire at the edge of the frame immediately preceding the goat's fall. For Lastra, this, together with other less obvious elements, is a purposeful tactic to draw attention to the essentially staged nature of the film. But Lastra argues that as with the goat, so with the Hurdanos: the result is a film that questions the tactics and motivations of ethnography while repurposing them for aesthetic ends. The film, writes Lastra, is "simultaneously a documentary and a dismantling of the documentary form," and "falls neither on the side of pure sympathy nor simple disgust but . . . insists on a constantly double movement embracing and repelling the Hurdanos at the same time, refusing a stable position."[21] This is a framing particularly apt in the representation of this group, which "resisted any homogenous representation as noble or ignoble. On the one hand they occupied a degraded place in the Spanish national body, while as Spaniards they were also said to *exemplify* Spanish

identity."[22] They were, therefore, denigrated in order to raise the value of
the other constituents of Spanish identity, a process that was "paradoxical,
since the Hurdanos were no alien community, but citizens well within the
heart of Spain itself, and therefore ineradicable."[23] Lastra argues that Buñuel thus "situates the Hurdanos on the border between the wholly inside
and the wholly outside, as a group hostile to both classifications."[24] This
paradoxical positioning of the partially alien subject is suggestively analogous to the position of the Jew in Europe, most particularly that of the
Jew as ethnographic subject within Europe. More concretely, the formal
aspect that this equivocation takes in Buñuel's film—the encroachment of
subversive content at its edges and through the juxtaposition of words and
image—is, I contend, recognizable in Vorobeichic's alternation between
straight photographs and complex montages and multiple exposures, an
alternation that he utilizes to toggle between the misery of the ghetto's
inhabitants and their joy.

Lastra takes his argument one crucial step further. Through a series
of subtle intertextual readings, he compellingly identifies the ultimate
referent in the film's chain of equivocal signs. It is a referent only able to
be present by virtue of its absence in the film, and indeed, its absence in
Las Hurdes—the Jews. Lastra points out that all of the ethnographic and
historical works on which Buñuel's film was based relate a local legend
accounting for the expulsion of the Jews from the region during the In-
quisition. A variant of the legend related by Buñuel has it that the original
inhabitants of the region were themselves Jews displaced by the Inquisi-
tion.[25] The final piece of evidence for the Jewish subtext—or even context—of *Land without Bread,* is the title appended to Buñuel's personal gift
of a print of the film to the Museum of Modern Art in New York in 1940:
Unpromised Land.[26] The Jewish subtext of the film is thus concretized.
The picture Lastra has painstakingly painted makes clear the profoundly
allusive potentialities for the representation of European Jews within the
context of modernist ethnographic representation.

As is clear from Buñuel's film, the appearance of realism does not pre-
clude a modernist underpinning. The same is true for the presence of
documentary photography in surrealism. Ian Walker has shown how surrealists used straight photography "as a simultaneous exploitation and

subversion of the standard realist frame," a manner akin to the equivocal dualism we have already seen in Buñuel.[27] This was particularly so in the avant-garde exploitation of ethnographic photography, a characteristic feature of *Documents* among other contemporaneous periodicals. *Documents* "was to offer a sort of ethnography of the everyday in which there was a two-way movement between the exotic and the commonplace.... The study of so-called primitive and exotic peoples was given no privileged status as ethnographic subjects. No methodological distinction was made between social facts taken from 'exotic' societies and those drawn from Western society."[28]

This two-way movement was also characteristic of the ethnographic and primitivist representation of Eastern European Jews in Europe, in large part due to the polyvalence of their constructed identities: Semitic (in "race") but European (in geography); Germanic (in language) but Slavic (again in geography); primitively religious but prone to excessive *Bildung* and assimilation. The collapse of exotic and mundane that was a signal achievement of the dissident surrealists was intrinsically present in the polyvalent identities of European Jews, which, however, was only capitalized on visually by Vorobeichic in his polysemic images. Whereas, for example, Buñuel's use of ethnography was simultaneously affirmative (in its reification of the conditions of production of ethnography) and critical (in the often jarring framing and contextualization that ethnographic representations were given), the tradition of visual representation of Eastern European Jews was based on an unproblematized use of ethnographic representational modes, which easily accommodated the valorization of the poverty, traditional religiosity, and noble sorrow of shtetl Jews. Characteristic examples of such images include works by Alter Kacyzne, a prominent Yiddish writer who earned a living running a portrait photography studio in Warsaw and traveled widely as a photographic correspondent for the New York Yiddish daily *Forverts*, as well as Roman Vishniac's prewar photographs of Eastern European Jews, which established his international reputation after the Holocaust.[29] Although their subjects embodied the binary of exotic and ordinary that avant-garde artists had to labor to achieve, the majority of photographers of Eastern European Jews adhered to a mixture of sentimental and ethnographic

FIGURE 9.4

Moyshe Vorobeichic. "Im Bethamidrasch (Lehrhaus)" (In
the Study Hall), "Zohar" (Radiance), in *Ein Ghetto im Osten*.
Zurich: Orell Füssli Verlag, 1931. Courtesy of Yossi Raviv.

realism. It was Vorobeichic who brought an avant-garde form to a subject
that was seemingly, in light of so many of its representations, quite distant
from the avant-garde.

He did this either by contrasting manipulated and straight photographs, as with the dual covers of the book, or through the juxtaposition of the images with the words surrounding them. The latter tactic, a
major element of the book, exploits the multilayered textual allusiveness
of Yiddish to create captions that offer sarcastic commentary on images
that on their own would appear to be in the typical sentimental mode.
These witticisms are lost in the translation of the captions, but the multiplicity of versions—many so distant from one another, they can hardly
be considered translations—mean that we cannot think of this book as
having three translations of one original. Rather, the book both visually

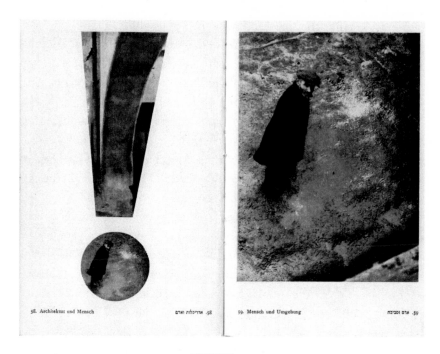

58. Architektur und Mensch   אדריכלות ואדם .58   59. Mensch und Umgebung   אדם וסביבה .59

FIGURE 9.5

Moyshe Vorobeichic. "Architektur und Mensch," "Adrikhalut ve-
adam" (Architecture and Man); "Mensch und Umgebung," "Adam
u-sevivah" (Man and Surroundings), in *Ein Ghetto im Osten*.
Zurich: Orell Füssli Verlag, 1931. Courtesy of Yossi Raviv.

and textually emphasizes its polysemy. Let us take, for example, an image of an empty room with blinding light reflecting off the flat surfaces
of the benches and lecterns scattered about (figure 9.4). The image carries the following captions (my translations appear outside the quotation
marks): German—"*Im Bethhamidrasch (Lehrhaus)*" (in the *bet ha-midrash*
[school]); Yiddish—"*in goens kloyz*" (in the synagogue of the Gaon of
Vilna); English—"In the '*Bethamidrash*' (Teaching House)"; Hebrew—
"*Zohar*" (Radiance). The English is clearly a translation of the German
(as is also clear from the mistranslation in image nine of "Thora Time"
for "*Talmudstunde*," or Talmud lesson).[30] But the Hebrew offers a pun in-

dependent of the other captions: *zohar* means brightness or radiance, but is also the name of the central book of the Kabbalah. The light reflecting off the lecterns in bursts of radiance is thus metonymically (and humorously) reinterpreted as the light of the Kabbalah, which would normally be studied from books lying on the lecterns.

Other pages parody the earnest conventions of ethnographic photography: a spread featuring two versions of an image of a man and his drab surroundings is captioned on the left as "Architecture and Man" and on the right as "Man and Surroundings" (figure 9.5). The generality of the captions seems to promise a subject of greater interest, but all that is shown is yet another bearded man, the wet ground on which he stands, and an unremarkable arch. Vorobeichic subverts the centrality of exoticism for ethnography by offering ordinary details that are in theory ethnographically satisfactory but that were all too often ignored in favor of prurience. He goes one step further than the conflation of exotic and everyday found in ethnographic surrealism by making the everyday take the place of the exotic.

Yet it is only the subject of these images that is ordinary; their overtly playful form is, in fact, where their real interest lies. By means of an elaborate visual pun, the spread humorously foregrounds the semiotic character of photography: the image on the right is of a poor man, slightly perspectivally compressed by the overhead camera angle; the image on the left duplicates the right-hand image in the form of an exclamation point. The transformation of image into typographic sign thus casts it as caption for its facing image, as well as a caption for the textual caption below it, rather than the other way around. Reading the photograph becomes a matter of recognizing its legibility and understanding its textuality rather than only interpreting its visual subject.

The duplication of the image echoes a simultaneity of meaning consisting of a visual pun on the Yiddish phrase *dos pintele Yid*.[31] Literally "the point of a Jew," it idiomatically means the essence of a Jew, an idiom that is itself already a word-play: the *pintele yud* is the point atop the letter *yud* in Jewish ritual script; when the letter yud becomes *yid*—Jew—the diacritic becomes a synecdoche for the essence of Jewish identity.[32] In insisting on the semiotic legibility of photography, Vorobeichic has gracefully and wittily deconstructed the essence of this idiom, simultaneously pointing toward the tropic and essentialized identity underlying the idea of the *pintele yid* as well as the image of the Ostjude. Reading the image textually, we see how the transformation of subject (yid) into punctuation (exclamation point) critically mirrors the process by which ethnography turned Jew into Ostjude. This image/exclamation point is not an ostensibly realist documentary photograph ready for interpretation (like its companion on the facing page), but an instance of what Rosalind Krauss calls the "language effect," spelling out an interpretation in itself, of itself.[33]

Despite the unmistakable ways in which Vorobeichic calls attention to the fundamentally nonrealist stakes of his work, contemporary readers, beginning with Zalman Shneour, seem not to have seen it this way. In his introduction, Shneour applauds what he sees as the documentary nature of the work, praising Vorobeichic for "doing without stereotypes, without sentimentality, without romanticism, leaving out everything that has no direct link to life in the Jewish street."[34] A few sentences earlier, in an opening paragraph present in the Hebrew and Yiddish, but not the German, he focuses on their ability to evoke sentiment: "The pictures arouse curiosity, light streams from the shadows, and shadow from light. ... How deep is Vilna; how mysterious her Jewish street."[35] What he does not comment on is the ways in which the photographs undercut both their status as documents and their sentimentality.

A review of the book from 1932 published in the German Jewish periodical *Menorah* similarly foregrounds the ethnographic dimension of the book while offering an answer to the question of its readership: the book, so writes the reviewer, is "a delight for any aficionado of Jewish folklore."[36] This identification of the book as ethnographic echoes Shneour's reading, in which he calls the book a "museum in miniature" and a "handbook for researchers."[37]

Political agendas could also instigate a superficial reading of the book. In a review of *Ein Ghetto im Osten* from the New York Yiddish daily *Forverts* in 1931, the eminent scholar of Yiddish Max Weinreich takes issue with what he characterizes as Shneour's confused interpretation of the book, producing an interpretation that likewise takes a narrow view on the book. In the images, Weinreich sees not mystery but Jews who "want

FIGURE 9.6

Moyshe Vorobeichic. "Vor dem Laden" (In Front of the Store),
"Parnasah be-shefa" (Abundant Livelihood), in *Ein Ghetto im Osten*.
Zurich: Orell Füssli Verlag, 1931. Courtesy of Yossi Raviv.

FIGURE 9.7

Moyshe Vorobeichic. "Dein Volk Israel ist reich," "'Ashirim 'amḥa
Yisra'el" (Your People Israel is Wealthy), in *Ein Ghetto im Osten*.
Zurich: Orell Füssli Verlag, 1931. Courtesy of Yossi Raviv.

a chance to come out of the shadowy, permanently dank corners into the
light of day." He further criticizes Vorobeichic for not including images
of modern Jews:

> Where is the gym class in a modern Yiddish school? Where is a match
> between two Jewish football teams and the faces of hundreds of adult Jews
> who wait breathlessly for their team to score a goal? Where is a Jewish
> workers' demonstration? A political mass meeting? The Jewish techni-
> cal school of the ORT? A troop of boy-scouts . . . ? Where is the Yiddish
> Scientific Institute [YIVO]?[38]

What these readings all have in common is the tendency to read Vorobeichic's photobook as if it were an entirely typical example of the representation of Eastern European Jews, and therefore an appropriate site for
engaging the usual questions of ethnographic or political utility.

But even those photographs that appear as if they might have been taken by Alter Kacyzne or Roman Vishniac turn out to be destabilizing. For example, an image of a woman sitting in her shabby storefront seems to sentimentalize the poverty of such storekeepers, while retaining a claim to documentary objectivity with the German caption "in front of the store" (figure 9.6). The Yiddish caption, by contrast, ironically subverts both the sentimental and the documentary readings of the image, offering instead "an abundant livelihood." Vorobeichic accomplishes a similar effect on the same theme with a formally challenging image (figure 9.7). Once again, the caption is sarcastic—"thy people Israel is rich"—but the image's heavily manipulated composition now participates in the commentary on the subject.[39] The premise of this commercial enterprise is cast as topsy-turvy; the disarray of the goods highlights their shabbiness; the shopkeeper herself seems just another pile of fabric for sale.

Taking the book as a whole, it becomes impossible to separate the various registers of the images: the book traffics in both the avant-garde and the authentic.[40] It is able to do so by virtue of its subversion of an ethnographic discourse, which was uniquely positioned to bridge avant-garde and traditional forms of representation, and to imbricate, or perhaps even combine, realism and modernism. *Ein Ghetto im Osten* shows that although visual figurations of Jews typically associated the ethnographic with the authentic and both with realist forms, this equation was not necessarily the case—the borders could be blurred. This blurring is the primary achievement of Vorobeichic's photobook, which, in its opposition to exoticized and abstracted notions of the primitive other could foster a modernist engagement with ethnography that is more than an affirmation of ethnography's tropes. But it is also something less than the aggressively critical critique of ethnography of the surrealists, who, for example, organized an anticolonial exhibition in 1931—the year in which Vorobeichic's book was published—as a rebuttal of the massive French colonial exposition of the same year. This anticolonial exhibition, *The Truth about the Colonies*, bespoke the maturation of the avant-garde engagement with ethnography and was of a piece with similar self-reflexive cultural products including Leiris's *L'Afrique fantôme* and Buñuel's *Las Hurdes*.[41] Vorobeichic's critique of ethnography was not as strident, because it did not share the resistance to the purported humanism of the ethnographic project percolating through such efforts. He did not have the luxury of distance such a position required—distance from his subjects and distance from the stakes of his work. For a Jewish artist depicting Jewish subjects, the identities of his subjects—as subjects—demanded acknowledgment, an acknowledgment that ethnography, as a discipline and as a network of representational tropes, could offer. Despite its resistance to primitivist aestheticization, the primitivist tendencies of the avant-garde still resulted in a stripping of subjecthood from its primitive subjects. For Vorobeichic, born in the city he depicted, speaking the same language and raised in the same religion as his subjects, what I have elsewhere called the plausibility of primitivism becomes a mitigating factor for the viability of his critique of ethnography.[42] He does not have the luxury of antihumanism when the status of his subjects and himself—as Jews and as humans—was so profoundly precarious.

The precarious situation of Jews in Europe in the early 1930s was clear. The "Jewish question" had an urgency for Jewish members of the avant-garde that the "human" question or the "ethnographic" question never had for the dissident surrealists, even considering the centrality of their critique of colonialism. These remained, ultimately, problems of other people. Not so for Vorobeichic, who immigrated to Palestine only a few years after the publication of his two seminal books in 1931. Whereas his political and artistic trajectory became increasingly clear and increasingly enmeshed in the formation of a Zionist visual idiom in Palestine and then in Israel, his stance was substantially less defined in the late 1920s and early 1930s. But this ambivalence, as I have shown, was deeply motivated; it prompted an engagement with his subject and subjects, but did not demand an answer to the questions underpinning his work.

Ein Ghetto im Osten expresses a playful awareness of the uses and misuses of the ethnographic tradition in the photographic representation of Jews. The book is, however, not a rejection of that tradition; it is, rather, an exploitation of it, which destabilizes the implicit ability of ethnography to create its own objects. Vorobeichic's imbrication of ethnographic and avant-garde photography opens up the possibility that his subjects have value originating outside the discourses to which he was reacting. This

ambivalence toward ethnography and toward the trope of the Ostjude
stems from a resistance to universalizing motivated by the photographer's
own identity. *Ein Ghetto im Osten* is thus a rarity in the avant-garde approach to ethnography, and by extension to colonialism, and beyond to
humanism—it is personal.

NOTES

1. "Reḥov ha-yehudim be-'or va-tsel," in *Reḥov ha-yehudim be-Vilna*, Schaubücher 27
(Zürich: Orell Füssli Verlag, 1931), 4.
My thanks to Jordan Bear for first bringing Vorobeichic to my attention and for his
perspicacity in responding to an early version of this essay; to Emily Beeny and to Kerry
Wallach for carefully commenting on subsequent drafts; and to Yossi Raviv—Vorobeich-
ic's son—for discussing his father's work with me by telephone and email.

2. The book saw three bilingual editions in 1931: German/Hebrew, English/Hebrew,
and German/Yiddish. The multilingualism pertains to the titles, captions, and introduction, while the images and their layout are the same in all editions. The book's German
title is *Ein Ghetto im Osten. Wilna* (A Ghetto in the East. Vilna); the Hebrew title is *Reḥov
ha-yehudim be-Vilnah* (The Jewish Street in Vilna); the Yiddish title is *Yidishe gas in Vilne*
(The Jewish Street in Vilna); and the English, leaning in a mildly quaint direction, is *The
Ghetto Lane in Vilna*. Since the book was published by a German-language Swiss press,
I will refer to the book by its German title (and a direct translation of that title), but will
specify from which edition all citations come. For information on the publication of the
book and the entire *Schaubücher* series, see Roland Jaeger, "Gegensatz zum Lesebuch
'Die Reihe Schaubücher' im Orell Füssli Verlag, Zürich," in *Autopsie: deutschsprachige
Fotobücher 1918 bis 1945*, ed. Manfred Heiting and Roland Jaeger (Göttingen: Steidl, 2012),
314–331.
I assume that Shneour's essay was written in Hebrew, since he begins it by referring to
his well-known Hebrew poem on Vilna. The distinction is important, since the versions
do diverge sometimes, mostly due to poor and occasionally erroneous translation. The
translations I offer of Shneour's introduction are mine and are from the Hebrew version,
unless otherwise specified.

3. The series also included titles of a more conventionally popular orientation, including *Das schöne Tier* (Beautiful Animals) and *Die Lüneburger Heide* (the Lüneburg Heath).

4. The others were *Ein Ghetto im Osten*; *An den Höfen der Maharadschas* (The Courts
of the Maharajas); *Von China und Chinesen* (On China and the Chinese); and *Frauenbilder
des Morgenlandes* (Women of the Orient).

5. Its post-Holocaust reception (though limited) took a different trajectory, split
between highly backshadowed evaluations and a small number of scholarly treatments.
Of the former, see Manfred Sapper, "Das Antlitz des ermordeten Volkes: Anmerkungen
zu den Fotos von M. Vorobeichic," *Osteuropa* 52, no. 9/10 (2002): 1338–1345. For scholarly
treatments of the book, the following four articles are, to my knowledge, the only examples. Nelson (in an article that echoes her dissertation) positions Vorobeichic's book as
a "New Vision" configuration of the spaces of Vilna. Zemel and Washton-Long contend

in similar ways that Vorobeichic recasts the diaspora Jew as a modern subject. Finally, Dmitrieva sees *Ein Ghetto im Osten* as an example of Vilna modernity. See Rose-Carol Washton Long, "Modernity as Anti-Nostalgia: The Photographic Books of Tim Gidal and Moshe Vorobeichic and the Eastern European Shtetl," *Ars Judaica* 7 (2011): 67–81; Carol Zemel, "Imaging the Shtetl: Diaspora Culture, Photography and Eastern European Jews," in *Diaspora and Visual Culture: Representing Africans and Jews*, ed. Nicholas Mirzoeff (New York: Routledge 2000), 264; Andrea Nelson, "Suspended Relationship: The Montage Photography Books of Moshe Raviv Vorobeichic," in *Time and Photography*, ed. Jan Baetens, Alexander Streitberger, and Hilde van Gelder, Lieven Gevaert Series 10 (Leuven: Leuven University Press, 2010), 141–164; Marina Dmitrieva, "Die Wilna-Fotocollagen von Moshe Vorobeichic," in *Jüdische Kultur(en) im Neuen Europa*, ed. Marina Dmitrieva and Heidemarie Petersen, Jüdische Kultur: Studien zur Geistesgeschichte, Religion und Literatur 13 (Wiesbaden: Harrasowitz Verlag, 2004), 69–84.

6. It is thus not as overtly political as some of its interpreters would have it, despite Vorobeichic's increasing dedication to Zionism and its cultural forms in the period. For such readings, see Zemel, and Long.

7. James Clifford, "On Ethnographic Surrealism," in *The Predicament of Culture: Twentieth-Century Ethnography, Literature, and Art* (Cambridge, Mass.: Harvard University Press, 2002), 117–151.

8. I use the turn-of-the-twentieth-century German term for Eastern European Jew, *Ostjude*, as a shorthand for these representational tropes. Although the term—which signified from its beginning a tropic image of Eastern European Jews—originated in German, I argue, in my in-progress book manuscript, that the discourse was by no means limited to the German context, and included, significantly, Yiddish texts from Eastern Europe. It also, of course, expanded westward. Vorobeichic's career indicates the geographical mobility of the discourse: he moved from Vilna to Germany to Paris, and published his book with a Zurich-based press that printed it in Leipzig.

9. The image reproduced here is the Hebrew cover of the German/Hebrew edition.

10. These techniques are all typical of the avant-garde photography of the Neues Sehen (New Vision), associated with the Bauhaus where Vorobeichic studied and first took up photography. His teacher László Moholy-Nagy was an important theorist and practitioner of the Neues Sehen. On German avant-garde photography books of the period, see Daniel H. Magilow, *The Photography of Crisis: The Photo Essays of Weimar Germany* (University Park: Pennsylvania State University Press, 2012) and *Autopsie: deutschsprachige Fotobücher 1918 bis 1945*, ed. Manfred Heiting and Roland Jaeger (Göttingen: Steidl, 2012); for examples of Moholy-Nagy's theoretical writings, see Christopher Phillips, ed., *Photography in the Modern Era: European Documents and Critical Writings, 1913–1940* (New York: Metropolitan Museum of Art: Aperture, 1989).

11. There was clearly a strong demand throughout the diaspora for nostalgic images from the "old country." But could Vorobeichic's book have tapped that same vein of sentimentality despite its striking modernism? Shneour's introduction and the publication history of the book suggest that the answer is yes.

12. It is true that museums also loom large in the mythology of the origins of primitivism and the avant-garde. The story of Picasso's inspiration in the Trocadéro Museum in Paris and subsequent transformation of *Les Desmoiselles d'Avignon* from a brilliant proto-cubist work into a primitivist masterpiece—the "first modernist painting," as it is sometimes called—is exemplary of the avant-garde appropriation (or at least apprecia-

tion) of ethnographic museums. Yet by the late 1920s museums were no longer a site of uncomplicated inspiration, but were a focus for the subversive primitivism and critique of colonialism of the ethnographic surrealists.

On the avant-garde critique of colonialism, see Janine Mileaf, "Body to Politics: Surrealist Exhibition of the Tribal and the Modern at the Anti-Imperialist Exhibition and the Galerie Charles Ratton," *RES: Anthropology and Aesthetics*, no. 40 (October 2001): 239–255; Jody Blake, "The Truth about The Colonies, 1931: Art Indigène in Service of the Revolution," *Oxford Art Journal* 25, no. 1 (January 2002): 35–58, doi:10.1093/oxartj/25.1.35. For further considerations of ethnography, primitivism, and the avant-garde, see Evan Maclyn Maurer, "In Quest of the Myth: An Investigation of the Relationships between Surrealism and Primitivism" (PhD thesis, University of Pennsylvania, 1974); Louise Tythacott, *Surrealism and the Exotic* (New York: Routledge, 2003); Marja Warehime, "'Vision Sauvage' and Images of Culture: Georges Bataille, Editor of Documents," *The French Review* 60, no. 1 (October 1986): 39–45; Ian Walker, *City Gorged with Dreams: Surrealism and Documentary Photography in Interwar Paris* (Manchester: Manchester University Press, 2002); Rosalind Krauss, "The Photographic Conditions of Surrealism," *October* 19 (December 1981): 3–34, doi:10.2307/778652; Julia Kelly, "Discipline and Indiscipline: The Ethnographies of Documents," *Papers of Surrealism* 7 (2007); Rosalind E. Krauss, Jane Livingston, and Dawn Ades, *L'amour Fou: Photography & Surrealism* (Washington, D.C.: Corcoran Gallery of Art, 1985). For general considerations of primitivism and art, see especially Robert Goldwater, *Primitivism in Modern Art* (Cambridge, Mass.: Harvard University Press, 1986); William Rubin, *"Primitivism" in 20th Century Art: Affinity of the Tribal and the Modern* (New York: Museum of Modern Art, 1990); Jill Lloyd, *German Expressionism: Primitivism and Modernity* (New Haven, Conn.: Yale University Press, 1991).

13. "Reḥov ha-yehudim be-'or va-tsel," 4.

14. On this discourse, see the definitive work: Johannes Fabian, *Time and the Other: How Anthropology Makes Its Object* (New York: Columbia University Press, 1983).

15. Shneour refers to an "album" since at the time he wrote the essay (it is dated October 1929 in the text), Vorobeichic's book had not yet been published; this date is obviously then the terminus ad quem for the images that were ultimately published in 1931.

16. He ultimately changed his name to Moshe Raviv in 1951, at the request of Ben Gurion.

17. By contrast, painting, exemplified by Chagall's "shtetl" works as well as primitivist artists from Gauguin to Nolde, was more readily able to portray primitivist subjects in modernist forms. It seems to me that the relative belatedness of modernist primitivism in photography is due to the heavy influence of anthropology on photography, or, to be more specific, of ethnographic and anthropological photography on the nonscientific photographic representation of primitivist subjects.

18. Clifford argued that the relationship of influence between ethnography and surrealism among the group around Georges Bataille and his journal *Documents* was not unidirectional (from ethnography to surrealism), but reciprocal, resulting in an ethnography that was, in essence, surrealist. This notion has been widely influential but also strongly criticized. See Jean Jamin, "L'ethnographie mode d'inemploi: de quelques rapports de l'ethnologie avec le malaise dans la civilisation," in *Le mal et la douleur*, ed. Jacques Hainard and Roland Kaehr (Neuchâtel: Musée d'ethnographie, 1986), 45–79; Jean Jamin, "Anxious Science: Ethnography as a Devil's Dictionary," *VAR Visual Anthropology Review*

7, no. 1 (1991): 84–91; Denis Hollier, "The Use-Value of the Impossible," trans. Liesl Oll-man, *October* 60 (April 1992): 3–24; Michael Richardson, "An Encounter of Wise Men and Cyclops Women: Considerations of Debates on Surrealism and Anthropology," *Critique of Anthropology* 13, no. 1 (March 1993): 57–75; Frances M. Slaney, "Psychoanalysis and Cycles of 'Subversion' in Modern Art and Anthropology," *Dialectical Anthropology* 14, no. 3 (January 1989): 213–234.

   19. James F. Lastra, "Why Is This Absurd Picture Here? Ethnology/Equivocation/Bu-ñuel," *October* 89 (July 1999): 51–68.

   20. Ibid., 52.

   21. Ibid., 53.

   22. Ibid., 57.

   23. Ibid., 58.

   24. Ibid., 67.

   25. Luis Buñuel, "Land without Bread," in *F Is for Phony: Fake Documentary and Truth's Undoing*, ed. Alexandra Juhasz and Jesse Lerner (Minneapolis: University of Minnesota Press, 2006), 92.

   26. See Lastra, 66; and Buñuel, 96.

   27. Walker, 5.

   28. Michael Richardson, *Georges Bataille* (New York: Routledge, 1994), 52.

   29. Indeed, Jeffrey Shandler calls this mode "the time of Vishniac." His reading of this representational mode is based, however, mostly on the post-Holocaust reception of Vishniac's works, and is premised on the mistaken contention that no photography books devoted to Eastern European Jewry were published before the war. See Jeffrey Shandler, "The Time of Vishniac: Photographs of Pre-War East European Jewry in Post-War Con-texts," *Polin: Studies in Polish Jewry* 16 (2003): 313–333.

   30. A mistake unfortunately echoed in Rose-Carol Washton Long's mistranslation of the same caption as "Talmud Hours": Long, 73.

   31. In pointing out the simultaneity of visual puns on Yiddish expressions in Chagall, Seth Wolitz has called this phenomenon "Marranism," since the dual meanings exist in two separate worlds. See Seth L. Wolitz, "Vitebsk versus Bezalel: A Jewish 'Kulturkampf' in the Plastic Arts," in *The Emergence of Modern Jewish Politics: Bundism and Zionism in Eastern Europe*, ed. Zvi Y. Gitelman (Pittsburgh: University of Pittsburgh Press, 2003), 172.

   32. Alternatively, the meaning could be based on the status of the letter yud as the smallest letter in the Hebrew alphabet—barely more than a "point" of ink, but just as important as any other letter. The phrase is clearly an item of popular theology, but I have been unable to find any sources that clarify its origins. Mendel Piekarz associates the phrase with nineteenth- and twentieth-century Hasidic thought on the subject of Jewish chosenness and essential Jewishness, and traces this theological strand to Yehuda Halevi and the Maharal (Yehudah Leib ben Beẓalel). This accounts for the theology of the phrase, but does not clarify its rather peculiar imagery or its origins. See Mendel Piekarz, *Ḥasidut Polin: megamot ra'ayoniyot beyn shetey ha-milḥamot u-vi-gzerot 700–705 ("ha-sho'ah")* (Jerusalem: Bialik Institute, 1990), chapter 5. Nevertheless, its meaning is clear, and both conjectural etymologies support my reading of Vorobeichic's word/image play.

   For a summary of the phrase's appearance in literary works, see Matthew Hoffman, "From 'Pintele Yid to Racenjude': Chaim Zhitlovsky and Racial Conceptions of Jewish-ness," *Jewish History* 19, no. 1 (January 2005): 66.

33. Rosalind Krauss, "Photography in the Service of Surrealism," in *Art of the Twentieth Century: A Reader*, ed. Jason Gaiger and Paul Wood (New Haven, Conn.: Yale University Press, 2004), 124.

34. M. Vorobeichic, *Ein Ghetto im Osten (Wilna): 65 Bilder*, ed. Emil Schaeffer (Zürich: Orell Füssli Verlag, 1931), 3 (in Yiddish).

35. Ibid.

36. "M. Vorobeichic: Das Ghetto von Wilna," *Menorah* 10, nos. 9–10 (September 1932): 440. The translation is mine.

37. "Reḥov ha-yehudim be-'or va-tsel," 7.

38. Max Weinreich, "A bilder-bukh fun der yidisher Vilne," *Forverts*, September 20, 1931, sec. 2, 4. The translation is mine.

39. This time the German caption retains the irony of the Hebrew and Yiddish, while the English elides it with a mistranslation: "The Material Wealth of Israel."

40. Devin Fore exposes the ways in which the false dichotomy between realism and modernism obscures a fruitful reading of literature and art in the period. See Devin Fore, *Realism after Modernism: The Rehumanization of Art and Literature* (Cambridge, Mass.: MIT Press, 2012).

41. On the anticolonial exhibition, see Janine Mileaf, "Body to Politics: Surrealist Exhibition of the Tribal and the Modern at the Anti-Imperialist Exhibition and the Galerie Charles Ratton," *RES: Anthropology and Aesthetics*, no. 40 (October 2001): 239–255; Jody Blake, "The Truth about the Colonies, 1931: Art Indigène in Service of the Revolution," *Oxford Art Journal* 25, no. 1 (January 2002): 35–58, doi:10.1093/oxartj/25.1.35; Lynn E. Palermo, "L'Exposition Anticoloniale: Political or Aesthetic Protest?," *French Cultural Studies* 20, no. 1 (February 2009): 27–46.

42. I elaborate on the concept in my in-progress book manuscript, *The Museum of the Jews: Salvaging the Primitive in German-Jewish and Yiddish Literature*.

PART 3.
SPACES OF JEWISH ETHNOGRAPHY
BETWEEN DIASPORA AND NATION

Zionism's Ethnographic Knowledge

Leo Motzkin's and Heinrich York-Steiner's Narratives of Palestine (1898–1904)

ALEXANDER ALON

THE CULTURAL ASPECT OF KNOWLEDGE PRODUCTION FOR THE ZIONIST MOVEMENT

Knowledge and science took on a central role in the Zionist movement. On the one hand, they were of practical use in the mass settlement of Palestine, and on the other hand, they were employed by the movement to culturally define Jewish identity. In 1895 Theodor Herzl wrote in his programmatic essay *Der Judenstaat*:

> When the peoples used to wander in historical times, they let themselves be carried, pulled, and hurled. Like locust swarms they used to go down unconsciously. The reason for this is because the earth was not known in the historical times.
> The new wandering of the Jews must happen according to scientific principles.[1]

Science is thus understood to guarantee the success of the Zionist project: the settlement of a land can only be successful if it is based on "scientific principles," and the very usage of these principles marks, for Herzl, a turning point in the history of the Jewish people from being a passive object of nature to becoming its active master. Simultaneously invoking different meanings of the Latin term *colere*,[2] Herzl charges science with the objectives of both cultivating the land and elevating "the Jews" to cultural agents.

However, despite the movement's lofty objectives, after four years of
Zionist activities, Zionist leader Max Nordau described the movement's
relation to necessary knowledge as still desolate. In a speech given at the
Fifth Zionist Congress in 1901, the noted physician and bestselling author
paints a gloomy picture of the Zionist movement. According to Nordau,
the organization, very embarrassingly, does not know who the potential
adherents of Zionism are. How many are there? What are their occupations? What do they wear? What do they eat, what do they drink? Nordau
argues that the previous generations of Jews were not willing to make use
of sciences such as anthropology, biology, or economics to register "exact
anthropological, biological, economical, and intellectual statistics about
the Jewish People."[3] To talk about the Jewish people without having acquired this knowledge, Nordau adds polemically, is futile, is nothing but
"empty chatter," is "at best poetry [Lyrik]." And he proceeds:

> We should deal with unchallengeable, iron numbers, but instead we don't
> have anything but general, indistinct feelings [Empfindungen]. From
> those few experts in the field we ask for information and we get moods
> [Stimmungen]. We look around searching for demography and what we
> discover is literature and art.[4]

This pleading for a thoroughly quantitative approach that is independent from the knowledge-producing subject is not shared by everyone in
the movement. One year later Leo Motzkin,[5] a mathematician by training
and one of the first statisticians for the Zionist movement,[6] while sharing Nordau's judgement of Zionism's ignorance, disagrees with Nordau's
discarding of "literature and art." On the contrary, in his article "Jüdische
Statistik und Zionismus" (Jewish Statistics and Zionism),[7] Motzkin
sketches a system to generate knowledge that indeed seems to oscillate
between the means of "poetry" and those of the sciences:

> [When studying the Jews,] scientific objectivity should more often than
> not exchange the statistician for the artist. Only he [the artist] would be
> capable of describing the transfers and intricacies of work, only he could
> catch a glimpse of the disordered occupations, not by giving them a name,
> but by analyzing and thus framing them.[8]

Motzkin thus postulates the artist as the ideal statistician of the Jews
by arguing that only his work can be deemed scientifically objective. Art,
defined here as the work of one single person, as subjectified knowledge,

so to speak, may generate scientific knowledge. It follows from this that art and science are not only interdependent; as systems for generating knowledge, they cannot be distinguished from each other.

While the difference between the approaches of Motzkin and Nordau seems clear enough, a closer look at the form in which they are clad also reveals significant similarities. Indeed, it is most conspicuous that both describe the production of knowledge for Zionism by employing aesthetic terms that refer to debates on the social role and the essence of literature: while Motzkin's concept of literature focuses on the description of social deficits, seemingly echoing literary programs close to French naturalism of the nineteenth century, Nordau gathers a whole arsenal of aesthetic concepts that are strongly connected to German Romanticism (witness "Stimmung," "Empfindung") and mentions a literary genre he obviously sees as a medium of subjectivity ("Lyrik," i.e., poetry), though he does so only to pit it, in a brutal dichotomy, against the sciences of his epoch.[9] Nordau thus seems to be paving the way for an interweaving of the discourses that he so skillfully detaches from one another in his talk. He does so by employing the concepts he pretends to despise, while being at the same time in obvious need of them to define a process of knowledge production that differs from systems that only generate "empty chatter."

This seemingly unavoidable interweaving of discourses one is faced with when analyzing the cultural aspect of Zionist knowledge production calls for a perspective of enquiry steeped in literary history, thus widening its scope to literary texts that negotiate the requirement to produce knowledge useful to the Zionist cause, and that reflect the methodological problems that accompany this enterprise. Due to their discursive entanglement with texts from a scientific discourse, such literary texts must be regarded as intertexts relevant both to the scientific and to the literary discourse.

The texts which will be treated in the following pages are set in both discourses. While the following section deals with the account of a knowledge-gathering expedition to Palestine undertaken by Leo Motzkin and presented to a political institution, the Zionist Congress, the two later sections deal with publicistic and explicitly literary texts, written by Heinrich York-Steiner for different newspapers with Jewish or Zionist affiliations.

All of these texts were published between the years 1899 and 1904. They thematize the mutual perception of foreignness and the cohesion of

Jewish entities and so focus on exemplary situations in which foreignness is either overcome or sustained. They also employ strategies to present these situations as paradigmatic for entire communities. This focus shows that these texts negotiate an essential question within ethnography, one that asks "how the *ethnoi*, the smaller and larger entities of human social life, organize themselves and how they produce cohesion between one another."[10] Additionally, these texts negotiate the debate raised by Max Nordau and Leo Motzkin regarding the essence and production of knowledge useful to Zionism, thus echoing methodological issues of this scientific endeavor. Ethnography, therefore, appears as a figure of thought to negotiate this debate.

AN EXAMPLE OF "ARTISTIC" SCIENCE: KNOWLEDGE PRODUCTION BY MEANS OF "IMPRESSIONS" IN LEO MOTZKIN'S EXPEDITION TO PALESTINE

From its first days, the World Zionist Organization, founded in 1897, exhibited an interest in assessing the Jewish population of Palestine's potential to contribute to the Zionist colonization of Palestine. In one of its first steps in this direction, it decided shortly before the Second Zionist Congress in 1898, upon Theodor Herzl's initiative,[11] to dispatch Leo Motzkin to Palestine, tasking him to "analyze the social and economical circumstances of the Jews" and to find out "what prospects the Palestinian elements offer for the future and if they are suitable to colonizational or industrial enterprises."[12] While Motzkin had agreed to spend the summer of 1898 in Palestine and to report on his expedition before the Congress in late August the same year, in his report he stated that at first he had deemed Herzl's task unacceptable, because lack of time would not allow for such "thorough work." He therefore left for Palestine only on the condition that he would be allowed to content himself with "casting a glance at present Jewish Palestine, collecting statistical data within reason and, first and foremost, presenting to the Congress sociopsychological and ethnopsychological [*völkerpsychologische*] impressions."[13]

Motzkin accords to both means of knowledge production—to Herzl's original task of "analyzing the social and economical circumstances of the Jews" and to the gathering of "sociopsychological and ethnopsychological impressions"—the potential to produce reliable results. While

Motzkin concedes, in his report to the Congress, that in the future one would have to investigate matters in a "much more thorough" way and for a longer amount of time, he claims at the same time to be "convinced . . . that my *general* views on the Jewish circumstances will also be confirmed after long and calm analysis [*Studium*]."[14] This is a remarkable statement, insofar as the "long and calm" analysis that Motzkin envisions is extremely rich and detailed: not only does he recommend to "study in detail the state and the idiosyncrasies of our Palestinian brothers" but also "to study the land exactly, to acquire a completely worked-out view on the climatological and hygienic circumstances [and] to determine the prospects and possibilities of new industries and to determine the legal circumstances."

On what grounds does Motzkin consider these two processes of knowledge production to be equivalent? One might be tempted to answer this question in the broad framework of ethnopsychology. In one of its founding texts, "On the Concept and the Possibility of an Ethnopsychology," published in 1851,[15] Moritz Lazarus describes the goals of the soon to be established science as "discovering the essence [*Wesen*] and the action of the folk spirit [*Volksgeist*] *psychologically;* discovering the *laws* to which the inner, the spiritual, or the ideal actions of a folk adhere, be it in life, the arts, or the sciences . . . and [discovering] the *reasons* . . . for the birth, development, and fall of a folk."[16] Lazarus places special emphasis on the process of knowledge production and states that "Ethnopsychology can only set out from the facts of folk life [*Völkerleben*]" and that "only from observation, ordering, and comparing of appearances [*Erscheinungen*] can it hope to discover the laws of the folk spirit."[17] However, *Völkerpsychologie*, as conceived by Lazarus in his founding text, does not employ the concept of "impression" that Motzkin associates with it. As a matter of fact, even Motzkin—a former student of Lazarus's at the Friedrich-Wilhelms-University in Berlin[18]—does not define it in his account of the expedition. Taking this metaphorical expression literally, "impression" seems to denote a process in which a certain issue marks a trail, so to speak, which in turn can be used to reconstruct the issue. From this, it can already be deduced that Motzkin's analytical concept runs against Lazarus's positivistic idea of knowledge production, thus begging the question of how "impression" is to be understood in this context. But what is the context?

In a nutshell, Motzkin's speech assesses the potential of the Jewish population of Palestine to turn away from a way of life dominated by religion and deemed economically and "morally" problematic and to become, instead, "Jewish peasants." To do this, Motzkin describes the problematic circumstances in Palestine: the economic situation of the Jewish inhabitants is precarious, and most of them live, or try to live, from *ḥaluka,* money sent by Jews in the diaspora to support the needy residents of Palestine. However, the support is meager and the system of dividing the money leads to unbalanced results, as the money is divided according to each person's membership in a *kolel,* a community of Jews of the same origin. For Motzkin this, in turn, leads to problems in the collection of data: as most Jews in Palestine are dependent upon the *ḥaluka,* they are also dependent on the image that potential donors have of them. Conscious of this dynamics, they try to find ways to influence it. This can easily lead to the observer obtaining a completely incorrect or distorted image of the "factual circumstances."[19] Poverty among the Jews in Palestine not only leads to their "fighting for bread"; according to Motzkin, it is also responsible for one of the gravest "plagues" (*Übel*) of the local Jewish community, namely their permanent appetite for scheming (*Intriguenthätigkeit*): "Fighting for bread leads to specific passions, heats up the *kolelim* against each other, and gives rise to a hypocritical fanaticism."[20] In other words, the *ḥaluka* creates an economic incentive to appear pious, as this heightens the probability of receiving a greater share of the donated money. On a more general note, this "appetite for scheming" can create the dangerous illusion that two different types of Jews are in fact identical. Motzkin remarks that, for instance, at the Wailing Wall in Jerusalem one can find

> the pious and the hypocritical Jews in the same way [*in gleicher Weise*], real feeling and showing off of artificial ecstasy side by side. Thus one can observe the external decay of our material existence and the degeneration [*Entartung*] of our inner being [*inneres Wesen*] at the same place.[21]

Two remarks can be made here. On the one hand, Motzkin claims to be able to perceive a difference between two types of Jews despite their behaving "in the same way," and despite their differing merely in their emotional attitude towards Judaism. On the other hand, Motzkin sees the observed Jews as evidence of a problem that he considers himself a part of. The encounter at the Wailing Wall is thus depicted as an encounter of the observer with his own—collective—identity.[22]

These remarks beg the question of how Motzkin generates his knowledge of the Jews of Palestine. Mirroring the importance of this question to him, Motzkin answers it in the beginning of his speech. Here, he describes how he countered the dissimulating actions of "scheming" by the Palestinian Jews with "systematic [*planmässig*] and conscious [*bewusst*] observation," through researching the matter and employing a certain amount of cunning:

> My system consisted in getting in touch with the most diverse circles and, most importantly, starting a conversation with as many ordinary people [lit., people of the folk] as possible and proceeding inattentively; to chatter on the subject of their lives.[23]

In other words, in conversations with the objects of his attention, Motzkin claims to have hidden from his interlocutors the specific interest that the conversation held for him. Motzkin thus answered the assumed dissimulation or scheming of his interlocutors with his own dissimulation.[24]

Motzkin's production of knowledge, which is part of his undertaking to produce an "ethnopsychological and sociopsychological impression," thus not only sets out from certain cultural assumptions regarding the "scheming" of the Jewish population but also ventures into the realm of the fictive. On the one hand, by claiming to have to extrapolate the true meaning of his interlocutor's speech, Motzkin admits that this meaning is actually constructed and not the fruit of a gathering of "facts of folk life," as Moritz Lazarus would have it.[25] On the other hand, extrapolating information from a conversation that does not even bear the marks of a scientific interview also suggests fiction, because it is a process in which one situation, an innocuous chat between two new acquaintances, is deliberately seen as another, that is to say as part of a systematic process designed by one interlocutor to gather reliable, scientific knowledge from the other. Without renouncing his claim to objectivity, the *investigator* Leo Motzkin thus presents himself also as the subjective *author* (or, to employ the previously mentioned term from 1902, the "artist") Motzkin, the sole creator of a world presented at the Zionist Congress, whose creation is dependent on the conversational and dissimulational skills that he employed during the research.

The "ethnopsychological and sociopsychological impression" that Motzkin considers equivalent to a detailed positivistic study (in its capacity to reveal "general views" on the situation) can therefore be described as a poetic procedure based on and requiring hermeneutics. The concept of knowledge production underlying this procedure seems to have been devised by Motzkin as a variation on the one suggested by Moritz Lazarus in his founding text of ethnopsychology. By adapting the methodology to his field of study, the Jews of Palestine and their idiosyncrasies (obviously too complex for Lazarus's methodology), Motzkin has innovated on Lazarus's idea of *Völkerpsychologie*. Meanwhile, Motzkin's assertion of the equivalence of the poetic and positivistic procedures implies that "the laws of the inner, spiritual, or ideal actions of a people" are to be determined by studying, living, and imagining interpersonal relationships.

This conclusion leaves several questions unanswered. To begin with, one must ask whether the absolute authority put in the hands of the investigator does not undermine Lazarus's mechanistic goal, "to discover the laws of the inner, spiritual, or ideal actions of a people." After all, it is not clear how the investigator Motzkin could always be so sure of understanding his fellow Jews, given their (and his) culture of deception. To put it differently: can one devise a systematic conceptualization of interpersonal relations? And if so, how?

While there is no historical evidence for it, the following texts by Heinrich York-Steiner seem to take up this very challenge. The comparison with his explicitly literary texts will be a first step in assessing the relationship between literature and science in Zionism.

A TEXT AS A CONCEPTUAL BASIS FOR ETHNOGRAPHICAL SITUATIONS: "DER TALMUDBAUER" BY HEINRICH YORK-STEINER

Between 1898 and 1904, or in the broader timeframe of Motzkin's expedition to Palestine and the debate on the relation between science and literature in Zionism, the author and Zionist functionary Heinrich York-Steiner (born in Szenitz 1859, died in Tel Aviv in 1934)[26] published a series in the German Jewish press with the Zionist publisher Jüdischer Verlag (Berlin), consisting of articles and narratives that focus on two issues: the social life of the Jews, and the Jewish settlement of Palestine. Institutionally, these texts were published within the context of a Herzlian Zionism: most of the articles appeared in the weekly *Die Welt,* which had been established following the First Zionist Congress in 1897 as an informative "propaganda instrument" for Zionism[27] and had became the official periodical of the World Zionist Organization a few years later. *Die Welt* featured on its cover the programmatic Basel declaration calling for a state in Palestine for the Jewish people: "Zionism aims at establishing for the Jewish people a home in Palestine to be secured under public law."

York-Steiner's *Talmudbauer* trilogy, a collection published in 1904 by Jüdischer Verlag, contains the tales "Die todte Frau" (The Dead Woman), "Maskir,"[28] and "Der Talmudbauer" (The Talmud-Peasant).[29] Throughout the three narratives, an anonymous omniscient narrator sketches a rigorous and methodic ordering of all ethnographical situations where love between Jews of different cultures might occur—a rhetorical strategy to convey the impression of authenticity.

In these ethnographic situations, it is a text that stands in the center, and human relationships originate from involvement with it. More precisely, it is the Talmud, and from the Talmud the concept of *kil'aim*—literally "diverse kinds," a term that gives its name to the eponymous Mishnaic tractate[30]—that structures the whole trilogy.

To employ a cinematic metaphor, the three texts contained in *Der Talmudbauer* are held together by a long tracking shot beginning at the turn of the nineteenth–twentieth century in a small village in the Austro-Hungarian Empire and, through several other villages, reaching the Jewish quarter of the Old City of Jerusalem, thereby connecting Europe and Palestine. As in a collection of case studies, this tracking shot allows the reader to study how one and the same question is addressed from Europe to Palestine: under which circumstances do Jews of different cultures establish emotional bonds with Jews and non-Jews? Will, for instance, an assimilated Jew be allowed by the non-Jewish inhabitants of his village to bury his wife at an honorable site in the local non-Jewish cemetery? The first narrative of the trilogy, "Die todte Frau," answers this question with a clear *no*: in the diaspora, Judaism is always perceived in an unfavorable way, even if one denies being a Jew. Emotional bonding between a Jew and a gentile is therefore seen as impossible. Can two assimilated Jews in the diaspora love each other, if one has a sentimental connection to Judaism, while the other one does not? The answer given in "Maskir" is negative as well. In a manner reminiscent of an experiment, the same question gives rise to several other case studies where Jews of different degrees of assimilation, national consciousness, and religiosity are paired in the diaspora as well as in Palestine. The result of the experiment is not surprising, given the Zionist context in which *Der Talmudbauer* was published: only in Palestine, and only under precise circumstances, is love possible. Still, it is interesting to see what the conditions of love in Palestine are.

It is in the narrative "Der Talmudbauer," the last work in the eponymous trilogy, where this question is negotiated, and it is precisely here that the link between text and human relationship is seen as crucial. Haim, the protagonist of the narration, is a young Talmud scholar who immigrated to Palestine with his parents in the late nineteenth century. He lives with them in extreme poverty in Jerusalem, dependent on the *ḥaluka*. The father, who taught his son the "Talmudic science"—the term *Wissenschaft* is explicitly used—is convinced that by educating his son to be a great scholar he will hasten the coming of the Messiah. Therefore, despite his nearly starving family, the father forbids Haim from getting a job that would save them all from hunger and thirst. Under these circumstances, the son does not see any other solution to the problem than to leave his family, and by a chain of significant coincidences he ends up in one of the Jewish settlements of the Old Yishuv, in Reḥovot. While Haim's father is constantly afraid that his son, having left Jerusalem and having very much limited the time spent on studying the Talmud, could socialize with unbelievers and thus delay the coming of the Messiah, this fear turns out to be unfounded, albeit in a surprising way. Indeed, in Reḥovot Haim meets Mirjam, a settler who has been studying the Talmud with her father, just like he has. In the central episode of their encounter, a Talmudic debate between them ceases to be centered merely on the Talmudic text and is suddenly contextualized within the present reality of the settlers' agricultural work in Palestine. The subject is a specific aspect of the Mishnaic tractate Kil'aim to which Mirjam directs Haim's attention:

In my opinion, the question of the Kil'aim is much more serious. According to the Law, one is not allowed to sow cereals between fruit or wine grapes. . . . This Law must be explained from a practical perspective. If the wine grapes are to grow well, they have to have all the power of the soil at their disposal; that is what the agronomists teach. . . . When the German colonists of the Templar community, who do not know our Laws, sowed cereals between the vines, their wine was so poor that they stopped doing so later on.[31]

Mirjam's interaction with the text differs significantly from Haim's, since Mirjam reads the Talmud as a document rooted in Palestine and as a text whose discussions, for instance on agriculture, can be useful to the practical agricultural work in the present settlement. Haim, on the contrary, has been brought up to regard the study of the Talmud as essential for its own sake, and the text itself as timeless. The encounter of the two youngsters, based on different readings of the tractate Kil'aim, is therefore also one of knowledge cultures. The fact that this tractate is central to the encounter of Haim and Mirjam, and that it also thematizes the rules for "mixing" items, shows that it might be programmatic for the whole narrative. Indeed, the correct handling of cereals is but one of the subjects dealt with in Kil'aim. The word is used in Leviticus 19:19[32] and Deuteronomy 22:9,[33] where it is employed to describe the laws on crossbreeding animals, crossbreeding seeds, and mixing wool and linen.[34] If read within the context of "Der Talmudbauer," it does therefore bear a distinctly biopolitical undertone, mirroring the central question of the trilogy, which considers the circumstances under which Jews of different cultures establish emotional bonds with other people. This programmatic significance of the Talmud can even be traced in the images employed in the text, for example in one of the scenes concluding "Der Talmudbauer," where the love between Haim and Mirjam finally blossoms and the mutual foreignness which had until then characterized the ethnographic situations that the two youngsters of different cultures were part of, dissolves:

They were standing under the pigeon shelter. There was a rush in the air. Mirjam looked up. A sparrow hawk flew by, the poor pigeons fled. As she lifted her face, he looked into her eyes; they were moist and gleamed. He asked about her pain, she lowered her head. And he saw that she was

crying silently. So he bent over and again she looked imploringly—as if
to say: "Go, please, go!" But he felt her breath and it was as if he was spellbound. His big strong body started to shiver, so that he had to cling to the
tender small girl. As he was holding her, she sank toward his broad chest
and now she burst into a loud sobbing. He heard the sound of complete
bliss [Seligkeit; lit., also "salvation"] in her crying which had filled [durch-
dringen; lit., "forced itself through"] the air on that evening of the Sabbath,
there, in Reḥovot. And he had not even said a word yet! So he hurried up,
wanting not to miss that beautiful hour which he had longed for so much.
And he spoke————Mirjam, for her part, stopped crying.[35]

The description of Haim's and Mirjam's sudden ability to feel the emotions of the other without having to utter a word stands for the occurrence
of love between the two, although the word is conspicuously absent: the
greatest bliss lies in mutual, effortless understanding. As can be seen when
Haim perceives Miriam's crying as a sound of "salvation," this occurrence
of love is given a strong religious relevance that can be detailed by focusing
on the images employed in describing this situation. Here, the pigeons are
especially relevant. Indeed, in one of the narratives of the trilogy, pigeons
are mentioned as the object of a Talmudic debate, in which questions of
sacrifice in the Temple in Jerusalem play a significant role. In the second
narrative in the trilogy, "Maskir," a young man with a Talmudic education,
unsure of whether to fully assimilate himself to his non-Jewish surroundings or to commit to the idea of a Jewish nation, remembers a situation in
his adolescence that had led him to quit the study of Talmud. His teacher
had brought up a Talmudic debate on the attributes of the pigeons that a
woman needs to bring to the Temple in Jerusalem after her menstruation,
to have them sacrificed.[36] The adolescent remembers having felt a sudden
sense of absurdity and a realization that these laws had lost their function,
given that the Temple had been destroyed and most Jews had lived outside
of Palestine for a very long time, making irrelevant the physical context in
which they used to make sense. Thus, he had seen his teacher's discussion
of this debate in class as anachronistic and irrelevant to contemporary
Jewish life and had quit studying the Talmud: "He didn't want to mea-
sure up altars which were never to be built and he did not want to choose
pigeons where there were no altars."[37] The occurrence of pigeons in the
encounter between Haim and Mirjam can therefore be read as the over-

laying of a Talmudic image. For the understanding of the text's content, this bears two consequences. On the one hand, the image can be read as anticipating the sexual encounter of Haim and Miriam, which would take place in present-day Palestine. On the other hand, it can simultaneously be read as anticipating a Messianic situation, where the Temple in Jerusalem is rebuilt and the aforementioned laws of the Talmud are again relevant to Jewish social life. Additionally, from a literary perspective, the employing of a Talmudic image is a clear hint that the Talmud is seen as a text that is able to conceptualize and at the same time serve as a basis for the most important element in Jewish life: the ethnographic situation with two young people as protagonists, whose relationship guarantees Jewish life (in Palestine) and guarantees the coming of the Messiah.

CONCLUSION: A LITERATURE MIRRORING SCIENTIFIC METHODOLOGY

It has been shown that literature and science are deeply entrenched in Zionism, as they not only share an interest in Jewish culture but also confront similar methodological problems and employ comparable strategies to solve them. According to my reading of Motzkin's concept of "impressions," interpersonal encounters and the fiction of understanding play a crucial role in determining "the laws of the inner, spiritual, or ideal actions of a people." Indeed, York-Steiner's texts seem to take this assertion to the extreme. On the one hand, *Der Talmudbauer* devises a comprehensive system, able to explain every possibility of Jewish encounters in the whole world. It does this by a systematic conceptualization of all possible interpersonal relations in Jewish society at the turn of the century, stating that mutual understanding is possible, but only if congruent knowledge cultures meet in discussing and practicing the Talmud. Thus, to quote Lazarus, it presents itself as a discovery of "the laws of the inner, spiritual, or ideal actions of a people," while tackling a methodological problem in Motzkin's procedure of knowledge production, namely that it lacks the concept of an ethnographical encounter.

On the other hand, *Der Talmudbauer* renounces one of the main features of scientific expeditions: to convey knowledge of a place and its inhabitants, one must visit it. Instead of a personal assertion from the narrator that he has seen with his own eyes what he is presenting to the reader, the text offers another proof of the correctness of its thesis; it employs a sort of poetic plausibility. As detailed, the constellation of the characters and the progress of the narrative are mirrored in the Talmudic principle of kil'aim. As this poetic relation is depicted as stringent, it is unnecessary to employ a (fictional) entity to witness the correctness of *Der Talmudbauer*'s thesis on Jewish society.

NOTES

This article has been written within the context of my dissertation, which is part of the project "The Knowledge of Zionism," funded by the Swiss National Science Foundation. Parts of it were researched and written while I was a visiting research fellow at the Rosenzweig Minerva Research Center at the Hebrew University in Jerusalem (January–July 2014). I thank Yfaat Weiss for the invitation and the ETH Zurich for granting me an exchange scholarship to sponsor my stay at the HUJI. I am especially indebted to Shaul Katz for bringing my attention to Leo Motzkin's expedition to Palestine and to Simon Milligan and Brian Tich for proofreading the manuscript. All the following translations from German are my own.

1. Theodor Herzl, *Der Judenstaat: Versuch einer modernen Lösung der Judenfrage von Theodor Herzl, Doctor der Rechte* (Leipzig: M. Breitenstein's Verlags-Buchhandlung, 1896), 71.

2. Regarding the historical semantics of the Latin term *colere*, cf. Hartmut Böhme, "Vom Kultus zur Kultur(wissenschaft):—Zur historischen Semantik des Kulturbegriffs," in *Literaturwissenschaft—Kulturwissenschaft: Positionen, Themen, Perspektiven*, ed. Renate Glaser and Matthias Luserke (Opladen: Westdeutscher Verlag, 1996), 48–68.

3. Zionisten-Congress, *Stenographisches Protokoll der Verhandlungen des V. Zionisten-Congresses in Basel 26., 27., 28., 29. und 30. December 1901* (Vienna: Verlag des Vereines "Erez Israel,"1901), 100.

4. Zionisten-Congress, *Stenographisches Protokoll 1901*, 102.

5. For a detailed biography of Motzkin, see Alex Bein, *Sefer Motzkin* (Jerusalem: ha-hanhala ha-tsionit ve-hanhalat ha-kongres ha-yehudi ha-ʻolami, 1939), כל—קמ.

6. Mitchell B. Hart, *Social Science and the Politics of Modern Jewish Identity* (Stanford, Calif.: Stanford University Press, 2000), 42.

7. Leo Motzkin, "Jüdische Statistik und Zionismus," in *Juedischer Almanach*, ed. Berthold Feiwel and Lilien Ephraim Mose (Berlin: Juedischer Verlag, 1902), 233–241.

8. Ibid., 236–238.

9. On naturalism, cf. Yves Chevrel, "Naturalistisch," in *Ästhetische Grundbegriffe*, vol. 4, *Medien-Populär*, ed. Karlheinz Barck, Martin Fontius, Dieter Schlenstedt, Burkhart Steinwachs, and Friedrich Wolfzettel (Stuttgart: Metzler, 2002), 404–431; on Romanticism, cf. Ernst Müller, "Romantisch/Romantik," in *Ästhetische Grundbegriffe*, vol. 5, *Post-*

moderne-Synästhesie, ed. Karlheinz Barck, Martin Fontius, Dieter Schlenstedt, Burkhart Steinwachs, and Friedrich Wolfzettel (Stuttgart: Metzler, 2003), 315–344.

10. Alexander Honold, "Das Fremde verstehen" (1997), http://www.inst.at/trans/1Nr /honold.htm.

11. Bein, *Sefer Motzkin,* 21f.

12. Thus Motzkin's own description of the task. Zionisten-Congress, *Stenographisches Protokoll der verhandlungen des II. Zionisten-Congresses gehalten zu Basel vom 28. bis 31. August 1898* (Vienna: Verlag des Vereines "Erez Israel," 1898), 99.

13. Ibid., 99.

14. Ibid., 101.

15. Moritz Lazarus, "Ueber den Begriff und die Möglichkeit einer Völkerpsychologie," in *Deutsches Museum: Zeitschrift für Literatur, Kunst und öffentliches Leben,* vol. 1 (Leipzig: Brockhaus, 1851), 112–126. On Völkerpsychologie and its reception, cf. Egbert Klautke, *The Mind of the Nation: Völkerpsychologie in Germany, 1851–1955* (New York: Berghahn Books, 2013).

16. Ibid., 112 f.

17. Ibid., 116.

18. Motzkin took a class with Lazarus in "Psychologie" in his first semester at the university, in 1887. He also studied with Wilhelm Dilthey, Georg Simmel, Emil Heinrich du Bois-Reymond, and Heinrich von Treitschke, but his main emphasis was on mathematics. Cf. his University documents at the Central Zionist Archives: CZA A126\6–5.

19. *Stenographisches Protokoll 1898,* 100.

20. Ibid. 109.

21. Ibid., 106. The elliptical syntax mirrors the German original.

22. This is not the place to discuss the implications of the term *Entartung* that Motzkin uses. A detailed history of it can be found in Karin Tebben, "Nachwort," in *Nordau, Max: Entartung,* ed. Karin Tebben (Berlin: De Gruyter, 2013), 773–776.

23. *Stenographisches Protokoll 1901,* 100f.

24. From a letter to Herzl, written to him while in Palestine, it even emerges that during his stay in Palestine Motzkin went as far as trying to hide that he was an emissary of the World Zionist Organization on a mission to gather information. Thus, on July 13, 1898, he writes to Herzl—who had seemingly asked him to publish a travel narrative for the Zionist newspaper *Die Welt* while traveling through Palestine—that it would be inconvenient to do so at this moment, as this would make it "almost impossible to get to know the life of the colonies. . . . presently I already have the problem that the aim of my travel, to study the lives of the Jews here and to report on it at the Congress, is frequently guessed." Central Zionist Archives CZA A126\207-2 and CZA A126\207-3.

25. Lazarus, 116.

26. Heinrich York-Steiner was one of the pseudonyms used by Heinrich Steiner; other names include "Henrik" and "Heinrich York." Cf. Michael Peschke, *International Encyclopedia of Pseudonyms* (Munich: Saur, 2006). Short biographical sketches can be found in Institut für Zeitgeschichte, Research Foundation for Jewish Immigration, New York, Werner Röder, and Herbert Arthur Strauss, eds., *Biographisches Handbuch der deutschsprachigen Emigration nach 1933* (Munich: Saur, 1980); and also in Joseph Gedaliyah ben Yehudah Leib Klausner, Benzion Netanyahu, Yeshayahu Leibowitz, Nathan Rothenstreich, Yehoshua Prawer, and Menachem Zvi Barkai, eds., *Ha-entsiklopediah ha-*

ivrit, klalit yehudit ve-eretsisraelit (1966); and in David Tidhar, *Entsiklopediah le-ḥalutsei ha-yishuv u-bonav: dmuyot u-tmunot* (Tel Aviv: Sfarim Rishonim). Cf. also Jacob Toury, "Herzl's Newspapers: The Creation of 'Die Welt,'" *Zionism*, 1/2 (1980): 159–172 regarding York-Steiner's collaboration with Theodor Herzl on the Zionist newspaper *Die Welt*, especially 164 and 168 f.

27. Achim Jaeger and Beate Wunsch, "Zion und 'Zionismus': Die deutsch-jüdische Presse und der Erste Baseler Zionistenkongreß," in *Positionierung und Selbstbehauptung: Debatten über den Ersten Zionistenkongress, die "Ostjudenfrage" und den Ersten Weltkrieg in der deutsch-jüdischen Presse*, ed. Achim Jaeger et al. (Tübingen: Niemeyer, 2003), 56, quoting *Die Welt* 1 (1897) no. 1 (June 4): 1.

28. A common abbreviation for the *Hazkarat neshamot*, a memorial prayer that expresses the hope that the departed souls of the dead will be granted eternal life. Cf. Meir Ydit, "Hazkarat Neshamot," in *Encyclopedia Judaica*, 2nd ed. vol. 8, ed. Michael Berenbaum and Fred Skolnik (Detroit: Thomson Gale/Macmillan Reference USA, 2007), 496–497.

29. Heinrich York-Steiner, *Der Talmudbauer und anderes* (Berlin: Jüdischer Verlag, 1904). *Die tote Frau, Maskir,* and the eponymous narrative *Der Talmudbauer* had been published separately before, in 1898 and 1899 resp., in the German Jewish press. *Die tote Frau* was published (under the title *Die todte Frau*) in *Die Welt* 1 (1898); *Maskir* was published in *Jahrbuch für jüdische Geschichte und Literatur* (1899); *Der Talmudbauer* was published in *Die Welt* 35–51 (1899).

30. For an English translation see e.g., *Kil'ayim*, trans. with notes by Rev. J. Israelstam, in *The Babylonian Talmud. Seder Zera'im*, trans. and ed. Rabbi Dr I. Epstein (London: The Soncino Press, 1978 [first pub. 1948]).

31. York-Steiner, *Talmudbauer und anderes*, 153.

32. Leviticus 19:19, in the words of the JPS Bible (1917): "Ye shall keep My statutes. Thou shalt not let thy cattle gender with a diverse kind [*kil'aim*]; thou shalt not sow thy field with two kinds of seed [*kil'aim*]; neither shall there come upon thee a garment of two kinds of stuff mingled together [*kil'aim sha'atnez*]."

33. Deuteronomy 22:9 in the words of the JPS Bible (1917): "Thou shalt not sow thy vineyard with two kinds of seed [*kil'aim*]; lest the fulness of the seed which thou hast sown be forfeited together with the increase of the vineyard."

34. The tractate is located in the first Order of the Mishna, namely Zera'im (Seeds), which deals with the agricultural laws of the Torah, in their religious and social aspects. Cf. I. Epstein, "Introduction to Seder Zera'im," in *The Babylonian Talmud. Seder Zera'im*, xiiif.

35. York-Steiner, *Talmudbauer und anderes*, 166f.

36. Cf. Leviticus 15:19–29. Leviticus 15:19 reads as follows: "And if a woman have an issue, and her issue in her flesh be blood, she shall be in her impurity seven days; and whosoever toucheth her shall be unclean until the evening." Lev. 15:29 reads as follows: "And on the eighth day she shall take unto her two turtle-doves, or two young pigeons, and bring them unto the priest, to the door of the tent of meeting."

37. York-Steiner, *Der Talmudbauer und anderes*, 46f.

Eastern Europe in Argentina

Yiddish Travelogues and the Exploration of Jewish Diaspora

TAMAR LEWINSKY

For a long time, travel has been a way for European Jewry to have both real and imaginary encounters with distant members of its religious community. The medieval Jewish traveler Benjamin of Tudela first described at length the conditions of Jewish communal, cultural, and economic life in the Mediterranean world and the Middle East. His famous *Sefer ha-Masa'ot* (Book of Travels) was widely read.[1] In the mid-nineteenth century, the Romanian lumber dealer Joseph Israel Benjamin adopted the pen name Benjamin II. Then he set off on a journey that in the following eight years would lead him to Constantinople, the Mediterranean, the Middle East, India, and Northern Africa. His search for the remnants of the ten lost tribes of Israel found approval from scholars such as Alexander von Humboldt and Carl Ritter.[2] The travels of these two Benjamins resonate in Mendele Moykher Sforim's quixotic *Kitser masoes Binyomin hashlishi* (The Brief Travels of Benjamin the Third) from 1878, in which a rather unheroic Benjamin III tries to leave his shtetl in search of the legendary Red Jews.[3]

While these travelogues originated in different times and speak of different outcomes—thus, the literary persona Benjamin III eventually finds himself not on the other side of the mystic Sambation river, but in the very heart of his native Tuneyadevke—they share a fundamental interest: the search for distant members of the Jewish diaspora. Therefore, a sense of unity and belonging can be seen as a driving force for both the real and fictional journeys. In addition, as narratives of travel, they are replete with ethnographic descriptions of peoples and local customs.[4]

In the twentieth century, the three Benjamins' travels find continuation in the prolific genre of Yiddish travel writing.[5] Although this genre includes descriptions of non-Jewish communities, it pays special attention to Jewish life in distant regions of the globe—from the United States to South Africa, from Palestine to the Soviet Union and, after the cataclysm of World War II, back to the remnants of Jewish life in Eastern Europe. In the majority of these later texts, as in their predecessors, the notions of dispersion and unity remain a crucial motif at the journey's outset. Yet by the twentieth century, because of the processes of emancipation, secularization, and politicization, and the mass migration that fundamentally changed Eastern European Jewry, the notion of diaspora had undergone a significant transformation. Diaspora was no longer a purely religious, but also a cultural and, especially, a national concept. As a result, Jewish diaspora refers both to the *Galut,* the Israelites' dispersion after the Temple's destruction in Jerusalem, and to the modern transnational communities that stemmed from migration. During the era of Jewish mass migration that began in the late nineteenth century, the transnational communities not only reached special importance, but also led to the emergence of Eastern Europe as the new (and/or additional) homeland from which the migrants considered themselves exiled. As twentieth-century travel writers explored the Jewish world, they found their attention drawn to the communities developing among Jewish migrants from Eastern Europe. Traveling Yiddish writers encountered Yiddish-speaking Jews even in the world's most distant regions and depicted that diaspora's exotic corners for their readers in the *alte heym,* the Eastern Europe homeland, as well as in the modern Yiddish culture's newly emerging and geographically expanding centers. Like travel writers in earlier centuries, these writers began with the assumption that the Jewish community they were to explore was, in one way or another, linked to their own history, while at the same time acknowledging that it could be markedly different. However, when describing immigrants' lives, the dichotomy between the observer and the observed—both belonging to the same transnational group— becomes less clear.

TRAVELERS AS LAY-ETHNOGRAPHERS

Taking into account the ever changing character of the Eastern European Jewish diaspora—the changes due to factors within the Jewish communities and geopolitical developments—this chapter traces the ethnographic impulse that can be discerned in Yiddish travel writing. Although not purposely composed as ethnographic texts, these travelogues, like travel writing in general, combine personal narrative and formal description. Modern ethnography—which until recently distanced itself from earlier, less scientific genres such as travel books, memoirs, and journalism—also uses this configuration. Even so, in modern ethnography, narrative is subordinate to the descriptive discourse, confined to personal narrative introductions or to other books that do not claim scientific accuracy.[6] As Mary Louise Pratt argues, "The authority of the ethnographer over the 'mere traveler' rests chiefly on the idea that the traveler just passes through, whereas the ethnographer lives with the group under study."[7] According to this distinction, the traveler gains comparatively superficial knowledge of the places he or she visits. Even though Yiddish travel writers live only temporarily with the groups they write about, they know intimately many aspects of their culture, language, and traditions. Arguably, then, they can enter these groups more quickly and deeply than the "mere traveler." Illustrating the encounter between the travel writers and the community groups, which, by and large, are Eastern European Jewish immigrant communities, this chapter explores how perceptions of differences and similarities are negotiated, and whether a specific methodology can be discerned.

To some degree, presumably, many Yiddish travel writers were familiar with and possibly influenced by a specific ethnographic (and also historiographic) tradition that had evolved in early twentieth-century Eastern Europe, in the context of modern Jewish, and especially Yiddish, culture and politics. Central to this national Jewish ethnography, which can be considered a form of autoethnography or native ethnography, were three aspects: a broad perspective regarding topicality and materiality; the collection of ethnographic information by *zamlers* (lay-ethnographers); and a focus on Ashkenazi Yiddish-speaking Eastern European Jewry.[8] The

YIVO ethnographic section outlined this type of Yiddish ethnography in its 1929 field manual *Vos iz azoyns yidishe etnografye?* (What is Jewish ethnography?; see Appendix 1). The manual emphasizes the importance of researching all segments of Jewish society, and it specifies a typology of material culture and folklore, as well as guidelines for the fieldwork itself. Moreover, this central text defines the field's dimensions as "the territory of the Yiddish language." Defining the territory linguistically is explained: "This in itself is a difficult enough task because of the dispersion of the Yiddish-speaking masses around the world, among foreign people and different ethnographic communities, which have without any doubt a strong influence on Jews."[9] While in *Vos iz azoyns yidishe etnografye?* the YIVO ethnographic section specified that all Eastern European and Yiddish-speaking emigration had to be understood as part of the field of research, studies were predominantly confined to Eastern Europe.[10]

Although only partly ethnographic in their intent, the travel writers, as mentioned above, followed the Jewish masses that had left Eastern Europe. Thus, if we consider the travel writers as lay-ethnographers of a Yiddish nation, they explored not only the folk culture of Jews in Eastern Europe, but also their transnational diaspora and ensuing transculturation processes. In doing so, travel writers realigned the field of research along the expanding and changing coordinates of Yiddish. They paid particular interest, however, to issues of migration and diaspora, both of which have entered the ethnographic field only in recent decades, thus enriching its methodology. Indeed, following migrational trajectories, the travel writers unknowingly touched upon issues that were to become key aspects of today's ethnography. The passage, the immigration process, the transfer to the final destination, and the process of integration and network-building are all part of the travelogues' stories. Or, to use James Clifford's well-known metaphor, they depicted culture being at once *rooted* and *routed*.

YIDDISH TRAVEL WRITERS IN ARGENTINA

Argentina, one of many destinations for Eastern European Jewish immigrants, appears regularly on the map of Yiddish travel writing. Four reports, created between 1914 and 1960, serve here as examples for exploring the Jewish diaspora through Yiddish travelogues: reports by Perets Hirshbeyn, Hersh-Dovid Nomberg, Mark Turkow, and Chaim Shoshkes, each originating from quite different historical and socioeconomic circumstances. Over the course of almost half a century, the Argentinean Jewish community not only increased substantially, but it transformed from an immigrant population into an integral part of urban Argentinean society.

When Perets Hirshbeyn (1880–1948), arguably the most prolific Yiddish travel writer, set out on his journey to Argentina on the eve of the Great War, the Eastern European Jewish community in Argentina numbered between 100,000 and 115,600. Significant immigration—initially with a high percentage of return migration—had begun in the late 1880s and peaked in 1906 and 1912, with roughly 13,500 new immigrants per year. At that time, the rural settlements of the Jewish Colonization Association (JCA) still absorbed a large number of newcomers, yet the most visible presence of Jewish life was in Buenos Aires.[11] Met with much interest, Hirshbeyn's travel images appeared in installments in the New York Yiddish daily *Der tog* (Day) and later in his travel accounts *Fun vayte lender* (From Distant Countries).[12] In the following decades, Hirshbeyn, the restless playwright, director, journalist, novelist, and traveler who had spent the first half of his life in Eastern Europe, published widely on his extensive journeys. In *Arum der velt: Rayze-ayndrukn (1920–1922)* (Around the World: Travel Impressions [1920–1922]),[13] for example, he gave an account of a two-year journey to Australia, New Zealand, Tahiti, and South Africa, which he undertook with his wife, Yiddish poet Ester Shumiatsher. Their five-year journey to South America, Japan, China, India, Palestine, and Europe, which also included a ten-month exploration of the Jewish agrarian settlements in Crimea, is documented in *Indye—fun mayn rayze in Indye* (India—From My Travel in India), *Shvartsbrukh*, and *Erets-Yisroel* (Land of Israel).[14]

In 1922 and 1923, at a time of renewed Jewish immigration from Eastern Europe to Argentina, Hersh-Dovid Nomberg (1876–1927), journalist, writer, activist, and longtime chairman of the Jewish Writers' Union in Warsaw, serialized his travel notes on a journey from Europe via Brazil, to Buenos Aires and the JCA colonies, for readers in the Warsaw Yiddish daily *Moment*. These accounts were later included as *Argentinishe rayze* (Argentinean Journey) in a collection of his feuilleton writings.[15] At the Czernowitz Yiddish language conference in 1908, Nomberg had proposed

declaring Yiddish a national Jewish language; he was a founder of the au-
tonomist Folkspartey in Poland, and a leading promoter of secular Jewish
education and modern Yiddish culture. So it comes as no surprise that he
was especially sympathetic to the lot of Yiddish activists among the Jewish Argentinean immigrants. Throughout Nomberg's journey, he stayed
in close touch with the Jewish writers who had arrived from Europe, even
encouraging them to organize. This effort was honored by their choice to
name the Argentinean Yiddish writers' union after him: *Literatn un zhur-
nalistn farband H. D. Nomberg*.[16] Further travels took him to Palestine, the
United States, and the Soviet Union.[17]

In the late 1930s, the readers of *Moment* were again presented with a
series of travel reports on South America. Mark Turkow (1904–1983) took
his readers to Uruguay and the Jewish farmlands of Argentina. Upon returning from South America, Turkow toured Poland and the free city of
Danzig, giving lectures on the problems of emigration and colonization
in South America. As the press reported, the success of his public pre-
sentations lay not only in the knowledgeable insights of a brilliant orator,
but also in their topicality.[18] In the postscript to the published reports
on Argentina,[19] titled *Oyf yidishe felder* (On Jewish Fields), the author
stressed that his book's main purpose was to provide an objective description of Jewish life in the agrarian settlements—not least for the future
emigrants among his readers.[20] Turkow himself left Europe for good in
1939 and settled in Buenos Aires, where he continued to serve as a communal activist. He was appointed director of the Hebrew Immigrant Aid
Society (HIAS) in South America, and became the Argentinean deputy
of the World Jewish Congress. Furthermore, he headed the Polish Jewish
landsmanshaftn association and was an editor of the Yiddish book series
Dos poylishe yidntum (Polish Jewry; Buenos Aires, 1946–1966), which delineated a topography of remembrance of the life and destruction of Polish
Jewry.[21]

Travels to South America are but one aspect of Chaim Shoshkes's
(1891–1964) *Mit yidn tsvishn indyaner, neger un araber* (With Jews Among
American Indians, Blacks, and Arabs), published in Israel in 1960.[22]
Shoshkes, an immigrant to the United States in 1940, was in no way in-
ferior to Hirshbeyn in his wanderlust. His journeys—first, a visit to the
Wembley British Empire Exhibition in 1924, and last, back to the Soviet

Union and the once-thriving Jewish communities in Russia and Poland in the 1960s—took him to five continents over the course of forty years.[23] He visited Argentina frequently, and this might explain why he chose to write about very specific aspects of Jewish life in Buenos Aires, instead of giving a more general description.[24] As in many of his post-World War II travelogues, Shoshkes delves into the Jewish community's centennial history in Buenos Aires. In fact, we learn very little about the Jewish community's plight in an atmosphere of growing public antisemitism, because Shoshkes focuses mainly on the community's historic struggle against the Jewish underworld.

From these four travelogues' range of subjects, I examine three recurring themes that lend themselves to an investigation of the ethnographic motives, the narrative and descriptive discourses, and the methodology operative in these texts: first, the urban immigrant generation; second, the Jewish settlers in the Argentinean agricultural colonies established from the late 1880s; and third, the mysterious world of the *teme'im*, the "ritually unclean," as the Jewish community of Buenos Aires termed the Jewish madams, prostitutes, and pimps of Buenos Aires.[25] All three topics seem especially appropriate for a discussion of the relationship between rooted and routed ethnography, since the writers are here concerned with immigrants' trajectories, the emergence and development of a new diasporic community, and generational changes challenging the notion of double rootedness on two continents. Moreover, the first and the third topics relate to the specific interest of Jewish ethnography in Eastern Europe in the urban spaces and the lower strata of society, including criminals and prostitutes.[26]

The Urban Immigrants

In his *Fun vayte lender,* Hirshbeyn sets out on a journey "to our faraway *goles*-land,"[27] the distant Jewish exile and its capital, Buenos Aires, his main purpose being "to travel and see how our Jews live in faraway countries."[28] Upon arriving in Buenos Aires, Hirshbeyn plans initially to spend at least a week exploring the city and its topography before looking for fellow Jews. However, feeling lost in the metropolis with only a few words of Spanish at his command (among them, of course, *judío*—

Jew),[29] he feels a strong urge to get in touch with the immigrant Jewish community. Following Yiddish theater advertisements, he finds his way into the heart of Jewish Buenos Aires and is soon surrounded by young Jews, who greet him "respectfully at the beginning and later with a simple open-heartedness . . . in short, Jews seized a Jew: a Jew found Jews."[30] This encounter between the locals and the visitor was facilitated through the guest's intimate knowledge of their language and culture, their linguistic and cultural codes. "In short, I am at home," the Yiddish cosmopolitan declares. "Vilna, Warsaw, New York, Chicago—or even Bobruisk—there is no difference. At home I am!"[31]

Hirshbeyn explores the immigrant community, a distant corner of the Jewish diaspora that had expanded through migration. Paradoxically, the Jewish world seems to have grown closer and become more familiar; the author muses,

> Who knows, maybe it is the fault of the Jewish people that the world has shrunk before my eyes? The Jewish people have dispersed around the wide world; wherever you go, you meet your friends from the *kheyder,* children of your *shtetl.* . . . Sometimes you start to think that the journey is not that long at all; that the captain has simply lost the way, turning around all the time in one single place.[32]

Throughout his account, Hirshbeyn paraphrases conversations and interviews with members of the immigrant community. He directs readers' attention to specific differences, linguistic and cultural, that have emerged as a result of migration and cross-cultural influences. But he also emphasizes the strong emotional connection the emigrants still feel with their old home, for example when describing the European-born owner of a Yiddish bookshop with whom he became acquainted. The immigrant tells her little son to greet a "Yiddish writer who comes from where mother's and father's home is."[33] Here and elsewhere, Hirshbeyn focuses clearly on differences between the first and second generation of immigrants— those from Europe and their descendants born in South America—and the gradual transition of Jews from immigrants to locals, from a mobile to a rooted community.

The life of the urban immigrants is also a pivotal aspect of Nomberg's *Argentinishe rayze,* and, as with Hirshbeyn, interviews are his main source of information, and interviewees are described and quoted at length. Nomberg also differentiates among various groups who arrived on the Rio de la Plata's shores over time: "You can still discern the specific waves of immigration: those of Baron Hirsch from the late eighties, the waves of 1905 and the last years before the war. It is as if you dig into the soil and, instead of a single compound, you see layers put on top of each other, not at all interspersed."[34] He is especially interested in the immigrant community's variety of subgroups or ethnographic groups that are defined by their members' provenance and social status: "To be a Polish Jew in Argentina is a little bit of hardship. *Litvakes* and even Bessarabian Jews treat the Polish Jew with contempt."[35] Moreover, Nomberg describes communal organizations, cultural life, libraries, schools, the press, and professional organizations established by immigrant Jews, but also their love of professional gambling, its impact on family structures and family life, and the social status of women in general.[36]

Nomberg stresses that manifold reasons stood behind individual plans to settle in Argentina, and that in many instances settling there was a matter of default rather than a real choice. One of his interlocutors, a Jew from Warsaw who had immigrated to Buenos Aires fifteen years previously, never managed to establish a connection with his new environment and still longed for the Vistula River. Only after World War I's disastrous events and the destruction of Jewish infrastructure in Eastern Europe did he understand that return migration was no longer an option; finally, he took in Jeremiah's words to the exiles to build houses and plant gardens.[37] Indeed, the trope of soil and rootedness—in contrast to uprootedness as a diasporic condition in traditional religious and Zionist discourses—is frequently invoked in the travelogues to describe the immigrants' process of establishing communities. Yet this organic trope has a special twist, in that a coexistent double-rootedness in the old and the new homeland is possible:

> And yet it is a Jewish settlement. And yet it is a branch, which grew out of an old trunk. The branch headed off too far from the trunk. Every rush of air bends it, every rush of air breaks it. And yet it is a Jewish settlement. A Jewish street. The Jewish language. . . . And yet it is a Jewish settlement. Groaning, they grow roots. Longing, they dig deep roots in the Argentinean soil.[38]

The Agricultural Settlements

The idea of Jews returning to farm their own land had been propagated by the JCA as a solution to the deteriorating conditions of Jews in tsarist Russia since the 1890s.[39] Initially, the JCA envisioned a large-scale project to resettle Russian Jews. Although these plans did not materialize, the agricultural colonies established on the JCA-owned territories absorbed thousands of Jewish immigrants. Especially during the formative first years, conditions were harsh, and many settlers left the colonies. A year before the outbreak of World War I, however, the population had risen to 18,900. It peaked in the mid-1920s, when 20,382 persons farmed their land in the Argentinean provinces of Santa Fé, Entre Ríos, La Pampa, Buenos Aires, and Chaco.[40]

Jewish agricultural settlements were a main destination for the travel writers, who appear to have been well informed about the history of the JCA, its colonies, and the settlement schemes; they were also familiar with the enterprise's failures and successes. The settlements' diversity in outlook, population, size, and economic prosperity over time are highlighted in the travelogues, where religious and secular institutions, schools, libraries, party life, and ideologies are depicted in great detail. While the latter aspects refer to a world that seems—at least in its general contours—familiar to the travel writers, the writers also collected stories on topics utterly foreign to them, such as the organizational structures of agricultural cooperatives; stories about the settlements' early stages, when year after year plagues of locusts destroyed the crops; the success of planting alfalfa and breeding cattle.[41] The travel accounts strongly emphasize description of the rural settlements. However, the personal narrative of the writer, negotiating differences and similarities, predominates over the informative aspects that might be directed at prospective immigrants.[42]

The landscapes, exotic to the Eastern European traveler's eye, are a perfect foil for the account of this foreign environment: "Facing the wilderness of nature, one easily understands what hard work the colonists have to endure, until they succeed in turning wild woods or empty, desertlike steppe into fertile soil."[43] The long, tiring journeys to both smaller and larger settlements are depicted in great detail. Hirshbeyn's journey to Moisesville is exhausting. Heavy rains block some of the roads, and swarms of locusts cloud the skies. In a somber mood, he arrives in the oldest agricultural colony and is soon surrounded by silent village Jews marked by years of hard work, but also by young, self-confident men. Unlike in the urban environment of Buenos Aires, Hirshbeyn does not immediately feel at ease with these Jewish settlers. Before long, however, he is reminded of his paternal relatives who dwelled in a small town in the Grodno region, and is reassured.[44] Almost a quarter of a century later, Turkow wrote a similar description of the people in Moisesville. The older generation receives visitors hospitably, especially those, writes Turkow, who bring back memories of the homeland: "When you meet the Jews of Moisesville, you get the impression that you are not in the wide open steppes of Argentina, but in a homey Lithuanian shtetl."[45] Memories can even create illusions. Nomberg recalls, "And tall trees . . . on the city square (plaza) [of Moisesville] . . . around the Lithuanian synagogue gave me the illusion of the long-forgotten sudden arrival of spring the way it used to be in my hometown before Passover."[46] The image of the shtetl, evoked as an expression of provincial backwardness and also as the bearer of an original yet vanishing culture, seems to draw the foreign closer.[47] In fact, the geographically remote region is confined to the realm of bygone times and is thus distanced in a temporal sense. This emotional search for the "authentic" Eastern European Jewish folk-culture in rural Argentina may also explain Turkow's disenchantment with some aspects of Jewish life in the colonies, particularly with the growing number of gentile settlers and the loss of traditional Jewish life. The settlers are well aware of these fundamental changes, and one of Turkow's interlocutors points out that the vernacular Jewish culture attracted earlier visitors like Nomberg and Hirshbeyn, who "were delighted by Moisesville. They found here a continuation of the Jewish folk-life we had brought over here from the old homeland. Today, everything is changing at a fast pace."[48]

Yet the travel writers also had an eye (and ear) for difference. They elaborated that, although aspects of regional distinctiveness and local traditions from the countries of origin were retained to some degree,[49] the new environment and influences produced a new type of Jewish farmer, the *Jewish Gaucho*, in the Jewish-Argentinean writer Alberto Gerchunoff's term. The transculturation processes behind this new type are described foremost as a generational change: while immigrant parents are depicted as still forming part of regionally distinct Eastern European communities, the native generation is described as rooted in the Argentinean pampas. Time and again, the differences in immigrant groups' temper, social status, trades, and organizational qualities resound in the descriptions of the agricultural settlements. Nomberg draws special attention to the children, with their wild appearance and Jewish names, who marvel at the rare event of snowfall in the pampas and from an early age ride horseback with ease.[50] Hirshbeyn closely examines the JCA colonies' trilingual, bicultural school system, in which heroic tales of San Martín infuse the children with patriotic feelings in Spanish, while the Hebrew-Yiddish instruction follows the traditional method of word-by-word translation of the Bible. The children encounter the latter with much less enthusiasm.[51]

Nomberg provides information about transferring local customs—like the settlers using the *bombilla,* from which the gauchos drink mate tea— and about linguistic influences from Spanish. Although the settlers still converse in Yiddish, they use Spanish expressions like *pampero* (strong wind), *chaco* (woodlands), *plaza* (square), or *criollo* (native) (with the typical Argentinean rendition of the *ll* as /ʒ/ and /ʃ/).[52] In the late 1930s, the Spanish influence on the settlers' spoken Yiddish becomes even more strongly felt. Turkow identifies the settlers' language as Lithuanian Yiddish. However, he criticizes the younger generation for degrading "the sounds of the juicy Lithuanian Yiddish language . . . by blending in Spanish words and even entire phrases."[53] Thus, while Nomberg was interested in linguistic change, Turkow followed a somewhat purist, normative agenda, worried by the notion that the second generation was taking roots in Argentina (to which he did not object) and would eventually become detached from the transnational Yiddish nation.

The World of the Teme'im

The travel writers also visit cemeteries, which Hirshbeyn defines as a marker of belonging. As he details in his description of Moisesville, where he is informed that 128 children died within a month's time, it is not the farming of their own land that connects immigrants to the Argentinean soil, but "the number of victims each family had to mourn created the bond between the weak Russian Jew and the young wild Argentinean nature." In other words, according to Hirshbeyn, it is not the number of trees they plant, but the cemeteries in which the farmers bury their children that make them stay.[54]

Yet one cemetery is not described in terms of a symbolic connection, but as an object of ethnographic research: both Nomberg and Shoshkes visit the cemetery of the *teme'im*, the Jewish pimps, madams, and prostitutes in Buenos Aires.[55] The cemetery visibly marks the communal structures established by the *teme'im*, who had been organized in mutual aid and burial associations since 1889.[56] Through these on-site visits, the writers look more closely at the Jewish underworld, but what they see and how they tackle the issue of Jewish involvement in human trafficking, which was then called "white slavery," are very much determined by the timing of their respective visits. Nomberg visited in 1922, during violent struggles by the official Buenos Aires Jewish community against organized crime. He reports critically on the luxurious cemetery being open only to the "bourgeoisie" of pimps and madams, while poor women are buried in the public cemetery's nameless graves, or their bodies are transferred to the university medical department.[57]

In Buenos Aires, "white slavery" and its Jewish involvement was a sensitive issue that tarnished the Jewish community's image. For Nomberg, the topic was present in press and literature, as for example Sholem Asch's famous and critically received play *Got fun nekome* (God of Vengeance) about a Jewish-owned brothel in the Warsaw region, yet, according to him, "dramatic scenes, stronger even than those Sholem Asch depicted . . . happened on the scene of real life in Buenos Aires."[58] Nomberg informs the reader about the human trade's "channels of distribution": "Each market procures its 'goods' from a different place. The market of Buenos Aires brought its 'goods' from Warsaw, Lodz, Kraków, Lemberg, and Odessa."[59] In addition to the transnational dimensions of this shady business, Nomberg amply describes the measures taken by the Buenos Aires Jewish community and provides a critical evaluation of the official actions and laws implemented to fight this phenomenon.[60]

Nomberg discusses the topic's perseverance in Jewish folklore: "Of Buenos Aires also the Jewish folksong has something to tell. When I collected folksongs many years ago, I often came across the word '*boyne*' and didn't understand its meaning."[61] *Boyne* (probably stemming from the Spanish *bueno*) was the expression the *teme'im* used for Buenos Aires. Driven by ethnographic interest, Nomberg explores the streets of Buenos Aires, collects stories about the world of prostitution, and discusses the specific "jargon" spoken in these circles.[62] However, he admits that he could not satisfy his curiosity with first-hand information. Making fun of himself, he confesses that his naïve initial intention for this urban ethnography was to find "the red Indians, the old inhabitants of Argentina and *khevre-layt*, the white-slavers; I thought that the streets abounded with them, that you could see them everywhere. I didn't find, though, any sign of them—not of the Indians and not of the white-slavers."[63] Beyond the jocular aspect of this observation, the comparison between the indigenous/rooted and the mobile/diasporic inhabitants suggests that the writer identifies both as ethnographic groups in their own right.

In the post-Peronist era, the late 1950s, Shoshkes visited the cemetery and reported that the last funeral had taken place five years earlier.[64] The ethnographic impulse is strongly felt in Shoshkes's descriptions. Jewish involvement in prostitution had declined in the 1930s. Thus, the moral standards by which this chapter in the history of Jewish migration was judged, as well as its political implications, had changed, and Shoshkes was eager to collect evidence and record information, especially since he had been informed that the municipality of Buenos Aires planned to close the place.[65] Like Nomberg, Shoshkes describes a luxurious cemetery that reminds him of graveyards in Italy. Helped by local informants and the non-Jewish gatekeeper, Shoshkes explores the individual life stories of those buried there, gathers information about specific rituals and commemoration practices conducted in the small adjacent prayer house, reads the Spanish and Hebrew inscriptions on the tombstones, and describes the portrait photographs found on the many richly worked monuments: "It was like skimming through a forbidden, juicy book that tells about an era which should be forgotten," he writes, but the luxurious tombstones demand that he record and analyze their story.[66] He also takes photographs—some of which are included in his travel report.

He does not oppose the closure of this "monument of shame," yet

First, we have to preserve somewhere in a community archive the photographs and inscriptions; it is material that after the passing of time will be an object of study, carried out with more detachment than now—since the living generation still remembers the fights they fought with the *teme'im* and the disgrace that Jews suffered because of them.[67]

Thus, Shoshkes focuses on collecting stories and material evidence. The Eastern European Jewish tradition of *zamlen* seems to resonate in his chronicles. His interest in the Argentinean Jewish underworld confirms the YIVO ethnographers' requirements defined in the interwar period: that all the ethnographic and social groups of the Yiddish-speaking diaspora of Eastern European Jews be researched, including all social strata, and all respectable and dubious trades.[68] Yet Shoshkes was also influenced by more contemporary ideas of ethnography and travel writing. Writing after the Holocaust and the founding of the State of Israel, he could not help but be conscious that he was collecting traces of material culture from a world that was no more.

CONCLUSION

The four travelogues presented here served various goals: they were produced for a broad audience and published in installments before they were eventually reprinted as individual volumes. The writers sought to entertain, to pique their readers' curiosity, but also—at least before the Holocaust—to inform Jews about a possible emigration destination. All four travelogues are knowledgeable and contain descriptive passages on the history of Jewish migration, on the Argentinean political situation, and on details of the colonies' development. As lay-ethnographers, the travel writers were interested in the mores, traditions, stories, material culture, and language of the Jews in Argentina. Although their descriptions of Jewish life in Buenos Aires and the Yiddish-speaking agricultural settlements differ in content and method, narrative elements outweigh descriptive passages. Moreover, the writers do not claim scientific objectivity, and, in most instances, they identify themselves as travelers with specific interests and preferences.[69]

The writers' use of tropes and images underscores their notion of a transnational East European Jewish diaspora connected through language, cultural traditions, and memories. While the linguistically assimilated Jews no longer form part of their field of interest, the writers do pay particular attention to issues of migration and diaspora. In traveling far west, their undertaking is, paradoxically, to document and preserve in writing distinctive aspects of Eastern European Jewish life. While doing so, they are well aware of the fluid and transitory qualities of the group, with its roots and routes.

Given that the globalized diaspora of Eastern European Jewry is a relatively recent phenomenon, highlighting the moment of its formation is highly significant. The diaspora of Eastern European Jewry is not at all given or fixed. Neither is the self-conception of the inhabitants of these transnational social spaces. Ethnologist Martin Sökefeld argues, "sentiments of belonging, attachment to a home and ideas of a place of origin do not constitute the 'substance' from which diasporas—like other identity groups—are made but the codes in terms of which 'a' diaspora is imagined." He suggests "defining diasporas as *imagined transnational communities,* as imaginations of community that unite segments of people that live in territorially separated locations."[70] Drawing on Benedict Anderson's concept of nations as *imagined communities,* this definition is especially meaningful for discussing the emergence of a diaspora of Eastern European Jewry in modern times. By describing specific émigré groups, twentieth-century Yiddish travel writers form part of the imaginative process that leads to the emergence of imagined transnational communities. At the foundation of this imaginative process stands Yiddish as an ideological, linguistic, and cultural link.

NOTES

1. See, for example, the critical English edition by Marcus Nathan Adler, *The Itinerary of Benjamin of Tudela: Critical Text, Translation and Commentary* (London: Oxford University Press, 1907).

2. Written in Hebrew, the travelogue was published in French translation in 1856 (*Cinq années en Orient, 1846–1851*). An enlarged German edition was published two years later: J. J. Benjamin, *Acht Jahre in Asien und Afrika. Von 1846 bis 1955. Zweite Auflage* (Hannover: Der Verfasser, 1858).

3. Mendele Moykher Sforim, *Kitser masoes Binyomin hashlishi* (Vilna: Rom, 1878).

4. For a discussion of travel literature in Yiddish fiction and the creation of Jewish spaces, see Leah Garrett, *Journeys beyond the Pale: Yiddish Travel Writing in the Modern World* (Madison: University of Wisconsin Press, 2003); on travel writing and ethnography, see Joan Pau Rubiés, "Travel Writing and Ethnography," in *The Cambridge Compan-*

ion to *Travel Writing*, ed. Peter Hulme and Tim Youngs (Cambridge: Cambridge University Press, 2002), 242–260.

5. There is no full bibliography of this specific genre. Some titles are listed in Mikhail Kizilov, "Hebrew and Yiddish Travel Writing," in *A Bibliography of East European Travel Writing on Europe (East Looks West*, vol. 3), ed. Wendy Bracewell and Alex Drace-Francis (Budapest: CEU, 2008), 229–241. In a random keyword search, Jack Kugelmass has found 139 digitized reprints of books dealing with travel (Jack Kugelmass, "A Yiddish Traveler in Peru," http://iijs.columbia.edu/files/Kugelmass%20Paper%202.pdf).

6. Mary Louise Pratt, "Fieldwork in Common Places," in *Writing Culture: The Poetics and Politics of Ethnography*, ed. James Clifford and George E. Marcus (Berkeley: University of California Press, 1986), 27 and 34–35. On the phenomenon of the ethnographers' two books: Vincent Debaene, *Far Afield: French Anthropology between Science and Literature* (Chicago: University of Chicago Press, 2014).

7. Pratt, "Fieldwork in Common Places," 38. See also Pratt, *Imperial Eyes: Travel Writing and Transculturation* (London: Routledge, 1992).

8. Itzik Gottesman, *Defining the Yiddish Nation: The Jewish Folklorists of Poland* (Detroit: Wayne State University Press, 2003); Kalman Weiser, *Jewish People, Yiddish Nation: Noah Prylucki and the Folkists in Poland* (Toronto: University of Toronto Press, 2011). On the problems of defining the scope of Russian Jewry in Late Imperial Russia, see Jeffrey Veidlinger, "The Historical and Ethnographic Construction of Russian Jewry," *Ab Imperio* 4 (2003): 165–184.

9. *Vos iz azoyns yidishe etnografye*, ed. Żydowski Instytut Naukowy (Vilna: YIVO, 1929), 8. I wish to thank Anna Lipphardt for reminding me of this text.

10. An exception is the folklorist Yehuda Leyb Cahan, who collected folksongs among immigrant Jews in London and New York. See Gottesman, xx.

11. Haim Avni, *Argentina and the Jews: A History of Jewish Immigration* (Tuscaloosa: University of Alabama Press, 1991), 21–92; "Argentina," in *Encyclopaedia Judaica*, 2nd ed., ed. Michael Berenbaum and Fred Skolnik (Detroit: Macmillan, 2007), 427–431. On Buenos Aires, see Victor A. Mirelman, *Jewish Buenos Aires, 1890–1930: In Search of an Identity* (Detroit: Wayne State University Press, 1990).

12. "Hirshbeyn, Perets," in *Leksikon fun der nayer yidisher literatur*, vol. III (New York: Alveltlekher Yidisher Kultur-Kongres, 1956), 152; Perets Hirshbeyn, *Fun vayte lender: Argentine, Brazil, yuni, november 1914* (New York: [s.n.], 1916). The book also includes depictions of his journey to Brazil during the early weeks of World War I, his dramatic passage to North America aboard a British liner that was sunk by a German war vessel, and his arrest and eventual arrival in New York aboard a freighter.

13. Perets Hirshbeyn, *Arum der velt: rayze-ayndrukn (1920–1922)* (New York: Literatur, 1927).

14. Perets Hirshbeyn, *Indye—fun mayn rayze in Indye* (Vilna: Kletskin, 1929); Hirshbeyn, *Erets-Yisroel* (Vilna: Kletskin, 1929); Hirshbeyn, *Shvartsbrukh* (Vilna: Kletskin, 1930).

15. "Nomberg, Hersh-Dovid," in *Leksikon fun der nayer yidisher literatur*, vol. VI (New York: Alveltlekher Yidisher Kultur-Kongres, 1956), 160–168; Hersh-Dovid Nomberg, "Argentinishe-rayze," in *Dos bukh felyetonen* (Warsaw: Rekord, 1924), 7–100; the accounts of Nomberg's travel to Argentina were again reprinted in his collected work (Nomberg, *Amerike: ayndrukn un bilder fun Tsofn- un Dorem-Amerike* [gezamlte verk, vol. 6] [Warsaw: Kultur-lige, 1928]), 36–84 of part three) and in his *Oysgeklibene shriftn*, published in the

Buenos Aires *Musterverk*-series: Hirshe-Dovid Nomberg, *Oysgeklibene shriftn: noveln, lider, eseyen* (Buenos Aires: Ateneo literario en el IWO, 1966). All citations are taken from the 1924 edition.

16. Yosef Mendelson, "Hersh-Dovid Nomberg in Buenos Aires," in *Zamlbukh*, ed. Yosef Mendelson, Avrom Zak, and Nekhemya Tsuker (Buenos Aires: Shrayber-fareyn H. D. Nomberg, 1962), 153.

17. Hersh-Dovid Nomberg, *Erets-Yisroel: ayndrukn un bilder* (Warsaw: Yakobson and Goldberg, 1925); Nomberg, *Mayn rayze iber Rusland* (gezamlte verk, vol. 5) (Warsaw: Kultur-lige, 1928); Nomberg, *Amerike*.

18. "A lebediker grus fun yidn in Argentine!" *Haynt*, February 8, 1938.

19. However, a planned second volume on his journeys to South America ("Oyf di shlyakhn fun di yidishe vanderungen"), advertised in Mark Turkow, *Oyf yidishe felder: a nesiye iber di yidishe kolonyes in Argentine* (Warsaw: [s.n.], 1939), was never published.

20. Turkow, *Oyf yidishe felder*, 193.

21. "Turkov, Mark," in *Leksikon fun der nayer yidisher literatur*, vol. IV (New York: Alveltlekher Yidisher Kultur-Kongres, 1956), 61–62.

22. Khayim Shoshkes, *Mit yidn tsvishn indyaner, neger un araber* (Tel Aviv: Y.L. Perets, 1960).

23. Khayim Shoshkes, *Lender un shtet* (Vilna: Kletskin, 1930), 9–29; Shoshkes, *Tsvishn yidn in vayte lender* (Tel Aviv: Hamenoyre, 1964). His travel writings include *Ekzotishe rayzes* (Warsaw: Yidishe univerzal-bibliotek, 1938); *Poyln—1946* (Buenos Aires: Farband fun poylishe yidn in Argentine, 1947); *Mayn rayze in der velt* (Buenos Aires: Undzer bukh, 1951); *Durkh umbakante lender* (Rio de Janeiro: Monte Scopus, 1954); *Masoes reb Khayim* (Rio de Janeiro: Tsiko, 1957); and *Fun Moskve biz eyver-ha-Yordn* (Tel Aviv: Y.L. Perets, 1961).

24. Shoshkes, *Mit yidn*, 51. For an earlier account from the Peronist era, see Shoshkes, *Durkh umbakante lender*, 360–366.

25. On this terminology, see Haim Avni, "Teme'im," *Saḥar be-nashim be-Argentinah u-ve-Yisra'el* (Tel Aviv: Yedioth Aharonot, 2009).

26. See, for example, Almi's "A Strange Experience," translated by Gabriella Safran in Appendix C of this volume.

27. Hirshbeyn, *Fun vayte lender*, 34.

28. Ibid., 40.

29. Ibid., 40–41.

30. Ibid., 48.

31. Ibid., 42–43.

32. Ibid., 13.

33. Ibid., 47.

34. Nomberg, "Argentinishe rayze," 60.

35. Ibid. Specific traits of the individual ethnographic groups are given in the following passages.

36. Ibid., 61–64.

37. Ibid., 62.

38. Hirshbeyn, *Fun vayte lender*, 60.

39. The philanthropic JCA, founded in 1891 by Baron Maurice de Hirsch, was central in facilitating emigration from Eastern Europe. It established emigration committees and founded agricultural cooperatives not only in Argentina, but also in Eastern Europe, the

United States, Palestine, and several other countries. See Ann Ussishkin, "Jewish Coloni-zation Association," in *Encyclopaedia Judaica*, vol. 11, 285–288.

40. Avni, *Argentina and the Jews*, 61; "Argentina," 429.

41. E.g., Nomberg, "Argentinishe rayze," 84–85; Turkow, *Oyf yidishe felder*, 10–11 and 87.

42. This becomes especially manifest when the travel writing is compared to informa-tive articles in migrants' newspapers, which are heavily loaded with accurate data. E.g., "Di yidishe kolonye in Argentine (fun a rayze-barikht)," *Der yudisher emigrant*, October 1, 1912.

43. Turkow, *Oyf yidishe felder*, 17.

44. Hirshbeyn, *Fun vayte lender*, 86–87.

45. Turkow, *Oyf yidishe felder*, 179.

46. Nomberg, "Argentinishe rayze," 80–81.

47. See Jeffrey Shandler, *Shtetl: A Postvernacular Intellectual History* (New Brunswick, N.J.: Rutgers University Press, 2014).

48. Turkow, *Oyf yidishe felder*, 187–188.

49. Ibid., 179.

50. Nomberg, "Argentinishe rayze," 70–71.

51. Hirshbeyn, *Fun vayte lender*, 93–96.

52. Ibid., 72, 74, 80, and 75–76.

53. Turkow, *Oyf yidishe felder*, 179.

54. Hirshbeyn, *Fun vayte lender*, 70.

55. Hirshbeyn only briefly touches on the subject by mentioning the abduction of Jew-ish daughters as a recurrent theme: "Buenos Aires. The capital of Argentina. . . . Uncanny things are told about the city of Buenos Aires. And the stories about Jewish daughters who have been abducted by unknown people and led away from their parents' home . . ." (Hirshbeyn, *Fun vayte lender*, 35). This is remarkable, since Hirshbeyn's *Barg arop* (Down-hill), a play about a seduced woman who ends up in a brothel, was staged in Buenos Aires in 1909. The local Po'ale Zion party organized the performance. When it was discovered that a large number of *teme'im* attended the play, the most dramatic commotion happened in the auditorium. See Shoshkes, *Arum der velt*, 75–76.

56. On the history of the cemetery and religious aspects among pimps, see Mir Yarfitz, *Polacos, White Slaves, and Stille Chuppahs: Organized Prostitution and the Jews of Buenos Aires, 1890–1939* (PhD thesis, UCLA, 2012), 182–196. On Jewish involvement in trafficking in women and prostitution, see Donna J. Guy, *Sex and Danger in Buenos Aires: Prostitution, Family and Nation in Argentina* (Lincoln: University of Nebraska Press, 1991); Sandra Mc-Gee Deutsch, *Crossing Borders, Claiming a Nation: A History of Argentine Jewish Women, 1880–1955* (Durham, N.C.: Duke University Press, 2010), 105–122; Avni, *Teme'im*.

57. Nomberg, "Argentinishe rayze," 51.

58. Ibid., 49.

59. Ibid., 44.

60. Ibid., 50–58.

61. Ibid., 44.

62. Ibid., 45–50.

63. Ibid., 46.

64. Shoshkes, *Mit yidn*, 57.

65. Ibid., 64.

66. Ibid., 59.

67. Ibid., 64.

68. *Vos iz azoyns yidishe etnografye?*, 10–11.

69. Turkow might be seen as an exception, insofar as he deliberately chose not to arrive as an official visitor or delegate but as a private traveler who did not want to attract too much attention: "My humble self," Turkow explains, "found itself in Moisesville very privately, in order to see, but to be seen as little as possible" (Turkow, *Oyf yidishe felder*, 178).

70. Martin Sökefeld, "Mobilizing in Transnational Space: A Social Movement Approach for the Formation of Diaspora," *Global Networks* 6, no. 3 (2006): 267.

PART 4.
POLITICS AND THE ADDRESSEE OF ETHNOGRAPHY

From Custom Book to Folk Culture

Minhag and the Roots of Jewish Ethnography

NATHANIEL DEUTSCH

In 1891, Rabbi Abraham Sperling (1851–1921) of Lemberg—now Lviv in Ukraine and then part of the Austro-Hungarian Empire—published his Hebrew language magnum opus, *Sefer Ta'amei ha-Minhagim u-Mekorei ha-Dinim* (Book of Reasons for Customs and Sources for Laws).[1] The book rapidly became the rabbinic equivalent of a bestseller. During Sperling's lifetime alone, at least six editions of the book were published, including a Yiddish translation in 1909; after his death, numerous official and bootleg versions were also published in various parts of Eastern Europe as well as in Germany, Hungary, the United States, and, most recently, Israel, likely making it the most widely produced book on Jewish custom in the modern period. Sperling's decision to write the book and its subsequent popularity reflected historical and ideological developments within Ultra-Orthodox or Haredi Judaism, writ large. Indeed, as we will see, *Sefer Ta'amei ha-Minhagim* is notable for its catholic approach to Jewish customs, including material drawn from the responsa of leading rabbis such as Moses Sofer (also known as the Ḥatam Sofer) of Pressburg, generally considered the ideological father of the Haredi movement, as well as multiple Hasidic sources. Yet, as I will argue in this essay, the book was also connected to more secular currents in turn-of-the-century European Jewish culture, including the *kinus* (ingathering) phenomenon and the creation of Jewish ethnography and folklore studies, in which *minhag* (custom) became a central, if theoretically problematic, category.[2]

Customs posed a conceptual challenge for the emerging discipline of Jewish ethnography because unlike the other major foci of the field—including tales, music, jokes, and sayings—minhag was considered a form of Torah, according to some traditional sources.[3] Even when minhag was not explicitly designated as Torah, it was accepted—albeit ambivalently at times—as an integral part of the halakhic framework that provided Jews with a normative and, in many cases, binding guide for behavior. Yet, unlike other aspects of this framework, minhag was not always seen as binding—though, as we will see, this changed dramatically with the advent of the Haredi movement in the nineteenth century—and individual minhagim were sometimes rejected for a variety of reasons, most notably when it was asserted that they had originated among non-Jews and therefore fell under the category of ḥukat ha-goy (the ways of the [gentile] nations) which Jews were forbidden to emulate.

The high status of minhag in traditional Ashkenazi societies, in particular—as Israel Ta-Shma, Jean Baumgarten, and other scholars have noted—was exemplified historically by their incorporation into standard legal codes, most notably the Shulḥan 'Arukh (Set Table), and by the creation of a distinctive literary genre devoted to minhagim and their te'amim (reasons), including the first printed Jewish custom book, Isaac Tyrnau's Sefer ha-Minhagim published in Hebrew in Venice in 1566, then in Shimon Guenzberg's Yiddish adaption (Venice, 1590), and thereafter in many editions in both languages.[4] These and other Jewish custom books both reflected popular practice and helped to shape it, especially in areas where displacement, disease, and other factors had undermined the transmission of customs and eroded knowledge of them.

The reception history of the Shulḥan 'Arukh reveals the degree to which minhagim functioned as an indispensible component of the practical halakhah. Initially composed by Yosef Karo (1488–1575), a sage of Sephardi or Iberian background, employing primarily Sephardi halakhic sources, the Shulḥan 'Arukh would never have been accepted by Ashkenazi Jewry were it not for the glosses that the Polish rabbi Moshe Isserles (the Rama; 1520–1572) added to the text.[5] These glosses, known as the Mapah (Tablecloth), consisted largely of Ashkenazi minhagim that Karo had not included in his original composition. Even then, there was dissent among some of Isserles's rabbinic contemporaries who claimed that the minhagim he cited were not representative of the full range of Ashkenazi customary practice.

Sperling's work participated in the centuries-old phenomenon of minhag literature published in Ashkenazi lands, yet it also possessed distinctive features that reflected its own specific historical context. Perhaps most significantly, the book embraced the explicitly ideological stance toward minhag articulated by the Ḥatam Sofer in response to the rise of the Reform movement in Germany, namely, that changing any Jewish custom was absolutely forbidden and concomitantly, that every Jewish individual, family, town, and region, should preserve and maintain their own distinctive minhagim.[6] Thus, for example, in a section titled 'al titosh torat imekha (do not forsake the teachings of your mother; Proverbs 1:8), a classic biblical proof text cited in support of customary observance, Sperling quoted a responsum of the Ḥatam Sofer that "to change a minhag of our ancestors, is an 'isur Torah [biblical prohibition]."[7] Halakhically speaking, this was the highest level of prohibition and reflected, in part, the regnant Haredi position that minhag was, itself, a form of Torah. As one of the haskamot (rabbinic approbations) appended to Sefer Ta'amei ha-Minhagim put it—quoting a popular saying—minhag Yisrael Torah hu (the minhag of Israel is Torah).[8] This stance was made even clearer on the cover of the 1909 Yiddish edition that stated, Un der minhog yisroel iz a toyre. Al keyn tor men nisht meshane zayn keyn shum minhog (And the minhag of Israel is a form of Torah. Thus, one should not change any minhag).[9]

Along with the Haredi valorization of minhag, which was only intensified by the followers of the Ḥatam Sofer—including Akiva Yosef Schlesinger (1837–1922), author of the incendiary work Lev ha-'ivri—Sperling's book also reflected the veritable explosion of new minhagim created by leaders of the Hasidic movement over the previous century-and-a-half and carefully preserved by their respective followers.[10] The encyclopedic approach taken by Sperling therefore mirrored the Ḥatam Sofer's position that each community should maintain its own traditional minhagim, as well as the normative Hasidic view that each rebbe or charismatic leader should serve as a behavioral model for his group of Hasidim or followers.

Largely originating in the western Oberland region of Hungary, the followers of the Ḥatam Sofer had long had a complicated relationship with

their Hasidic counterparts in the eastern region known as Unterland—
critiquing, competing, and cooperating with them, at turns.[11] Against
this backdrop, Sperling's book represented a notable example of literary
consolidation, bringing together broader Haredi and Hasidic sources under a single umbrella, with the intent of producing a practical guide for
traditional Jews of different backgrounds who were nevertheless united
in their common veneration of minhag.

One of the most striking aspects of Sperling's work was his exclusive
stress on literary sources rather than oral tradition or observed behavior.
Thus, in his introduction, Sperling described himself as "nothing more
than a copyist of books who had rewritten the things therein on new paper."[12] Elsewhere, Sperling listed the names of forty-five "holy and famous
[Hasidic] tsadikim whose holy words are found in this volume [including]
a number of new Torah insights and tales from famous tsadikim . . . which I
collected from holy books, good and sweet words, precious like pure gold,
which I organized alphabetically."[13] As we will see below, this represents
a major contrast with the approach taken by later Jewish ethnographers
in Eastern Europe, who, despite their common interest in minhagim, emphasized the importance of oral traditions and contemporary practice
rather than literary sources, which they typically dismissed as an invalid
source of current folk practice.

Yet in its stress on gathering texts from a wide variety of traditional
sources, *Sefer Ta'amei ha-Minhagim* may be fruitfully compared with the
massive literary anthologies produced during roughly the same period by
participants in the kinus movement, whose seeds were already planted
by Leopold Zunz as early as 1819. As Israel Bartal has written, "One of the
horizons in the creation of 'national culture' was the project of *kinus* ('ingathering'), the collection, editing, and preservation of the nation's cultural creative assets."[14] By the first few decades of the twentieth century,
the kinus project had inspired Micha Yosef Berdichevsky's compilation of
aggadic folklore, *Mimekor Yisrael* (originally published in German as *Der
Born Judas*); Hayim Bialik and Yehoshua Ravnitsky's *Sefer ha-'Agadah*;
Louis Ginzburg's *The Legends of the Jews*; and Martin Buber's famous retellings of Hasidic tales, which drew on some of the same Hasidic literary
sources as did Sperling's work, albeit to dramatically different ends.

Despite sharing their approach to "ingathering" Jewish literary traditions, *Sefer Ta'amei ha-Minhagim* parted ways with these other works in at least three important respects. First, Sperling took great pains to deny that he had creatively altered or transformed any of the material he had dutifully copied from the "holy books" he employed as sources, writing, "It was not my intention to lie or to boast, God forbid, to do or invent something in order to be glorified."[15] Indeed, Sperling's insistence on recording traditions exactly as he found them anticipated the instructions later given by Eastern European Jewish ethnographers to *zamlers* to be as precise as possible when recording folk material in the field. Second, unlike his counterparts in the kinus movement, Sperling did not intend his collection of Jewish traditions to serve as the raw material for largely secularized national Jewish culture, or as a way of introducing these traditions to an audience consisting of already assimilated Jews as well as non-Jews. Instead, *Sefer Ta'amei ha-Minhagim* both reflected and sought to reify an alternate vision of Jewish peoplehood, one that claimed the mantle of "tradition," despite its own radical ideological elements. Somewhat paradoxically, one of the things that provided unity for this version of Jewish peoplehood was precisely its ideological acceptance, even fetishization, of the many local differences in customs that had developed over time: this was not a case of tolerating difference but of mandating it.[16]

This stance led to the third major difference between Sperling and figures like Bialik, Berdichevsky, and Buber: Sperling intended *Sefer Ta'amei ha-Minhagim* to serve as a practical guide for how to live. For this reason, he organized his book according to the structure of the *Shulḥan 'Arukh*, the most important Jewish legal code and itself a compendium of *dinim* (laws) and minhagim, especially once Rabbi Moshe Isserles had appended his glosses to satisfy the needs of Ashkenazi readers. As Sperling wrote in his introduction, "I composed everything according to the *Shulḥan 'Arukh* so that people could find what they were looking for easily."[17] Like earlier Jewish custom books, *Sefer Ta'amei ha-Minhagim* focused on three main areas, the Jewish life-cycle, the holidays, and folk medicine—all topics of great interest for Jewish ethnographers, as well. To expand his audience and help ensure that the book could be used with greater ease, Sperling also wrote in a clear and accessible Hebrew style.

The popular, even folkloric dimension of Sperling's work was emphasized in the fully vocalized Yiddish translation published in Lemberg in
1909, whose cover boldly announced that the book was appearing in *ivri
taytsh* (a Yiddish typically employed to translate holy books), "so that
big and small can understand it." The table of contents that followed interspersed a list of mundane topics such as "matters concerning *tsitsis*
[fringed garment]," "matters concerning *tefillin* [phylacteries]," and "matters concerning reading the Torah," with brief descriptions of wondrous
tales guaranteed to attract and entertain, presumably when reading about
various minhagim—at least temporarily—lost its appeal. Thus, like one of
the chapbooks popular with Yiddish audiences, the text sought to tempt
potential readers and attract book buyers with amazing tales about a rabbi
"whom robbers wanted to kill"; a "student of Ramban who became a her-
etic and then performed repentance"; "the Arizal [Isaac Luria] and *gilgulim*
[reincarnations]"; a "man who appeared to his children in a dream so that
they would rebury him," and so on. Significantly, then, in its combination
of tales and minhagim, the Yiddish version of *Sefer Ta'amei ha-Minhagim*
highlighted precisely those elements of Jewish folk culture—along with
songs, jokes, and healing traditions—that constituted the core of Jewish
ethnography and folklore study.

The Yiddish version of the book explicitly advertised its narrative elements as a way of attracting a broader audience, though, in fact, they constituted a relatively minor proportion of the overall text. In this regard,
the Yiddish work, despite its populist gestures, fit the broader profile of
the custom book genre, in which tales were subordinated to descriptions
of minhagim and their "reasons." This format reflected the desire of custom book authors to situate their works within a halakhic literary world
in which narrative material might be embedded in legal discussions for
didactic purposes but was not the primary mode of discourse. From a
literary point of view, therefore, custom books were something of a "mid-
dle-brow" legal genre, since they did not require the extensive rabbinic
education that more elite halakhic works expected and, in some cases,
were even translated into Yiddish, but were nevertheless pitched toward
readers—or, at least, buyers—who were interested in having a book that
was primarily about proper practice rather than entertainment or edifica-

tion and which usually included statements to the effect that minhag itself was a form of Torah.

By contrast, the classic works of the kinus project, such as *The Legends of the Jews, Sefer ha-'Agadah,* and *Tales of the Hasidim,* emphasized narratives—typically aggadic midrashim and tales or *ma'asiyot*—rather than halakhic material, however broadly construed. References to customs as well as descriptions of them appear in these literary collections, but they generally serve as only one of many elements within an overall narrative structure instead of as their primary focus. Thus, for example, Martin Buber included many customs in his retellings of Hasidic tales, including multiple references to the minhag of eating a *se'udah shelishit* (third meal) on the Sabbath (not coincidentally a favorite time for storytelling), but documenting or illuminating the reasons for these customs was not the point of the tales.[18]

"OF THE PEOPLE?"

Insofar as minhagim reflected the ways in which Jews of all socioeconomic classes celebrated holidays, performed life-cycle events, and engaged in a wide variety of mundane activities, they appealed to Jewish ethnographers and folklorists seeking to document the everyday life of the people. This was especially the case for Jewish ethnographers in Eastern Europe, such as An-sky, who were heavily influenced by Russian populism and various strands of socialism. But was minhag a populist phenomenon? On the one hand, minhagim sometimes originated among groups of people—workers, women, and, in some cases, non-Jews—who were not part of the scholarly elite that produced other elements of the halakhah. On the other hand, the personal habits of famous rabbis—or, once Hasidism spread throughout Eastern Europe, *tsadikim* (Hasidic holy men)—were frequently imitated and transformed into minhagim by their followers. In short, minhagim were an expression of both populist and elite elements within traditional Jewish society.

Similarly, Jewish ethnographers tended to stress the oral and mimetic transmission of minhagim, just as they fetishized "authentic" folk songs and tales that purportedly had not been influenced by printed music

or published texts. Yet, as we have already seen, minhagim were fully
integrated into normative legal codes and also inspired their own literary genre, the custom books, of which Abraham Sperling's *Sefer Ta'amei
ha-Minhagim* is just one example. Indeed, there are striking parallels between the efforts of the traditional scholars who collected and recorded
minhagim in custom books and the Jewish ethnographers and amateur
fieldworkers—known as *zamlers* in Yiddish—who documented the same
minhagim in their studies of Jewish folk culture. We might even describe
the rabbinic authors of the custom books as practicing a kind of ethnography *avant la lettre,* while a significant number of early Jewish ethnographers had either studied in yeshiva, received rabbinic ordination, or were
currently rabbis.

This was the case, for example, with Max Grunwald (1871–1953), a con-
gregational rabbi in Hamburg, Germany, who in 1896 published an ethnographic questionnaire along with a public call for his fellow Jews to
collect folk traditions, followed in 1898 by the founding of the Gesellschaft
für Jüdische Volkskunde, its journal, the *Mitteilungen der Gesellschaft für
Jüdische Volkskunde,* and the Museum für Jüdische Volkskunde. In 1952
Grunwald, whom Dov Noy has called "the founder of Jewish folkloristics,"
published an autobiographical account of his long career in the pages
of the *YIVO Bleter,* the Yiddish language academic journal of the YIVO
Institute for Jewish Research in New York.[19] At the end of his remarks,
Grunwald asserted, "I see in Jewish custom [*minhag*] the spinal cord of
Judaism. In places where it continues to function, there Judaism exists."[20]
It was as powerful a statement about the great significance of minhag in
Jewish life as any made by Abraham Sperling or the Haredi sources he
cited in his work. Rather than record minhagim in traditional custom
books, however, Grunwald believed that they should be the subject of
Jewish folklore studies or as he put it, "Comparative Jewish folkloristics
must build a scientific infrastructure to research Jewish minhagim as I
myself tried."[21]

Within the Russian Empire, meanwhile, many of the young men who
participated in the Jewish Ethnographic Expedition that An-sky led into
the Pale of Settlement between 1912 and 1914 and who contributed to his
massive ethnographic questionnaire, *The Jewish Ethnographic Program,*
had been educated in a yeshiva or a rabbinical seminary and, in some

cases, had actually received rabbinic ordination (e.g., Yekhiel Ravrebbe, Shmuel Shrayer, and Avrom Rekhtman).[22] Ravrebbe, who was born in the Volhynian shtetl of Baranovka to a Hasidic family that followed the Makarov Rebbe, exemplified the kind of individual whose expertise An-sky relied upon. As a youth, Ravrebbe earned a reputation as an 'ilui (prodigy) and was known as a "walking encyclopedia" for his vast knowledge of Jewish tradition.[23]

In short, many of the young contributors to An-sky's *Jewish Ethnographic Program* shared the same cultural and educational backgrounds as the authors and readers of the traditional custom books. Most, if not all, had drifted—in some cases, very far—from their own youthful observance of the literally thousands of minhagim which they mentioned in the questionnaire. The encyclopedic knowledge of customary practices they embedded in the questions reflected two factors: their immersion in the traditional cultural milieu that still considered minhagim to be important and their knowledge of halakhic works, such as the *Shulḥan 'Arukh,* that incorporated many minhagim, as well as custom books, perhaps including Sperling's *Sefer Ta'amei ha-Minhagim* itself.

In the years following World War I, the center for Jewish ethnography in Eastern Europe shifted to Poland, including the historically Lithuanian city of Vilna that was included in its territory, though some activities continued in the Soviet Union, especially in St. Petersburg, Minsk, and Kiev. As early as 1918, Yehuda Zlotnik (also known by the surname Avide), a Polish rabbi who wrote under the pen name Yehuda Elzet, published a groundbreaking essay on minhagim in the first volume of the journal *Reshumot.* Dedicated to Jewish ethnography and folklore, the journal was the brainchild of Alter Druyanow, Hayim Bialik, and Yehoshua Ravnitski, and was initially published in Odessa before moving to Tel Aviv following the publication of the second volume.

Elzet was born in Plotsk, served as a town rabbi in Gombin, and helped to found the Polish Mizraḥi (religious Zionist) Party before moving to Montreal (he ultimately settled in Israel where he died in 1962).[24] The fact that Elzet chose to write under a pseudonym indicates tension between his identity as an Orthodox rabbi and his involvement in Jewish ethnography, an activity that was generally perceived as the purview of secularized Jews, albeit some with a yeshiva background. In a note to Elzet's Hebrew language essay on minhag, the editors informed readers that, "With the permission of our esteemed author, who wishes his name to be concealed, we reveal that he is a rabbi in a Polish town."[25] It would appear that having a Polish rabbi in the inaugural volume lent the new publication some cachet and, given the subject of the essay, a greater claim to authenticity.

The subtitle of the essay described it as a "Collection of minhagim that have not yet been recorded in a book or whose full significance has yet to be explained." Most of the piece is, in fact, dedicated to describing different minhagim that Elzet collected via his own fieldwork in Jewish communities throughout Poland and Lithuania, beginning with those connected to eating and including other sections on holidays, engagement and weddings, pregnancy, and childhood.[26] As he put it, "I recorded in my notebook: 1) Minhagim which I did not find listed in books and which are currently practiced in my district, that is the district of Warsaw—(In the case of the minhagim which I saw in other districts I explicitly recorded their place of origin next to them). 2) Minhagim which I saw a need to comment on, to add to, or amend some matter to, concerning the minhag itself or its reason or source."[27]

In his essay in *Reshumot,* Elzet generally stressed current practices, in some cases even stretching the boundaries of what could be considered a custom, for example: "In recent years a new folk saying has become widespread. When the child cries during the circumcision, afterwards people say: 'He has good reason to cry—he's already prohibited from living in Moscow! [i.e., due to the stringent residency restrictions of Jews in the Russian Empire].'"[28] In other instances, however, Elzet referred to traditional halakhic literary sources, such as Moshe Isserles's glosses to the *Shulḥan 'Arukh* or to the works of the medieval sages known collectively as the Rishonim, when explaining the source or meaning of various minhagim.[29]

In addition to describing different minhagim and discussing their origins and significance, Elzet did something more, something that had never been done in the brief history of Jewish ethnography. At the beginning of the essay, he formulated a methodological introduction to the study of minhag as an ethnographic practice. True to his background as a rabbi, Elzet began by quoting a number of rabbinic sayings that emphasized the great importance of minhag, including: "Minhag annuls halakhah," "The

Minhag of our ancestors is Torah," and "Leave it [the decision concerning an uncertain halakhah] to the people of Israel. If they are not prophets, they are the children of prophets." In other words, Elzet employed precisely the same proof texts as the Haredi authors of contemporary custom books.[30] Moreover, he explicitly and emphatically located minhag within a normative halakhic framework, writing: "When we examine many minhagim we are astonished to see how great the love of the commandments [mitzvot] and the fear of sin was among our people and how extensively the knowledge of the laws of the Torah [hukei ha-Torah] must have been disseminated among all segments of the nation, so that some customs of women and the common folk are nothing but the reflection of a reflection, if it is possible to say, of a known law [din]."[31] Further, Elzet stressed, in an echo of the standard Haredi position, "each and every minhag was important, even the most seemingly insignificant."[32]

Historically, one of the chief ways that rabbinic authors had invalidated a particular minhag was to assert that it had originated among non-Jews, for instance, the so-called darkei ha-'Emori (the ways of the Amorite) mentioned in the Talmud and elsewhere.[33] Like these sources, Elzet was also interested in distinguishing between minhagim of Jewish and non-Jewish origin, but he saw this difference in primarily national-cultural rather than halakhic terms: "In order that knowledge of the people's minhagim become important and serve, in truth, as a key to the soul and spirit of the people, it is necessary for us to determine the source and reason for every minhag and whether it is a native product with a source in the soul of the people or something borrowed from another nation. . . . And it is also incumbent upon us to clarify whether the reason for a minhag was borrowed from the foreign nation or if a new reason was given in a new spirit ... providing them with an understanding concerning holy purity."[34]

At this point in his text, Elzet parted ways with Wissenschaft des Judentums scholars who merely sought to explain the "scientific" origin of a given minhag, by historicizing the phenomenon as follows: "And there is another thing I need to point out: It is impossible to be satisfied with a purely scientific reason for a particular minhag, discovered following extensive research, rather it is our duty to know all of the reasons, that the people themselves gave for that minhag from the point that it was incorporated among them and integrated into their lives, for we find that in different times they gave different reasons for the same minhag."[35] In other words, Elzet was not only interested in why a minhag was created— what he called "the scientific reasons which reveal the initial source and principal origin"—but also in how the people themselves interpreted and reinterpreted the reasons for performing a minhag during different periods based on changing historical and social circumstances.

Significantly, Elzet explicitly addressed the relationship between the new ethnographic literature on minhagim and the traditional custom books, arguing that ethnography should document contemporary practices for future generations just as custom books had done for minhagim in the past: "And since it is impossible to know about the minhagim of past generations except what was recorded in the books of those generations— and what was already documented in those books will not be lost and it will always be possible for someone qualified in such things to gather all the material and clarify it—we will commit a great sin against our nation if the memory of a particular minhag from among those that are practiced in our own day is lost from our spiritual treasury."[36] In proposing that ethnography should now take over the documentary function of traditional custom books, Elzet appeared to be ignoring or at least dismissing the significance of contemporary works such as Sperling's *Sefer Ta'amei ha-Minhagim*. Elzet went even further, however, by suggesting, "It appears as if, in general, the end of minhagim has already arrived, that they are going and falling away one by one from our web of life."[37] While the popularity of Sperling's work may be seen as giving the lie to Elzet's claim, seen from another perspective, the Haredi fetishization of minhag may also be understood as reflecting the same fear that traditional customs were in danger of disappearing.

"A YESHIVE-BOKHER TYPE"

In the decade following the publication of Elzet's essay, the ethnographic study of Jewish customs would grow dramatically in Poland due to the establishment of the Yidisher Visnshaftlekher Institut (Yiddish Scientific Institute) or as it became popularly known, YIVO. Founded in Vilna in 1925 by a number of figures including Max Weinreich, Elye Tsherikover, Zalmen Reyzen, and Nokhem Shtif, the last of whom had written a kind of literary call to arms in 1924, entitled "Vegn a yidishn akademishn institut" (On a Yiddish Academic Institute), YIVO quickly emerged as the hub for Jewish ethnographic research in Eastern Europe through the activities of its Ethnographic Commission.[38] In the same year, the Amerikaner Opteyl (American Section) of YIVO—known as the "Amopteyl" for short—was established in New York City by Jacob Shatsky and Yehuda Leyb Cahan, who headed its Folklore Committee.[39]

In August 1927, Cahan, a native of Vilna who had arrived in New York City in 1904 during the great wave of Jewish immigration from Eastern Europe, sent a letter addressed to his "very important friend" in Kiev, Nokhem Shtif, who had recently moved to the Soviet Union and become one of the key figures in the Chair for Jewish Culture at the Ukrainian Academy of Sciences, later known as the Institute of Jewish Proletarian Culture (Institut Evreiskoi Proletarskoi Kul'tury, or IEPK). Cahan offered Shtif "heartfelt thanks" for the copy of *The Jewish Ethnographic Program* he had sent him—which at the time was extremely difficult to acquire—but he was ambivalent at best concerning its usefulness: "It is a great and important work, though it turns out that I can make little use of it. . . . An-sky's Program is no more and no less than an enormous questionnaire, concerning which one can say, that one fool can ask more than ten clever men can answer. I say this with all due respect and only in jest. We must therefore have twenty professors, trained, stubborn zamlers who should set out among the people and seek answers."[40] The most practical approach, he continued, would be to divide the unwieldy program into smaller, more manageable questionnaires on specific topics, which could then be published and distributed to various communities, "just as [Max] Weinreich has done at YIVO [in Vilna]. Someday this could bring good results, if the proper zamler were found."

Elsewhere in his letter to Shtif, Cahan emphasized that no single zamler could ever do justice to all the different subfields of Jewish ethnography, "I would like to select suitable people for each specialized branch of investigation. In any case, the ethnographic or folklore realm is so extensive, that one person, even with the best abilities, could never achieve command over it in a single lifetime. Therefore, I would like to suggest that for each branch of folklore a suitable zamler should be selected."[41] According to Cahan, there were four main areas of Jewish ethnography—folksongs, folk tales, folk music, and folk beliefs and minhagim—and each required a zamler with a different personality and background.

To collect Jewish folksongs, Cahan recommended a "young man with a pleasant voice who can sing a bit. He can possess other attributes but those are the most important"; for folk tales, "a good storyteller with a considerable stock of different stories, humorous and fantastical"; for folk music, "a professional musician, with a feeling for folk-melodies. He is able to work independently." Finally, for folk beliefs and minhagim, Cahan recommended a "yeshive-bokher type; not a rationalist, but rather a bit mystical; one who himself has an inclination to believe in supernatural things, although he can explain them according to reason. He should not discuss or debate, seldom ask anything, only see, hear, and record."[42]

Just as fieldworkers who collected stories or music had to have skills in those areas, so the fieldworker who collected minhagim had to possess a certain background and temperament that was suited to his subject matter. But what did it mean to be talented in the area of minhagim? First, according to Cahan, such an individual needed to have a base of knowledge that could only come from receiving a yeshiva education, like Yehuda Elzet and the students of the Jewish Academy who had helped An-sky compose the Jewish Ethnographic Program. This individual was probably no longer fully immersed in the culture of traditional Judaism, or else it is unlikely that he would devote himself to ethnography. Yet he needed to be drawn to the supernatural realm in which many minhagim and folk beliefs were imbricated. Able to offer rational explanations for these phenomena when necessary, he nevertheless had to avoid expressing skepticism when working in the field. In short, this "yeshive-bokher type" had to have one foot in and one foot out of the world to which Abraham Sperling and his Haredi readers remained fully committed or, to borrow the original subtitle of An-sky's play *The Dybbuk*, he had to be *tsvishn tsvey velt* (between two worlds).

CONCLUSION

For the emerging field of Jewish ethnography at the turn of the twentieth century, minhagim were among the most important stuff of Jewish folk culture, and traditional custom books, such as Abraham Sperling's

Sefer Ta'amei ha-Minhagim, served as critical antecedents, as well as coun-terpoints. In theory, early Jewish ethnographers stressed the importance of oral traditions over and against written sources, and yet when it came to minhagim, they were clearly influenced in a variety of ways by a liter-ary genre that not only provided a wealth of information about current and historical Jewish folk practices but also served as a literary model for collecting, organizing, and documenting these practices.

Ideologically, Jewish ethnography was predicated on the fundamental claim that Jews were a people or folk in their own right, rather than a parasitic economic caste lacking its own culture—a view that united an-tisemites from Western to Eastern Europe. Indeed, Jewish ethnographers were not only sympathetic to the various forms of Jewish nationalism that emerged during this period; they were, almost without exception, fellow travelers in these movements. Within this context, minhagim had particular significance because they demonstrated that the common Jew-ish people had always possessed a set of practices and beliefs that were distinctive on the one hand, yet that also revealed important parallels with the folk cultures of surrounding peoples, on the other.[43]

At the same time, unique among the various subjects of Jewish ethnog-raphy, including music, jokes, tales, and so on, minhagim were an integral, if frequently contested, part of the Halakhic system that stood at the cen-ter of traditional Judaism. The decades immediately preceding the rise of Jewish ethnography had witnessed the ideological elevation of minhag within Haredi circles, largely in response to the rise of the Reform move-ment and the spreading effects of cultural assimilation, which had eroded or eliminated many traditional Jewish practices and behaviors. Against this backdrop, minhag was seen as the outermost ring or, in traditional Jewish parlance, the "fence around the law"; concomitantly, if Jews gave up their practice of minhagim, they would soon find reason to abandon the Torah, in general, and would cease to exist as a "kingdom of priests and a holy nation" (Exodus 19:6). Thus, while their paths diverged in ways large and small, both Jewish ethnographers and Haredi thinkers came to see minhag as a defining element of Jewish peoplehood.

NOTES

1. References are to the recent Israeli edition, Abraham Isaac Sperling, *Sefer Ta'amei ha-Minhagim u-Mekorei ha-Dinim* (Jerusalem: Shay Lamora, 1999).

2. Throughout this article I will generally use the phrase *Jewish ethnography*, though, to a great degree, the terms ethnography and folklore studies (or folkloristics) were employed interchangeably to describe the same phenomenon. In some cases, however, an attempt was made to distinguish them. See, for instance, the discussion of YIVO's evolving distinction between folklore and ethnography in Itzik Gottesman, *Defining the Yiddish Nation: The Jewish Folklorists of Poland* (Detroit: Wayne State University Press, 2003), 121, "'Folklore' became the term used only for the texts, the material. 'Ethnography' defined the academic discipline that studied these materials." See also, Barbara Kirshenblatt-Gimblett, "Di folkloristik: A Good Yiddish Word," *The Journal of American Folklore* 98, no. 389 (1985): 331–334.

3. For an introduction to the topic and a discussion of traditional sources, see, in Hebrew, Daniel Sperber, *Minhagei Yisrael: mekorot ve-toldot*, 8 vols. (Jerusalem: Mosad Ha-Rav Kuk, 1998–2007); in English, Daniel Sperber, *The Jewish Life Cycle: Custom Law and Iconography: Jewish Customs from the Cradle to the Grave* (Ramat Gan: Bar-Ilan University Press, 2008).

4. Jean Baumgarten, "Prayer, Ritual and Practice in Ashkenazic Jewish Society: The Tradition of Yiddish Custom Books in the Fifteenth to Eighteenth Centuries," *Studia Rosenthaliana* 36 (2002–2003), 121–146.

5. On the contentious reception history of the *Shulḥan 'Arukh* in Ashkenazi communities, see Joseph Davis, "The Reception of the 'Shulhan 'Arukh' and the Formation of Ashkenazic Jewish Identity," *AJS Review* 26 (2002), 251–276.

6. For the Ḥatam Sofer and his ideological approach, see Michael Silber, "The Emergence of Ultra-Orthodoxy: The Invention of a Tradition," in *The Uses of Tradition: Jewish Continuity since Emancipation*, ed. Jack Wertheimer (New York: Jewish Theological Seminary, 1992), 23–84.

7. Sperling, *Sefer Ta'amei ha-Minhagim*, 551.

8. Sperling, *Sefer Ta'amei ha-Minhagim*, 9 (Introduction).

9. Abraham Sperling, *Sefer Taamei ha-Minhugim oyf Ivri Taytsh* (Lemberg: Verlag A. J. Sperling, 1909).

10. On Schlesinger's attitude toward minhag, see Silber, 50–84.

11. Ibid., 40–47.

12. Sperling, *Sefer Ta'amei ha-Minhagim*, 7 (Introduction).

13. Ibid., 4.

14. Israel Bartal, *"The Kinnus Project: Wissenschaft des Judentums and the Fashioning of a 'National Culture' in Palestine,"* in *Transmitting Jewish Traditions: Orality, Textuality, and Cultural Diffusion*, ed. Yaakov Elman and Israel Gershoni (New Haven, Conn.: Yale University Press, 2000), 311.

15. Sperling, *Sefer Ta'amei ha-Minhagim*, 7.

16. A variety of reasons were offered in traditional sources for why Jews should retain their specific customs. On the Ḥatam Sofer's explanation for why Ashkenazi and Sephardi Jews should preserve their customary forms of prayer, see Sperber, *Minhagei Yisrael*, 3: 5–13.

17. Sperling, *Sefer Ta'amei ha-Minhagim*, 7.

18. See, for example, Martin Buber, *Tales of the Hasidim: Book One: Early Masters and Book Two: The Later Masters* (New York: Schocken Books, 1991), 101, 214, 255, 276.

19. Max Grunwald, "Zikhroynes un briv: kapitlekh fun an oytobiografye," *YIVO-bleter* 36 (1952): 241–251. It was an interesting, even provocative, venue for a German Jewish folklorist and rabbi to publish his reminiscences. Yet, as Grunwald explained within its pages, critics had earlier leveled "attacks against 'Mauscheln,' that is, against Yiddish. The fact that thanks to the Jews of Eastern Europe this 'Mauscheln' had become a world language . . . encouraged me to deal seriously with this jargon." Perhaps because of the conceptual challenges posed by minhag that I discussed above, Dov Noy, "Yerushalayim shel minhag," *Meḥkarei ha-merkaz le-ḥeker ha-folklor* 6 (1982), 1, has asserted that "In the past, Jewish folkloristics dealt extensively with folk literature, songs and music, and folk art but relatively little in folk beliefs and minhag and their reciprocal relationship." Noy's claim is overstated, given the consistent inclusion of minhag as one of the major foci of Jewish ethnography and the extensive efforts to collect minhagim via ethnographic questionnaires and the activities of zamlers on the ground. Indeed, in the continuation of his remarks, Noy acknowledges that even though Grunwald, himself, did not engage extensively with minhag in his published books and articles—at least relative to other subjects—the topic nevertheless "occupied a notable place within the totality of his thought and scientific undertaking."

20. Grunwald, "Zikhroynes un briv," 246. Noy discusses this statement in "Yerushalayim shel minhag," 2. A Hebrew translation of an excerpt from Grunwald's autobiographical essay in *YIVO-bleter* appears in *Meḥkarei ha-merkaz le-ḥeker ha-folklor* 6 (1982): 9–12.

21. Ibid. As an example of this kind of research, Grunwald mentioned his book *Hygiene der Juden* (Dresden: Verlag der historischen Abteilung der internationalen Hygiene-Ausstellung, 1911), which included, inter alia, essays such as Samuel Weissenberg, "Hygiene in Brauch und Sitte der Juden," and M. S. Bamberger, "Die Hygiene des Schulchan Arukh." Weissenberg was a Russian Jewish physician and anthropologist who also served on the planning committee for An-sky's Jewish Ethnographic Expedition. On his life and work, see John Efron, *Defenders of the Race: Jewish Doctors and Race Science in Fin-de-Siècle Europe* (New Haven, Conn.: Yale University Press, 1994), 91–122.

22. On the expedition and the Jewish Ethnographic Program, see Nathaniel Deutsch, *The Jewish Dark Continent: Life and Death in the Russian Pale of Settlement* (Cambridge, Mass.: Harvard University Press, 2011).

23. On the influence of these institutes on the Jewish Academy in St. Petersburg, see Brian Horowitz, *Jewish Philanthropy and Enlightenment in Late-Tsarist Russia* (Seattle: University of Washington Press, 2009), 201.

24. See Rebecca Margolis, *Jewish Roots, Canadian Soil: Yiddish Cultural Life in Montreal, 1905–1945* (Montreal: McGill-Queens University Press, 2011), 51.

25. Yehuda Elzet, "Mi-minhagei Yisrael: kovets minhagim shelo nizkeru od 'o shelo nitba'aru 'adayin ke-khol tsorkham," *Reshumot* 1 (1918): 336.

26. Jewish food was a particular interest of Elzet; he published a pioneering book on the subject, *Yidishe maykholim* (Warsaw: n.p., 1920).

27. Elzet, "Mi-Minhagei," 337–338.

28. Ibid., 367.

29. See, for example, ibid., 339.

30. David Assaf, in Yekhezkel Kotik, *Journey to a Nineteenth-Century Shtetl: The Memoirs of Yekhezkel Kotik*, ed. David Assaf (Detroit: Wayne State University Press, 2008), 96 n.132, writes in reference to Elzet, "We must also note that similar feelings moved Orthodox rabbis to engage in source-collecting projects."

31. Elzet, "Mi-Minhagei," 335.

32. Ibid., 336.

33. See, for instance, Babylonian Talmud Shabbat 67a.

34. Elzet, "Mi-Minhagei," 337.

35. Ibid.

36. Ibid.

37. Ibid.

38. Initially the Commission worked together with the An-sky Vilna Jewish Historic-Ethnographic Society; then it functioned independently. See the entry on YIVO by Cecile Kuznitz in *The YIVO Encyclopedia of Jews in Eastern Europe*, http://www.yivo encyclopedia.org/article.aspx/YIVO

39. See the entry on Cahan by Chana Mlotek in *The YIVO Encyclopedia of Jews in Eastern Europe*, http://www.yivoencyclopedia.org/article.aspx/Cahan_Yehudah_Leib.

40. Yehuda Leyb Cahan, *Shtudyes vegn yidisher folksshafung* (New York: YIVO, 1952), 133.

41. Ibid., 131.

42. Ibid., 131–132.

43. On this topic, see An-sky, "Mutual Influences between Christians and Jews," as translated by Golda Werman, in "Ansky Lives!" ed. David Roskies, trans. Golda Werman, *Jewish Folklore and Ethnology Review* 14, no. 1–2 (1992): 66–67.

In Search of the Exotic
"Jewish Houses" and Synagogues in Russian Travel Notes

ALLA SOKOLOVA

Pan Tadeusz, Or the Last Foray in Lithuania: A Gentry Tale of 1811 and 1812, in Twelve Books of Verse (1834), the best-known poem of the canonical Polish Romantic poet Adam Mickiewicz (1798–1855), contains a description of an "old Jewish inn." First Mickiewicz describes an indoor courtyard, known "by the more rustic name 'byre,'" for horses, goats, and poultry; then he mentions a "huge room" with a "long, narrow, many-legged wooden table," and guest rooms, "chambers narrow and long," in the tavern itself. Mickiewicz also pays attention to carved wooden columns on the façade.[1] This description fancifully combines biblical allusions and anthropomorphic images: the inn resembles both Noah's Ark and the Temple of Solomon;[2] from a distance, it also brings to mind a devout Jew "nodding at prayer."[3] Apparently, Mickiewicz considered that the architecture of synagogues, inns, and other Jewish buildings bore the imprint of the ancient style invented by Phoenician carpenters from the city of Tyre. He believed that "the Jews had adopted" this style of architecture and "carried it through the world" wherever they settled.[4] Mickiewicz defined such buildings as "the heritage of Gothic art," perhaps because he discerned the influence of Arab architecture.[5]

Mickiewicz's description of the inn invites us to examine representations of architectural and ethnographic reality marked as Jewish. It allows us to trace how romantic ideas about the ancient biblical roots of Polish Lithuanian Jewry combined with an Orientalist system of stereotypes,

which developed as part of the European tradition of constructing differences between East and West.[6] On the one hand, then, we might recognize
pro-Jewish sentiment in Mickiewicz's admiration of the carved decorations, reminiscent of Sabbath candlesticks, in the inn's façade. On the
other hand, he was apparently subject to certain anti-Jewish prejudices
of his time, as evoked by the comparisons of the inn's "smoky and dirty"
walls with a "black *lapserdak*" (Jewish traditional clothing), and its roof
with "a cap and Jewish beard."[7]

Travelogues of the nineteenth and early twentieth centuries about the
western provinces of the Russian Empire contain both pro- and anti-Jewish perspectives on local Jewish ethnographic realia (with the exception
of essays in Jewish publications, which were prone to exhibiting Jewish
"ethnic pride"). The authors, like Mickiewicz, sometimes alternate between these perspectives in a single description. An analysis of the origins of Jewish stereotypes is beyond the scope of this article;[8] however,
I use these travelogues to consider the prehistory of Jewish ethnography
and the study of Jewish architectural history in Russia. Having first read
these travelogues while studying the built environment of the shtetl in
the Vinnitsa region of Ukraine, I show that they remain valuable for researchers, despite their contradictions and their old-fashioned approach
to the material.[9]

Under the influence of nineteenth-century imperial policy, some of the
Russian educated elite began to see the western provinces as "primordially
Russian Orthodox lands" that had been, in bureaucratic jargon, "returned
from Poland."[10] These territories were surmised to contain locales "not
trampled underfoot by tourists"[11] that needed description. Sergey Kozlov
notes that "frankness, vividness, and breadth of exposition" were characteristic of travel writing, along with everything "from sketches of everyday
life to lengthy treatises on the mores, traditions, and particularities of the
national character of other peoples."[12] Thus some travelers to the western
provinces digressed from reflections on "ancient Russian architecture"[13]
and "Russian folk culture," to manifestations of ethnic and religious diversity—in particular, Jewish architectural and ethnographic realia. The
first part of this chapter focuses on travelers' descriptions of houses constructed from local building materials in primitive ways. I consider how
authors of travelogues justified giving these houses the status of a Jewish

"folk dwelling," which functioned as a kind of hall pass into the field of ethnography and from there to the world history of architecture. In the second part of the chapter, I consider travelogues describing synagogues as monuments of "Jewish olden times." Historians of architecture, in discussing "monuments of olden times," distinguished between architectural masterpieces and historical monuments, taking care to underline the ethnic specificity of both types.

Referencing Hans Rogger, Alexander Etkind writes that the creation of the Pale of Jewish Settlement "was tantamount to the establishment of a Jewish colony."[14] Of course, he does not mean that Jews were seen as active participants in the colonization of these lands. Although they had played that role before the Polish partitions, the Russian imperial authorities deemed them a "people" with no right to the land on which they lived. Orthodox Russians were assigned the role of "native people," and the three hundred years of Jewish residence were interpreted as "*temporary.*"[15] Etkind notes: "Having colonized its multiple territories, Russia applied typically colonial regimes of indirect rule—coercive, communal, and exoticizing—to its population." Jews stood out in this framework as *hyper*-exoticized colonial subjects,[16] and travelers, accordingly, imbued their observations of Jews in the Pale of Settlement with an Orientalizing flavor, even though, geographically, the Pale lay to the west of the "interior provinces." While discussing the effects of colonialism, Robert Bernasconi mentions that "the simplest way of excluding the possibility of dialogue" is to declare that "a partner belong[s] to the exotic, primitive culture."[17] This kind of representation can express not only the observer's distance from this culture, but also an active interest in observing it,[18] which explains how travelogue authors could simultaneously exoticize Jewish ethnographic reality and describe some of its phenomena clearly. Russian architectural studies and ethnography followed this exoticizing, colonial research paradigm. From the 1870s onward, the quality of scientific research on architectural monuments improved and a genre of essays on "architectural olden time (starina)" appeared.[19] Such essays described buildings recognized as valuable monuments and theorized about the origin, style, and national distinctiveness of their architectural forms. Their authors took on the role of the traveler, and so this genre is often indistinguishable from the travelogue. The first Jewish historical and ethnographic expedition in Russia, organized by the writer and public figure Semyon Akimovich An-sky,[20] would go to the Pale only in 1912; by then, ethnography and architectural studies had already formed as scientific disciplines with methodologies for describing "folk dwellings" and architectural monuments.

This chapter considers how travelogue authors[21] converted the heuristic potential of Orientalism into richly detailed representations of "Jewish inns" and synagogues, which I compare to descriptions in belletristic accounts and scholarly articles by their contemporaries. Among my travelers, some traveled independently, others at public expense as part of government service. The earliest essay discussed is "Notes of a Russian Traveler from 1823 to 1827" by Andrey Glagolev, published in 1837;[22] the latest is Eleazar Lissitzky's "The Synagogue of Mogilev," based on his recollections of a 1916 journey and published in 1923.[23] Lissitzky's essay is a travelogue that described his direct impressions of the synagogue, famous for its paintings; it is also a critique of what Lissitzky saw as vulgar ethnographic tendencies in the developing field of Jewish architecture studies, including the work of my authors. I consider how travelers functioned as researchers and experts, rather than as belletrists primarily interested in making vivid impressions. Researchers who dare to approach the object of their study with a willingness to doubt their preconceptions gain a special ethnographic vision, which allows them to experience the power of these objects while maintaining them at a distance. The descriptions of architectural and ethnographic realia examined here show that these authors were successful in tempering the tendency of their imaginations to rely on literary (including biblical) allusions,[24] and also in developing a critical approach to the scholarly and quasi-scholarly works of their predecessors.

The texts I consider at greatest length were written by the following seven individuals:

1. Andrey Gavrilovich Glagolev (1793–1844), who had a doctorate in literature, traveled outside Russia from 1823 to 1828, then worked at the Department of Foreign Religions in the Ministry of Internal Affairs.

2. Alexander Stepanovich Afanas'ev (Chuzhbinsky; 1816–1875) traveled to study the life and customs of Russian river and coastal

regions in 1856 at the suggestion of Grand Prince Konstantin Nikolaevich, then wrote a series of articles, later collected in a two-volume ethnographic work, *Poezdka v Iuzhnuiu Rossiiu* (Trip to Southern Russia). *Part I: Ocherki Dnepra* (Essays about the Dnieper). St. Petersburg, 1861; *Part II: Ocherki Dnestra* (Essays about the Dniester). St. Petersburg, 1863.

3. K. M. (full name and dates unknown) traveled in the late 1870s and wrote *Putevye ocherki. Podoliia* (Traveler's Essays: Podoliia), in *Kievskaia starina* (Kievan Olden Time), May 1884–April 1885, parts I–X.

4. Andrey Pavlovich Subbotin (1852–1906), Russian economist and writer.

5. George Kreskent'evich Loukomsky (1884–1952), historian, art critic, artist, and secretary of the Paris group "Mir iskusstva" (World of Art), wrote books on Russian architecture and art, including *Russisches Porzellan* (Russian Porcelain), *Russische Baukunst* (Russian Art in Wood), and *Jewish Art in European Synagogues (From the Middle Ages to the Eighteenth Century)*.

6. Semyon Akimovich An-sky (Shloyme Zanvl Rappoport, 1863–1920), Russian Jewish scholar, playwright, ethnographer, and political activist.

7. Eleazar (Lazar Markovich) Lissitzky (1890–1941), better known as El Lissitzky, graphic artist, designer, typographer, art theorist, and architect, and important avant-garde figure, was active from 1916 to 1918 in the Jewish art movement. In 1916 he undertook an expedition with the artist Isakhar-Ber Rybak (1897–1935) to Belarus and Lithuania, where they copied paintings in wooden synagogues.

THE TRANSFORMATION OF "JEWISH INNS" INTO EXOTICIZED "FOLK DWELLINGS"

Glagolev considered himself a classicist, but his "Notes" show that he was more of a sentimentalist, no less prone to Orientalism than Mickiewicz. He writes that he "got [his] first notion about the Jews"[25] in Zhytomyr (Volyn); he represents Berdichev stereotypically as an "eternally

FIGURE 13.1

Korchma (Inn). Samgorodok. Berdichev district. Drawing by
Elena Rusova. Second part of the nineteenth century. Collection
of the Russian Geographic Society, Razriad 112, op.1, d. 898.

hustling flea market of Jews."[26] One section of his essay, "The Jews," is dedicated to a systematic ethnographic description of Jews, including their
appearance, costume, religious rituals associated with observance of the
Sabbath, their houses, and even a special *brichka* (Jewish chaise), "worthy
of Orlovsky's own brush."[27] Glagolev calls Jews the "descendants of the
ancient Israelites" in a quasi-theological statement that they had been
"condemned to wander from one country to another, almost as though
only to demonstrate to the world that certain decisions of God's justice
are immutable."[28] He draws attention to "Oriental" physical features that
betray Jews' "origins in ancient Zion."[29] He describes the Jewish "folk
dwelling": "in the construction of their houses, the Jews . . . have retained
the imprint of Asian architecture."[30] Unlike Mickiewicz, he avoids biblical
allusions: "Despite the severity of the climate, they [Jews] often open wide

FIGURE 13.2

The Inn (detail from photo). Yiddish caption on reverse
reads: "Houses in Kozin." Collection "Photo-archive of An-
sky's Expeditions" at the Center "Petersburg Judaica."

the tall doors of their rooms, which they call *stantsy*,[31] as if to catch a breath
of wind from all parts of the world."[32] This idea of a "national psyche"
exerting a defining influence on the character of the "folk dwelling" was
widespread until the early twentieth century.[33] Glagolev gives a detailed
description of the layout and furnishings of "the Jewish *korchma*" (inn).
He was particularly impressed by the covered courtyard at the rear border
of the heated part of the building, which for Mickiewicz recalled Noah's
Ark: "A covered courtyard is protected from rain and snow, but during
the night it is so dark there that you can hardly get past the carriages
and horses without a lighted lantern."[34] Such observations, testifying to
the author's immediate impressions, are particularly valuable for me as a
supplement to my own field observations.

A more detailed and systematic description of the Jewish inn appears in
"Essays on the Road: Podoliia," under the pseudonym K. M.[35] The author
notes that Jewish houses in small towns in Podoliia were "completely unknown quantities for a resident of, let us say, left-bank Ukraine."[36] He (or

FIGURE 13.3

Jewish korchma (inn). Lithograph from drawing by L. A.
Belousoff (1806–1854). *Costumes de la Petite Russie*. Paris:
Publie par Daziaro à Moscou et St. Petersbourg, 1845.

she) draws the accurate conclusion that all Jewish houses in this region
are "built according to one and the same architectural type."[37] He defines
the layout principles of this type of house, and calls it the "Jewish *zaezd*"
(inn, a house with a hallway, called *anfur* in Yiddish).[38] In order to describe
such houses as a kind of ethnographic curiosity, K. M. employs the term
zhilishche (dwelling). Like Glagolev, K. M. found that the architecture of
the "Jewish *zaezd*" reveals the Jewish "national character," but he used
different evidence, noting that the covered courtyard to the side of the
rear wall of the heated part of the inn was littered with "all kinds of slop
and kitchen leftovers, because it takes longer to take them out onto the
street."[39] If Glagolev mentions the "untidiness" of Jewish inns in passing,[40]
K. M. repeatedly describes this disorder, as well as the dirt in and around
Jewish houses, as characteristic of Jews.

K. M.'s observations about "Jewish dirt" echo Alexander Afanas'ev
(Chuzhbinsky)'s ethnographic research work, "Essays of the Dniester,"[41]
and K. M. mentions that Afanas'ev had visited the same places "twenty
years earlier."[42] Afanas'ev's essays contain no descriptions of "Jewish

FIGURE 13.4

Jewish korchma or *Little Russian tavern*. Popular print (lubok) published
by E. Iakovlev from metal-plate engraving. Moscow, 1857. (Lithographic
version of this image was published by A. Loginov in 1851 in Moscow.)

dwellings," but his representation of Jewish streets is a striking example
of exoticization. He uses grotesque images that express both aversion to
what he saw and interest in it. For example, he defines local towns and
townships as "hotbeds of the children of Israel"[43] where Jews "nest,"[44] and
at night, they "move swiftly and abruptly, far and near."[45] The marketplace
in the town of Khotyn is "crowded with Jews nesting in the mud, because
no matter how hot the sun's rays shine, they cannot get into this kingdom
of dampness and harmful fumes . . . it is a *real maze* here, and even though
the shops stretch out in two lines, sometimes you have to walk in such a
roundabout way that you wonder where all these bends and curves came
from" (emphasis mine).[46] K. M. depicts the old part of Khotyn in almost
the same words: "First [you see] the old town, which looks like a *real maze*
of curves, narrow and impassably dirty streets, and mostly Jewish houses,
each intended for trade or commerce" (emphasis mine).[47]

It is no coincidence that K. M. mentions "dirt" in the preamble to his description of the "exterior of a [typical] little town in Podoliia" and of the "architecture of Jewish houses." He needs this preamble to help the reader experience the moment of crossing the boundary between suburb and trade center and to heighten the contrast between the "rows of beautiful peasant huts" and the "dirty, shabby Jewish dwellings."[48] Indeed, before the end of the nineteenth century, this lack of land improvements was as typical of small towns in the Jewish Pale as in the empire's central provinces. There too, travelers compared the "ramshackle houses and rotten fences"[49] in the towns to the peasant huts; though these were no less ramshackle, they were "buried in gardens" and therefore declared beautiful. When similar comparisons were drawn in the western region, with its entirely Jewish small towns, the dirt of the town was seen as testimony to the Oriental "national character" of the Jews.

Unlike Glagolev, Afanas'ev, and K. M., Andrey Subbotin,[50] the author of the 1887 essay "In the Pale of Settlement . . ."[51] examined the houses of Jews exclusively in search of signs of poverty. Perhaps that is why he only incidentally mentions "the inns or visiting houses (in Yiddish, *akhsanie*)"[52] and the residences of "wealthy" Jews, which look like European buildings."[53] His description of a house of "poor Jews" in the town of Ostropol' (Volyn) is typical: "In one such hut, sagging and propped up on stakes, resembling not so much a human habitation as a barn, lived five young orphans. These children were looked after by the owner of this edifice: a poor old Jewish peddler woman. Despite this hut's miserable appearance and almost complete lack of utensils, it turned out to be much cleaner inside than we expected."[54] Subbotin repeatedly raises the idea of Jewish cleanliness, as if to challenge the notion that dirt was an essential attribute of Jewish space.[55] Subbotin does find dirt in the streets around "poor Jewish houses," but he finds the interiors relatively clean. His reflections testify to a paternalistic attitude and skepticism toward anti-Jewish stereotypes.

The comparatively neutral characterization of the bad sanitary conditions of poor Jewish streets and houses at the start of the essay gives way to a description tinged with Orientalism. The author describes his trip "from lively, rich Bialystok . . . to the nest of Jewish poverty and gloom, their famous [Jewish] center—Berdichev."[56] Subbotin writes, "the town-

ship Polonnoe is infested with Jews . . . the filth and stench in their court-
yards should undermine the strength of this already weak tribe."[57] Such
statements mark the author as an Orientalist, albeit one paternalistically
inclined toward the "weak tribe." Among his sketches of poor "Jewish
huts," two relatively short ones stand out. Of the poorest quarter of Minsk,
Subbotin notes:

> Even the poorest Jewish huts have chimneys that send out smoke without
> getting it into the room. The windows are larger than in peasants' houses,
> about 1.5–2 *arshins* [yards] in height. There are always several rooms in the
> hut and they try to keep them discrete: one room is kept clean, another
> serves as the bedroom, and the fireplace is always located separately. At
> the entrance to the house, to the right side of the door, there is usually a
> tablet encased in glass [*Mazuzia*][58] with the Jewish sign, hanging askew
> from the ledge to which it is nailed. . . .[59]

Here is Subbotin on a street in the little town of Ostropol': "Small wattle
and daub huts of 6–8 square *sazhens* (fathoms) with direct access onto the
street, all with balconies or porches, a shop or workshop usually located in
the front room. . . ."[60] These observations focus on details, thereby weak-
ening the didactic representation of Jewish poverty. The author, it appears,
has been "captured" by his own observations of reality and distracted
from his own ideology. Unlike Glagolev and K. M., Subbotin does not
generalize from his observations but confines himself to "fleeting impressions and observations in the spirit of narrative," because he prides himself
on his ability to gather factual material in an unbiased way; he believes
that his work will benefit "*otchiznovedenie*" (literally, "fatherland studies,"
i.e., regional studies).[61]

Subbotin was probably familiar with the authoritative ethnographic
study of Jews in the southwest, *Proceedings of the Ethnographic and Statistical Expedition to the West Russian Region,* edited by Pavel (Pavlo)
Chubynsky and published in 1872 by the Imperial Russian Geographical
Society.[62] The section of this work on Jewish "home life," "Jews of the
Southwestern Region," offers disparate observations of the "Jewish dwelling"; for example, "in the [houses of] Jews of the middle and even lower
class, the main exit more often than not leads directly onto the street."[63]
Chubynsky notes that a characteristic element of the façade of a Jewish
house in a small town is the gate through which one can enter the "inner

courtyard," which is under the same roof as the house.[64] He concludes, "Jewish dwellings are somewhat different in their external and internal architecture from the houses of Christians ... due to the particularities of Jews' occupation and lifestyle."[65] Chubynsky's statement revises the conclusions drawn eleven years earlier by Moisei Berlin, a "learned Jew" in the Department of Religious Affairs of Foreign Confessions. In "Essay on the Ethnography of the Jewish Population in Russia" (St. Petersburg, 1861), Berlin argues that there are no significant differences between Jewish and Christian "dwellings":[66] "Jewish dwellings, *in essence,* do not differ from local [dwellings] in the region where they [Jews] are settled" (emphasis mine).[67]

It appears that Chubynsky, like Berlin, did not consider the "Jewish dwelling" worthy of systematic architectural and ethnographic description because it was constructed from local building materials in a "primitive" way (that is, according to local methods of folk production). Ethnographers and the authors of ethnographically oriented travelogues believed that these techniques belonged exclusively to the rural "native population," which did not include Jews. In the grip of an ideology that negated the possibility of something authentically "Jewish" in the architecture of Jewish houses, these writers could describe such Jewish architectural elements only when speaking relatively informally about their own impressions, but not when generalizing in a more scholarly tone. The examples of Berlin and Chubynsky indicate that travelers who presented systematic ethnographic reports were particularly unable to remove their blinders. In contrast, contemporary vernacular architectural studies allow us to consider the Jewishness of a building in different terms: one could explain how the layout of shtetl houses stems from distinctive features of their utilitarian and symbolic use by their owners, Jews or non-Jews, including interaction with visitors, travelers, or researchers.[68]

PLACING THE EXOTICIZED SYNAGOGUE IN JEWS' AND NON-JEWS' CULTURAL HERITAGE

Chubynsky's "Jews of the Southwestern Region" offers scattered references to synagogues, mainly in the chapter "Customs and Rituals," while K. M. and Afanas'ev drew attention to Orthodox churches, cathedrals, castles, even mills and inns, but none of the numerous local synagogues. K. M. reasoned about the need to "preserve and study as many monuments of the olden time as possible, especially monuments of ancient architecture.... [This architecture] is preserved almost exclusively in the remains of churches and monasteries...."[69] He did not includes synagogues among such "monuments." In contrast, in Subbotin's essay, a lengthy description of the Minsk synagogue follows his observations about Jewish charity and his sympathetic remarks that Jews' "cheerfulness of spirit is supported by their religiosity."[70] Subbotin finds synagogue structure predictable: "In the city center, near the [Russian Orthodox] cathedral and the main Roman Catholic church, there is an expansive synagogue yard, before which stands a massive, cubic synagogue building with the inevitable chandeliers, the ark, the podium for the cantor, benches."[71] He moves on to things he finds more interesting, such as the sale of synagogue seats and "the queue for reading the Torah." Subbotin characterizes the main Old Synagogue in Vilna similarly: it is "highly revered by the Russian Jews, and the seats are very expensive."[72] "The synagogue building," he writes, "is large, in cubic form; it is very spacious inside; its dome is supported by four large columns. In this synagogue, as in [the one in] Minsk, there are always a lot of people."[73]

Glagolev's essay displays deeper interest in synagogue architecture— to be more precise, in a single synagogue building. In the "ethnographic" chapter entitled "The Jews," he writes only, "[in a town] where there is no synagogue, the place of prayer is often an inn or a tavern."[74] A description of the synagogue building and of some of the rituals that take place inside is included in the next section on the Austrian town of Brody. Significantly, he decided to visit the synagogue only after he left Russia for Austria. Before that, he had visited Novgorod-Volynsky, Ostrog, Kremenets, and Dubno and observed a variety of architectural monuments, from ancient earthen fortifications to "a military depot constructed in 1817 in Dubno,"[75] but did not mention the monumental synagogues that were among the most important landmarks of the town centers.

Just after crossing the Russian–Austrian border, he writes that he has finally "fallen into the hands of the Jews."[76] Once in Brody, he imagines that he has "appeared in Judea."[77] Perhaps this is why Glagolev was somewhat annoyed not to find in the architecture of the Brody synagogue the

FIGURE 13.5

Interior of the Great Synagogue in Brody. Drawing by W. Leopolski
(1828–1892). *Tygodnik ilustrowany* "Kłosy." Warsaw, 1874, vol. 19, no. 486, 260.

FIGURE 13.6

Great Synagogue in Brody. Photo by Alla Sokolova, 2000.

similarities he sought with the Temple of Solomon. But he did not waste
the opportunity to demonstrate before the local Jews his awareness that
"the altar of the Jerusalem Temple was located at its western wall . . . and
the entrance [to the Temple] was from the east,"[78] upon discovering that
the entrance to the synagogue in Brody was "from the west, through large
iron gates or small doors on the left side of the gate."[79] Glagolev was definitely disappointed with the architectural form of this "big stone building" constructed in 1741: "This shul [the synagogue] has a square layout
and the simplest architecture."[80] Nonetheless, he describes the architecture of the synagogue in Brody, especially its prayer hall, in detail. He
mentions that the Ark of the Covenant was "veiled with a green curtain";
"on one of the benches of the pulpit" lay "two crimson velvet cushions
for the circumcision of infants"; "the pillars supporting the arch of the
synagogue were all octahedral, and on each face was a printed sheet of
the Commandments framed in glass."[81] With some irony, he observes,
"the Jews believe that one can find another such synagogue as this only
in Prague."[82] This statement indicates that Glagolev discussed the build-

ing with local Jews; it seems that the Brody Jews deemed their synagogue
building an outstanding architectural masterpiece and did not mind being
examined by the Russian traveler. It appears they considered Prague one
of the most important centers of the Jewish world. Glagolev's search for
resemblance between the monumental architecture of the Brody synagogue and the Temple was atypical for Russia, though common to the west
(as in Poland): Sergey Kravtsov cites eighteenth- and nineteenth-century
Polish artistic depictions of synagogues that disclose the artists' intention
to show these synagogues as architectural heirs of the Temple.[83]

In Russia, the journal *Evreiskaia starina* (Jewish Olden Time), published from 1908 by the Jewish Historical and Ethnographic Society
(JHES), demonstrates the emergence of a systematic interest in the
architecture of synagogues in the Pale as monuments of Jewish olden
time.[84] Each issue contains a notice asking readers to send documents
and "monuments of olden time" (Jewish ritual objects no longer in use)
for the JHES archive and museum, and they received, among other things,
twenty-six photographs of seven synagogues from the end of 1908 to the
end of 1912 (but not a single photograph of a "Jewish dwelling").[85] The
preface to the legend of the synagogue recorded by Z. Averbukh in his
native town of Semiatichi and published in *Evreiskaia starina* exemplifies
the new tendency.[86] The publisher's interest in the architecture of this "big
stone synagogue" is emphasized. He mentions that the building was built
in 1755, and writes: "Thanks to the artificial hill on which the synagogue
is located, it is not only higher than the Uniate Church, but almost level
with the local Roman Catholic church."[87] "The synagogue has a pyra-
midal shape [roof], and the interior is designed in the Oriental style."[88]
Averbukh regrets that the "old painting that had once covered the ceiling"
of the synagogue was destroyed after its repair. After presenting the "curious stories" of the synagogue's construction, he calls it "a monument of a
former landlord's whim."[89]

The appearance of narratives of the history of synagogue architecture
in Russia was driven by discussions about national art in general and
Jewish art in particular. For example, the meeting of the JHES held on
February 2, 1911 was devoted to the "historical review" of synagogue architecture from the Temple of Solomon to the synagogues of the twelfth
through nineteenth centuries. The keynote speaker, artist and art critic

Lev Antokolsky, drew attention to what were called Polish synagogues. Simultaneously, one of the most respected publications, *The History of Russian Art,* edited by Igor Grabar, ran an article by Grigory Pavlutsky on these wooden synagogues.[90] Pavlutsky reasoned that "the Jews could not have brought [the secrets of] wooden architecture from Judea, since there were no forests there," and that is why the "Jewish character" was not definitely expressed in the architecture of the wooden synagogues.[91] Owing to a supposed similarity between these wooden synagogues and certain (unfortunately lost) "halls of local gentry with old Russian roots," Pavlutsky assumed them to be part of the Russian national heritage; they have since been classed as monuments of "secular wooden architecture in Ukraine."[92]

Pavlutsky's reasoning elucidates the meaning of the "tradition of folk architecture" as a concept employed by historians and amateurs, including the authors of travelogues. As mentioned, this concept was linked to the idea of transmitting secrets of architectural mastery from one generation to the next. The process of sacralization—the classification of artisans' experience as somehow sacred—could happen only in a place considered "the cradle of folk culture." According to Pavlutsky, since the Jews were not the indigenous population of Ukraine, Jewish builders and carvers could not create anything unique but only blindly copy local "folk production." Pavlutsky might have evaluated the originality of the wooden synagogues' architecture differently had he supposed the "cradle" of Eastern European Jews was in Eastern Europe rather than the Middle East.

Reasoning about "ethnic stylistic features"[93] in synagogue architecture in Volyn and Galicia can also be found in travelogues by the famous art critic and artist George Loukomsky, based on trips in 1913 and 1914.[94] He photographed and sketched the synagogue along with other architectural "monuments of olden time," and wrote: "if . . . Jewish synagogues and Armenian churches do not contain a completely Polish appearance, they still remain pan-European in character, and *there is nothing specifically Russian about them*" (emphasis mine).[95] This conclusion might be a response to Pavlutsky's proposal to categorize wooden synagogues, with the "halls of local gentry," as possessing Old Russian roots. This idea probably seemed wrong to Loukomsky; he critiqued it in his 1947 book *Jewish Art in European Synagogues*,[96] published many years later. In his travel

FIGURE 13.7

Synagogues in Zaslav. Photo of 1912 by G. Loukomski (1884–1952).
Photographic Department of the Scientific Archive of the Institute of Material
Culture of the Russian Academy of Sciences, St. Petersburg, photo O.471/892.

essays on Volyn and Galicia, he limits himself to a brief description of the
synagogues, with practically no art-critical analysis. He is not entirely
consistent in his statements about the pan-European nature of the architecture of synagogues in Galicia: among them, "there are examples of
wonderful construction, deprived of clear ethnic stylistic traits, but still
very curious."[97]

Both essays include lengthy descriptions characteristic of the travelogue. For example: "The urban landscape of present-day Volyn presents a
sad picture. After the high hills with the swamp forests and purple sunset
in the background, the black roofs of miserable Jewish inns rise before
you. . . . Long-skirted figures of Jews, trudging up the black road behind
the dirty ragged *balagula* [in Yiddish, a coachman; Loukomsky mistakenly uses this word to denote the entire vehicle], are replaced by Jews
wandering the streets of the town and making a din. . . . Over there is a
synagogue. A unicorn and a lion holding the Tablets of the Covenant are
on the front of its roof. Around it is a crowd, a black Jewish buzzing crowd,

scampering about, thronging. . . ."[98] In his essay on the old architectural monuments of Galicia, Loukomsky compiles a list of the most impressive synagogues: in Zholkva, "one of the most beautiful"; in Przeworsk, "Baroque"; and in Belz, "with a huge gable pediment."[99] He considers the synagogues in Zaslav "very characteristic of the original attributes of their architecture,"[100] easily recognizable among other buildings. He draws attention to the "whole group of synagogues, painted in bright (blue and orange) colors," and mentions, "Here, as in Dubno and Kremenets, you see the same love of bright colors."[101] The mention of this "love of bright colors," and the "curious" architecture of synagogues, shows Loukomsky in the role of a "white master," burdened with knowledge of art history. This continues with his condescending wonder at the uncivilized tastes of the "black Jewish buzzing crowd."[102] Nonetheless, his observations, photographs, and especially drawings of the synagogue buildings are of great value to researchers of synagogue architecture.

Several of the synagogues in Volyn that Loukomsky mentions in his essay were photographed during An-sky's ethnographic expedition of 1912–1914. An-sky did not write travel essays, but his small article about Dubno compares visits to the town before and after World War I.[103] A description of the Dubno synagogue, destroyed in 1914 by artillery fire, occupies a prominent place. We can compare the assessments of this synagogue by Loukomsky, who sought markers of ethnically specific style, whether Polish, Russian, or Jewish, in the architecture of various buildings, and An-sky, who was concerned with the construction of a Jewish cultural heritage. They both hoped to find "Jewish traits" in its architecture. Loukomsky was certain that they were there, but An-sky disagreed. According to An-sky, it was a "huge stone building of a somewhat strange type of architecture that almost never occurs in Volyn."[104] Later, he writes: "The synagogue was as simple and devoid of decoration on the outside as it was richly furnished on the inside."[105] Loukomsky also mentions this synagogue in his essay about Volyn: "There are several interesting buildings in the town of Dubno, including the synagogue—it is one of the most typical [for the architecture of the area] because of its mass and the pilasters partitioning its walls."[106] Loukomsky's opinion seems more measured than An-sky's. The Dubno synagogue (completed in 1794 after twelve years of construction) is a typical example of stone

FIGURE 13.8.

Great Synagogue in Dubno. Photo from the collection "Photo-archive
of An-sky's Expeditions" at the Center "Petersburg Judaica."

synagogue architecture in Volyn and its neighboring regions. Although
An-sky's assessment of the architecture of the Dubno synagogue appears
simply inaccurate, his comments on the history of its construction clarify
his skepticism about the search for Jewish traits in it. An-sky writes: "Like
many other stone synagogues in the towns and townships of Poland and
Ukraine, it was built with the assistance of the local *pan* (landlord)—in
this case, Prince Mikhail Lubomirsky, who donated bricks and wood or
sold them at a cheap price, and assigned his serfs to the construction at
a low fee."[107] This point was important for An-sky, who wanted to delin-
eate as precisely as possible the sphere of true "folk production," meaning
objects made by Jewish craftsmen.[108] An-sky considered the stone synagogues that testified to the "landlords' whims" to be valuable primarily as
historical landmarks. He articulates this viewpoint in his novel *V novom*

FIGURE 13.9.

Great Synagogue in Dubno. Photo by Alla Sokolova, 2003.

rusle (On a New Course): "the old synagogue in the town of N [Vitebsk], which had no architecture, no dome, no decorations, no external distinctions . . . was considered a landmark" because it "had been built during the reign of Catherine, and had witnessed the French invasion, several massacres, and numerous fires."[109]

An expedition photograph depicting the stone synagogue in Dubno could illustrate An-sky's essay or Abram Rekhtman's memoirs of the expedition. Rekhtman writes about the "[stone synagogues], which, in their greatness and luster, their sanctity and mystery, [towered over] the low, adobe-walled houses, covered with straw and half-sunken into the ground."[110] Still, Rekhtman maintains that it is not stone synagogues but wooden ones whose architecture is "original and one-of-a-kind [with] intricate cornices and porches."[111] An-sky probably agreed; he considered wooden synagogues among the masterpieces of Jewish "folk production," and he "rebuilds" the wooden synagogue in his play *The Dybbuk*. This synagogue was "rather squat" from the inside, with "tear-stained walls that

FIGURE 13.10.

Synagogue in Mogilev on the Dnepr. View of the Western Façade. Collection
"Photo-archive of An-sky's Expeditions" at the Center "Petersburg Judaica."

you cannot whitewash."[112] From the outside it was "high . . . , blackened,
with a whole system of roofs, one above the other."[113]

An-sky was involved in "educating the [Jewish] people"[114] and held
in high esteem "examples of folk production collected in the expeditions
[that] demonstrate that Jews have their own artistic line, their own colors. . . ."[115] Abram Efros,[116] a famous art critic, uses the same expressions
in his article "Aladdin's Lamp," commissioned by An-sky for the album
The Jewish Artistic Heritage and drafted in 1918, but never published.[117] In
unison with An-sky, Efros encouraged readers to extract "the common
structure of the folk aesthetics of forms and learn the laws governing Jewish line, color, plane, and space. . . ."[118] He wanted to find "an inimitable
combination of forms through which the national blood and its artistic

FIGURE 13.11.

Synagogue in Mogilev on the Dnepr. Painting on the eastern
part of the vault. Collection "Photo-archive of An-sky's
Expeditions" at the Center "Petersburg Judaica."

predilections can sing,"[119] and proclaimed a search for the "internal laws"
and "internal structure" of the artistic forms of Jewish "folk art," which
he described, using highly Orientalizing language, to be "tightly and carefully swaddled like an ancient mummy."[120]

The idea that a commitment to the Orient was a constant of "Jewish
taste" led to a search for eastern motifs in Jewish works. For example,
Rachel Bernstein-Vishnitser, an authoritative art historian, wrote in her
first major article on Jewish art that "researchers of the Polish Jewish synagogues were astonished by the common abundance of oriental motifs in
their interior decoration and ornamentation of [synagogue] utensils."[121]
Vishnitser could not give up the search for eastern influences in the interior paintings of synagogues constructed during the seventeenth and

eighteenth centuries in Poland. She explained the arabesque character of these paintings not through the fashion for oriental ornamentation in eighteenth-century Poland, but rather through connections between Polish Jews and their "eastern brothers."[122]

Such statements on monuments of synagogue architecture as exotic curiosities encountered sharp criticism in El Lissitzky's essay on the Mogilev synagogue.[123] This essay was written as a travelogue in 1923. While examining a painting in this synagogue's prayer hall, Lissitzky asked, "Where does it come from, this flow, whence these clouds drank their fill so as to pour forth such miraculous rain?"[124]—that is, he was interested in the mental outlook of professional artists and in their iconographic sources.[125] As for the problem of "national moments," or traces of specifically Jewish taste and style, in the wall painting of the Mogilev synagogue, Lissitzky first proposes that its solution be left to "psychologists and ethnographers." He then immediately disavows this idea, mentioning that "the kinship between forms present in the painting of the Mogilev synagogue and forms present at the same time in the art of other nations looks very serious."[126] Lissitzky elucidates his meaning with examples showing how professional skills allow talented craftsmen to transcend the borders of an alien cultural space and even create works that define its character. "The Italian Fioravanti built the Uspensky Cathedral in the Kremlin, and his compatriot Aloysius built the Kremlin itself. It was the Phoenician Hiram who built the Temple of King Solomon."[127] Lissitzky needed these examples (the last one clearly aimed at historians of Jewish art) to argue against the idea of national styles. This was not just because he was groping artistically toward what would eventually come to be known as the International Modern or International Style; it was more important for him to prove the futility of trying to understand the Jewish architectural and artistic heritage on the basis of ideas about a timeless "Jewish style" and "the laws of Jewish line, color, plane, and space." This idea, referenced by Mickiewicz in his description of the "Jewish inn," played an important role in Efros's reasoning on the continuity of a posited Jewish architectural tradition that retained "an ancient mummy"—that is, the sacred experience accumulated from the construction of the Temple of Solomon in Judea—through space and time. Lissitzky denounced this idea as fruitless.

CONCLUSION

In all our travelogues, including Lissitzky's, synagogues and Jewish houses are exoticized to a greater or lesser degree. Authors used exoticization as a kind of "optical device" to facilitate their observation of ethnographic realia marked as Jewish. Travelogue authors exoticized such objects regardless of their other attitudes—that is, whether they wished to minimize their own association with these phenomena, or on the contrary, to claim them as their cultural heritage.

I would like to mention a few points supporting the case for wider attention to travelogues of the nineteenth century to the present day. First, the travelogue genre allows writers to focus on their first impressions or "raw" direct observations, leaving their interpretations for the future. Of course, even such observations are influenced by the prevalent stereotypes. But sometimes the authors are so captivated by their observations of ethnographic reality, so immersed in an alien cultural space, that they free themselves from the power of these stereotypes; this happens most often when the description of the observed phenomena is included inside the narrative of the observations themselves. Second, travelogue authors' descriptions and interpretations of their own reflections on the ethnographic reality of the observed phenomena resemble ethnographic field notes. Field researchers, like travelogue authors, tend to compare their perceptions of phenomena with earlier descriptions and interpretations. Both groups want to recognize in the phenomena of ever-changing ethnographic reality what has already been recognized before, and they want to produce new interpretations and discover new phenomena. It is due precisely to this that the personal impressions of travelogue authors are so important, even if their interpretations sometimes lack impartiality, "courage," and depth.

NOTES

1. I thank Sergey R. Kravtsov for drawing my attention to this text.

2. The description of the inn in Mickiewicz's text is not detailed enough to create a graphic reconstruction of its layout. We may assume, however, that it was built in the shape of a *T*, with the main façade of the heated part of the building (the tavern itself) facing the street, and the part containing the indoor courtyard attached to the back. See

for instance: figures 20, 21 in Tadeusz Chrzanowski, *Karczmy i zajazdy polskie* (Warsaw: Arkady, 1958). Mickiewicz refers to the butt-end façade of the indoor courtyard as the main one, perhaps to strengthen the similarities between the inn and the Temple of Solomon.

3. I use Marcel Weyland's translation: http://www.antoranz.net/BIBLIOTEKA /PT051225/PanTad-eng/PT-Start.htm.

4. Ibid.

5. Despite criticism, the so-called Arab/Moorish theory of the origin of the Gothic was disseminated in the seventeenth century and remained popular during the first half of the nineteenth century. According to Nikolai Gogol, Gothic architecture is "extraordinary, Christian, national for Europe. . . . To give it an Arab origin would be in vain. . . ." N. Gogol, "Ob arkhitekture nyneshnego vremeni" (1835), http://feb-web.ru/feb/gogol/texts /pso/ps8/ps8-056-.htm.

6. In my view, Mickiewicz employs ethnographically significant details in descriptions of various realia only to lend his historical epic vividness and an air of authenticity. It seems that Mickiewicz's historical imagination is most productive in this text, recalling what Galit Hazan-Rokem in this volume calls the "exegetical" and the "ethnographic" imagination, meaning the impulse to interpret what one sees according to a literary model, as opposed to the impulse to simply describe what lies before one's eyes.

7. Ibid. See Marcel Weyland's translation from the Polish.

8. See, for instance, Michael Weisskopf, *The Veil of Moses: Jewish Themes in Russian Literature of the Romantic Era* (Leiden: Brill, 2012).

9. See, for instance, Alla Sokolova, "The Podolian Shtetl as Architectural Phenomenon," in *The Shtetl: Image and Reality. Papers of the Second Mendel Freidman International Conference on Yiddish*, ed. Gennady Estraikh and Mikhail Krutikov (Oxford: Legenda, 2000), 36–79; Alla Sokolova, "House-building Tradition of the Shtetl in Memorials and Memories (Based on Materials of Field Studies in Podolia)," *East European Jewish Affairs* 41, no. 3 (2011): 111–135.

10. Mikhail Dolbilov, *Russkii krai, chuzhaia vera: Etnokonfessional'naia politika imperii v Litve i Belorussii pri Aleksandre II* (Moscow: Novoe literaturnoe obozrenie, 2010), 15.

11. See the preface to one of these essays, K.M. (full name unknown), "Putevye ocherki: Podolia," in *Kievskaia starina*, Parts I–X (May 1884–April 1885), I: 5.

12. Sergey Kozlov, "Russkie puteshestvenniki novogo vremeni: imperskii vzgliad ili vospriiatie kosmopolita?" in *Beyond the Empire: Images of Russia in the Eurasian Cultural Context* (Sapporo: Slavic Research Center, Hokkaido University, 2008), 134, http://src-h .slav.hokudai.ac.jp/coe21/publish/no17_ses/07kozlov.pdf.

13. Thanks to the Slavophiles, ancient Russian art fell into the category of folk production. In travel essays, ethnographic observations of different "nations"—of their language, clothing, housing, and cuisine—were therefore placed side-by-side with descriptions of the ruins of monumental buildings, as well as with information on the history of settlements and the legends surrounding them. On the history of the study of this topic, see: Pavel Rappoport, *Zodchestvo Drevnei Rusi* (Leningrad: Nauka, 1986), http://www.gumer .info/bibliotek_Buks/History/rapop/01.php.

14. Alexander Etkind, *Vnutrenniaia kolonizatsiia: Imperskii opyt Rossii* (Moscow: Novoe literaturnoe obozrenie, 2013), 236.

15. Andrey Subbotin, *V cherte evreiskoi osedlosti: Otryvki iz ekonomicheskikh issledovanii v zapadnoi i iugo-zapadnoi Rossii za leto 1887 g.* (St. Petersburg: Izd. Red. "Ekonomichashk-ogo zhurnala," 1888–1890), no. I, 2.

16. See for details: Etkind, *Vnutrenniaia kolonizatsiia*, 108.

17. Robert Bernasconi, "Levy-Bruhl among the Phenomenologists: Eroticization and the Logic of 'the Primitive,'" *Social Identities: Journal for the Study of Race, Nation and Culture* 11, no. 3 (May 2005): 242.

18. We should agree with Robert Bernasconi that even a keen interest in an unknown culture might be caused not by the necessity of an equal dialogue with its carriers, but by a craving for the exotic.

19. See, for example: Pavel Rappoport, "Osnovnye itogi i problemy izucheniia zodchestva Drevnei Rusi," in *Drevnerusskoe iskusstvo. Khudozhestvennaia kul'tura X–pervoi poloviny XIII v.* (Moscow: Nauka, 1988), 8. http://archi.ru/files/publications/articles/rap_zodch.htm.

20. Semyon Akimovich An-sky (Shlomo Z. Rappoport, 1863–1920), Russian Jewish scholar, dramatist, ethnographer, and public figure.

21. An exception is the description of the synagogue in the town of Brody, included in the essay by Andrey Glagolev. After the first partition of Poland, Brody was annexed by Austria; the border with the Russian Empire passed in its vicinity.

22. Andrey Glagolev, *Zapiski russkogo puteshestvennika s 1823 po 1827 god.* In his travel essays, Glagolev compares Europe with Russia, and finds the first one rotten and decrepit in comparison with the young and mighty Russia. While passing through Switzerland, he portrays the miserable condition of the people of this country and calls their freedom imaginary. Andrey Gavrilovich Glagolev (1793–1844), who held a doctorate in literature, left Russia on a trip in 1823 and returned in 1828. He then worked at the Department of Spiritual Affairs of Foreign Confessions at the Ministry of Internal Affairs.

23. L[issitzky]., E[leazar]., "Vegn der Molever Shul," in *Milgroim*, ed. M. Vishnitzer and M. Kleinman, art ed. R. Wishnitzer, Issue 3 (1923): 9–13. Eleazar (Lasar Markowitch) Lissitzky (1890–1941), better known as El Lissitzky, was a graphic artist, designer, typographer, art theorist, and architect. He was an important figure of the Russian avant garde. Starting in 1916, he participated in the Jewish Society for the Encouragement of the Arts. In 1918, in Kiev, Lissitzky became one of the founders of the Jewish avant-garde artistic and literary association "Kulturlige." In 1916, he undertook an expedition to a number of small towns in Belarus and Lithuania with the artist Isakhar-Ber Rybak (1897–1935), where they copied paintings of wooden synagogues.

24. Such allusions and their sources, examined by Galit Hasan-Rokem in this volume, fall outside the scope of this article.

25. Glagolev, *Zapiski russkogo puteshestvennika*, 106.

26. Ibid., 107.

27. Ibid., 132. The author has in mind the artist Alexander Osipovich Orlovsky (1777–1832), a representative of the Russian national Romanticism movement in painting, who played an important role in Russian–Polish cultural relations of the time.

28. Ibid., 123.

29. Ibid., 129.

30. Ibid., 130.

31. From French *stanca* or Italian *stanza*, meaning a room allotted for guests.

32. Ibid. Most likely, these were the doors of shops, taverns, and workshops, traditionally located in Jewish houses on trade streets and squares of townships.

33. In a number of articles on Russian folklore, Glagolev expresses his idea of folk production as "a reflection of the psychology of the nation." See P. A. Nikolaev, ed., *Russkie pisateli, 1800–1917: Biograficheskii slovar'* (Moscow: Sovetskaia entsiklopediia, 1989) 1: 571.

34. Glagolev, *Zapiski russkogo puteshestvennika*, 130–131.

35. In previous articles I have mistakenly identified K.M. as Mikhail Karinsk. The true identity of K.M. remains unknown.

36. K.M., *Putevye ocherki. Podoliia*, part IV, 364.

37. Ibid., 365.

38. Ibid., 364–365. Not accidentally, the thick description of a typical Jewish house in travel essays by K.M. attracted the attention of the leading Ukrainian historian of architecture Sergei Taranuschenko. In his working notebook he included a number of excerpts from essays by K.M. about the "Jewish *zaezd*." See the Central Scholarly Library (Kiev), Manuscript Department, f. 278 (Collection of S. A. Taranushchenko), nos. 63–71.

39. Ibid.

40. Glagolev, *Zapiski russkogo puteshestvennika*, 110.

41. Alexander Stepanovich Afanasiev (Chuzhbinskii; 1816–1875) traveled to study the life and customs of the river and coastal regions of Russia in 1856 at the suggestion of Grand Prince Konstantin Nikolaevich. His research resulted in a series of articles later collected in a two-volume ethnographic work, *Poezdka v Iuzhnuiu Rossiiu*, part I. *Ocherki Dnepra* (St. Petersburg: Ministry of Marine Affairs, 1861); part II; *Ocherki Dnestra* (St. Petersburg: Ministry of Marine Affairs, 1863).

42. K.M., *Putevye ocherki. Podolia*. Part VI, 69.

43. Hereinafter cited from *A. S. Afanas'ev (Chuzhbinskii), Sobranie sochinenii*, vol. VIII, *Poezdka v Iuzhnuiu Rossiiu. Ocherki Dnestra* (St. Petersburg: German Hoppe, 1893), 22.

44. Ibid., 68.

45. Ibid., 77.

46. Ibid., 98.

47. K. M., *Putevye ocherki. Podoliia*. Part IV, 389.

48. Ibid., part VII, 363.

49. Vasiliy Ivanovich Zuev, "K voprosu o neobkhodimosti ozdorovleniia gorodov," *Zodchii*, no. 2 (1897): 9–12. The author notes the deplorable state of cities in Russia: they are "striking in their extremely unsightly appearance, in some kind of dissoluteness, in their complete lack of urban development, and in the imprint of extreme poverty, from unpaved, dusty streets to rickety houses and rotten fences . . ." (Ibid., 11).

50. Andrey Pavlovich Subbotin (1852–1906), Russian economist and writer.

51. A. P. Subbotin, "V cherte evreiskoi osedlosti."

52. Ibid., no. I, 6. It is significant that the author has found it necessary to acquaint the reader with the word for inn in Yiddish, as was customary for ethnographically marked realia.

53. Ibid.

54. Ibid., 39.

55. This opinion was supported by such paradigmatic pearls of classic literature as Pushkin's line about "the dirty shops of the Jews" (See Alexander Pushkin, "Iz pis'ma k Vigeliu," *Polnoe sobranie sochinenii v 10 T.* [Moscow: Akad. Nauk SSSR, 1959, 2: 154]) or Gogol's description of the Jewish street in Warsaw, "which bore simultaneously the names 'Dirty' and 'Jewish.'" See Nikolai Gogol, *Mirgorod, Sobranie khudozhestvennykh proizvedenii v 5 T* (Moscow: Akad. Nauk SSSR, 1959), 2: 184.

56. A. P. Subbotin, "V cherte evreiskoi osedlosti," Issue 2, 65.

57. Ibid., 94.

58. This is the name Subbotin gives a *mezuzah*, a piece of parchment inscribed with specified Hebrew verses from the Torah, rolled up, and placed inside the case.

59. Ibid., issue 1, 39.

60. Ibid., issue 2, 86.

61. Ibid., issue 2, 1–2.

62. Pavel (Pavlo) Platonovich Chubynsky, *Trudy etnografichesko-statisticheskoi ekspeditsii v Zapadno-Russkii krai, snariazhennoi Imperatorskim Russkim geograficheskim obschestvom: Materialy i issledovaniia, sobrannye P. P. Chubynskim*, vol. 7 (St. Petersburg: Imperatorskoe russkoe geograficheskoe obshchestvo, 1872). Pavel (Pavlo) Platonovich Chubynsky (1839–1884), ethnographer and folklorist who specialized in ethnic studies in Ukraine and Russia.

63. Chubynsky, *Trudy etnografichesko-statisticheskoi ekspeditsii* 7:22.

64. Ibid.

65. Ibid.

66. In the preface to the section "Jews of the Southwestern Region" of the "Proceedings of the Ethnographic and Statistical Expedition to the West Russian Region," Chubynsky calls the essay by Berlin "the first systematic work on the ethnography of the Jews" (P. V.). For this study, Berlin was elected a member of the Imperial Russian Geographical Society, but his research has never been considered "historiographical." See Vassilii Shchedrin, "Neizvestnaia 'Istoriia khasidizma': Raboty M. I. Berlina v kontekste russko-evreiskoi istoriografii XIX v.," in *Arkhiv evreiskoi istorii* (Archive of the Jewish History) 1 (Moscow: ROSSPEN, 2004), 172.

67. Moisei Berlin, *Ocherk etnografii evreiskogo naseleniia v Rossii*, 9.

68. See for details A. Sokolova, "House-building Tradition of the Shtetl in Memorials and Memories (Based on Materials of Field Studies in Podolia)," *East European Jewish Affairs* 41, no. 3 (December 2011): 111–135.

69. K.M. (full name unknown), *Putevye ocherki. Podoliia, Part VIII*, 482.

70. Subbotin, "V cherte evreiskoi osedlosti," Issue 1, 41.

71. Ibid., 42.

72. Ibid., 95.

73. Ibid.

74. Glagolev, *Zapiski russkogo puteshestvennika*, 128.

75. Ibid., 113.

76. Ibid., 135.

77. Ibid., 136.

78. Ibid., 141.

79. Ibid., 137.

80. Ibid., 141. The date of construction is indicated in the cartouche, preserved on the eastern façade of the synagogue in Brody.

81. Ibid., 139–140.

82. Ibid., 141.

83. See for details Sergey R. Kravtsov, "Synagogue Architecture of Volhynia," in *Synagogues of Volhynia*, ed. S. R. Kravtsov and V. Levin (Jerusalem: Bet Tfila, forthcoming 2015).

84. The JHES was founded in St. Petersburg on November 16, 1908.

85. In 1909, the JHES received the following photographs from nonresident members: a single photograph of the synagogue in the town of Grozny, sent by A. Isakovich; eight photographs of the synagogue in the town of Lyuboml (Volyn) sent by barrister I. P. Kelberin from Kiev ("The Annual Report of 1909," *Evreiskaia Starina*, vol. 1 [1910]: 16). In 1910: three photographs of the synagogue in the town of Feodosiia sent by B. I. Toporo-

vsky from the city of Ekaterinoslav ("The Annual Report of 1910," *Evreiskaia Starina*, vol. 1 [1911]: 8). In 1911: one photograph of the synagogue in the town of Starokonstantinov, sent by M. Kliachko; three photographs of the synagogue in the town of Jurburg, sent by L. A. Boner; four photographs of the synagogue in the town of Ostrog; four photographs of the synagogue in the town of Feodosiia ("The Annual Report of 1911," *Evreiskaia Starina*, vol. 2 [1912]: 8). In 1912: two photographs of the synagogue in the town of Lutsk, sent by B. I. Toporovsky from Ekaterinoslav ("The Annual Report of 1912," *Evreiskaia Starina*, vol. 2 [1913]: 10).

86. Z. Averbuch, "Semiatichskaia sinagoga i predaniia o nei," *Evreiskaia Starina*, vol. 4 (1911): 563–567.

87. Ibid., 563.

88. Ibid.

89. Ibid., 567.

90. Grigory Grigorievich Pavlutskii, "Starinnye dereviannye sinagogi v Malorossii," in *Istoriia russkogo iskusstva*, ed. I. Gragar (Moscow: I. Knebel' Publishing, 1911), 2:377–382. Grigory Grigorievich Pavlutskii (also Pavluckiy; 1861–1924), a well-known historian of architecture and art critic, professor at Kiev University.

91. Ibid., 380.

92. Pavlutskii, "Ancient Wooden Synagogues in Ukraine," 382.

93. George Kreskent'evich Loukomsky, *Galitsiia v ee starine: Ocherki po istorii arkhitektury XII–XVIII vekov* (Petrograd: Comradeship "R. Golikov & A. Vilborg," 1915), 96.

94. I refer to Loukomsky's essay mentioned in the previous note, as well as to another of his essays: *Volynskaia starina*. Separate print from the magazine *Iskusstvo Iuzhnoi Rossii* (Kiev, 1913). George Kresken'tevich Loukomsky (1884–1952), historian, art critic, artist, a secretary of the Paris group "Mir iskusstva," released works on Russian architecture: *Russisches Porzellan, Russische Baukunst*, and others.

95. Loukomsky, *Volynskaia starina*, 14.

96. George Kreskent'evich Loukomsky, *Jewish Art in European Synagogues (from the Middle Ages to the Eighteenth Century)* (London: Hutchinson & Co., 1947), 24.

97. Loukomsky, *Galitsiia v ee starine*, 96.

98. Loukomsky, *Volynskaia starina*, 43.

99. Loukomsky, *Galitsiia v ee starine*, 96.

100. Loukomsky, *Volynskaia starina*, 29.

101. Ibid.

102. Ibid., 43.

103. S[emyon]. An-sky, "Dubno," *Evreiskaia nedelia*, no. 31 (1916): 38–40; no. 32 (1916): 24–25.

104. Ibid., no. 32, 24.

105. Ibid.

106. Loukomsky, *Volynskaia starina*, 26.

107. An-sky, "Dubno," 24.

108. The following question was mentioned in the program for historical and regional studies compiled by An-sky: "Do you know a Jewish artist, engraver, etc.? [Do you know] if there is anyone who has his works?"

109. S[emyon]. An-sky, "V novom rusle," in *Pervyi evreiskii sbornik* (Moscow: S. Skirmunt, 1907), 251.

110. Abram Rekhtman, *Yidishe etnografye un folklor* (Buenos Aires: YIVO, 1956), 38.

111. Ibid.

112. See, for example, S[emyon]. An-sky, "Mezh dvukh mirov," in *Polveka evreiskogo teatra 1876–1926* (Moscow: "Paralleli" Publishing, 2003), 329.

113. Ibid., 346.

114. See: Benjamin Lukin, "'. . . Akadmiia gde budut izuchat' folklor.' An-skii—ideolog evreiskogo muzeinogo dela," in *Evreiskii muzei* (St. Petersburg: "Symposium" Publishing, 2004), 62.

115. From the review of An-sky's lecture dedicated to Jewish folk art, which took place in the Jewish Public Assembly, May 11, 1918. Publications of the Jewish ethnographic expedition, in *Evreiskaia nedelia*, No. 11–12 (1918): 20.

116. Abram Markovich Efros (1888–1954), Russian art historian, literary critic, and translator.

117. Hereinafter the quotations are taken from the English translation of the article by Abram Efros, which was published in the album S[emen]. An-sky, *The Jewish Artistic Heritage* (Moscow: "Mosty kul'tury," 1998), 7–51.

118. Ibid., 14.

119. Ibid., 11.

120. Ibid., 14.

121. R. Bernstein-Vishnitser, "Iskusstvo u evreev v Pol'she i Litve," in *Istoriia evreiskogo naroda* vol. 11, no. 1, *Istoriia evreev v Rossii* (Moscow: Comradeship "MIR," 1914), 391.

122. Ibid.

123. Lissitzky, "Vegn der Molever Shul," 9–13.

124. Ibid., 12.

125. Lissitzky notes that decorations in books brought from afar and kept in the synagogue often became sources for artists (Ibid., 13).

126. Ibid.

127. Ibid.

Ballads of Strangers

Constructing "Ethnographic Moments" in Jewish Folklore

DANI SCHRIRE

To Galit Hasan-Rokem

When and where does ethnography begin? When and where does it end? With the recognition that knowledge is in constant flux, it may be helpful to think in terms of ethnographic moments, which form at one and the same time the beginning and the end of any ethnography. After a short conceptual discussion, this chapter analyzes two moments of encounter—two fragments in the history of Jewish ethnography. This analysis informs a reflection on the project of Jewish ethnography in broader terms, leading to a discussion of the complex relations between folk-narratives, performance, literature, historical writing, and ethnographic sciences.

* * *

Several ethnographers have reflected (implicitly or explicitly) on the meaning of the ethnographic moment. According to the British social anthropologist Marilyn Strathern, "the ethnographic moment is a moment of immersement . . . that is simultaneously total and partial, a totalizing activity which is not the only activity the person is engaged [in]";[1] this partiality derives from the complex relations between the "field" as the site of ethnography and the "field" established when observations are organized in written accounts. The totalizing effect of this moment is a result of the fundamental ways in which emotions and feelings partake in experiencing the moment and the way such experiences are remembered, interpreted,

and written about.[2] Greg Dening, an Australian ethnohistorian who studied encounters between natives and European strangers on the beaches of
various Pacific islands, expands the horizons of the experiential scope of
such moments, referring to ethnographic moments as "the space between
cultures filled by interpretation, occasions of metaphorical understanding and translation. The first product of the ethnographic moment is interpretation, an understanding of what is new and unexperienced in the
light of what is old and experienced."[3] Hence, ethnographic moments call
into question experiences—both collective and individual—in the *longue
durée,* helping one arrive at different understandings as well as creating
many misunderstandings. Ethnographic moments demonstrate the kind
of attention everyday culture demands; their space is a classic example of
a geography that goes beyond representation.[4]

When thinking of Jewish ethnography, the question then becomes:
who is involved? What cultures are these, separated by the void of the
ethnographic moment? What experiences should be accounted for, and
how? It seems that any serious consideration of ethnographic moments
transgresses boundaries (national, linguistic, social, etc.). It can transform
the language of "mapping" Jewish ethnography (as in "East"-"West" or
"Russian"-"German") into a language of "routing" itineraries, drawing
trajectories and contact points.[5] Jewish ethnography can then be conceptualized as a wide array of fault-lines that are situated in different spatial
and epistemological contexts, in both science and literature.

WHEN IS THE JEWISH ETHNOGRAPHIC MOMENT?

While this may not seem intuitive, perhaps the first question that
should be put forward is: when is the Jewish ethnographic moment? This
question is closely related to the broader issue of the time of ethnographic
moments and to the way ethnography in general negotiates premodernity:
for example, whether the category of *folklore* can be applied to ancient
times.[6] Furthermore, it is not clear in this sense how ethnographic sciences are related to other forms of ethnography, such as literary ones.

One answer to the question of time is that ethnographic moments have
been with us for as long as natives have encountered strangers. They are
narrated in scientific accounts as well as in literary, historical, and reli-

gious works. As an example, we may refer to the New Testament, where we find the encounter between a Samaritan woman and Jesus Christ. After Christ asks her for a drink to quench his thirst, she replies: "How is it that you, a Jew, ask a drink of me, a woman of Samaria? Jews do not associate with Samaritans" (John 4:9). The Gospel narrative demonstrates how an interpretation of Others is transformed in one moment in relation to previous experiences of what Jews do or do not do.[7] It should be noted that there is nothing in this narrative itself that relates to an ethnographic moment, or to ethnography at all. Indeed, there is a second possible answer to the question of the time of ethnographic moments, according to which they are an outcome of modernity. To be sure, the development of a scientific discourse on ethnography had a great impact on the content and meaning of ethnographic moments—in fact, on their very possibility. Modern scientific narratives of encounters form our understanding of such moments.

The puzzle we confront here is similar to the one posed by Bruno Latour—one of the key figures in Science and Technology Studies and the cofounder of what has become known as actor-network-theory—who addressed a different scientific endeavor, asking whether ferments existed before they were discovered by Louis Pasteur.[8] Surprisingly, he answered this question negatively, explaining that time has to be considered along two axes: linear succession of time, where 2013 precedes 2014, and sedimentary succession of time, where the content of 2013 is retrofitted in 2014, 2015, and so on. Hence, by relating to the encounter between Christ and the Samaritan as an ethnographic moment, we transfer modern terms to antiquity, reconceptualizing encounters between people from different backgrounds as "ethnographic moments." This process reconfigures the narrative of the Gospels as well as Jewish ethnography itself, extending ethnography to a period thousands of years before it emerged as a concept. A similar dialogic and relational approach was offered by folklorists Amy Shuman and Galit Hasan-Rokem in their discussion of folk-genres.[9]

In short, to answer the question of "when is the ethnographic moment," it is necessary to understand the interconnectedness of modern "moments" and premodern "moments." The way ethnographic discourse of the nineteenth and twentieth centuries constructed the meaning of such moments cannot be divorced from hundreds of years of experience negotiating moments where experience is challenged. In addressing Jewish ethnographic moments, I suggest following experiences of modernity as well as experiences that preceded the rise of ethnographic sciences, without assuming the primacy of one experience over the other.

UNDER THE SHADOW OF HOFFMANN-KRAYER

The rise of modern ethnographic sciences was important in constructing the image of an encounter between two "types" of people, categorized in polar terms: "Westerners"-"Others," "educated"-"primitives," "city-dwellers"-"peasants," "inauthentic subjects"-"authentic subjects," "rational people"-"spiritual people," "young men"-"old women," "literate cultures"-"oral cultures," and so on. Such divisions were based on the assumption that modernity had not reached some "traditional" people; knowledge was likewise divided between "high" and "low."[10] Thus, in his 1902 work titled *Die Volkskunde als Wissenschaft* (Folklore as Science), Eduard Hoffmann-Krayer, the founder of the Swiss Society for folklore, pointed to the difference between *vulgus* and *populus*. According to folklorist and cultural anthropologist Regina Bendix,

> He wanted to differentiate two tasks that folklorists had faced thus far. The term *Volk* had two distinct semantic meanings, political-national (*populus*) and social-civilizational (*vulgus*). Folklorists more likely would be preoccupied with the social-civilizational, and while Hoffmann-Krayer intended *vulgus* to be an objective term, his definition was permeated by an upper-class or "high-cultured" distancing.[11]

This theory of a two-layered society was soon criticized by Adolf Strack from Giessen.[12] Nevertheless, Hoffmann-Krayer's work was crucial in informing ethnographic moments. To criticize such ideas today in scientific contexts is perhaps unnecessary, yet the idea that ethnography relates to an encounter between people from two "layers" is far from obsolete, and it has certainly had an impact beyond scientific circles. In this context Jewish ethnography was often approached as an encounter between Jews from different "strata," constructed along any of the aforementioned binary oppositions.[13] Such a binary way of thinking was the result of various meta-discursive assumptions that are at least as old as modernity itself, as folklorists Charles Briggs and Richard Bauman convincingly show in their *Voices of Modernity*.[14] This modern legacy (burden?) stands at the basis of our understanding of ethnographic moments and informs the choice and method of my engagement with the two ethnographic moments that I examine here. The first begins with a pictorial representation, which in itself seems to reaffirm Hoffmann-Krayer's ideas.

KREMENETS 1913: PEOPLE ARE STRANGE
WHEN YOU'RE A STRANGER

An ethnographic moment becomes a "classic" when it is frozen, reproduced, re-presented. Captured in Yudovin's camera, this ethnographic moment is stored in the YIVO archive and appears on their website with the caption, "Zusman Kisselhof on the S. An-sky Ethnographic Expedition making sound recordings of Jewish folklore. Kremenets, 1912."[15]

It is not clear what one sees in this picture: is it a preparation before the recording of the children? Perhaps the expedition members were trying to "enchant" their audience by playing sounds from the phonograph?[16] In any case, we have here "two Jewish cultures" performing together in one moment that would be followed by two crucial transformations: first, the sounds recorded on these wax cylinders in Kremenets would be taken thousands of kilometers away and stored in dusty archives in Kiev or St. Petersburg (before the latter would be named Petrograd, Leningrad, and then St. Petersburg again); and even if these sounds survived the poor recording technology, the distance, the passing of time, and the violence of revolutions and we could still listen to them, what we would hear would be very different from what took place in this multisensory performance. On the other hand, this ethnographic moment would also be recorded in the minds of the expedition's participants, and as part of their communicative memory it would be told and retold, written down, and then translated over the years, finally becoming "primary sources" in the hands of the historians who, in their dialogue with twenty-first-century publishers and readers, would write the history of a key event in modern Jewish culture.[17] This dual representation enhances the point made by the Dutch anthropologist Johannes Fabian in his now classic *Time and the Other*, which relates to the coevalness of anthropological engagements.[18]

FIGURE 14.1

Zusman Kisselhof and the People of Kremenets: An Ethnographic Moment.
From the Archives of YIVO Institute for Jewish Research, New York.

The two trajectories whereby this moment has been communicated to us
in the last century go hand-in-hand with the continuously reproduced
communicabilities of historical knowledge vis-à-vis folkloric knowledge.
By referring to "communicabilities" I use the terminology offered by the
folklorist and anthropologist Charles Briggs in his account of the circulation of folklore.[19] Briggs goes beyond discussions that emphasize prag-
matics and genres, accounting also for various scientific procedures that
enhance the circulation of folklore. As he shows, some of these procedures
are discursive, but others are material (e.g., the communicability of folk-
art undergoes drastic changes in folklore museums). Importantly, Briggs
stresses that communicability is itself "viral." When knowledge is considered "folklore" or "history," its communicability changes accordingly.
Thus, in a process strange, but not extraordinary, *History* has made the
gaze of An-sky and the members of his expedition familiar to us, turn-

ing the outsiders who arrived at the scene from the Big City into familiar
subjects, while simultaneously marking these Jews native to the shtetl as
anonymous strangers with peculiar forms of knowledge. Instead of split-
ting this ethnographic moment into "Jewish folklore" on the one hand
and "Jewish (modern) History" on the other hand, I try to follow Dening
in doing

> ethnohistory both of "primitive" and "civilized" and of cultures in the
> past and in the present . . . I think I do ethnohistory when I try to describe
> Strangers in contact with Natives and Natives in contact with Strangers,
> interpreting what is new in the light of what is old and, in that, remaining
> the same and changing.[20]

There are immediate problems in presenting a symmetric narrative of
this ethnographic moment: how can we get closer to the bewildered gaze
of those residents of Kremenets as they observed the expedition members?
Gabriella Safran's insightful biography of An-sky has made his enigmatic,
wandering figure intimately familiar to a twenty-first-century audience.[21]
Hence, it has become quite difficult to make him appear a stranger anymore. Perhaps a quote from a memoir written by one of the expedition
members, Yitzhak Gur-Aryeh, can help characterize An-sky as a figure
operating in strange ways:

> The second episode in Kremenets is connected to the Roykhel house, an
> important Zionist house. The mother and the father knew Hebrew and
> educated their children in it . . . from our close relation with the Roykhel
> house we learnt that the grandmother knew how to sing the lullaby
> that according to tradition would get the Rabbi from Opatów to sleep.
> Unfortunately, she was an observant woman who refused to sing in front
> of men in general and strangers like us in particular. An-sky was so eager,
> he went to talk to her. After that she was so enchanted she agreed to sing
> in front of the women of the house in one room while we heard her from
> the other room . . . and how great was her *surprise and grief* when she heard
> her voice on record, recorded by the musicologist Kisselhof, without her
> noticing."[22]

Unfortunately, we do not have direct access to the angry voice of the
woman who sang the lullaby, but we do have a voiceover from one of the
expedition members who correctly portrays himself and his fellows as
strangers to the shtetl. We can still gain certain insights into the point of

view of the residents of Kremenets, from which this ethnographic moment seems much less heroic than the picture itself might suggest. While
for Gur-Aryeh this was an amusing and even admirable episode, when
one contemplates a grandmother's surprise and grief, this moment can be
somewhat disturbing. Indeed, by modern ethical standards, Kisselhof's
performance as an ethnographer is absolutely unacceptable.

In addition to Gur Aryeh's Hebrew memoir, which was written in Israel, another memoir provides a clearer idea of the way the residents of
Kremenets viewed An-sky and his fellows. It was composed long after An-
sky became part of Jewish History, as part of the *yizkor* (memorial) book
of the town, written originally in Yiddish by Henekh Gelernt in New York:

> Sh. Anski came to Kremenets with his two companions: B. Kisselhof, a
> teacher in the Modern Talmud Torah in Petersburg ... and Y. Yudovin, a
> relative of Anski's from Vitebsk and an artist who specialized in Jewish or-
> naments and liked to photograph everything. The guests stayed at Moshe
> Melamed's hotel, and through him Anski met Duvid Roykhel and Henekh
> Gelernt. Melamed was very impressed by the guests from Petersburg, who
> spoke to him in Yiddish.
>
> "... Some strange Jews have arrived"—Melamed said to Gelernt—"and
> they registered at the hotel as coming from Petersburg. Even before they
> washed and refreshed themselves after such a long journey, they asked to
> see you." ... Since H. Gelernt didn't dare go by himself, suspecting that
> they were undercover agents, Melamed agreed to go with him.
>
> As he entered the room, H. Gelernt realized that the man's face was
> familiar from a photograph he'd seen. Sh. Anski gave him a very warm
> welcome. Soon Duvid Roykhel arrived, too, and from the next room came
> Anski's two assistants, B. Kisselhof and Y. Yudovin. They joked about
> Anski's attire, which was modern, not Hasidic: on his head he wore a
> modern hat.... The news about the mysterious Jewish "delegates, sent by
> the Petersburg minister himself," spread through town like wildfire. On
> Friday night, the streets were usually filled with young people; this time,
> they all gathered around the hotel and envied the group that was privi-
> leged to be inside.[23]

Although this text was written in retrospect, taking into account the
"historical significance" of the moment, it still offers a perspective on
the expedition in which the expedition members are considered "guests,"
"mysterious," even "strange." Most interestingly as a *mise en abyme*, the
stranger becomes familiar only through the aid of another photograph,

one that we, as readers of the account, are unable to view. When this text and Gur Aryeh's are aligned next to Yudovin's picture, they operate as a double-exposure, presenting a more symmetric ethnohistory of this moment a hundred years later. When Gelernt's suspicion that An-sky and his men were undercover agents is placed next to Gur Aryeh's testimony, we can see that Gelernt was not totally wrong; agency was indeed manipulated, and some truths were kept undercover. It is to be hoped by now the expedition members, with their strange habit of photographing "everything" (as Gelernt put it), seem at least as foreign to our eyes as they did to the residents of Kremenets. To be sure, in this ethnographic moment, not only were ethnographically trained Jewish scholars busy "ethnogging" the "simple" Jewish folk, but the so-called "simple" ones also "ethnogged" these strangers, examining their attire and their laughable modern hats.

Even when this moment in Kremenets is examined from a number of perspectives, it seems to me unsatisfactory: one may still get the wrong impression that an ethnographic moment is based on social binaries, somehow surrendering to the logic of Hoffmann-Krayer's *vulgus in populo* and a notion of fixed social "layers." This double exposure of Kremenets may support a conception of Jewish ethnography as an interaction exclusively between Jews. In my second example, which focuses on an encounter between Israelis and a German, it becomes clearer that Jewish ethnography relates neither to an engagement with two "social layers," nor to Jews alone.

JERUSALEM 1961: ANOTHER ETHNOGRAPHIC MOMENT

Unlike the Yiddish and Russian voices that could be recorded or heard in the phonograph positioned in Kremenets on the eve of the Great War, the Israeli soundscape of 1961 was filled with German voices coming out of radio reports of the Eichmann trial. Less widely known is that a German voice could also be heard in public at the Third World Congress for Jewish studies, which opened at the end of July that year in the Mazer building of the newly built campus of Giv'at Ram at the Hebrew University of Jerusalem. Among the many lectures of the section for art and folklore, Ingeborg Weber-Kellermann delivered a lecture titled: "Die Volksballade von der schönen Jüdin im europäischen Zusammenhang mit dem Lied von den zwei Königskindern" (The Folk-Ballad of the Pretty Jewess in the Context of the Song on the Two Kings' Children). Although Weber-Kellermann is virtually unknown among scholars of Jewish folklore or ethnography, she took part in an incredible ethnographic moment.

Born in 1918, Weber-Kellermann, like many of her generation, joined the Bund Deutscher Mädel in der Hitler-Jugend (the League of German Girls in the Hitler Youth). During the war she studied in Berlin, producing an ethnographic study of a village in Slavonia (Slawonien).[24] After the war she resided in West Berlin, continuing her work with her doctoral mentor, Adolf Spamer, in East Berlin at the Akademie der Wissenschaften.[25] In an interview with *Die Zeit* published in 1989, she tells of her experience as a nurse positioned in Czechoslovakia, where she encountered Jewish refugees.[26] This (ethnographic) moment led her to reassess her previous work; she was one of the first German folklorists to integrate sociological dimensions into the discipline.[27] In a paradigmatic article that she published in 1959, she went against the earlier assumptions of her essentialist dissertation, now emphasizing interethnic relations.[28] When Spamer died, he was replaced by Wolfgang Steinitz, a committed communist who served as the vice-president of the Akademie.[29] Under his leadership she published a monumental work on ballads, based on a nineteenth-century collection.[30] During that time she lived in the western part of Berlin, but in 1960, shortly before the Berlin Wall was erected, she left Berlin for Marburg in West Germany. There, she wrote her habilitation, becoming one of the most influential professors in postwar German Volkskunde until her retirement in 1985 and practically until she died in 1993.[31]

This condensed account of an important scholar provides very few hints that could explain her participation in a Jewish studies conference. My knowledge of what took place in Jerusalem and the emotions that were connected to it is derived from a comparison of three versions of Weber-Kellermann's paper. Two of these appeared in the proceedings of the conference, one in German (the only lecture to appear in the proceedings in German, indicating that her talk was in this language) and another in Hebrew, which is *almost* identical to the German version. The third version was a longer article that was published a year later in the Swiss journal of *Volkskunde* and was explicitly based on the presentation in Jerusalem (this is marked in a footnote).[32]

Weber-Kellermann's paper was devoted to a ballad type that is very common in the Deutsche Volksliedarchiv in Freiburg. The general motif of the ballad runs as follows: a lake separates two lovers; the boy attempts to cross the lake swimming; the girl signals him the way with a candle; the light blows out; the boy is lost in the water and drowns; the following morning the girl recovers his body and commits suicide by jumping into the water. This is the narrative known as Hero and Leander in Greek mythology. Weber-Kellermann noted that several versions of this ballad involve a family feud as in *Romeo and Juliet,* where the lake plays a symbolic role. In her article, Weber-Kellermann mentions modern versions of this theme, such as *West Side Story.*[33] Nevertheless, the ballad Weber-Kellermann discussed is much more morbid; in her lecture she described a particular version, titled "Die schöne Jüdin" (the pretty Jewess), which is fully reproduced here in the original German with an English translation:

1. Es war einmal eine Jüdin,
Eine wunderschöne Dam.'
Sie hat eine einzige Tochter,
Ihr Haar war ihr geflochten,
Zum Tanz war sie bereit.

2. "Ach Mutter, Herzensmutter,
Mein Köpfchen tut mir weh.
Lassen Sie mich ein klein Weilchen
Spazieren gehn in der Heide.
Auf daß es mir wieder vergeh."

3. "Ach Tochter, Herzenstochter,
Das kann und darf nicht sein.
Lieber leg ich dich in dein Bette,
Und schlaf mit mir in die Wette.
So wird dir's wohlergehn."

4. Und als die Mutter schlafen tut,
Die Tochter ihr entsprang.
Sie sprang wohl über die Gassen,
Wo alle Leute saßen.
Dem Jäger in die Arm'.

5. "Ach Jäger, Herzensjäger,
Mein Köpfchen tut mir weh.
Laß du mich ein klein Weilchen
In deinen Armen stehen,
Auf daß es mir wieder vergeh."

6. "Ach Jüdin, wunderschöne Jüdin,
Das kann und darf nicht sein.
Lieber will ich dich lassen taufen,
Wilhelmine Magdalena sollst du heißen
Und eine Christin sein."

7. "Und eh ich mich tu taufen lassen
Und eine Christin sein,
Lieber will ich mich erhenken,
Ins tiefste Meer einsenken
Und keine Christin sein."

1. There once was a Jewess,
A beautiful lady.
She had an only daughter
Her hair was braided
And she was ready to dance.

2. "Oh mother, dearest mother,
My little head aches.
Let me for a little while
Walk in the meadow
So that it [my headache] will go away."

3. "Oh daughter, dearest daughter,
That can't and must not be.
My love, I would rather lay you down in your bed
And sleep with me on a bet [on who sleeps longer]
So that you feel better."

4. And as the mother falls asleep,
The daughter found her way out.
She jumped over the alleys
Where all the people were sitting
Into the hunter's arms.

5. "Oh hunter, dearest hunter.
My little head aches

Let me for a little while
Stay in your arms
So that it will go away."

6. "Oh Jewess, beautiful Jewess
That can't and must not be.
I would rather have you baptized.
Wilhelmine Magdalena you should be called
And be a Christian."

7. "And before I let myself be baptized
And be a Christian,
My love, I shall rather hang myself,
Drown myself in the deepest sea
And not be a Christian."

Evidently, the version Weber-Kellermann presented at the conference
is odd: like many ballads it is structured around dialogues and the final
dialogue carries a promise of death, but this death is not fully realized in
the narrative; the Jewish girl does not die. It should be stressed that of the
eight versions found in Weber-Kellermann's book from 1957, this version
(#321 in the book) was the only one to end abruptly. Despite that, it is
this version that appears in the five-page German lecture summary. Yet
in her published article, Weber-Kellermann presents a different version,
from the Deutsche Volksliedarchiv (DVA Nr. A 146384)—a much more
complete and typical version that includes the last stanza:

8. Sie schlug auf ihren Mantel
Und stürzt sich in den See:
"Ade herzliebster Vater und Mutter,
ade herzliebster Jäger,
wir sehn uns nimmermehr!"

8. She opened her coat
And threw herself into the lake:
"Farewell dearest father and mother
Farewell dearest hunter
See you never again!"

How can one explain Weber-Kellermann's choice to present for her
Jerusalem audience a version with a truncated ending when she knew of

so many complete versions? Moreover, this ballad was not unknown: a version of it was published in the beginning of the nineteenth century, in Achim von Arnim and Clemens Brentano's classic *Des Knaben Wunderhorn* (The boy's magic horn), where it is titled "Die Judentochter."[34] In fact, Johannes Brahms later set it to music. Numerous versions of this ballad were recorded over the years, and some were collected in fieldwork as late as the 1970s.[35] Weber-Kellermann's academic performance can be explained as a refusal to assume the role of someone who "kills" the Jewish daughter in words. She spared her, she spared the audience, and most of all she spared herself.[36]

It is evident from both the lecture summary and the published article that Weber-Kellermann put much weight on the ballad's meaning. The ballad was seen as a prism through which social relations between Jews and Christians in post-Reformation Germany were discussed. It exemplified a Christian German view of the Jewish daughter who chose death rather than conversion. In the tense year of 1961, Weber-Kellermann was hoping that such a discussion would help foster a German–Israeli academic dialogue, a hope that is also manifested in the report on the congress that she addressed to her German colleagues.[37]

Considering that Israel and West Germany formed official diplomatic relations only in 1965, Weber-Kellermann's choice to approach historical Jewish–German relations in Jerusalem in the German language was very brave; alternatively, it may have been too hasty, lacking the necessary reflectiveness. Indeed, Weber-Kellermann left only the Christian gaze on the poor Jewish daughter. It is only later, in her article, that she mentions one Jewish version of the ballad, recorded by Alexander Eliasberg and published in his *Ostjuedische Volkslieder.* This version is very similar to the version published by von Arnim and Brentano.

In the Hebrew summary of the lecture—and only in the Hebrew—another Jewish version is mentioned, one collected in Kovno (Kaunas) and published in Ginzburg and Marek's *Yidishe folkslider in Rusland* (#356). This classic collection, published for the first time in 1901, was republished years later by Dov Noy, the founder of academic Israeli folklore.[38] Noy was born in Kolomea, Galicia, and from his entire family there the only one who survived the Shoah was his brother, Me'ir Noy, an important collector of Jewish folksongs of Eastern Europe. It is very likely that this bibliographical addition in the Hebrew version was a personal initiative of Dov Noy, who was in charge of the folklore section in the congress. In this Yiddish version of the ballad, the Jewish daughter is confronted with only a single option: to marry a Christian and become one herself. In the end, she does not die physically, but rather dies spiritually, something that may be seen by the Jewish folk narrator as much worse. Noy's dissatisfaction with the German ballad is also attested by the fact that Weber-Kellermann's lecture and her article were found in his personal archive in a file that he titled "Antisemitic folklore."[39] Such a frame of reference for this ballad is perhaps extreme, especially if German perceptions of the pretty Jewess are compared to English ballads bearing the title "The Jew's Daughter" (the Hugh of Lincoln or Little Sir Hugh ballads). Like its German counterpart, this English ballad can be traced to some of the oldest ballad collections; it appeared in Percy's *Reliques of Ancient English Poetry* (1765) as a Scottish ballad and was later published in major collections, including Francis Child's *English and Scottish Popular Ballads* (Child # 155). Many scholars of the Lincoln blood libel analyzed this ballad, which tells of a Jewish daughter who tempted a Christian boy playing ball, brutally murdering him and dumping his body in a well. This ballad was read in the context of medieval chronicles of Hugh of Lincoln as well as in connection with Chaucer's *Canterbury Tales* ("The Prioress's Tale"). Interestingly, Herder translated it into German in his *Volkslieder* book (Leipzig, 1778: 120–123), where it is titled "Die Judentochter," a generation before von Arnim and Brentano published the German ballad with the same title, which is discussed above.[40]

Nevertheless, other than the version documented by Ginzburg and Marek, in the Israeli National Sound Archive there are no further Yiddish ballads of the Hero and Leander type. It is therefore dangerous to rush to clear-cut conclusions. Since Ginzburg and Marek's collection was the first of its kind in the history of Jewish folklore, it seems that this ballad gradually disappeared from the repertoire of Jewish performers at the turn of the twentieth century. One may speculate that this reflects a growing internalization of Enlightenment ideals among Jews in Eastern Europe. However, there are abundant versions of the Hero and Leander type in the Judaeo-Spanish (Ladino) Romance tradition, known as "Tres Hermanicas eran."[41] In many versions of this romance a promiscuous daughter is banished by her father, who sends her to a castle on the island of Rhodes, where a knight passes by, kisses her, and takes her to the castle where they jump into the sea. As the romance collector and scholar Moshe Attias notes in relation to the version he collected (Attias #61), many Jewish versions of this story end abruptly when the daughter is taken by the knight;[42] according to his interpretation, this truncated version does not include the sour ending. However, when this romance is examined alongside the ballad of Ginzburg and Marek, one may hypothesize that in the Jewish *oikotype* of Hero and Leander, the physical death was replaced in the folk-imagination by a spiritual one, which was viewed as the worst possible fate for the Jewish girl. Still, since some of the versions of this romance include the ending where the lovers jump into the sea, this hypothesis needs further investigation.

The fate of the Jewish girl was continually negotiated by modern literary writers. For the audience listening to Weber-Kellermann's talk, such modern forms of creativity were important in their experience of this ethnographic moment. One of the most important voices to engage with this ballad theme was Shaul Tchernichowsky, the most famous and influential *literary* Hebrew ballad writer. Tchernichowsky was born in 1875 in Russia, and he attended medical school in Germany before finally settling in Palestine in 1931. In 1942, a year before he died, he published a cycle of "ballads of Worms," in which he reread medieval Jewish–German relations in the context of contemporary Jewish–German relations.[43] Two ballads from the cycle offer a reflection of the folk-ballad discussed by Weber-Kellermann. In the first one, the Jewish daughter commits suicide rather than falling into the hands of the German knights. In the second, which takes the form of a dialogue between the rabbi's daughter and her mother, the daughter is convinced that a German knight has fallen in love with her, but in the last stanza her mother tells her that the knight will sit on the porch watching as she is thrown into the fire. Tchernichowsky, in 1942, completely denied the possibility of Jewish–German love relations. Just as in Weber-Kellermann's truncated version, the end of his poem is not unambiguous, but here the fate of the Jewish daughter is left in the hands of the German knight, outside the daughter's own control.

Tchernichowsky inferred what became perhaps more apparent in 1961 during the testimony at the Eichmann trial—that unlike how the Jewish or German folk-imagination had envisioned it, the fate of Jews would be determined almost exclusively by Germans.

I am unaware of attempts to interpret Tchernichowsky's literary ballads in the context of folk-ballads; the most famous of his ballads relating to a relationship between a Jewish girl and a non-Jew appeared in his "The Rabbi's Daughter's" from 1924, in which he rereads the history of the Khmelnitsky massacres of the seventeenth century in the context of the Jewish massacres that took place in Ukraine in the aftermath of World War I. Katznelson, who wrote about the sources for this poem, suggests that Tchernichowsky relied on the chronicles of Nathan (Nata) ben Moses Hannover on the Khmelnitsky massacres, but added other literary influences, namely a Polish literary ballad titled "Laszka" (The Polish Girl) published in 1838 by the Polish poet Tadeusz Łada-Zabłocki— itself influenced by a Polish chronicler of the sixteenth century named Stryjkowski.[44] Although Katznelson notes that the editor of the publication in which the Laszka ballad appeared also relied on Christian legendary sources, Katznelson himself refrains from proposing that Tchernichowsky may have been influenced by traditional sources such as folk-ballads. Although Katznelson admittedly regards Łada-Zablocki as an unknown poet, he never considered examining Tchernichowsky in the context of folklore, maintaining an unspoken division between the modern Hebrew literary canon and folklore, and thereby internalizing Herder's distinction between *Kunstpoesie* and *Naturpoesie*.[45] In contrast, I argue that when we consider the context of this ethnographic moment, it is important to recognize the role and relevance of literature in its widest sense, relating to several "canons." In her discussion of literary canon production, the American literary theorist Barbara Herrnstein-Smith responds to folklore as a "different kind" of canon:

> the entire phenomenon that we call "folklore," which occurs through the same or the corresponding mechanism of cultural selection and re-production as those described ... specifically for "texts," demonstrate[s] that the "endurance" of a verbal artifact ... may be more or less independent of institutions controlled by those with political power.[46]

In contrast to Herrnstein-Smith's romantic claim that folklore is "more or less independent of institutions," the communicability of folklore is much more complicated; folklore is certainly tied to powerful institutions.[47] Nevertheless, she demonstrates the potential of folklore to destabilize key notions in literary critique. For example, in the important and influential discussion of the "Modern Hebrew Canon" undertaken by Hannan Hever, a key figure in the critical study of modern Hebrew literature, folklore is never mentioned as a point of reference, in the same way that folk-ballads are not discussed as a context for Tchernichowsky's ballads.[48] While Hever's anti-hegemonic reading deconstructs many of the boundaries within the Zionist literary canon, he does not undermine the communicability of Literature (with a capital "L") in itself.[49]

Such views separating folklore from literature are unable to account for the range of experiences that unfold in ethnographic moments. Thus, although folklore can be a relevant context for interpreting the work of a great poet such as Tchernichowsky, the reverse is also true, as the work of Tchernichowsky can be pertinent in framing this ethnographic moment in Jerusalem in 1961. The relevance of Literature as an apt context stems from the differences between the communicability of Literature and the communicability of folklore: even if much of Weber-Kellermann's audience consisted of folklorists who were well acquainted with Jewish folklore, they were also influenced by Tchernichowsky's interpretations of traditional themes.

Another intertextual trajectory that can shed light on the audience's experience emerges from a comparison of Tchernichowsky's literary writings to his historical writings, in a way similar to my earlier analysis of the ethnographic moment in Kremenets in 1913.[50] There is no a priori reason to attribute more value to historical narratives produced by chroniclers or historians than to literary writings. In that sense, the debunking impulse of scholarship on the "invention of tradition," which was spearheaded by historians in the 1980s, is irrelevant in explaining experiences as frameworks for ethnographic moments.[51] A comparison between the communicability of historical narratives found in literature and folklore (e.g., folk-narratives, festivals, and rituals) and the communicability of historical narratives written by professional historians is more fruitful for that.

How, then, can we interpret what happened during this ethnographic moment in Jerusalem in 1961? The fluidity between previous experiences generated by the imagination—found in ethnographic writings, literature, history, and folklore performance—afforded various possible reactions to this moment. As we can see, Weber-Kellermann's position is reflected in her choice to present a truncated German ballad that spared the Jewish daughter. Her performance was influenced by folklore and historical narratives. The addition of a bibliographical reference by Noy may indicate a certain unease around the exclusive German perspective on the Jewish daughter, motivating the integration of a Jewish–Russian folk-ballad perspective. Finally, modern literary attempts may help in interpreting the possible reactions of the audience present at that moment. Those different gazes on the beautiful Jewish daughter may have informed what took place between a German scholar and her Israeli colleagues in the Mazer building at the Giv'at Ram campus of the Hebrew University of Jerusalem. While typically one thinks of folkloristics or Volkskunde as the context of folklore, here a scholar performed academically in front of two different audiences: the Israeli folklorists who attended her talk and the Volkskundlers who later read her article. In the Hebrew version, an Israeli scholar performed a Jewish perspective on the Jewish daughter by adding an additional reference to the paper. These different scholarly performances took place in relation to a tense moment, one that involved cross-cultural interpretations based on previous experiences. In this moment, folklore, literature, historical writings, and probably also journalistic reports from the Eichmann trial formed the basis of the experiences that framed the performances of these scholars.

*   *   *

When and where does Jewish ethnography begin? When and where does it end? What can ethnographic moments tell us about the scope of Jewish ethnography? Drawing from the two examples revisited here, it is clear that ethnography takes place beyond the "vulgus in populo." Ethnographic moments can also take place between people and texts.[52] Jewish ethnography is made by Jews and non-Jews performing together, cutting through fixed coordinates of "East" and "West." Ethnographic moments are conditioned by the failure of previous knowledge and experiences to give adequate explanations, and so they are saturated with new feelings and emotions that are inseparable from processes of interpretation. Because of the crucial role that both ethnographic sciences and literature (as well as other artistic forms) of the nineteenth and twentieth centuries played in Jewish modernity, particularly in coping with the anxieties of novel encounters, it is important to notice that sometimes ethnographic science can serve as the context of literature, while simultaneously it is folk-literature, and literature more broadly, that can serve as the context of ethnographic science.

NOTES

This article is based on the paper I delivered at the conference on Jewish ethnography that took place in September 2013 at the ETH in Zürich. I would like to thank all participants for their fruitful ideas. I am particularly indebted to Alexander Alon, Regina Bendix, Anna Juraschek, Sabine Kienitz, Michael Lukin, Amos Noy, and Edwin Seroussi for their comments and help at different stages of this study. This work was carried out while I was a postdoctoral fellow at the Franz Rosenzweig Center and a Warburg postdoctoral fellow at the Folklore Research Center—both at the Hebrew University of Jerusalem.

1. Marilyn Strathern, *Property, Substance and Effect: Anthropological Essays on Persons and Things* (London: The Athlone Press, 1999), 1.

2. Prost goes further, likening the ethnographic moment to a moment of epiphany: Audrey Prost, "Caught in an (Ethnographic) Moment: Negotiating Religious Loyalties in and out of the Field," *Anthropology Matters Journal* 5, no. 2 (2003), http://www.anthropologymatters.com.

3. Greg Dening, *Performances* (Chicago: University of Chicago Press, 1996), 195.

4. See especially in the work of Thrift, a British geographer and theorist: Nigel Thrift, *Spatial Formations* (London: Sage, 1996); Nigel Thrift, *Non-representational Theory: Space, Politics, Affect* (New York: Routledge, 2008).

5. Michel de Certeau, *The Practice of Everyday Life*, trans. Steven F. Rendall (Berkeley: University of California Press, 1984), 118–122; James Clifford, *Routes: Travel and Translation in the Late Twentieth Century* (Cambridge, Mass.: Harvard University Press, 1997).

6. This key question was addressed extensively in Hasan-Rokem's folkloristic readings of the Midrash: Galit Hasan-Rokem, "Did the Rabbis Recognize the Category of Folk Narrative?," *European Journal of Jewish Studies* 3, no. 1 (2009): 19–55. For a critique, see Dina Stein, "Let the 'People' Go?: The 'Folk' and Their 'Lore' as Tropes in the Reconstruction of Rabbinic Culture," *Prooftexts* 29, no. 2 (2009): 206–241.

7. Galit Hasan-Rokem discusses other narratives found in Leviticus Rabbah, interpreting other encounters between Jews and Samaritans and exposing the diverse experiences of such ethnographic moments: Galit Hasan-Rokem, *Tales of the Neighborhood: Jew-*

ish Narrative Dialogues in Late Antiquity (Berkeley: University of California Press, 2003), 42ff.

8. Bruno Latour, *Pandora's Hope: Essays on the Reality of Science Studies* (Cambridge, Mass.: Harvard University Press, 1999), 145–173.

9. Amy Shuman and Galit Hasan-Rokem, "The Poetics of Folklore," in *A Companion to Folklore*, ed. Regina Bendix and Galit Hasan-Rokem (Malden, Mass.: Wiley-Blackwell, 2012), 55–74.

10. This is particularly evident in accounting for where "theory" stems from, as if theory is something that comes from "above." As Naithani has shown in her discussion of folklore collectors in the British Empire, theory was discussed from below, by folklore collectors. The Comaroffs, who are known particularly for their postcolonial anthropologies, have lately turned the geographical imagination of theory on its head: Sadhana Naithani, *The Story-Time of the British Empire: Colonial and Postcolonial Folkloristics* (Jackson: University Press of Mississippi, 2010); Jean Comaroff and John Comaroff, *Theory from the South: Or, How Euro-America Is Evolving toward Africa* (Boulder, Colo.: Paradigm Publishers, 2011).

11. Regina Bendix, *In Search of Authenticity: The Formation of Folklore Studies* (Madison: University of Wisconsin Press, 1997), 109.

12. Sigmar Berrisch, *Adolf Strack: Ein Beitrag zur Volkskunde um 1900* (Gießen: Universitätsbibliothek Gießen, 2005).

13. One of the best examples of this is Max Grunwald, the founder of Jewish folklore, who noted in a Hebrew memoir published on his seventy-fifth birthday that "folklore begins with a grandmother"—see Max Grunwald, "Ha-folklor ve-'ani," (The Folklore and I), *Edoth* 2 (1946): 7–12 [Hebrew]. In this short piece, Grunwald depicts his encounter with two older women in Hamburg. Some other binaries are illustrated in An-sky's construction of social margins in his expedition, as well as in the work of some Zionist folklorists who have turned their gaze to Mizraḥi Jews, constructing a binary between modern European Jewry and traditional Oriental Jewry; this is characteristic of many of the articles published in *Edoth*, edited by Raphael Patai between 1945 and 1948.

14. Richard Bauman and Charles L. Briggs, *Voices of Modernity: Language Ideologies and the Politics of Inequality* (Cambridge: Cambridge University Press, 2003).

15. The date is probably incorrect, since Kisselhof (Kiselgof) joined the expedition only in its second season, so in actuality this moment probably took place in 1913; a less likely alternative is that the location was different since wooden houses were not typical for Kremenets at the time. I thank Benjamin Lukin and Lyudmila Sholokhova for their insights in this regards. For Kisselhof's role in the expedition, see James Benjamin Loeffler, *The Most Musical Nation: Jews and Culture in the Late Russian Empire* (New Haven, Conn.: Yale University Press, 2010), 82–93; 159–171; Gabriella Safran, *Wandering Soul: The Dybbuk's Creator, S. An-sky* (Cambridge, Mass.: Harvard University Press, 2010), 200.

16. This practice is mentioned in Deutsch's work: Nathaniel Deutsch, *The Jewish Dark Continent: Life and Death in the Russian Pale of Settlement* (Cambridge, Mass.: Harvard University Press, 2011), 20ff.

17. In the last two decades, many key publications by An-sky about his work and the expedition have appeared, attesting both to An-sky's lasting influence and to the status of the expedition as a monumental event in Jewish modern history, e.g., David Roskies, "S. Ansky and the Paradigm of Return," in *The Uses of Tradition: Jewish Continuity in the Modern Era*, ed. Jack Wertheimer (New York: Jewish Theological Seminary of America, 1992),

243–260; S. Ansky, *The Enemy at His Pleasure: A Journey through the Jewish Pale of Settlement during World War I*, trans. Joachim Neugroschel (New York: Metropolitan Books/ Henry Holt and Co., 2002); Gabriella Safran and Steven J. Zipperstein, eds., *The Worlds of S. An-sky: A Russian Jewish Intellectual at the Turn of the Century* (Stanford, Calif.: Stanford University Press, 2006); Eugene M. Avrutin et al., eds., *Photographing the Jewish Nation: Pictures from S. An-sky's Ethnographic Expeditions* (Waltham, Mass.: Brandeis University Press, 2009); Safran, *Wandering Soul*; Samuel Spinner, "Salvaging Lives, Saving Culture: An-sky's Literary Ethnography in the First World War," *Österreichische Zeitschrift für Volkskunde* 113 (2010): 543–567; Deutsch, *The Jewish Dark Continent*.

18. Johannes Fabian, *Time and the Other: How Anthropology Makes Its Object* (New York: Columbia University Press, 1983).

19. Briggs has devoted a number of articles to the communicabilities of knowledge; see especially his programmatic article that engages the communicabilities of folklore: Charles L. Briggs, "What We Should Have Learned from Américo Paredes: The Politics of Communicability and the Making of Folkloristics," *Journal of American Folklore* 125, no. 495 (2012): 91–110.

20. Dening, 45.

21. Safran, *Wandering Soul*.

22. Yitzhak Gur Aryeh, "Etnografya ve-folklor," *Yitzhak Gur Aryeh z"l. Mehanekh, hoker-hafolklor ve-ish ha-tarbut, shenatayim le-moto*, ed. Yom-Tov Lewinsky (Jerusalem: Hotsaat ha-mishpaḥah u-Moetset ha-morim le-ma'an ha-keren ha-keyemet le-Yisrael, 1959). This episode was narrated also by Deutsch: Deutsch, *The Jewish Dark Continent*, 19ff.

23. Chanokh Gelernt, "The Anski 'Expedition' in Kremenets," in *Pinkas Kremenits; Sefer Zikaron*, ed. Abraham Samuel Stein (Tel Aviv: Irgun 'ole Kremenits be-Yisra'el, 1954): 367–375. English translation by Yocheved Klausner on the JewishGen website, http:// www.jewishgen.org/yizkor/kremenets/kre367.html.

24. Ingeborg Weber-Kellermann, *Josefsdorf (Josipovac): Lebensbild eines deutschen Dorfes in Slawonien* (Leipzig: Hirzel, 1942). This study was based on a language-enclave approach (*Sprachinsel*) that was popular in German Volkskunde at the time, focusing on ethnographic studies of German minorities, especially in southeastern Europe. These studies are exemplary of the narrow-nationalist Volkskunde practiced at the time.

25. Spamer, who was born in Mainz in 1883, was a key scholar in German Volkskunde in the interwar period, though he was dismissed from some of his academic positions in 1938. His legacy is ambivalent: although he opposed the practice of Nazi racial Volkskunde, his studies were used by some of these scholars. As Brinkel shows, after the war he managed to establish Volkskunde in East Germany, partly due to his prewar connections. He was active both in Dresden and in Berlin, where he helped form a commission for Volkskunde in the renewed Akademie der Wissenschaften (1947). Like his West German colleagues, Spamer did not confront the past of his discipline, which scholars began to negotiate starting only in the 1960s and much more in the decades that followed. See Teresa Brinkel, "Institutionalizing Volkskunde in Early East Germany," *Journal of Folklore Research* 46, no. 2 (2009): 141–172. For a more general context of the negotiation with the past, focusing on West Germany, see Mary Beth Stein, "Coming to Terms with the Past: The Depiction of 'Volkskunde' in the Third Reich since 1945," *Journal of Folklore Research* 24, no. 2 (1987): 157–185.

26. Friederike Herrmann, "Ingeborg Weber-Kellermann: Weg mit dem Weihnachtsmann," *Die Zeit* (December 22, 1989), http://www.zeit.de/1989/52/weg-mit-dem-weihnachtsmann.

27. This is evident in her short introduction to German Volkskunde, subtitled "between German studies and social sciences": Ingeborg Weber-Kellermann, *Deutsche Volkskunde: Zwischen Germanistik und Sozialwissenschaften* (Stuttgart: Metzler, 1969).

28. Ingeborg Weber-Kellermann, "Zur Frage der interethnischen Beziehungen in der "Sprachinselvolkskunde," *Österreichische Zeitschrift für Volkskunde* 62 (1959): 19–49.

29. Steinitz was born in 1905 in Breslau to a middle-class Jewish family. Due to his communist tendencies and his Jewish background he had to resign his position in 1933, going into exile in Leningrad the following year and later residing in Stockholm before his return to Berlin, where he took a position in 1951. He rejected Spamer's work and directed Volkskunde to a "new socialist consciousness." His political commitment may have influenced Weber-Kellermann's reorientation. See Brinkel, "Institutionalizing Volkskunde in Early East Germany"; Teresa Brinkel, *Volkskundliche Wissensproduktion in der DDR: Zur Geschichte eines Faches und seiner Abwicklung* (Münster: LIT Verlag, 2012), 52–71.

30. Ingeborg Weber-Kellermann, *Ludolf Parisius und Seine Altmarkischen Volkslieder* (Berlin: Deutsche Akademie der Wissenschaften zu Berlin, 1957).

31. Weber-Kellermann's career was discussed in Elke Gaugele, "Von Zeiten und Zeichen. Ingeborg Weber-Kellermann (1918–1993)," in *Maß nehmen-Maß halten: Frauen in der Fach Volkskunde*, ed. Elsbeth Wallnöfer (Vienna: Böhlau, 2008), 79–112; Gabriele Schlimmermann, "Ingeborg Weber-Kellermann mit Adolf Spamer und Wolfgang Steinitz zwischen 1946 und 1960 in Berlin (Ost)," in *Fachfrauen—Frauen im Fach*, ed. Andrea Eichner et al. (Frankfurt am Main: Institut f. Kulturanthropologie u. Euro. Ethnologie der U. Frankfurt a.M., 1995), 45–59; Friedemann Schmoll, "Vor Marburg. Ingeborg Weber-Kellermann und die deutsch-deutschen Volkskundebeziehungen un den 1950er Jahren," in *Ansichten, Einsichten, Aussichten: Beiträge aus der Marburger Kulturwissenschaft*, ed. Antje van Elsbergen, Franziska Engelhardt, and Simone Stießbold (Marburg: Makufee, 2010), 309–318.

32. Ingeborg Weber-Kellermann, "Die Volksballade von der schönen Jüdin im europäischen Zusammenhang mit dem Lied von den zwei Königskindern," *Schweizerisches Archiv für Volkskunde* 58 (1962): 151–164.

33. A better modern Hollywood oikotype can be seen in Buster Keaton's *Our Hospitality* (1923), in which the climax takes place in the gushing water as Keaton saves his lover to end the family feud.

34. Ludwig Achim von Arnim and Clemens Brentano, *Des Knaben Wunderhorn: Alte deutsche Lieder*, 1st ed. (Heidelberg: Mohr und Zimmer, 1806), 252.

35. Philip Vilas Bohlman and Otto Holzapfel, *The Folk Songs of Ashkenaz* (Middleton, Wis.: A-R Editions, Inc., 2001), 15–23.

36. Notably, I do not know which version was presented orally, though I assume it is the one that appeared in the written summary. In any case, the summary stands for itself.

37. Ingeborg Weber-Kellermann, "Der 3. Weltkongreß für jüdische Studien (Third World Congress of Jewish Studies) vom 25. Juli bis 1. August 1961 an der Hebrew University in Jerusalem," *Hessische Blätter für Volkskunde* 51–52 (1961): 152–154.

38. Shaul M. Ginzburg and Peysekh S. Marek, *Yiddish Folksongs in Russia*, ed. Dov Noy (Ramat Gan: Bar-Ilan University Press, 1991).

39. I would like to thank Amos Noy for this information.

40. For a discussion of the Hugh of Lincoln ballad, see Karl Heinz Göller, "Sir Hugh of Lincoln: From History to Nursery Rhyme," in *Jewish Life and Jewish Suffering as Mirrored in English and American Literature*, ed. Bernd Engler and Kurt Müller (Paderborn: Schöningh, 1987), 17–31; Brian Bebbington, "Little Sir Hugh: An Analysis," in *The Blood Libel Legend: A Casebook in Anti-Semitic Folklore*, ed. Alan Dundes (Madison.: University of Wisconsin Press, 1991), 72–90; Richard Utz, "The Medieval Myth of Jewish Ritual Murder: Toward a History of Literary Reception," *The Year's Work in Medievalism* 14 (1999): 22–42.

41. These versions are noted in Seroussi's comparative remarks in Alberto Hemsi, *Cancionero Sefardí*, ed. Edwin Seroussi (Jerusalem: The Jewish Music Research Centre, the Hebrew University of Jerusalem, 1995), 82–83.

42. Moshe Attias, *Romancero Sefardi* (Jerusalem: Instituto Ben-Zewi; Universidad Hebrea, 1956), 159–161.

43. This ballad, and other modern Hebrew literary examples where the Jewess negotiates outside oppression, are discussed in Nehama Aschkenasy, *Eve's Journey: Feminine Images in Hebraic Literary Tradition* (Philadelphia: University of Pennsylvania Press, 1986), 231–241.

44. Gideon Katznelson, "'Bat ha-rav'—mekorot ve-ha'aracha," ("The Rabbi's Daughter"—Sources and Evaluation), *Moznayim* 27 (1968): 343–349.

45. Bauman and Briggs, 163–196.

46. Barbara Herrnstein Smith, "Contingencies of Value," *Critical Inquiry* 10, no. 1 (1983): 30. This quotation is also marked by folklorist Ben-Amos in relation to the concept of "tradition" employed by American folklorists: Dan Ben-Amos, "The Seven Strands of Tradition: Varieties in Its Meaning in American Folklore Studies," *Journal of Folklore Research* 21, nos. 2–3 (1984): 97–131.

47. Briggs, "What We Should Have Learned from Américo Paredes."

48. Hannan Hever, *Producing the Modern Hebrew Canon: National Building and Minority Discourse* (New York: New York University Press, 2002).

49. In contradistinction, Antonio Gramsci's radical antihegemonic ideas were inseparable from his serious consideration of folklore: Antonio Gramsci, "Observations on Folklore," in *Selections from Cultural Writings*, ed. David Forgacs and Geoffrey Nowell-Smith, trans. William Boelhower (Cambridge, Mass.: Harvard University Press, 1985), 188–195. See also Stephen Olbrys Gencarella, "Gramsci, Good Sense, and Critical Folklore Studies," *Journal of Folklore Research* 47, no. 3 (2010): 221–252.

50. Israel Yuval, who is particularly known for his cultural history of Rhenish Jews in the Middle Ages, has looked at two Tchernichowsky poems that retell historical events in which Jews were massacred, involving Jewish martyrdom: in the war of Mohammed in 627, and during the Crusaders' massacres of 1096 in Mainz. Yuval points to commonalities between historical chronicles and the Tchernichowsky poems that retell these historical events, though he stresses that Tchernichowsky's historicity was harnessed by a future-oriented national ethos: Israel Jakob Yuval, "Was tun Historiker und Schriftsteller der Geschichte an? Zwei Testfälle: Medina und Mainz," in *Recht—Gewalt—Erinnerung: Vorträge zur Geschichte der Juden* (Trier: Kliomedia, 2004): 63–77.

51. E. J. Hobsbawm and T. O. Ranger, eds., *The Invention of Tradition* (Cambridge: Cambridge University Press, 1983). This critique was made initially by Charles Briggs and reiterated in his discussion of communicability: Charles L. Briggs, "The Politics of Discursive Authority in Research on the 'Invention of Tradition,'" *Cultural Anthropology*

11, no. 4 (1996): 435–469; Briggs, "What We Should Have Learned from Américo Paredes," 106.

52. Fenske's encounters in archives bring to life such ethnographic moments, engaging
theoretically with the relations between archive-based historical-ethnography and the
ethnography of the present: Michaela Fenske, "Micro, Macro, Agency: Historical Ethnography as Cultural Anthropology Practice," *Journal of Folklore Research* 44 (2007): 67–99.

APPENDIXES

NOTE TO READERS

The following appendices contain English translations of three Yiddish source texts that are particularly important for the history of Jewish ethnography: a 1929 handbook for collectors published by YIVO; a 1928 handbook published in the Soviet Union; and a memoir about a 1921 incident during which a young folklorist was imprisoned in a brothel.

Appendix A.

What Is Jewish Ethnography? (Handbook for Fieldworkers)

NAFTOLI VAYNIG AND KHAYIM KHAYES

TRANSLATED BY JORDAN FINKIN

Naftoli Vaynig and Khayim Khayes, *Vos iz azoyns yidishe etno-grafye? (Handbikhl far zamler)* (Vilna: Yidisher Visnshaftlekher Institut, Serye "Organizatsye fun der yidisher visnshaft," no. 6, 1931)

What is Jewish Ethnography? (Handbook for Fieldworkers) was written by Naftoli Vaynig (1897–1943), an ethnographer and literary critic, and Khayim Khayes (d. 1941), an energetic leader of the YIVO Ethnographic Committee.[1] Their pamphlet, first published in 1929, was the most concise and usable practitioner's handbook for the collection of ethnographic data among Yiddish-speaking Jewish communities. In keeping with the aims of YIVO, by focusing on specifically Yiddish language, materials, sources, and technical vocabulary the *Handbook* effectively created the field of Yiddish ethnography.

* * *

The activities of the Ethnographic Committee of YIVO (the Yiddish Scientific Institute) up until now have shown that there are hardly any fully prepared fieldworkers; they must be *trained*. A large portion of the correspondence which the Ethnographic Committee conducts has been directed at educating its collaborators, so by virtue of that experience the present handbook has been prepared. Here we have taken into account those doubts with which fieldworkers often come to us, and as far as possible we have tried to resolve these questions and difficulties in a colloquial form and in limited space. We hope that this booklet will clarify the task for the older collaborators and also bring to us many new fieldworkers.

This brochure was prepared by N. Vaynig and Kh. Khayes with the help of M. Weinreich.

With regard to the ethnographic terminology (see below) the authors ask that it be taken into account that this work is nothing more than an attempt for which they alone take responsibility. Future notes and corrections will be gratefully considered.

The Ethnographic Committee of YIVO, February 15, 1929

WHAT IS THE GOAL OF ETHNOGRAPHY?

It is quite common that to such things whose meaning or significance we do not know we tend to attach little value or overlook them completely. The majority of our intelligentsia still today do not understand the importance of collecting and protecting Yiddish folklore and look on that work with contempt. In the folk-man (*folksmentsh*) this is expressed in suspicion or distrust. Today, still, the peasant watches uneasily the botanist collecting flowers in the field, or the geologist creeping up the mountain gathering stones in a bag. For that same reason the folk-man does not willingly wish to tell or sing something. The folktales, he knows, are only good for children; a man who reads books does not pay heed to such things except as an enjoyable diversion. But why would one write it down? Are there really no better things? Surely he will be ridiculed and made a fool of in public. More than once the fieldworker has stopped short, not knowing how to respond when asked: why do you need all these foolish things?

*   *   *

Thick books are published on life in the big cities, their culture and their entertainments. But what does he do in his far-flung little shtetl, in his dark urban backstreet, that folk-man who reads neither newspapers nor books, who neither goes to the theater nor listens to music? We know very little about it.

Ethnography[2] merely wished to fill in that gap. We know that being cut off from modern life, separated and secluded in his little shtetl or village, the folk-man constructed his own particular culture. He does not study medicine, but he has his own remedies and cures, his own explanations for various natural phenomena. He does not read novels, but has his own storytellers, folk-singers. He does not go to the theater, but he has his own entertainments, folk plays, etc.

Where did he derive all of these things?

Inquiring after the meaning of a custom we often encounter an answer like this: my father also did it this way. He often tells a story that happened to his father or grandfather in order to confirm a belief or custom. In a word, the folk-man lived and continues to live today with that tradition which is preserved and passed on from generation to generation. The tradition is for him the book, the school, from which he derives his knowledge, a source of a great lived experience that his ancestors have passed on to him as an inheritance, and he in turn enriches it with his observations and passes it on to his children.

The tradition is holy. It changes only very slowly and lives its particular life for hundreds of years. The silk gaberdine at which the Polish intellectual often laughs is no more than an old Polish garment that Jews adopted and preserved to this day. And so it is with other customs as well. They sometimes impart to us more information, and in a more lively way, than what the remaining documents tell us. So, for example, in some cities in Poland to this day there remains a custom of heating the ovens on the eve of Passover; this could be a commemoration of the blood libels that regularly took place on that night.

Those customs, songs, and stories that live to this day among the people vividly communicate to us the moods of ages long past. So we must investigate precisely the life of the folk-man, everything we have learned from the power of tradition.

For a long time other peoples have accomplished much in this field. Great edifices were devoted to preserving every tiniest crumb that might tell of the past (and what can't the earnest researcher be told?): old Frankish clothing, examples of houses, inside and outside, household objects, utensils, jewelry, old forms of baked goods, etc., etc. Large collections are published of folk tunes, songs, stories, plays, dances, and so forth. For years researchers will go in search of a forgotten tune, a verse from a song.

A very great labor awaits us. Much has already been worn away by modern culture; much has been driven off into the far-flung shtetls and is there dying off. We must collect what can still be saved.

To this the Ethnographic Committee of the Yiddish Scientific Institute (YIVO) devotes itself.[3]

THE MATERIAL OF JEWISH ETHNOGRAPHY

Ethnographic Groups

In the course of its historical development the Jewish tribe has divided itself into various groups that differentiate themselves from one another: on one side that large group of Ashkenazim, on the other side the Sephardim and the smaller or more exotic groups, such as the Yemenites, the Bukharans, the Caucasians, the Chinese, etc.

Each in its own particular way these groups have developed their own peculiar way of life; they live partly with their inheritance from the old Jewish tribe, and partly under the influence of their neighbors and surrounding relations.

Theoretically considered, that is, Jewish ethnography encompasses the way of life of all Jewish groups. However, taking on all of them would mean taking on too much. For the present, therefore, we will limit the area of our ethnographic work. *The territory of our ethnographic investigations is in the first place the territory of the Yiddish language.*

On its own this poses sufficient difficult problems given the diffusion of the Yiddish-speaking masses all over the world, among foreign peoples and different ethnographic communities that doubtless had a great effect on the Jews. Not going into it too deeply, it is worth merely pointing out the differences that exist, for example, between the Polish, Lithuanian, and Galician Jews, or indeed between Polish and Hungarian Jews, or even now on the western border of Poland, between the Jews of the shtetl Konin, which had belonged to the sphere of influence of Posen (Poznań), and its near neighbors from Congress Poland.

Not only did that process take place in Jewish life, but simultaneously another one did as well. Here and there we are dealing with withered or nearly withered branches of the Jewish people. The process of history has leveled out such groups as the Jews of Holland, Alsace, Bohemia, Moravia, or Posen and they no longer live such an active existence as the great community of Eastern Jews.

This means that Yiddish-speaking Jews can be distinguished into particular groups that have led and continue to lead their own peculiar life. The difference is not insignificant for ethnographic work. We cannot call them *ethnic* groups, because the signs of their separate existence are not extremely sharply delineated; but we do have here, within the confines of the Eastern European Jewish community, such groups that one must consider according to their distinctive characteristics and according to a certain methodology in the present work as *ethnographic groups.*

Thus we will be able to distinguish such ethnographic groups as: Lithuanian, Belorussian, Polish, Ukrainian, Eastern Galician, Western Galician, between which the difference is not solely one of dialect. And among them we will be able to single out further smaller subdivisions.

And even though it may seem that these groups have much in common, it is still of interest to ethnography to know to what degree these groups preserve certain distinctive features.

Work on this aspect among Jews is much more difficult than among other peoples because it is more difficult to apply the territorial principle. Other peoples have firmly established groups that have lived continually in one area, and the ethnographer investigates all aspects of their way of life, producing monographs on individual regions or villages. The Polish ethnographer Kolberg collected in thirty-eight volumes the ethnographic wealth of the Polish territory according to a geographic division, such as the Kraków region, Posen, the Lublin region, etc. This is somewhat more difficult for us, and the taxonomist will still have to determine to what degree that territorial designation applies for us. Meanwhile, we must demand of fieldworkers that they *absolutely* precisely indicate where the material they record comes from.

Social Groups

Every ethnographic group is further divided into various social strata. First and foremost are *professional groups.*

It is well known that the individual professional groups even have their own particular prayer houses or religious quora (*minyonim*). And not only do they each have their own jargon and terminology, but also their own customs, superstitions, sayings, and anecdotes. Familiar is the little song about how a cantor came to a shtetl for the Sabbath and each one of the craftsmen, in his own way and according to his understanding, judged the cantor's manner of praying.

Among these professional groups let us mention shopkeepers, market women, fair merchants, second-hand clothing dealers, tailors, cobblers, butchers, coachmen.

The way of life of such groups among us is still little studied. Incidentally, much material can also be found in Yiddish literature.[4]

As objects of ethnographic investigation there are also actors, school children, children of preschool age, yeshiva students, etc.—in general every group which for the most part leads a life of its own, with its own interests and its own norms. In previous YIVO collections the section "Children's Creations" occupies a prominent place, but still more needs to be collected.[5]

An interesting grouping consists of those whom one might call the "underworld" or "lumpenproletariat"; it is a stratum on its own, which consists both of déclassé and professional elements.

Not far from the border of that grouping stand *musicians.* Till now their way of life was best described by Sholem Aleichem in his novel *Stempenyu*.[6]

Meanwhile, from the actual underworld thieves have attracted the most attention. In part this interest stems more from a romantic sentiment than from a purely scientific impulse. In literature the thieves' way of life is reflected in Sh. Asch (*Motke ganef*) and F. Bimko (*Ganovim*).[7]

Ethnography must also investigate the language and way of life of prostitutes and other "hidden" people, including sayings, songs, superstitions, etc. Science is interested in all branches of life because social relations also find expression in what is wanton and repellant.[8]

To the underworld also belong the wandering organ grinders, beggars, and street performers. And one must collect not only individual moments that involve them, but also extremely important are general descriptions of their way of life.

This is more or less the manner of dividing the groups. This division is both natural and at the same time facilitates this work since one is afforded the opportunity of proceeding in one's research gradually and systematically.

THE DOMAINS OF JEWISH ETHNOGRAPHY

Material Culture

All of folk culture can be divided into three domains: (1) material culture; (2) social culture; and (3) spiritual culture.

This is the order in which these three domains are arranged among the peoples of the world, and there it is entirely justified. Where we are dealing with a community firmly attached to the land the ethnographer must concern himself with the layout of the village, the form of housing construction, agricultural tools and implements. Setting aside the effect of material culture on social and spiritual culture, all questions of material culture are important on their own as well.

For us the proportion of the three domains is quite different, because the questions of material culture must in our research occupy a much smaller space. This is a fact arising from the historical conditions in which we live. Jews did not cultivate their own style of constructing settlements, and moreover with respect to architecture, given these conditions, our achievements are not great. But precisely because we possess so little we need with all the more diligence and interest to preserve and secure what there is.

Folk Art

A friend writes of a Polish shtetl: in their synagogue one finds an old volume of Psalms, its pages adorned with drawings. Sometimes German artists would come and copy the drawings; today it lies about somewhere with the synagogue wardens.

Our synagogues and study houses are, in part, little museums of old Jewish folk art: the curtains of the ark, candelabra, fescues, paintings, alms plates, adornments on the walls, etc. The largest portion of Jewish art used to be concentrated in the synagogues. Today everything is abandoned, covered in dust; and how many relics have been lost!

The style of the synagogues themselves is often peculiar. Some old wooden synagogues are built according to the manner of the old Polish courts with Jewish study-house windows; only a few remain today, and no one takes care of them in order that one fine day they might not collapse and disappear.

But it is not only the synagogues that maintain for us a piece of Jewish art.

The gravestones in the cemeteries are often decorated with ornaments, images, stylized letters.

And in the pious old houses there are also:

Old *mizrekhn,*[9] embroideries of scenes from the Pentateuch; spice boxes, holiday linen robes, Matzah covers, old wine goblets, etc.

So much has already completely disappeared, but much more is being lost before our eyes. Whatever possible must be brought by unbidden hands into the museum of YIVO. Whatever cannot be moved one must see to being photographed or described as precisely as possible.

If there is no photographer, sometimes a good draftsman can take his place. However, one must always bear in mind that the best copy is no substitute for the original.

The point is that one must always stand guard over our old folk art and remember that should the remnants of what is left be lost, *we* bear the responsibility.

Clothing, Baking, Food

There are still several other domains of material culture that need to be investigated.

First of all, *clothing.* The old-fashioned clothes for men, women, and children were not completely different from what is worn today. But a couple of things should be mentioned: long-sleeved coats, short coats, women's kerchiefs, hairbands, brooches, medallions. All of these things must be collected for the YIVO museum; in the worst case, they must be photographed or described.[10]

It is also important to collect and describe current styles of men's, women's, and children's clothing. One must never rely on the fact that "everybody knows that."

Jewish *baked goods* baked especially for the various holidays are also expressions of our distinctiveness. Such goods should be collected and sent to the Ethnographic Committee.

Weekday, Sabbath, and holiday *dishes* must also be described, including: the order of the meals, their names, even how they are prepared. It must also be noted whether those dishes are adopted by poor people, wealthy people, or people of moderate means.[11]

SOCIAL AND SPIRITUAL CULTURE

Superstitions

Nothing is looked upon as derisively as folk beliefs, or as they are sometimes called, superstitions, household remedies, etc.

More than once we are astonished to see how credulously a folk-man carries out some "wild" superstitious act, with what engrossment various ceremonies are performed.

Where do they come from?

Here we are dealing with the remnants of past times, in part from those distant ages when everyone lived as many peoples in Africa and Australia still do.

A first glance it seems to us that the whole conduct of such primitive peoples (one calls them "wild" even though in truth they are often no wilder and no more barbaric than the so-called civilized peoples) is strange. But such an appraisal comes only from not understanding their way of thinking or their interpretation of various natural phenomena.

The primitive man believes that the whole world around him is full of good and evil spirits that wish either to help him or cause him harm. One encounters signs of them at every step. Should he wish to *avoid* a

misfortune he must read the signs well and do the "divine" will. From this
originate the largest number of apotropaisms with which the primitive
man seeks to defend himself from misfortune. When he builds himself a
house he must first beg the spirits' pardon for disturbing their rest: so he
brings a sacrifice, first of people and later of animals. Today still, when one
builds a house one puts into the foundation some money or a chicken; "it
should be for good luck," it is explained. This explanation is a modern one,
but the act itself is a remnant from that primitive time.

The primitive man is terrified of the unseen spirits that lurk everywhere
around him. It pains him inside, that is, when an evil spirit enters his body
and it must be driven out (cf. "dybbuk").

Or when someone hiccups one often says: someone is talking about
you. We do not at all think that here we are saying the same thing as the
"wild" Negro of Africa. For us this is mostly nothing more than a bit of
fun; for the primitive African or Australian, however, this is something
deeply serious. The hiccup indicates that a spirit has entered the person.
But it does not harm him; that is, if it is a *good* spirit that has entered him
for a while—it might be the spirit of an ancestor whom he has recalled.

Similar is when someone sneezes. One responds: *tsu gezunt, tsu lebn*
(to health, to life), and one intends it as nothing more than an expression
of courtesy. For the primitive man we can get down to the true source of
the precatory custom. Its meaning is more serious: he asks the spirit that
has spoken through his body to intend life not death, health not illness.

Furthermore, the primitive man believes that the representation of
a thing can summon the thing itself. Desiring to destroy an enemy, one
must make a doll from rags that represents the enemy and pierce it. That
is enough for the enemy to lose his power and be weakened.

Compare this to what we do: when someone closes a lock while the
bride and groom are standing under the marriage canopy, that affirms
their good luck. When someone is buried, a little lock is sometimes put
into the grave so the dead man should come to closure.

Things that were once in contact still maintain their affinity, even when
no longer in contact. For example, when the Negro walks through a forest he is fearful lest he, God forbid, should brush against a tree and leave
a bit of his garment hanging from a branch, because should it fall into a
sorcerer's hands he might perform spells with it. The primitive man fears

his own footsteps and looks to wipe them away. Upon this same belief is built a large number of our superstitions and remedies. For example, a remedy for getting rid of warts or healing a wound involves wiping a fine piece of ribbon over the place where the growth is and then laying it on the road; whoever picks it up will take on that affliction.

These are the most important foundations upon which all superstitions and beliefs are based.

Until the late Middle Ages they were generally widespread. Medieval medicine is full of various remedies and charms. The first chemists still sought the philosopher's stone, and the first astronomers still read men's fortunes in the stars. However, in the age when the upper strata of society ascended step by step, the simple people, the toiling and tormented, lived in darkness, relying only on their own experience and the experience of their parents and grandparents. Tradition thus became something sacred.

Today, when we collect all of these superstitions, remedies, and customs among our folk-people, we are gathering together the remnants of the thousand-year labor of the human mind to wrest the secrets from nature.

Here, too, belongs the whole matter of *magic*.[12]

Folksongs, Folktales

We love to hear the beautiful, sweet songs that are sung in all the corners of the world where the Jewish masses live. Who composed them? No one knows. Somewhere there, by the workbench, or on the coachbox, someone sang a little song, and it passed from mouth to mouth, from city to city, and became a folk possession.

Often, when such a song is brought from one city to another, or when it is sung by many people, it gets changed, a stanza is added, it is mixed with another song, a couple of verses drop out. Thus songs grow or pass away.

Folksongs grow together with melodies. A folksong is only ever sung. The tune first gives the song its soul. Without it the folksong has no life. Sometimes the melody came before the song.

Collectors of folksongs must always remember this and neither scrimp on their energy nor spare their effort in attracting to this work musicians and those who can read music in order to record these Jewish melodies.

Sometimes a song is borrowed from foreign sources; but this too is important because it gives an idea of the flavor of the choice and *how* the foreign element was adapted.

The same applies to folktales that to this day are told and listened to with such intensity by young and old alike. Who devised them? No one knows. They exist and they wander from settlement to settlement, from country to country, from generation to generation. In every shtetl there are folk storytellers.

Sometimes these are poor people who wander the shtetls listening to various stories and retelling them; peddlers who travel the fairs; musicians; Hasidim who love to tell of the wondrous miracles of their great holy men.

The folk storyteller is often also the tale's co-creator. His imagination is at work while he tells, and he adds color, exalting the hero, expanding the story in order to make it finer, more captivating. He lives to tell about the wonder of enchanted worlds, about palaces that sparkle in silver and gold, about the olden times when wonder-working rabbis would come and bring good fortune into every Jewish home. Here he weaves in his dream, the dream of a people living in poor, dark houses and in bitter need. Here he quenches the thirst of the masses for a bit of sunlight, a bit of glory, a bit of happiness.

They are told less and less today, but there are still enough to collect.

We wish to gather together and publish in the bright light of day all of these forgotten and nearly forgotten songs and stories.[13]

Jokes

The playful joke that makes one laugh or smile is also an element of scientific ethnography. However many of these are collected is still far fewer compared with the great number of jokes and witticisms circulating among the people. Great scholars, philosophers, and psychologists have tried to discover what makes a good joke, why it makes one happy and carefree. But no matter how one looks at the matter, all acknowledge one thing: the *Jewish* joke takes the seat of honor; we must collect and describe it.[14]

Joke production among the people never stops for a moment; but lively, stormy times provide more material for sharp minds and tongues. Therefore our age—the time of war, of revolutions, of the founding of states—has provided limitless material for new jokes. They must all be described; where necessary an explanation should be added.[15]

Proverbs and Sayings

· When one shears the sheep, the lambs tremble.
· Let a dog on the bench and he'll jump on the table.
· Haste makes waste.
· Money—shmoney! But is then shmoney money?

A deep worldly wisdom speaks from the folk-sayings of every people. A worldly intelligence, built on experience, on people's sharp observations, opinions, and actions.

And all of this is expressed in a compressed form, short and sharp. Like a mnemonic formula.

And in truth in every people these sayings were and often still are today the way in which parents communicate to their children their view of the world.

Today a mother still says to her child: "Remember, God does not send down from aboven when you sit idle by the oven" or "Just know, a gentile will lose, a nobleman will find, and a Jew gets picked on."

How much bitter experience lies in this tiny sentence!

Tremendously rich is the treasury of sayings. A true folk-man has a quip and a comparison ready for every occasion—sometimes with biting irony and sometimes with healthy humor.[16]

Names and Nicknames

It seems, what interest can there be in collecting names? And yet onomastics is an important branch of science. A collection of family names at a certain point is like a mirror of Jewish occupations in past times, of cities and countries of origin, sometimes even an expression of folk humor.[17]

No less interesting is collecting *nicknames*. "It is possible," Dr. Vaysenberg says, "that nicknames preceded individual and family names. . . ." As primitive society became more abundant in number, there arose the need to be able to differentiate people with the same name. This began to act on the folk imagination; focusing, depending on the conditions, on the physical or intellectual characteristics of the individual he was given a surname and was thereby made known to the people.

In recording nicknames one must always indicate the *real* name and the family name of the bearer of the nickname. It should be noted whether that nickname is connected to a whole family. As far as possible an explanation should also be given.[18]

Finally, it is also very useful to designate the specific *geographic* names that Jews have created for cities, shtetls, sections of cities, and streets.[19]

Words

There is a field where ethnography meets linguistic research, and that is the field of word collections. A collection of words that are characteristic of a particular city or region (an *idioticon* is what such a collection is called) often allows us to learn much about its customs, its spiritual condition, its preoccupations.[20]

Riddles

Among primitive peoples the mind is sharpened through riddles. The cleverness of both children and adults is tested.

Still during the Middle Ages in the monastery schools, children were taught the foundations of the Bible by riddles, composed similar to our "Who Knows One" from the Haggadah.

Today riddles belong only to the world of children; they are a component of children's games.

That is nothing new: many aspects of former primitive human life remain among children in the form of play. So, for example, the counting rhymes that children use today as a game were sometimes employed as a means of selecting a messenger, and sometimes also for ferreting out a guilty man.[21]

Dramatic Plays

Every people has its dramatic plays.

Among other peoples at the conclusion of the old year there begin the great "carnivals," folk celebrations. One goes out into the street and "goes crazy," greeting the new year with wild abandon.

We also possess our dramatic plays. These are the *purim-shpiln* (Purim plays).

Purim was formerly a true folk holiday, and on that day, through his purim-shpil, the simple folk-man brought some healthy laughter into his grey existence.

The older ones among us still remember these plays, the cobblers and coachmen who used to change their clothes and perform the great "*Yoysef-shpil*" (Joseph play).

In those days they played all the roles: the writers, the directors, the players.

And today, in times of great theaters and operas, when Purim comes and in Vilna there is performed an old antiquated play about Ahasuerus or the Selling of Joseph, the hall is always filled beyond capacity and the play is accompanied by a bright laughter from beginning to end.

For our purim-shpiln possess such uncontrived humor that is often lacking in contemporary comedy. Oftentimes they have a distinct feeling for dramatic effect that makes us wonder how that could be achieved by cobblers and coachmen who never had anything to do with art.

Purim-shpiln still wander about the cities and shtetls; of many plays today we know only fragments, crumbs, and of many others we know only their names.

As many plays as possible must be rescued. Wherever old Purim-players live we must seek them out and record whatever they can still remember of the old texts and melodies, gathering as many details as possible about the old methods and costumery. Not only are we dealing with something that is a great thing for science, but also the new Yiddish theater can find here a source of authentic folk art.[22]

Books

In every old Jewish house, in attics, in prayer houses, among old book-sellers, one can find Yiddish or Hebrew books with stories, rabbinical eulogies, women's prayers, Bible translations, etc.

These printed materials, however small or worthless they may seem, can often hold a great significance. In them is Jewish folk creativity often-times reflected. One must gather together what one can of them for YIVO.

Jews in Foreign Folklore

It is often very curious for us to see how the Yiddish language and Jewish customs, religion, etc., are reflected in the minds of the surrounding peoples. As far as possible one must see to noting down both serious and derisive songs about Jews, descriptions of a Jewish holiday by a non-Jewish narrator, tales and legends in which one encounters Jewish heroes, etc.[23]

Customs

When certain customs, songs, etc., take place as part of an expression of a collective activity we call this a phenomenon of the *social* culture. With regard to studying the social culture of Jews the holidays are very impor-tant; for those YIVO has published a special questionnaire.[24]

Also relevant here are *family celebrations* (birthdays, first haircuts, bar mitzvahs, weddings); customs connected to *death*; the conduct of estab-lished *sodalities* (burial societies, etc.); the conduct of rabbinical courts. Also important are the *juridical*[25] concepts of the people.

We are speaking here principally about the old Jewish way of life be-cause in the course of the long centuries it was refashioned and took on fixed forms. To be sure, the *new* way of life must also be chronicled, includ-ing the extent to which it has assumed particular forms.[26]

With regard to all of the phenomena of social culture it is better not to give individual pieces of information but rather *linked descriptions*. Once again: do not be put off by the notion that something has probably already been described! The smallest distinction can have value for the history of the custom, and moreover the geographical *distribution* of a custom is also very useful to know.

∗   ∗   ∗

BRIEF ETHNOGRAPHIC TERMINOLOGY

I. Folk Beliefs

(1) *Customs (minhogim).* These are the customs that are directly relevant:
   - (a) to certain moments in a person's life, such as birth, *kheyder,* bar mitzvah, wedding, death;
   - (b) to various holidays;
   - (c) here also belong the customs of various established sodalities or groups (we are familiar with the customs of the burial society, yeshiva students, etc.).
(2) *Superstitions (zabobones).*
   - (a) This is what we call the folk-man's belief in spirits, good and ill days, hours, moments; in the power and influence of various objects on a person's life and fortune, for example, one mustn't empty waste-water after midnight; one mustn't sew on oneself lest one lose one's mind.
   - (b) The various means by which one guards against and staves off possible misfortune, or conversely how one seeks to bring about a desired outcome.

This we call a "magic act."

> · "When one pours out waste-water one says three times: *hit zikh!* [watch out]"
> · "If you sew on yourself, you must chew something."
> · "If you want the spice cakes in the oven to rise, lift the spatula up in the air."

In fact, every superstition is connected to a magic act. However, wherever there is no such connection it is a sign that we have not received the superstition in its complete form.

(3) *Folk Medicine.* Folk medicine employs not only natural remedies but also magical ones. Therefore we distinguish:

(a) *Cures (refues).* So we call all of the herbs, the various materials such as iron, knives, liquids, and also the living things that are used as means of healing without any magic acts.

· "If you have a cold, hold a *smoking feather* under your nose."
· "If your face is swollen, apply a *seashell* to it."
· "If you have rheumatism, bring a guinea pig into your house."

(b) *Remedies (sgules).* These are all of the magic acts that are performed as means of healing or that add a stronger power and a more certain effectiveness to the cures (refues).

· "If someone breaks his back, he should be laid down on the threshold and a firstborn son should step over him."
· "Against jaundice one should put on *golden* objects."
· "If one wishes to get rid of freckles, one should wash one's face in the *first and last snow*."

(c) *Charms (opshprekhenishn).* This is a magic act in the form of an incantation which is supposed to bring about healing.

· Against the Evil Eye: "Three women stand upon a cliff, one says 'Ill' and one says 'Not ill,' etc."
· "Mousey, mousey, here's a [tooth] of bone, give me one made of iron!"

(d) *Apotropaisms (shmires).* These are used to avert illnesses, misfortunes, etc.

· In order to protect oneself against the Evil Eye one ought to wear an amulet.

(4) *Folk Meteorology.* This entails reading various phenomena to predict the weather.
> · "If one sees a stork flying, it is going to rain."
> · "If a goose stands on one foot, there will be a frost."

Just as folk meteorology is concerned with divining what will come, so it is also connected to a whole group of folk beliefs at the heart of which lies informing a person of what will happen to him in the near future. The curiosity to know what the morning will bring has produced various ways of learning about it. All of these we may divide into passive and active kinds.

The passive ones are those phenomena which come on their own and show the future without human participation. In the active ones, however, those conditions or moments from which the future may be deduced are consciously produced. To the passive category belong:

(5) *Signs (simonim).*
> · "It is a bad sign when a black cat crosses one's path."
> · "If someone dies on a Friday it is a sign that he was a holy man."
(6) *Dreams (khaloymes).*
> · "If one dreams of a living fish, it is a sign of money."

To the active category belong:

(7) *Occurrences (trefenishn).* One tries to read one's fortune, one's destiny, the length of one's years, etc., from a shadow, a mirror, from card-reading, from books (the so-called *trefers* [fortune-tellers]), from the hands (palmistry), from the face (physiognomy), from the stars (the Zodiac and astrology).
> · "When one leaves synagogue on Hoshanah Rabbah, look around. Whoever does not see his shadow will die in the coming year."
> · "From the Yom Kippur candles one can read who will live longer."
(8) *Magic (kishef).* An overt act designed to summon an image that might show the future.

Ordinary people are not always fit for interpreting these phenomena, or indeed for summoning them. To a much greater degree *fortune-tellers* and *sorcerers* have this ability.

II. Children's Creations (kindershafung)

(1) *Counting Rhymes, Mocking Rhymes (tseylungen, oysvarfenishn).*
   · "*Eyns, tsvey, dray, azer liber lay.*" (One, two, three, fiddle, diddle, dee.)

(2) *Children's Games.*
   · *In khapenish* (Blindman's bluff); *Sheli-shelokh* (Red Rover)

(3) *Children's Songs.*
   (a) with melodies (in circle-games—a song connected with a game);
   (b) children's incantations (recitative).

(4) *Chain-Songs.*
   · "*Moyshele mayn kind, vern zolstu blind, blind zolstu vern . . .*" (Moyshele my child, you shall go blind, blind shall you go . . .)
   · "*Ov iz a foter . . .*" (*Ov* is a father)

(5) *Children's Riddles.*
   · "A woman sits on the roof and minces farfl, what is that?"

(6) *Kheyder Songs.* These are the distinctive songs that *kheyder* children sing.

(7) *Joking and Mocking Songs.*
   · "*Itsik shpitsik nodl teshl . . .*"

III. Folk Tales

(1) *Wonder Tales.* These are what one calls all kinds of fantastic tales of princes, princesses, hidden treasures, supernatural worlds and events in which there appear spirits, imps, demons, talking birds, etc.

The tales of Hasidic rabbis contain a great trove of wonder tales.

(2) *Legends.* These are tales connected to certain places (cities), holy sites (synagogues, cemeteries), holy people (the Prophet Elijah), historical personalities (Yoynosn Preger, Napoleon), historical facts and events.

Legends are either *generally diffused,* for example those about the Prophet Elijah, or Rothschild; or they are *local,* known only in certain areas, for example the Ger Tsedek; or only in a single place (for example, legends about certain synagogues).

(3) *Moralistic Tales (magides).* These have an explicit moral. These tales are commonly told by preachers (*magidim*), for example the tales of the Dubner Magid.

(4) *Tall Tales (ployderayen).* These are tales in which things which never happened are strung together. For example: "In Tammuz, during the great frosts, we sat in the Sukkah...."

(5) *Exaggerations (guzmoes).* These are exaggerations of events and occurrences. For example: one person says that he saw a fly on the top of a tower and the other says he saw the fly yawning. Here belong the tales of the town fabulists, etc.

(6) *Anecdotes.* These are what one calls little humorous stories.

A special place is occupied by:

    (a) the anecdotes of Hershele Ostropolyer,
    (b) Motke Khabad,
    (c) Froyim Greydinger,
    (d) the innumerable anecdotes of the fools of Chelm.

(7) *Jokes.* These are short, sharp anecdotes, usually in a dialogic form.

(8) *Verses* of the Bible that are humorously interpreted, as, for example, is the practice of many of Sholem Aleichem's heroes.

(9) *Children's Stories,* which one tells to children and which children tell each other. (Here can also be included all of the enumerated categories of stories.)

IV. Songs[27]

(1) *Religious Songs,* whose subjects are God, prayer, and good deeds. Here belong, for example, women's supplicatory prayers (*tkhines*), "God of Abraham."
(2) *Moralistic Songs.*
(3) *Holiday Songs* include both serious and celebratory songs. They are connected to Purim, Simchat Torah, etc.
(4) *Ballads* are songs of an epic character that narrate an event.
(5) *Historical Songs.* Here belong pogrom songs, war songs, revolutionary songs, and in general all songs that are connected to a certain public event at a certain time.
(6) *Lifeways Songs* (*shteyger-lider*). These arise from classes or groups in a community and sing of their way of life, their joys and sorrows. One can include in this group workers' songs, work songs, soldiers' songs, coachmen's songs, songs of the underworld, etc.
(7) *Songs of Family Life,* such as: bride-and-groom songs, wedding songs, lullabies.
(8) *Love Songs.*
(9) *Songs of Varied Content.*

In a special category are:

(10) *Songs of Wedding Entertainers* (*badkhonim-lider*).

V. Proverbs and Sayings (*shprikhverter un vertlekh*).

(1) *Proverb* (*shprikhvort*). The proverb proper is a common opinion, expressed in a fixed phrase.
   · "Better an ugly face than a wicked heart."

· "Neither by cursing nor by laughing can one change the world."

(2) *Bon mot, Witticism (glaykhvort, glaykhvertl)*. This is a kind of proverb with a more humorous content.

"A pawn at home means peace in the pocket" (*mashken babayis sholem bekeshene*)

"Noble ancestry in the grave, but miseries at home" (*yikhes na kvores, a doma tsores*)

(3) *Saying (vertl)*. A saying is an aphorism, a dictum, whose source can be derived, or, when uttered, its source is mentioned. Here belong all the sayings of Hasidic rebbes, holy men, etc.
   · "Holiness comes not by inheritance" (*kedushe kumt nit biyrushe*; the "Ha-khoyze")
   · "An idler for himself, a wise man for someone else" (*a batlen far zikh, a khokhem far yenem*; the "Radoshitser")
   · "Settled up is half paid" (*opgerekhnt iz halb batsolt*; the Pshiskher)

(4) *Idiom (rednsart)*. This is a proverbial form constructed on a comparison or a certain concrete example, and its content displays a certain linguistic or cultural-historical value.

The principle mark of an idiom is that it does not stand alone as a proverb, but is rather bound to a sentence.

   · "[He takes] the fish before the net."
   · "[He writes] *Noah* with seven mistakes."

Often the comparison is comical:

   · He shines like the moon in an oven.
   · He runs like a mouse over a cimbalom.

Here also belong such expressions as:

· "A Sodom deed" (*mayse-sdom;* i.e., an act of cruelty)

· "Old Terakh" (*alter terakh;* i.e. an old fool).

(5) *Epigram* (*zogvort*) appears as the conclusion to a little story or anecdote:

> · "The beadle calls people to the synagogue and then lays himself down to sleep."
>
> · "Once a fool fell, and he no longer wished to go."

(6) *Interpolation* (*tsushprokh*). So one calls an expression that is added in certain cases, either for purely religious reasons, or in order to avert an ill effect.

> · "God willing" (*mirtseshem*); "heaven preserve us" (*nitogedakht*); "may it never happen to the Jews" (*nit far keyn yidn gedakht*); "don't open your mouth to Satan" (*al tiftakh pe lesotn*); "without vowing" (*bli neyder*).

(7) *Mockery* (*shpet-loshn*). So one calls words which the people alter in order to ridicule:

> · "Money—shmoney" (*gelt-shmelt*); "love—shmove" (*libe-shmibe*).
>
> · "Sonny-in-law" (*geneydem*).[28]
>
> · "*Daytshun*" (a derisive word for a German Jew; from *daytsh* [German]).
>
> · "*Shlepure*" (a derisive word for a beggar or bum; from *shleper* [beggar, bum]).
>
> · "*Lererushke*" (a derisive word for a teacher; from *lerer* [teacher]).

(8) *Blessings* (*brokhes*).

(9) *Curses* (*kloles*).

(10) *Oaths* (*shvues*).

(11) *Well-wishing* (*vintshenishn*).

*   *   *

HOW TO COLLECT

(1) Every fieldworker must carry with him a notebook and a pencil, and not only when he goes out to collect, but always; right in the street, or in a house he happens to have entered, he might hear something of value.

It is better not to rely on one's memory and rather to record something on the spot.

Whenever one cannot record everything someone says, one must note down as much as possible: distinctive words, phrases, etc. Upon returning home one must write down the story.

In recording any materials one must stick to our rules for fieldworkers, which are included at the end of this book.

(2) Usually when one asks someone to relate some information one receives the answer: I don't know what to tell. Sometimes he really cannot remember anything and one must always, with careful questions, help the speaker to remember whether he knows something of a custom or has heard of something similar, etc.

Such orientational questions are always given in the questionnaires.

It is better not to show the questionnaire to the person from whom one wishes to elicit something.

While talking and recounting, that person might mention things that perhaps do not relate to the question; however, one must not lose the opportunity to record that as well.

Lose nothing that may have value!

(3) Everyone can lend a hand in this; whoever has even a little desire or understanding of the matter can be useful to Jewish science.

In particular, many can help, including:

   (a) those who are close to folk-people, who have their trust, who are very familiar with their lives;

   (b) teachers who in their work might draw in school children, their parents and friends;

   (c) cultural organizations, youth groups, clubs, etc.

(4) This work is laborious and can be divided up if undertaken by a circle of fieldworkers (though it must not be a large group). Common work strengthens one's determination.

(5) A fieldworker must constantly seek to attract new people into the work of collecting, not only in a city, but also in the surrounding shtetls. Everywhere and at every opportunity he must explain why it is necessary to preserve our folk creativity.

(6) In order to popularize this idea, one may take advantage of the local dramatic circles, choirs, and declaimers, and organize evenings of Jewish folk music, folk dancing, evenings of Jewish songs, stories, etc.

*   *   *

RULES FOR FIELDWORKERS

(1) *You must never think that you do not need to record something because "It has certainly already been recorded." Always bear in mind: better too much than too little.* It is possible that such a thing has indeed already been recorded, but in a slightly different form; and moreover, it is important for science to determine how far the area extends in which an ethnographic phenomenon is diffused.

(2) One must first of all disclose those things of which one is completely certain. If you have any doubts add "it seems," "people say," "so-and-so says." If you are filling in a questionnaire leave blank any question to which you do not know the answer.

(3) *It is better to submit materials piece by piece.* If something is not clear to you, ask.

(4) *As far as possible one must record according to the local pronunciation, not the "literary" one,* even though it may be

ungrammatical. Words of Hebraic origin, too, must be written according to that pronunciation (*mirtseshem, shimshn agiber*).

(5) Do not rely too heavily on your own memory. If you hear something interesting, write it down soon.

    (a) Before you begin recording something, ask your informant whether he had read in a printed book what he is going to tell or sing to you.

    (b) *One must on no account ever prompt or correct the narrator or singer.*

(6) Indecent, coarse things must also be recorded. Ethnography does not come with an aesthetic gauge and records everything that exists in folk life.

(7) *Record as accurately as possible what the informant says,* whether that includes empty words ("for example," "well . . . ," "about," "as one says . . .") or repeated phrases. *Throw nothing away,* add nothing. One ought not be tempted to make something "prettier"; one must faithfully communicate every phrase and saying just as one heard them.

(8) If you are providing folk-words that are known only in your region, or if they are used in literature in a different meaning, add that in the commentary.

(9) The Ethnographic Committee must review a large amount of material, so as far as possible you must see to saving everything leftover of your work.

Therefore, act as follows:

    (a) *Record each phenomenon (song, belief, tale, etc.) on a separate piece of paper;* for smaller entries use 9 11 cm notes (a quarter of the size of a notebook page); for larger entries— double or quadruple size notes.

    (b) When you begin writing, leave a finger's breadth margin free at the top; then above note down the city, the district, and the province in which you recorded the information.

    (c) If it is a matter of small entries (for example, proverbs) that you do not wish to write down on separate notes, *absolutely*

leave a two-finger's breadth space free between one entry
and the next.

(d) If the material was heard from another person, below add
from whom (his name, family, parents, and occupation).
If that informant is from another city, one must indicate
that city. If that informant heard the material from still
another person, one must also indicate that person's name,
etc., as well as the time when he heard it. Right underneath
indicate the date and your name.

(e) By all means write only on one side of the paper, in ink.

(10) The address for everything to be sent to the Ethnographic
Committee is:

T-wo Przyjaciół Żydowskiego Intsytutu
Naukowego, W. Pohulanka 18, Wilno.

NOTES

1. All notes—with the exception of those added by the translator and marked
"(trans.)"—appear as they are found in the original essays.

2. *Ethnography* is a Greek word (*ethnos*—"folk"; *graphein*—"write"); in Yiddish one
can translate it as *folkskentshaft* (knowledge of the folk).

3. The bibliography provided in the present volume is not intended to be exhaustive.
Its aim is merely to help the reader and the fieldworker orient themselves. Therefore, only
works in Yiddish are mentioned, and only in extract. Many further materials on Jewish
ethnography can be found in the journal *Yidishe filologye* (Yiddish Philology, Warsaw
1924), in the philological publications of YIVO (here noted as the *Filologishe shriftn fun
YIVO*), in the American *Pinkes* of YIVO, in the Minsk *Tsaytshrift*, etc.
Those important collections not in Yiddish include *Mitteilungen zur jüdischen Volkskunde*
(German) and *Reshumot* (Hebrew).
S. An-sky, *Di yidishe folksshafung*, an off-print from the pedagogical monthly *Di naye shul*,
published by the Jewish Central School Organization, Vilna, 1921.
S. An-sky, *Gezamlte shriftn*, vol. 5, Farlag Anski, Vilna—Warsaw—New York, 1927.

4. Y. Elzet, *Der vunder-oytser fun der yidisher shprakh*, vol. II: *Melokhes un baley-
melokhes* (Warsaw, 1920), 42. Noyekh Prilutski, *Kremer-loshn*, in *Yidishe filologye*, 93. Y.
Rivkind, *Der bal-melokhe in an alt yidish lid*, in *Filologishe shriftn fun YIVO*, I, 41–56 (this
is of ethnographic interest even though it properly belongs to literary history). Y. Kats,
Terminologye fun stoleray, in *Filologishe shriftn fun YIVO*, I, 211–218. Sh. Vinter, *Tsu der
terminologye fun melokhes*, in *Filologishe shriftn fun YIVO*, III, 415–424. A. Trivaks, *Ba-
legole-loshn*, in *Bay undz yidn*, 172–173. (In the area of technical jargons the Ethnographic
Committee met with the Terminological Committee of YIVO, which already possesses
a number of materials; but its collections still need to be greatly expanded; and the cor-

respondence of the Ethnographic Committee must therefore help according to their abilities.)

5. Sh. Lehman, *Di kindervelt*, in *Bay undz yidn*, 111–149. In Polish there is the work of Regina Lilienthal, *Dziecko Żydowskie*, published in 1927 by the Krakow Academy, 97. M. Shveyd, *Aktyorn-shprakh*, in the American *Pinkes* of YIVO, I, 257–259.

6. Concerning musicians there is a chapter in Y. Elzet's *Vunder-oytser*. A. Trivaks gives a dictionary of their language in *Bay undz yidn*, 167–171. And Noyekh Prilutski: *Loshn ha-klezmorim be-poloniyah*, in *Reshumot*, I, 272–291.

7. Concerning the Jewish thieves' language (or as it is sometimes called, thieves' cant [*hentshke-loshn*]), there are numerous works, but most of them are not in Yiddish. A. Trivaks gives a dictionary in *Bay undz yidn*, 159–167; and F. Bimko adds an appendix to his above-mentioned drama. Sh. Lehman, *Ganovim un gneyve (rednsartn, tsunemenishn, uaz"v)*, in *Bay undz yidn*, 45–91.

Thieves' songs: P. Graubard, *Gezangen fun thom*, in *Bay undz yidn*, 19–41. Sh. Lehman, *Li-belider fun ganovim*, in *Filologishe shriftn fun YIVO*, I, 291–308. Sh. Lehman, *Ganovim-lider (mit melodyes)* (Warsaw, 1928). On the effect of the Jewish thieves' language on the German one see the work of Dr. R. Glants, *Di oysforshung fun dem yidishn eygns in dem eltern [daytshn] hentshke-loshn*, in *Filologishe shriftn fun YIVO*, II, 353–368.

8. In P. Graubard's above-mentioned "*Gezangen fun thom*" there are also prostitutes' songs.

9. The *mizrekh* is a form of ornamentation on the eastern wall of a house indicating the direction of prayer (trans.).

10. An interesting historical overview of the recent past is given by Noyekh Prilutski, *Dos gevet*, 14–159.

11. There is interesting material in Yehude Elzet, *Der vunder-oytser fun der yidisher shprakh*, vol. III: *Yidisher maykholim*, 122. In Prilutski's just mentioned "*Gevet*," pages 1–13 are devoted to explanations of "noodles" (lokshn) and "challah" (koyletsh).

12. R. Lilienthal, *Ayin-hora*, in *Yidishe filologye*, 245–271. A. Sosnovik, *Materyaln tsu der yidisher folksmeditsin in vaysrusland*, in *Yidishe filologye*, 160–168. S. Vinter, *Kedorim un makhasheyfim*, *Yidishe filologye*, 394–396. M. Vaynraykh, *Lantukh, di geshikhte fun a heymishn nitgutn*, in *Filologishe shriftn fun YIVO*, I, 217–236. Prof. Y. Tsoller, *Lilis*, in *Filologishe shriftn fun YIVO*, III, 121–142.

13. Sh. Ginzburg and Sh. Marek, *Evreiskie narodnye pesni v Rossii* (Jewish Folksongs in Russia) (St. Petersburg: Voskhod, 1901). Noyekh Prilutski, *Yidishe folkslider*, vol. I, *Religyezishe un yontevdike* (Warsaw: Bikher far ale, 1911); vol. II, *Lider un mayselekh fun toyt, balades un legends mit un on a muser-haskl* (Warsaw: Nayer farlag, 1913). A. Landoy, *Bamerkungen fun Noyekh Prilutskis "Yidishe folkslider"*, in *Yidishe filologye*, 151–160. Y. L. Kahan, *Yidishe folkslider mit melodyes*, vol. I; vol. II, 2nd edition (New York, 1920). Sh Lehman, *Arbet un frayhayt, zamlung fun lider, vos zenen antshtanen in folk in der tsayt fun "frayhayts-bavegung" in tsarishn rusland* (Warsaw: Folklor biblyotek, 1921). Sh. Bastom-ski, *Baym kval*, II, *Yidishe folsklider* (Vilna: Naye yidishe folksshul, 1923). A. Landoy, *Bamerkungen tsum yidishn folklor*, in *Filologishe shriftn fun YIVO*, I, 13–22. V. Anderson, *Dos lid vegn der mobilizatsye*, in *Filologishe shriftn fun YIVO*, II, 401–413. Y. L. Kahan, *Folksge-zang un folkslid*, in *Filologishe shriftn fun YIVO*, II, 139–154. Y. L. Kahan, *Yidishe folkslider*, in the American *Pinkes* of YIVO, I, 65–128. Y. Goldberg, *Bamerkungen vegn dem poetishn shteyger fun yidishn folkslid*, in *Tsaytshrift*, I, 105–116. Y. Goldberg, *Di yidishe mishshprakhike*

un fremdshprakhike folkslider, in *Tsaytshrift,* II, 589–606. A. M. Bernshteyn, *Muzikalisher pinkes,* vol. I (Vilna: Oysgabe fun der historish-etnografisher gezelshaft a"g fun sh. an-ski, 1927). See further concerning thieves' songs.

    Sh. Bastomski, *Yidishe folksmayses un legends,* I. II, [Yoysef dile rayne] (Vilna: Di naye yidishe folksshul). Y. L. Kahan, *Yidishe folksmayses,* in the American *Pinkes* of YIVO, I, 217–234.

    14. Y. Kh. Ravnitski, *Yidishe vitsn* (Berlin: Moriyah, 1922). Sh. Lehman, *Ganovim un gneyve,* in *Bay undz yidn,* 59 ff. Sh. Beylin, *Loymdishe un maskilishe vitsn,* in *Filologishe shriftn fun YIVO,* III, 497–514. Sh. Beylin, *Anekdotn, rednsarten . . .* , in *Tsaytshrift,* II–III, 859–868.

A theoretical work on Jewish jokes was presented in Hebrew by Alter Druyanov in the introduction to his *Sefer ha-bedichah ve-ha-chidud* (Frankfurt-am-Main: Omanut, 1922), 12–55. The jokes themselves, which the author includes (pp. 59–260), have, in their translation into Hebrew, lost much of their freshness.

    15. Sh. Lehman, *Milkhome-vitsn.* [In *Corrigenda* (p. 4): Sh. Lehman, *Di eyropeishe milkhome: A zamlung fun yidishe folksvertlekh, anekdotn, remozim, briv, gramen, lider, mayses un legends, vos zenen geshafn gevorn in der tsayt fun krig,* in *"Leben"* (*Heftn fun tsayt tsu tsayt far literatur, kunst un publitsistik unter der redaktsye fun Moyse Shalit*)—*Fun di milkhome yorn* I (Vilna, 1922), 5–28. Sh"s Roman, *Lider un gematriyoes, vos hobn a shaykhes tsu der velt-milkhome,* in ibid., 105–108.]

    16. Ignaz Bernstein, *Yidishe sprikhverter un rednsarten,* 2nd expanded edition (Warsaw, 1908). B. Vakhshteyn, *Di oysbreyterung fun Ignaz Bernsteins lebnsverk,* in *Filologishe shriftn fun YIVO,* I, 28–38. Y. Pirozhnikov, *Yidishe shprikhverter nokhn inyen geteylt in bezundere opteylungen* (Vilna, 1903). N. Prilutski and Sh. Lehman, *Yidishe shprikhverter, glaykhvertlekh . . . Vegn lender, gegndn, shtet un shtetlekh,* in *Noyekh Prilutski zamlbikher,* I (1913): 9–87; II (1917): 161–173. Y. Elzet, *Der vunder-oytser fun der yidisher shprakh, folkstimlekhe rednsarten, glaykhvertlekh, u"a* (Warsaw, 1918–1920)—I: *Dos davnen* (1918); II: *Melokhes un baley-melokhes* (1920); III: *Yidishe maykholim;* IV: *Der mentshlekher kerper.* Sh. Bastomski, *Baym kval: Yidishe shprikhverter, vertlekh, glaykhvertlekh . . .* (Vilna: Di naye yidishe folksshul, 1920). Sh. Rubinshteyn, *Shprikhverter un rednsarten,* in *Filologishe shriftn fun YIVO,* I, 411–426. Z. Khrapkovski, *Folklorzamlung,* in *Tsaytshrift,* I, 117–132; II, 831–860.

    17. Sh. Vaysenberg, *Di yidishe familye-nemen af ukrayne,* in *Filologishe shriftn fun YIVO,* III, 313–366.

    18. Sh. Vaysenberg, *Di tsunemenishn fun yidn in yelisavetgrader krayz,* in *Filologishe shriftn fun YIVO,* I, 79–90.

Relying on onomastics Dr. Y. Shiper posed an interesting hypothesis (*Der onheyb fun loshn ashkenaz* [*Yidishe philologye*], 101–112, 272–287). On this question see also Dr. A. Landoy, *Yidishe philologye,* 330.

    19. Y. Taglikht, *Di yidishe geografishe nemen fin tshekhoslovakay* (Filologishe shriftn fun YIVO, III, 585–588).

    20. F. Alfabet, *Materyaln tsu an idyotikon fun shtetl pyosk,* in *Yidishe filologye,* 61–72. M. Lerer, *Materyaln tsu an idyotikon fun khelem,* in *Filologishe shriftn fun YIVO,* 201–206. Sh. Vinter, *Kortnshprakh,* in *Filologishe shriftn fun YIVO,* 319–324. M. Lerer, *Fun poylish-yidishn verter-oytser,* in *Filologishe shriftn fun YIVO,* II, 369–380. Y. Toyb, *Materyaln tsu an idyotikon fun loyvitsh,* in *Filologishe shriftn fun YIVO,* III, 143–152. A large amount of material of this sort is spread throughout the works of N. Prilutski, especially in *"Dos gevet,"* as

well as Y. Elzet, *Der vunder-oytser.* N. Prilutski, *Grins af shvues,* in *Yidishe filologye,* 87–89.
N. Prilutski and Z. Reyzen, *Purimdiks,* in *Yidishe filologye,* 89–90.
On humorous words and forms of expression cf. N. Prilutski, *Shpet-loshn,* in *Yidishe filolo-gye,* 33–45, 123–140, 338–382.

21. Sh. Bastomski, *Yidishe folksretenishn,* 2nd ed. (Vilna, 1923). Hershele, *Funem folksmoyl,* in *Bay undz yidn,* 104–106.

22. N. Prilutski, *Purim-shpiln,* in *N. Prilutskis zamlbikher,* I, 88–125; II, 57–160. Y. Shiper, *Geshikhte fun der yidisher teaterkunst un drame,* vols. I–III (Warsaw, 1923–1927). Y. Shatski, *Di ershte geshikhte fun yidishn teater,* in *Filologishe shriftn fun YIVO,* II, 215–264. M. Vaynraykh, *Tsu der geshikhte fun der elterer akhveyresh-shpil,* in *Filologishe shriftn fun YIVO,* II, 425–452. Sh. Bastomski, *Purim-shpiln* (Vilna, 1926).

23. N. Vaynig, *Dos poylishe folkslid* Wojna Żydowska (Filologishe shriftn fun YIVO, III, 411–466).

24. YIVO, series *Organizatsye fun der yidisher visnshaft,* number 4: *Etnografishe anketes,* vol. I: *yomtoyvim* (Vilna, 1928). N. Vaynig, *Homen-figur un shmate-mentsh,* in the American *Pinkes* of YIVO, I, 62–64.

25. Moyshe Lerer, *An amolike yidishe khasene in khelem,* in *Yidishe filologye,* 392–394. Kh. Khayes, *Gleybungen un minhogim in farbinding mitn toyt,* in *Filologishe shriftn fun YIVO,* II, 281–328. S. An-sky, *Der toyt in dem yidishn folksgloybn,* in *Filologishe shriftn fun YIVO,* III, 89–100.

26. M. Gromb, *Gasn- un hoyf-reklame [in varshe]* (Filologishe shriftn fun YIVO, III, 283–296).

27. The terminology for songs is based on the divisions of N. Prilutski and Y. L. Kahan's folksong collections.

28. An ironic play on *eydem* (son-in-law) and *ganeydn* (paradise) (trans.).

Appendix B.

Research Your Shtetl!

H. ALEKSANDROV

TRANSLATED BY JORDAN FINKIN

H. Aleksandrov, Forsht ayer shtetl! (Minsk: Institut far vaysruslendisher kultur, Yidisher sektor, Sotsyal-ekonomishe komisye—Byuro far kantkentenish, 1928)

The literary critic and historian Hillel Aleksandrov (1890–1967) was
active in the Jewish section of the Institute for Belarusian Culture. Produced at about the same time as YIVO's *What Is Jewish Ethnography?*,
Aleksandrov's pamphlet offers a distinctly Marxist take on the practice
of Jewish ethnography.[1] Instead of the YIVO folkloric and philological
focus, Aleksandrov's text is concerned with social forces and the evolving
socioeconomic relationships in the communities being studied, taking the
shtetl as the primary research object.

* * *

I.

(1) Every socioeconomic investigation in the area of local folklore
must observe two factors: first, it must be timely; that is, connected to certain problems in the surrounding reality as far as
they appear in everyday life. Second, it must at the same time
offer well worked-through material that can be used for further
scientific investigations that will bear a more general, nonspecial-

ized local character. Both factors are suitable for the dual goal of current local folklore: the goal of production on the one hand, and scientific research on the other.

The shtetl comprises, in the indicated details, much appreciated material for local research. Among the problems of Soviet work on the Jewish street the shtetl-problem occupied one of the most important places, being so closely connected to the tasks of changing the socioeconomic structure of the Jewish population in the direction of agriculture and industrialization. It is now placed on our agenda thanks to the decree of the Ratfolkom (Soviet People's Committee) of the BSSR concerning the economic organization of the shtetls. We must, however, state that the indicated works always come up against a great obstacle: material on the shtetl is lacking. Our Jewish economic literature is in general very poor, and beyond journalistic articles that speak of the shtetl in general terms, we possess nearly nothing. General political journalism and science have also very little interest in the shtetl.[2] From before the revolution we can point to only two monographic descriptions of the shtetl: Y. Leshtsinski's work in *Ha-Shiloach* from 1903 ("Statistik fun a shtetl"), and Dr. L. Rokhlin's study "Dos shtetl krasnopolye" (in Russian; published by "Yeko" in 1909). There is a small amount of material in our older periodical press.

The task of monographic descriptions of shtetls must today be accomplished insofar as the task of economic reconstruction of the shtetl can be solved only on the basis of precise familiarity with every shtetl. The method of monographic investigations, which already occupies a large place in local Russian research literature on the village (the well-known works of Prof. Fenomenov, "Sovremennaia derevnia," A. Bolshakov, "Derevnia 1917–1927," etc.), must also be applied to the shtetl. This can be carried out by special expeditions from our state and scientific institutions; this can be carried out by the local organizations for regional folklore and their various sections.

(2) We must first of all study the shtetl as an economic unit, that is, as a particular socioeconomic type of settlement that developed

over the course of decades and centuries. We must imagine the shtetl not only as a "Jewish settlement"[3] but as a settlement with heterogeneous national composition, which came into being thanks to the specific conditions of the economic development of our region. The shtetl must be investigated in close connection with the entire territorial and social environment—first of all with the surrounding peasant environment with which it is closely connected. A certain exception can be made in this with regard to the few industrial shtetls that are more linked to the city than to the village. Here the underlying premise lies on the foundation both of our program as a whole and its individual parts. The shtetl set against its surrounding social and economic background, either of today or of the past: so must it be understood and investigated.

That same principle must be considered in investigations in the area of lifeways and cultural life. Here one must bear in mind the process of cultural interaction that appeared in various folk customs, language, etc. Very recently, for example, works have shown up among us that deal with investigating the interaction of the Yiddish and Belarusian languages (M. Shulman's article in the journal *Shtern,* 1927), or Ukrainianisms in the Yiddish language (B. Lyubarski's article in the collection of the Odessa Institute for Folklore). This work can and must be continued locally.

(3)　Our program begins with studying the local condition and appearance of the shtetl, the connection of the shtetl with the region. The causes which have contributed to the development of a given shtetl settlement, and which are to a large extent produced by geographic factors, must be studied precisely. Material on this subject can be obtained by excursions around the shtetl, familiarizing oneself with the old habitués of the shtetl and its region, if such people remain, and asking around among the older people, etc. One can learn about the region from those materials which are found in the Rayoysfirkom (Regional Executive Committee). The latter supply every year precise reports on the condition of the region—they can and must serve as the first source for the understanding the region. To this end one may use the so-called "Gedenk-bikher" (memorial books, pamiatnye knizhki), materials from the censuses from the years 1897 and 1926, materials from the former district archives, etc.

(4) The historical part occupies a large place in our program. This is explained by the fact that our local history is still nearly unknown; at the same time, the local history can supply very important material for the Marxist understanding of Jewish history.[4]

In order to study the older history of the shtetl one may use those historical materials found in various specialized studies (Prof. Semyonov's work on the Vitebsk province; Dembovetski's description of the Mohilev province; the three-part Polish geographic dictionary; Semyonov's Rusland, vol. 9 [on Belarus]). One should use various historical legends that are connected to the "birth" of a shtetl (these are mainly prevalent in the so-called noble shtetls), histories of streets, old houses, etc.

Historical material that deals with the social life of the Jewish population can be found in the pinkosim (community record books). Even though more than anything these books reflect the religious way of life, one can still very often find in these religious forms echoes of social disparities (very informative in this regard are the works of F. Marek, who made extensive use of the socioeconomic material from our shtetl and city pinkosim [in Voskhod, Evreiskaia starina, etc.]). Of chief importance is understanding the aspects of Jewish history of the nineteenth century, when the social disparities had the character of a social struggle (Hasidim and Mitnagdim, the Haskalah movement). There must also be gathered together material on the history of the revolutionary movement in which the shtetl played an important role. There must also be gathered together the memories of participants, printed and written proclamations, etc.

For this local history to this day almost no use has been made of local archives—from district cities and rural areas. In those places can be found a wealth of material related to the history of the shtetl in general—both of the Jewish and the non-Jewish populations. Because of this, use can also be made of material from the former *Gubernskie vedomosti* (Provincial Records) from the Yiddish, Russian Jewish, and Hebrew presses.

The period from right after the October Revolution can be preserved on the basis of materials that have survived in various forms—local decrees, memories of local authorized representatives, various official documents, etc. This work can have a durable character—by systematically gathering current material of local social life of historical importance (reports of the Rik [Regional Executive Committee], various state and social institutions, minutes of local congresses, etc.).

(5) In studying the population and its economic activity one must first of all make use of current statistical material to be found in the local state and social institutions—the Rik, cooperative institutions, trade unions, local organizations. Here one must chiefly pay attention to the dynamic nature according to which we get an idea not only of the condition of the shtetl today, but also of that "in which it grew."

In order to familiarize oneself with the movement of the population, one must bear in mind not only the natural factors (births, mortality rate), but also the mechanical ones (internal and external emigration), that play an exceptionally important role in our shtetls.

The economy of the shtetl now presents an image of various phenomena in which are mixed together elements of old and new ways of life. On the one side we have a considerable number of productive elements—peasants and home craftsmen; on the other side—the rest of the intermediary professions (small businesses, trade in the villages and at the fairs) and the so-called "undefined" professions. In investigating the local economy it is important to use the questionnaire-method of studying in a place itself the composition of the various strata of the population, its various economic institutions. Such questionnaires are now published widely in various publications on local research; they are also administered by various local institutions. In these investigations what must be above all emphasized is the aspect of struggle between the private-capitalist and the socialist sectors in our economy, which is keenly reflected in the shtetl economy.[5]

With regard to those institutions that serve the population in various areas, one can get the relevant information from the institutions themselves (schools, libraries, reading rooms; clinics; pharmacies, etc.).

(6) It is very important to study the kind of culture a shtetl has. On one side we independently have very important remnants of the moldy past (kheyders, preachers, etc.); and on the other side— aspects of the new way of life (Komsomol, Pioneers, etc.). Very often these aspects are reflected in our press; the relevant material must be recorded, gathered together, and systematized. Such material has already been dealt with in the collection *Evreiskoe mestechko i revoliutsiia* (The Jewish Shtetl and Revolution, edited by Prof. Tan-Bogoraz, 1926) and can easily be applied locally.

With regard to gathering ethnographic material, we intend to publish a special set of guidelines—therefore, we will not dwell on that here; we have only sketched out in our program the most important materials of folklore that must be collected locally.

The most important thing that local researchers must always bear in mind is: the material that they obtain and on which they work must be well and thoroughly documented.

Considering the great interest that is shown today in the problems of the shtetl,[6] we hope that our local leaders (teachers, agronomists, employees of social institutions, students, etc.) will undertake the work of researching the shtetls, simultaneously collaborating with the state, social, and scientific institutions.[7]

II. PROGRAM: RESEARCHING THE SHTETL

(1) Site and Appearance of the Shtetl. Geographical situation, general characteristics of the shtetl; how far is the shtetl from the regional center, district city, capital. Number of houses—wood, brick; number of stores; other buildings. The market. Number of streets, their names, general appearance. Map of the shtetl.

The shtetl as a regional center. General information about the regional borders, area of the territory, the number of village councils and their population; the soil in the region; natural resources; the economic condition of the region—division of land and livestock, development of larger and smaller industry. Map of the region. The train station in the shtetl and its economic importance; post, telegraph, telephone. Connection to the nearest cities and shtetls.

(2) History of the Shtetl. Where and when was the shtetl founded—historical facts and legends connected to it; where did the name of the shtetl come from. Old and new streets in the shtetl; where did their names come from. Family names in the shtetl as material for history. The nobleman—proprietor of the shtetl, his connection with the population (tax, other duties; stories about the lord).

When did Jews appear in the shtetl, the legal foundations of their settlement; the Jewish population in the villages around the shtetl settlement, their connection to the shtetl. Growth of the Jewish population in the shtetl, occupations, social groups. Relations with the non-Jewish population (facts of competition, intercession against expulsion of the Jews, etc.). The Community and its work. The Community and organs of self-rule, the Community and the surrounding nobility, struggle for leaseholdings (arendes), tenure claims; the Community and various strata of the Jewish population (the activities of alcohol-sellers, merchants, rabbis; struggles of craftsmen with the Community). Internal socioreligious struggle (arguments about rabbis, kosher butchers, etc., particular study-houses and religious quora of craftsmen, sodalities); persecution of freethinkers. Religious teaching institutions—kheyders, yeshivas.

The non-Jewish population in the shtetl (the villages that are directly connected with the shtetl; "goyish" streets), its economic structure, relationship with the Jewish population. The shtetl in the first half of the nineteenth century. The expulsion of the Jewish population from villages, how this affected the shtetl; struggle with the newly arrived. The condition of the Community; intensification of the social and cultural-religious struggle (Hasidim and Mitnagdim, the first maskilim). The War of 1812 in the shtetl. Nicholas I's "reforms" and their reflection in the shtetl—cantonist recruits' "German" clothing, "state" schools. Emigration to Ukraine (Volhynia, agricultural colonies), kosher-meat tax and candle tax.

The shtetl in the second half of the nineteenth century (after the emancipation of the serfs). The change of the economic structure of the shtetl—development of wholesale trade, factories and mills, effect of the railroad; emigration to larger centers. Emigration to America in the last decades of the nineteenth century and the beginning of the twentieth.

Sociopolitical orientations—Haskalah, Hibat Zion, the first socialists; folkist circles and the Jewish youth; the beginning of worker movements—social democratic organizations. "Iskra," participation of Jewish workers; participation in the Bolshevik organization. The Bund, Socialist-Zionists, Poalei-Zion. Zionists and religious-political parties ("Agudat Yisrael," etc.). The year 1905 in the shtetl—intensification of the economic struggle, strikes, participation of particular parties and people. The connection of the revolutionary movement in the shtetl to the village—participation of shtetl organizations in the agrarian movement. Reaction in the shtetl—pogroms, expulsions of workers and peasants.

The shtetl during the war. The economic effects of the war on the shtetl (homelessness, impoverishment of the working classes, speculation). The February Revolution in the shtetl. The relationship of the various strata of the population and parties to the February Revolution. The soviets in the shtetl; struggle before October. The shtetl Community. October in the shtetl. The first steps of Soviet power. The Civil War and its effect on the shtetl (the various powers, pogroms, guerillas). Military Communism and its effect on the shtetl economy (the expulsion of shopkeepers and middlemen, emigration to the larger centers of Belarus, RSFSR, Ukraine). NEP and the shtetl. Facts of the latter years.

Various local facts that had an effect on the life of the shtetl (fires, special decrees, etc.).

(3) Population. Division of the population according to sex, age, nationality, profession, number of families. Natural growth of the population for the various nationalities (births, deaths, weddings). Mechanical growth of the population (emigration to larger cities in Belarus, Ukraine, RSFSR, outside of the Soviet Union). Social composition of the population according to nationalities before and after the Revolution.

(4) Economy of the Shtetl.

(a) Agriculture. Number of agriculturally oriented population in the shtetl according to nationality, amount of land, division of the land according to national and social groups. The character of shtetl agriculture, as related to the suburban kind. Various forms of agriculture—crop fertility, cattle breeding, gardening, orchard-keeping, how they are distributed. Other forms of agricultural occupation. Trade. Budget of the shtetl peasant; place of nonagricultural income in the budget of the shtetl peasant. Soviet farming and collectives in the shtetl.

Jews on the land before and after the revolution. Jewish colonies and collectives near the shtetl—their history, development, condition today. Possibilities for further land distribution of the Jewish population.

(b) Artisanry. Division of artisans according to nationality and specialty; social differentiation. Distribution of certain specialties, and the reasons for it. Economic condition of the artisans before and after the revolution. How raw goods are received, how merchandise is sold. Connection to the village. General amount of production. Participation of youth in artisanry (members of a family, apprentices). Perspectives on the development of artisanry.

(c) Trade. General nature of local trade before and after the revolution (pointing out special forms of trade if they exist). Division of stores according to nationality and category.

Volume of trade among the private shopkeepers. Large and small shop owners; merchants in the village. Fairs, their distribution, volume of trade. State trade in the shtetl.

(d) Light and Heavy Industry. Number of firms of various kinds, their character, process of manufacture, technical equipment, number of workers, volume of manufacture. History of the factory, its development, relationship among the managers and workers.

(e) Workers and Employees. National composition, division according to categories and institutions. Minimum, average, and maximum wages, growth for various periods. Unemployed according to sex, nationality, age, profession.

(f) Indefinite Professions. The place of this group in the shtetl before and after the revolution, what they live on. Dependents, on whose salary they live, nature of their support.

(g) Cooperation and Its Forms. (1) Use-Cooperation, its history and development, its condition today. Struggle with private trade. (2) Credit-Cooperation—loan- and savings-banks; their condition before and after the revolution. The number of participants, number and size of loans, other functions (in various periods). What they do to receive raw materials and sell the manufactured products. Connection to the central cooperative associations. Agricultural credit and its place in the shtetl economy. (3) Trade-Cooperation. Artel and workers' cooperatives, their history and development, condition today (compared to various periods). Connection to the cooperative associations.

(h) Support from Other Countries (America, etc.). Number of families that receive support, the nature of that support, the amount.

(i) The Shtetl as Administrative Center. The administrative condition of the shtetl before the revolution. Local administration—district police, constabulary, their relation to the population. District administration, its connection to the shtetl. Local administration, local elders, municipal rabbi.

(5) Soviet organization in the shtetl. Shtetl soviets and national councils, their condition, the work of their sections. Political activity of the population—number of participants in the elections in the various years, number of people who do not have the right to vote. The budget of the soviet for various years. Results of the work of the soviet in the shtetl (in the sense of improving the economic condition, taxes, land distribution, distribution of welfare, etc.).

(6) Education in the Shtetl. Nature of education before the revolution. Kheyders (their number), basic elementary schools, yeshivas; number of students and teachers. State schools—primary schools, middle schools, number of children according to national and social composition. Children from the shtetl who studied in other cities. Other cultural institutions.

The October Revolution and education in the shtetl. Literacy of the population according to sex, nationality, age. General and national schools, number of children according to national and social composition, teacher composition. General information about the composition of the schools—housing, supplies, tools, etc. The connection of the school to the population. History of the school. Extramural institutions—library, reading rooms, popular hall, clubs—their work. Shtetl youth who study in other cities—colleges, polytechnics, etc.

(7) Organization and Sanitary Condition. General appearance of the streets, houses. How the houses are built. Water provision. Lighting. Baths. Medical help—doctors, medical practitioners (feldsher), clinics, pharmacies, hospitals—before and after the revolution. General information about the condition of these institutions.

(8) Political and Social Organizations in the Shtetl. Trade unions— number of members in particular unions, their work. The work of insurance funds. Home-craftsmen societies and their work. Mutual aid societies and their work. Shtetl philanthropy before the revolution, information about charitable institutions; shtetl philanthropy today.

Gezerd[8] and its work. MOPR,[9] Osovyakhim.[10] Local folklore
societies. Other societies. Clericalism in the shtetl and its effect.

(9) Way of Life and Culture. General cultural condition of the population. Piety; how the study houses, prayer houses are attended.
The activity of religious representatives. The new way of life and
family life (mixed marriages, uncircumcised children, etc.).

Folk medicine among the various nationalities (magic healing,
superstitions). Materials on the local language (local nicknames,
sayings, where they came from; Belarusian words in the Yiddish
language and vice versa, etc.).

The rest of material culture in the shtetl (old study houses,
prayer houses, interesting buildings—their style and architecture, old valuables; photographs).

(10) Biographies of Local Personages—social and political activists,
writers, artists, etc.

NOTES

1. All notes—with the exception of those added by the translator and marked
"(trans.)"—appear as they are found in the original essays.

2. I have dwelt upon precisely this question in the article "Vyvuchen'ne miastechka,"
published in *Pratsy II-ga usebelaryskaga Kriyaznaichaga Zyezdu,* 73–80.

3. Such a conception is today quite incorrect and does not conform to the official
materials concerning the national composition of our shtetls. On precisely this, see my
article "Di yidishe bafelkerung in di shtetl fun vaysrusland," *Tsaytshrift* vol. 2–3: 307–378.

4. We recommend the interesting article by S. Archangelskii, "Lokal'nyi metod v is-
toricheskoi nauke," *Kraevedenie* 2 (1927).

5. On precisely this see the instructional methodological book by Dzens-Litovski and
Abramov, *Poznanie mestnogo kraia.*

6. We take this opportunity to note the initiative in this regard of the Jewish Section
of the Mozirer Society for Folklore.

7. The same program is published in Belorussian in the journal *Nash krai,* no. 2 (1928).
There as well, there is a corresponding bibliography, assembled by Kh. A. Faleyes.

8. Yiddish acronym for Gezelshaft far aynordnen af erd arbetndike yidn (Society for
Settling Working Jews on the Land). (trans.)

9. Russian acronym for the International Organization of Aid to Revolutionaries.
(trans.)

10. Russian acronym for the Union of Societies of Assistance of Defense and Aviation-
Chemical Construction. (trans.)

Appendix C.

"A Strange Experience"

A. ALMI

TRANSLATED BY GABRIELLA SAFRAN

A. Almi, *Momenten fun a lebn: Zikhroynes, bilder un epizodn* (Buenos Aires: Tsentral farband fun poylishe yidn in argentine, 1948), 121–128.

A. Almi (Eliyahu Hayim Sheps, 1892–1963) was a Yiddish writer in multiple genres. As Almi notes at the end of this excerpt, the story of the folklorist's misadventure in a brothel turned into folklore in its own right. It is often cited in scholarship on the Warsaw Yiddish folklorists. Both Safran and Werberger's chapters in this volume discuss the episode at length. The original text showcases the folklorist's use of dialect terms, here the language of the criminal underworld, set off with quotation marks, such as "araynfetsn" for "to stab."

* * *

When I was gathering folklore—folksongs, stories, women's Yiddish prayers, and, not to ignore the distinction here, material from the world of criminals—first just for myself, later for Noah Pryłucki's[1] folklore collections, I had a tough moment when I was sure I was about to die—as a victim of folklore. . . . It is a strange tale that really smells like a cheap thriller.

Other young people who gathered folklore among Warsaw criminals also had all sorts of unpleasant experiences, but they got away with getting beaten up. I didn't get beaten at all. The Jewish prostitutes and their pimps saw me as a sucker who wrote down stupid songs and stories and paid money for them.

If I paid money (money that came from Noah Pryłucki's pocket), of course no one would beat me up for that. They had a different attitude to those folklore collectors who came to chatter and waste their time without paying. They would drive them away, sometimes with broken bones.

Once a Jewish prostitute from whom I had transcribed some songs of the criminal underworld told me that the girls who "worked" in a certain "house" in Mokotów (a suburb of Warsaw) knew a ton of songs and stories. I went straight there.

The madam, a Jewish women in a traditional wig, received me nicely, but when she heard why I had come she looked at me with wonder, as at a madman. The whole thing seemed suspicious to her, and she summoned a man from another room, a tall, broad-shouldered young man with a pock-marked face—a perfect representative of the Warsaw underworld.

The pock-marked man put me through a kind of "cross-examination"; he simply could not understand why I needed the songs and stories. I had to give him and the madam an entire lecture about the importance of folklore, assuring them that there are folklore collections in all languages and if they did not believe me they could make inquiries. I don't know whether they understood what I said or not, but finally the pock-marked young man said to the madam, "After all, he's paying! What do we care what he gets for his money?"

They led me into a big room where five girls were sitting, four Jewish and one Polish. He explained to the girls what I wanted from them. They exchanged glances and started to laugh. The pock-marked young man got angry and yelled, "Shut your traps and give him the goods!"

He and the madam closed the door after themselves and I stayed with the five girls. Surprisingly, it was the Christian girl who started to speak first—in Yiddish no less. She boasted that she could not only speak Yiddish but sing Yiddish songs as well.

One of the girls looked very young—about 15 or 16. She carried herself in a more dignified way than the others and she even looked ashamed.

The girls sang songs for me, but I had already recorded most of them from other prostitutes. Only two or three were ones I was hearing for the first time.

In the next room I heard a door slam and the voices of two men. The madam appeared and called two of the girls—some regulars were here! Customers....

Then the young embarrassed girl told me that she knew a lot of songs, only she did not have a good singing voice—but she would try.

She began to sing a melody I knew from another song, but with different words. Soon I grasped what she was after. She had simply let me know about her personal misfortune: she was a prisoner, she had been bought. I don't remember the words, but the content was this: "Dear man, I am a respectable Jewish girl from Lublin. I came to Warsaw to find work. I was tricked into coming here. Help me escape."

My hands started to tremble as I wrote down her "song" and with a wink I let her know that I understood what she meant. She looked at me with gratitude.

Another girl was called out. A few minutes later, the door banged open and the pock-marked young man ran in furiously. His face flushed, he grabbed the young girl by the arm and pulled her out of the big room into another room, slamming the door.

I realized that one of the girls had heard what the one from Lublin had "sung" and had informed on her. I began to get ready to leave the brothel. But the door banged open again and the pock-marked young man was back.

He looked at me fiercely and, without saying a word, hit me with his iron-hard hand and pulled me up. I was sure he would throw me out. But it turned out worse. He carried me into another room. There he kicked a door and before I could look around, he pushed me into a big room where all sorts of rags had been thrown and barrels had been set along the wall. The room had a small window, the size of a calendar page, right by the ceiling.

The pock-marked young man disappeared, then locked the door from the outside. Left alone, I began to think about my situation. I grasped that the pock-marked young man had imprisoned me because I knew a secret, the secret of the girl from Lublin, who had been tricked by people who traffic in women. But what would he do with me? Would he leave me there until I died of hunger, or would he kill me?

I was sure that I was going to die. I thought that perhaps the young man would bury me in the empty fields of Mokotów, near the brothel, and no one would ever know what had happened to my bones. . . .

I tried to pry the door open, but quickly gave up. I got up onto a barrel and looked out the little window, but saw nothing more than an empty field covered with scrap metal and bricks. Even if I yelled, no one would hear me. The only thing I could do would be to write a note and throw it out the window—and maybe someone would find it long after I had become a resident of the "other world". . . .

But that plan was soon destroyed. I heard the sound of a key in the door. The pock-marked young man appeared and yelled, "Give me what you scribbled down!"

Before I could make a move, he went through all my pockets and pulled out all my papers, my pencils, my watch, my few rubles, even my address book, and put it all loose into his pockets.

While he was emptying my pockets I kept trying to talk to him, to beg him to let me out, assuring him that I would not tell any stories. He didn't answer, even a single word. When he had finished his noble work, he left and locked the door again from the outside.

The hours went on interminably. They were hard, painful hours. This was how a person sentenced to death must feel in the death chamber. I had no doubt that death awaited me too. But when? I shuddered at every rustle. . . . He was coming after me. . . . What would he do? Shoot me? No, maybe he would stab a knife into my heart—which was the style in the Warsaw criminal underworld.

These thoughts tormented me all night and morning and into the day. It felt to me as though a year had gone by. Suddenly I heard steps, and a click from the door of the room. The pock-marked young man had come in. This time he did not look as angry as the day before.

"Does anyone know that you came here?" he asked and looked into my eyes.

"Of course people know," I lied. "My parents know, and so does the lawyer Noah Pryłucki, who sent me here to transcribe songs."

"Come!" he ordered me.

He led me through the other rooms. They had all been emptied of furniture. Nor was there any trace of the madam and the girls. They had, as they say, run off.

The pock-marked young man put ten kopecks into my hand, probably for the tram back into the city. Then he opened the door and pushed me outside.

When I was already outside, he called after me, "You'd better shut your mug, and nothing will happen to you."

I didn't even pay attention. I strode ahead. The free air refreshed me.

Since then I have not gone after folklore in the criminal underworld....

*   *   *

Soon after that, once I had come to America, Noah Pryłucki reminded me of the incident in a letter to me. Asking me to collect folklore among the Jewish immigrants to America, he informed me that he had accumulated a big collection of folklore from the Jewish criminal underworld and he wanted to publish it in a separate collection. Maybe I could find a publisher for it in New York?

By the way, he told me that a pock-marked young man—and he gave the name—had come to ask him, the lawyer Noah Pryłucki, to defend him. What was this about? Someone had "come up with a rumor" that the young man was a human trafficker, and the trial was set for a few months away. When Pryłucki refused to defend him he reminded him that once a young man had come to transcribe the songs of some girls, his "acquaintances," and he told him then that he, Herr Pryłucki, had sent him and for that reason he was very good to me ...

Pryłucki's letter also had interesting details about my experience with the trafficker. Years later I gave the letter to YIVO, along with a lot of other letters from the Pryłuckis, Hillel Zeitlin, Perets, Spektor, and Sholem Aleichem.

I described the whole story in 1921 in the Lodz *Folksblat,* edited by Lazar Kohan, who invited me to write for the newspaper. Then the story was republished in many Yiddish newspapers in various countries. My father wrote to me then that the old Pryłucki[2] was mad that I had not published it in *Moment*—not because of the sensationalism of the story, but because in *Moment* he would have taken out his son's name. He was afraid that it would be interpreted badly that Noah had sent a young kid to such places to collect folklore. The "old man" had a grudge against me anyway, because, being a regular writer and American correspondent for *Moment* in Warsaw, I was writing at the same time for *Folksblat* in Lodz. For that reason, he later raised my salary so that I could stop working for the Lodz newspaper, and that is what I did.

NOTES

1. On the influential Yiddish folklorist Noah Pryłucki, see Kalman Weiser, *Jewish People, Yiddish Nation: Noah Prylucki and the Folkists in Poland* (Toronto: University of Toronto Press, 2011).

2. Noah Pryłucki's father Tsevi Pryłucki was a powerful figure in the Yiddish press.

CONTRIBUTORS

ALEXANDER ALON is working at ETH Zurich on his doctoral thesis within the project "Das Wissen des Zionismus" (The Knowledge of Zionism), funded by the Swiss National Science Foundation. He collaborated from 2010 to 2013 on the German edition of Louis Ginzberg's *Legends of the Jews,* and he has published on M. J. Berdyczewski and Aleksandar Tišma and other Jewish subjects.

NATHANIEL DEUTSCH is Professor of History and the Neufeld-Levin Endowed Chair of Holocaust Studies at the University of California, Santa Cruz. He received a Guggenheim Fellowship for his most recent book, *The Jewish Dark Continent: Life and Death in the Russian Pale of Settlement* (2011).

EVA EDELMANN-OHLER is a postdoctoral fellow in Literature and Cultural Studies at ETH Zurich. She is the author of *Sprache des Krieges. Deutungen des Ersten Weltkriegs in Zionistischer Publizistik und Literatur* (1914–1918) (Language of War: Interpretations of the First World War in Zionist Press and Literature [1914–1918]).

JORDAN FINKIN is an independent scholar. A specialist in modern Jewish literatures, modernism, and Hebrew and Yiddish poetry, he is the author of *A Rhetorical Conversation: Jewish Discourse in Modern Yiddish*

Literature (2010) and most recently *An Inch or Two of Time: Time and Space in Jewish Modernisms* (2015). His current projects include studies of the Yiddish poet Leyb Naydus as well as the creation of high-art literature in Yiddish and Hebrew.

GALIT HASAN-ROKEM is the Max and Margarethe Grunwald Professor of Folklore and Professor emerita of Hebrew Literature at the Hebrew University of Jerusalem Among her many publications in folkloristics and Jewish studies are *Companion to Folklore* (2012), coedited with Regina F. Bendix, and *Louis Ginzberg's* Legends of the Jews: *Ancient Jewish Folk Literature Reconsidered,* coedited with Ithamar Gruenwald (2014).

SYLVIA JAWORSKI is writing a dissertation at ETH Zurich on the dynamics of assimilation and Jewish religion. She is the coeditor of *Am Rand: Grenzen und Peripherien in der europäisch-jüdischen Literatur* (2012) and the author of articles and reviews in Jewish cultural history.

ANDREAS KILCHER, a professor at ETH Zurich and a scholar of German Jewish literature and culture, Kabbalah, and the European tradition of esotericism, is the author of *The Linguistic Theory of Kabbalah as an Aesthetical Paradigm* and other publications on the encounters between European and Jewish cultures from the sixteenth century through the present, with a focus on the twentieth century, among them the standard work *Dictionary of German-Jewish Literature.*

TAMAR LEWINSKY is a curator for contemporary German Jewish history at the Jewish Museum in Berlin. She is the author of *Displaced Poets. Jiddische Schriftsteller im Nachkriegsdeutschland* (2008) and coeditor of *East European Jews in Switzerland* (2013). She has published in the field of Yiddish Studies.

GABRIELLA SAFRAN is the Eva Chernov Lokey Professor in Jewish Studies at Stanford University, where she teaches in the department of Slavic Languages and Literatures. She is the author of *Wandering Soul: The Dybbuk's Creator, S. An-sky* (2010); currently she is working on Russian and Yiddish literatures and the history of listening.

DANI SCHRIRE is a lecturer in the Program for Folklore and Folk-Culture and the Program in Cultural Studies at the Hebrew University of Jerusalem. His dissertation, "Collecting the Pieces of Exile: A Critical View of Folklore Research in Israel in the 1940s–1950s" is forthcoming from the Hebrew University Magnes Press.

ALLA SOKOLOVA is the Curator of the Judaic Collection at the State Museum of the History of Religion in St. Petersburg and a Lecturer at the Center for Jewish Studies at the European University of St. Petersburg. She is the author of many studies of Russian Jewish architecture and material culture.

SAMUEL SPINNER is a postdoctoral fellow in Yiddish Studies at the Johns Hopkins University; from 2012 to 2014 he was the Ross Visiting Assistant Professor of Yiddish and Jewish Studies at UCLA. He specializes in modern Yiddish and German Jewish literature and visual culture, and has also translated the oldest Yiddish book written by a woman, *Meneket Rivkah* (2008). His forthcoming book is titled "The Museum of the Jews: Salvaging the Primitive in German-Jewish and Yiddish Literature."

LILIANE WEISSBERG is the Christopher H. Browne Distinguished Professor in Arts and Sciences and Professor of German and Comparative Literature at the University of Pennsylvania. She has published widely in the field of German Jewish Studies. Among her recent book publications are *Hannah Arendt, Charlie Chaplin, und die verborgene jüdische Tradition* (2009); *Affinität wider Willen? Hannah Arendt, Theodor W. Adorno und die Frankfurter Schule* (ed., 2011); *Über Haschisch und Kabbalah. Gershom Scholem, Siegfried Unseld und das Werk von Walter Benjamin* (2012); *On Writing with Photography* (ed. with Karen Beckman, 2013); and *Juden. Geld. Eine Vorstellung* (ed., 2013).

ANNETTE WERBERGER is Professor of Comparative Literature at the European University Viadrina in Frankfurt/Oder, Germany. She has published on the poetics of Osip Mandelstam, on folklore and ethnography, and on Russian, Yiddish, Polish, and Austrian literatures. Her main topics are currently *Weltliteratur* as entangled literature, literature and folklore, and literary primitivism.

INDEX